IDENTIFYING & MANAGING PROJECT RISK

FOURTH EDITION

Essential Tools for Failure-Proofing Your Project

IDENTIFYING & MANAGING PROJECT RISK

FOURTH EDITION

TOM KENDRICK

HarperCollins
LEADERSHIP

AN IMPRINT OF HARPERCOLLINS

Published by HarperCollins Leadership, an imprint of HarperCollins Focus LLC.

Any internet addresses, phone numbers, or company or product information printed in this book are offered as a resource and are not intended in any way to be or to imply an endorsement by HarperCollins Leadership, nor does HarperCollins Leadership vouch for the existence, content, or services of these sites, phone numbers, companies, or products beyond the life of this book.

Book design by Aubrey Khan, Neuwirth & Associates, Inc.

ISBN 978-1-4002-4000-5 (eBook)
ISBN 978-1-4002-3998-6 (TP)

Library of Congress Cataloging-in-Publication Data
Library of Congress Cataloging-in-Publication application has been submitted.

Printed in the United States of America
23 24 25 26 27 LBC 5 4 3 2 1

CONTENTS

INTRODUCTION

Your mission, Jim, should you decide to accept it . . .

So began every episode of the classic TV series *Mission: Impossible*, and what followed chronicled the execution of that week's impossible mission. The missions were seldom literally impossible, though; careful planning, staffing, and use of the (seemingly unlimited) budget resulted in a satisfactory conclusion just before the deadline—the final commercial.

Today's projects should also probably arrive on a tape that "will self-destruct in five seconds." Compared with project work done in the past, current projects are more time-constrained, pose greater technical challenges, and rarely seem to have enough resources. All of this leads to increased project risk—culminating too often in an "impossible project" that seems overwhelmingly likely to fail.

As a leader of complex projects, you need to know that techniques exist to better deal with risk in projects like yours. Used effectively, these processes will help you recognize and manage potential problems. Often, they can make the difference between a project that is impossible and one that is merely difficult. This is what *Identifying and Managing Project Risk* is about. Throughout this book, examples from modern projects show how to apply the ideas presented to meet the challenges you face. This is not a book of theories; it is based on data collected in the recent past from hundreds of complex projects worldwide. A database filled with this information, the Project Experience Risk Information Library (PERIL), forms the foundation for this book. These examples are used to identify sources of risk, and they demonstrate practical responses for typical project challenges.

The structure of the book also reflects current thinking about project risk management, embodied in publications from the Project Management Institute (PMI®, the professional society for project managers), such as its *Practice Standard for Project Risk Management*. This book also addresses the related concepts of VUCA (Volatility, Uncertainty, Complexity, and Ambiguity) that complicate modern projects.

The first half of the book addresses risk identification, relying heavily on project definition and planning. The initial six chapters show the value of building a thorough understanding of the work in uncovering sources of risk. The remainder of the book covers the assessment and management of risk, at the detail (activity) level as well as at the project level—and above. These chapters cover methods for assessing identified risks, establishing an overall risk plan for the project, making project adjustments, ongoing risk tracking, project closure, and the relationship between project risk management and program, portfolio, and enterprise risk management.

It is especially easy on modern projects to convince yourself that there is little to be learned from the past, and that established ideas and techniques "no longer apply to *my* project." Tempting though it is to wear these "hindsight blinders," wise project managers realize that their chances of success are always improved when they take full advantage of what has gone before. Neither project management in general nor risk management in particular is all that new. Broad principles and techniques for both have been successfully used for much more than a century. Even though many lessons can be learned from current projects (as the PERIL database illustrates), there is also much to gain from earlier work.

As a potent reminder of this, each chapter in this book concludes with a short description of how some of the principles discussed relate to a very large, historical project: the construction of the Panama Canal. Taking a moment every so often to consider this remarkable feat of engineering reinforces the importance of good project management practices—and may provide some tropical relief from what can be occasionally dry subject matter.

Risk in projects comes from many sources, including two that are generally left out of even the better books on the subject: (1) the inadequate application (or even discouragement) of project management practices, and (2) the all-too-common situation of wildly aggressive project objectives that are established without the foundation of any realistic planning. These risks are related, because only through adequate understanding of the work can you detect whether objectives are impossible, and only by using the information you develop can you hope to do anything about it.

Identifying and Managing Project Risk is intended to help leaders of today's complex projects (and their managers) successfully deliver on credible commitments. Whether you develop products, provide services, create information technology solutions, or deal with complexity in other types of projects, you will find easy-to-follow, practical guidance to improve your management of project risk along with effective practices for aligning your projects with reality. You will learn how to succeed with seemingly impossible projects by reducing your risks with modest incremental effort.

IDENTIFYING
& MANAGING
PROJECT
RISK FOURTH
EDITION

CHAPTER 1

WHY PROJECT RISK MANAGEMENT?

"Those who cannot remember the past are condemned to repeat it."

—GEORGE SANTAYANA

F ar too many modern projects retrace the shortcomings and errors of earlier work. Projects that successfully avoid such pitfalls are often viewed as lucky, but there is usually more to it than that.

The fate of the Fukushima Daiichi nuclear facility on the coast of Japan is a well-known story. A massive offshore earthquake in March 2011 and the tsunami it caused led to a reactor meltdown that destroyed the facility and made part of the Fukushima prefecture uninhabitable. Unknown to most, another nearby reactor, the Onagawa nuclear power plant, was similarly situated near the water and was even closer to the earthquake's epicenter. When the earthquake hit, it was inundated by the forty-meter wall of seawater and experienced the most violent tremors ever experienced by a nuclear power plant. Despite this, the Onagawa plant suffered no permanent damage.

The difference between these two vastly different outcomes, summarizing Juliette Kayyem's *The Devil Never Sleeps: Learning to*

Live in an Age of Disasters, was that the operators of the Onagawa plant saw this scenario as a possibility, and determined how to fail safely. In this part of Japan tsunamis have long been a recognized threat, with warnings carved high on the overlooking cliffs about the dangers of building below them. The power plant staff at Onagawa had extensive emergency training and had rehearsed for this scenario. When the disaster hit, they had the means to respond and quickly shut the plant down.

Preparation for risk can make a massive difference.

THE RISKY PROJECT

All projects involve risk. There is always at least some level of uncertainty in a project's outcome, regardless of what the Microsoft Project Gantt chart on the wall seems to imply. Projects involving technology (and today that's nearly all projects, to some degree) are particularly risky, for several reasons. First, technical projects are highly varied. These projects generally have unique aspects and objectives that significantly differ from previous work, and the environment for technical projects evolves quickly. In fact, the very opportunities that give rise to modern technical projects contain significant uncertainty, giving rise to much more difference from one project to the next than in past projects. In addition, today's projects are frequently "lean," challenged to work with minimal funding, staff, and equipment. To make matters worse, there is a pervasive expectation that, however fast the last project may have been, the next one should be even quicker. The number and severity of risks on such projects continue to grow. To avoid a project doomed to failure, you must consistently use the best practices available.

Good project practices come from experience. Experience, unfortunately, generally comes from bad project management. We often learn what not to do by doing it and then dealing with the consequences. Fortunately, we can also benefit from experience even when it is not our own. The foundation of this book is the experiences of others—a large collection of mostly plausible ideas that did not work out as well as hoped.

Projects that succeed generally do so because their leaders do two things well. First, they recognize that much of the work on any project, even the highest of high-tech projects, is never entirely new. For this work, the notes, records, and lessons learned on earlier projects can be a roadmap for identifying, and in many cases avoiding, multiple potential problems. Second, they plan project work thoroughly, especially the portions that require innovation, in order to understand the challenges ahead and to anticipate many of the risks.

Effective project risk management relies on both of these ideas. By looking backward, past failures may be understood and dealt with, and by looking forward via project planning, many future problems can be minimized or eliminated.

RISK

In projects, a risk can be almost any uncertain event associated with the work. Not all risks are equally important, though. Project leaders must focus on risks that can materially affect project objectives, or "uncertainty that matters." There are many ways to characterize risk. One of the simplest, from the insurance industry, is:

Loss multiplied by likelihood

Risk is the product of these two factors: the expected harmful consequences of an event and the probability that the event might occur. All risks have these two related but distinctly different components. Employing this concept, risk may be assessed in aggregate for a large population of events (macro-risk), or it may be considered on an event-by-event basis (micro-risk).

Both characterizations are useful for risk management, but which of these is more applicable differs depending on the situation. In most fields, risk is primarily managed in the aggregate, in the macro sense. As examples, insurance companies sell a large number of policies, commercial banks make many loans, gambling casinos and lotteries attract crowds of players, and managers of mutual funds hold large portfolios of varied investments. The literature of risk management for these fields (which is extensive) tends to focus on large-scale risk management, with secondary treatment for managing single-event risks.

As a simple example, consider throwing two fair, six-sided dice. In advance, the outcome of the event is unknown, but through analysis, experimenting, or guessing, you can develop some expectations. The only possible outcomes for the sum of the faces of the two dice are the integers between 2 and 12. One way to establish expectations is to figure out the number of possible ways there are to reach each of these totals. (For example, the total 4 can occur three ways from two dice: 1 + 3, 2 + 2, and 3 + 1.) Arranging this analysis in a histogram results in figure 1-1. Because each of the thirty-six possible combinations is equally likely, this histogram can be used to predict the relative probability for each possible total. Using this model, you can predict the average sum over many tosses to be 7.

If you throw the dice many times, the empirical data collected (which is another method for establishing the probabilities) will

■ **Figure 1-1:** Histogram of Sums from Two Dice

generally resemble the theoretical histogram. However, because the events are random it is extraordinarily unlikely that your experiments rolling dice will ever precisely match the theory. What will emerge, though, is that the average sum generated in large populations (100 or more throws) will be close to the expected average of 7, and the shape of the histogram will also be similar to the predicted theoretical distribution. Risk analysis in the macro sense takes notice of the population mean of 7, and casino games of chance played with dice are designed by "the house" to exploit this fact. On the other hand, risk in the micro sense, noting the range of possible outcomes, dominates the analysis for casino visitors, who may play such games only once; the risk associated with a single event—their next throw of the dice—is what matters to them.

For projects, risk management in the large sense is useful to the organization, where many projects are undertaken. But from the perspective of the leader of a single project, there is only the one project. Risk management for the enterprise or for a portfolio of projects is mostly about risk in the aggregate (a topic explored in chapter 13). Project risk management focuses mainly on risk in the small sense, and this is the primary topic of this book.

Macro-Risk Management

In the literature of the insurance and finance industries, risk is described and managed using statistical tools: data collection, sampling, and data analysis. In these fields, a large population of individual examples is collected and aggregated, and statistics for the "loss and likelihood" can be calculated. Even though the individual cases in the population may vary widely, the average loss times likelihood tends to be fairly predictable and stable over time. When large numbers of data points from the population at various levels of loss have been collected, the population can be characterized using distributions and histograms, similar to the plot in figure 1-2. In this case, each "loss" result that falls into a defined range is counted, and the number of observations in each range is plotted against the ranges to show a histogram of the overall results.

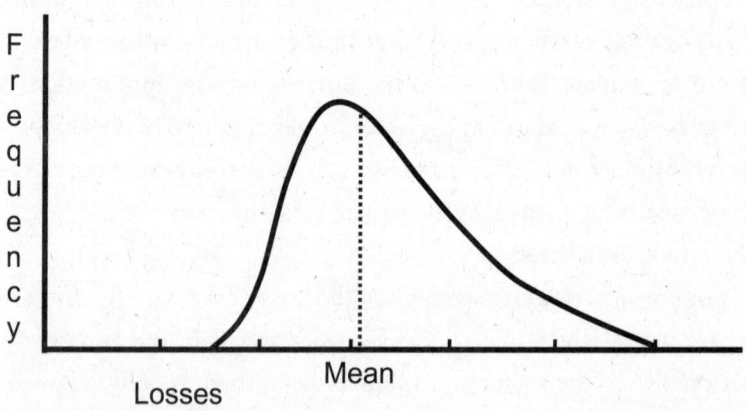

Figure 1-2: Histogram of Population Data

Various statistics and methods are used to study such populations, but the population mean is the main measure for risk in them. The mean represents the typical loss—the total of all the losses divided by the number of data points. The uncertainty, or the amount of spread for the data on each side of the mean, also matters, but the average sufficiently characterizes the population for most decisions.

In fields such as these, risk is managed mostly in the macro sense, using a large population to forecast the mean. This information may be used to set interest rates for loans, premiums for insurance policies, and expectations for stock portfolios. Because there are many loans, investments, and insurance policies, the overall expectations depend on the average result. It does not matter so much how large or small the extremes are; as long as the average results remain consistent with the business objectives, risk is managed by allowing the high and low values to balance each other, providing a stable and predictable overall result.

Project risk management in this macro sense can be useful at the project portfolio and enterprise levels. If all the projects undertaken are considered together, performance primarily depends on the results of the "typical" project. Some projects will fail while others achieve spectacular results, but the aggregate performance is what matters to the business's bottom line. Chapter 13 explores managing risk for a collection of projects and the relationship of portfolio and enterprise risk management to project risk management.

Micro-Risk Management

Passive measurement, even in the fields that manage risk using large populations, is never the whole job. Studying averages is necessary, but it is never sufficient. Managing risk also involves taking action to influence the outcomes.

In the world of gambling, which is filled with students of risk on both sides of the table, knowing the odds in each game is a good starting point. Both parties also know that if they can shift the odds, they will be more successful. Casinos shift the game in roulette by adding zeros to the wheel but not including them in the calculation of the payoffs. In card games such as blackjack casino owners employ the dealers, knowing that the dealer has a statistical advantage. In blackjack the players may also shift the odds by keeping track of the cards recently played, but establishments minimize this advantage through frequent shuffling of the decks and barring known card counters from play. There are even more effective methods for shifting the odds in games of chance, but most are not legal; tactics like stacking decks of cards and loading dice are frowned upon. Fortunately, in project risk management, shifting the odds is not only completely fair, it is an excellent idea.

Managing risk in this small sense considers each case separately—every investment in a portfolio, every individual bank loan, every insurance policy, and, in the case of projects, every significant exposure faced by the current project. In all of these cases, standards and criteria are used to minimize the possibility of large individual variances above the mean, and actions are taken to limit adverse results. Screening criteria are applied at the bank to avoid making loans to borrowers who appear to be poor credit risks. (Deviating from this policy by offering so-called subprime mortgages led to a disastrous worldwide economic downturn in 2008.) Insurers either raise the price of coverage or refuse to sell insurance to people who seem statistically more likely to generate claims. Insurance firms also use tactics aimed at reducing the frequency or severity of the events, such as auto safety campaigns and programs encouraging fire prevention. Managers of mutual funds work to influence the boards of directors of companies whose stocks are held by the fund. All these tactics work to shift the odds—actively managing risk in the small sense.

For projects, risk management is almost entirely similar to these examples, focusing on specific aspects of each project. Thorough screening of projects at the overall business level attempts to select only the best opportunities. It would be excellent risk management to pick out and terminate (or avoid altogether) the projects that will ultimately fail—if only it were that easy. As David Packard noted many years ago, "Half the projects at Hewlett-Packard are a waste of time and money. If I knew which half, I would cancel them."

Project risk management—risk management in the small sense—works to improve the chances for each individual project. The leader of a project has no large population, only the single project; there will be only one outcome. While in most other fields risk management is primarily concerned with the average outcomes of large numbers of independent events, for project risk management *predictability* matters most. For this we must strive to manage the variation of possible results for each project.

For a given project you can never know the precise outcome in advance. However, through review of data from earlier work and project planning, you can improve the results that you can expect. Analysis and planning will help you to better understand the odds and take action to improve them. The goals of risk management for a single project are to establish credible plans consistent with business objectives and then to shrink the range of possible outcomes, particularly undesirable outcomes.

One type of "loss" for a project may be measured in time. The distributions in figure 1-3 compare timing expectations graphically for two similar projects. These plots differ from the plot in figure 1-2, which was based on empirical measurements of a large number of actual, historical cases. The plots in figure 1-3 are projections of what might happen for these two projects, based on estimates and assumptions for each. These histograms are speculative and require you to imagine executing each project many times, with varying results. Developing this sort of risk characterization for projects is explored in chapter 9, about quantifying and analyzing project risk. For the present, assume that the two projects have expectations as displayed in these two distributions.

Figure 1-3: Possible Outcomes for Two Projects

For these two projects, the average (or mean) duration is the same, but the range of expected durations for Project A is much larger. Project B has a much narrower spread (the statistical variance, or standard deviation), and so it will be more likely to be completed close to the expected duration. The larger range of possible durations for Project A represents higher risk, even though it also includes a small possibility of an outcome even shorter than that expected for Project B. Project risk increases with the level of uncertainty, both negative and positive.

Project risk management uses the two fundamental parameters of risk—likelihood and loss—just as any other area of risk management does. Likelihood is generally characterized as probability and may be estimated in several ways for project events (though often by guessing, so it can be quite imprecise). For projects, loss is generally referred to as impact, and it is based on the consequences to the project if the risk does occur. Impact is usually measured in time (as in the examples in figure 1-3) or cost, particularly for quantitative risk assessment. Other risk impacts include increased effort, issues with stated deliverable requirements, and a wide range of other more qualitative consequences that are not easily measured, such as team productivity, conflict, and impact on other projects or other operations. Applying these concepts to project risk is covered in chapter 7.

Managing project risk depends on the project team understanding the sources of variation in projects, and then working to minimize threats and to maximize opportunities wherever it is feasible. Because projects of most types are unlikely to be repeated enough times to develop distributions based on measured, empirical data like those in figure 1-2, project risk analyses rely heavily on projections and range estimates.

OPPORTUNITIES AND RISKS

The topic of opportunities arises frequently when discussing risk. In the project environment, there are at least three types of opportunity management for projects:

1. Overall project goals and scoping choices
2. Project planning choices
3. Uncertain project events having potential benefits

The first relates to choices made concerning the specifications and other aspects of the expected project deliverable, and often this precedes the project. The second type of opportunity management for projects relates to decisions made as the work is planned and executed and involves evaluating trade-offs among project parameters (such as reducing a schedule by increasing the work done in parallel). A third type of opportunity involves uncertain project activities that may result in either damaging or beneficial results (similar to the duration estimates in figure 1-3). The first two are choices, not uncertainties, but all three types of opportunity relate to project risk management, and each is addressed in some detail in this book.

To a great degree, project risk management is necessitated by the first kind of project opportunity. Projects are always unique undertakings, so the results they are expected to deliver inevitably involve unknowns. The business case for most projects rests on the assumption that the value of the outcome will significantly exceed the project's cost. Especially at the outset of the work, however, there are generally significant unknowns, so there will be a range of possibilities. If the ranges for cost and value are realistically represented by the curves in the upper portion of figure 1-4, then the expected net returns can be expected to look something like the distribution in the lower portion of the figure. The mean expected return will be approximately the difference between the average of the assumed values and costs.

This all assumes that the initial expectations are realistic, based on historical performance, some analysis, and reasonable

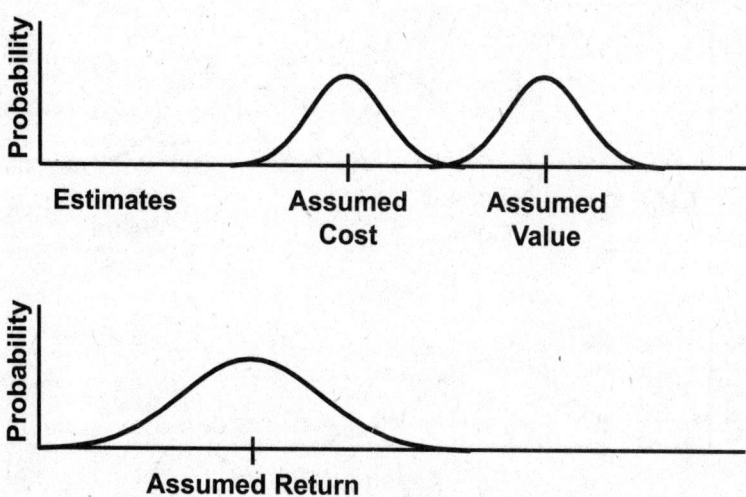

Figure 1-4: Assessing Typical Return for a Project

assumptions. In most cases, however, the initial project assumptions may be based more on wishful thinking than on reliable, analytical analysis. For projects initiated based on "stretch" goals—with aggressive expectations outside of what might reasonably be expected—the picture changes. If there is pressure to assume that costs will be near the low end of the realistic range, and increase the expected value of project results to the most optimistic possibilities, the range for project returns will resemble figure 1-5.

Again, the assumed return is the difference between the assumed project value and cost, and on that basis it looks excellent. The range of possible net return outcomes, though, should cause great concern. When project sponsors and stakeholders impose aggressive "stretch goals" (based sometimes on no more than a lack of understanding), it steeply tilts the playing field. This creates an environment where all uncertainty and project risk is on

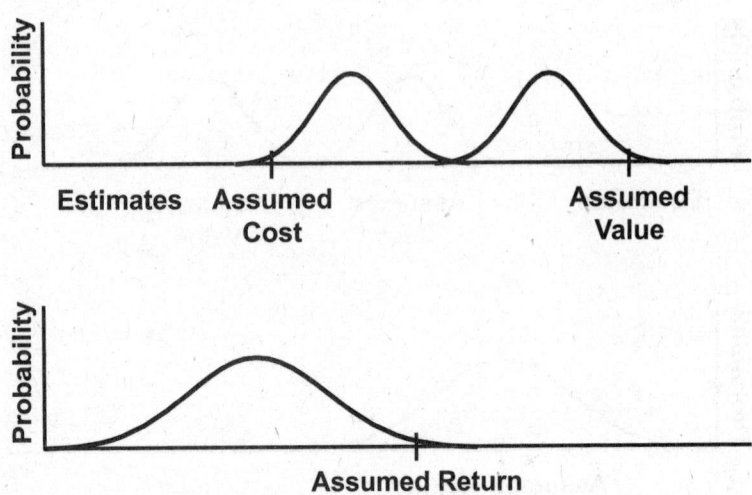

Figure 1-5: Returns for a "Stretch" Project

the downside, and makes it almost certain that the project will be unsuccessful, or at least "challenged." This type of project opportunity is based on choices for objectives and constraints. Chapters 3 through 5 explore identifying risks associated with unrealistic project constraints and questionable objectives.

A second type of project opportunity management also involves choices, this time in how you plan to do the work. It is common for projects to find that their bottom-up plans fall short on timing, cost, or other initial expectations. This may be a direct result of aggressively setting goals, as discussed previously. Striving to meet aspirational objectives, project leaders work to optimize the workflow by adopting alternatives that compress plans, save money, or use other trade-offs to better align with key stakeholder expectations. Even when these tactics appear to address project constraints (such as aggressive deadlines), the adjustments and tactics adopted will inevitably increase risk and create new failure modes. Chapter 6 explores the self-inflicted risks that emerge from managing project constraints.

The third type of project opportunity involves beneficial uncertainties associated with planned activities. There may be little opportunity of this kind, however, because on many projects optimistic expected results and aggressive constraints cause uncertainties to skew heavily toward adverse consequences. That said, considering these cases certainly falls to the project leader, and you can often find at least a few potentially beneficial uncertainties if you look. Chapter 6 explores uncovering such "positive risks," and chapter 7 addresses techniques for managing them.

BENEFITS OF PROJECT RISK MANAGEMENT

Is it even possible to manage risk? This fundamental question is unfortunately not trivial, because uncertainty is intrinsic to project work, regardless of how we approach it. If "managing risk" means completely removing all risks and uncertainty, for projects this is certainly impossible. However, we can work to understand significant sources of risk and take prudent actions to reduce failure modes and increase our chances for project success.

Because our ability to manage risk is at best only partially effective, it's fair to ask a second question: Should we even bother to try? As with any business decision, a good answer depends on costs and benefits. Developing a project plan with thorough risk analysis unquestionably involves effort, which some may see as unnecessary overhead. Project risk management can also provide many benefits, though. For complicated projects, the benefits gained from grappling with risk generally far outweigh the costs.

A summary of the benefits of project risk management follow, and each is amplified in later chapters. Specific project risk management costs are outlined in the following section.

Less VUCA

In recent years the acronym VUCA has become part of the conversation around business risk. It originated with the military in the wake of the 9/11 terrorist attacks in 2001. Leaders at the Pentagon used VUCA to characterize the shifts emerging internationally. VUCA stands for:

- **Volatility:** Unpredictable change
- **Uncertainty:** Lack of predictability
- **Complexity:** Difficulty understanding interactions
- **Ambiguity:** Insufficient clarity

All of this relates generally to today's business environment, and particularly to projects. The seventh edition of the *PMBOK®* *Guide* from the Project Management Institute (PMI®), while mostly de-emphasizing risk management, does define an Uncertainty Performance Domain containing *"Uncertainty, Ambiguity, Complexity, Volatility,* and Risk." Effective project risk management aims to understand these challenges and works to minimize them.

VUCA environments are chaotic, stressful, and demotivating, so reducing the effects of VUCA can lower the frustration caused by avoidable problems, and reduce the cost and effort of late project rework. Identifying root causes of potential project problems uncovers weaknesses and helps in constructing more robust plans. Deeper understanding of project challenges enables project teams to avoid pitfalls.

Justifying Project Reserves

Risk analysis quantifies project uncertainties, so it is useful in establishing reserves for schedule and/or project resources. It's always more appropriate to define a schedule range (or budget window) than single-point fixed objectives for risky projects. Commitments for high-risk projects are best established with goals that reflect the risks. Setting a target date with schedule reserve establishes a project deadline further out. Having a range for acceptable project performance visibly communicates the uncertainty. For example, the target schedule for a risky project might be six months, but the committed schedule, reflecting potential problems, may be set at seven months. Completion within (or before) this range defines a successful project; only if the project exceeds seven months will it be considered a failure. Project risk assessment data provides both the rationale and the magnitude for required reserves. Chapter 10 addresses this in more detail.

Increased Project Control and Understanding

Risk management efforts build awareness of project exposures for the project team, showing when, where, and how painful the problems could be. This causes people to work in ways that tend to make project difficulties less likely, similarly to driving carefully in adverse weather conditions.

Risk data also provides deeper understanding of project exposures and more vivid and convincing messaging about possible consequences. Using information about the likelihood and consequences of potential problems can be very convincing in discussions with stakeholders, and provides increased leverage to project leaders in defining objectives, determining budgets, obtaining staff, setting deadlines, and negotiating project changes.

Improved Overall Management

Increased awareness of project risk also improves management of projects across an organization. Sharing risk assessment and status information among projects can materially raise the chances of projects achieving their objectives. Although there are never any guarantees, broader awareness of common failure modes and ideas that make projects more robust can significantly improve the odds for success. In addition, risk management processes help in identifying infeasible or otherwise problematic projects so they can be avoided, quickly aborted, or at least modified. Risk analysis can also reveal opportunities for improving projects and increasing the value of project results.

Effective risk management also helps in defining appropriate project priorities. Thorough, clear information makes setting relative priorities between projects more objective and logical. High-risk projects with substantial expected benefits may warrant increased support and attention. (High risk does often align with high reward.) You can raise your project's priority by generating a thorough risk plan, displaying your competence and readiness for dealing with possible problems. Projects that gain higher priority significantly reduce their overall risk—doors are opened, obstacles disappear, needed resources are allocated, and queues for services shrink.

An additional benefit of thorough risk management will be better portfolio management for all ongoing and future project work. An appropriate mix of projects will include both lower- and higher-risk (and return) projects in proportions aligned with overall business objectives. Achieving and maintaining a suitable mix of ongoing projects requires realistic risk information. Chapter 13 covers the process for project portfolio management.

COSTS OF PROJECT RISK MANAGEMENT

Project risk management has many potential benefits, but it is not free. Managing risk entails work, and this requires investment in both time, effort, and funding. Directly confronting project risks can also temper the enthusiasm and performance of project contributors. Both of these factors are undeniable and must be considered (and managed) along with the benefits.

Incremental Effort, Cost, and Time

Done effectively, the overall investment for uncovering project risks need not be large. Risk identification is best done as part of overall planning, making note of risks, uncertainties, and challenges as you develop your plans. Throughout the process you can keep track of unknowns, worst cases, and other potential problems as a part of your efforts to understand the work.

Analysis of risks also need not be a major undertaking, especially if you have assembled a thorough risk register and apply straightforward assessment processes. Developing responses for key risks is similarly not typically a great deal of extra work—and in fact mostly falls under the category of "doing your job as a project leader." (Ultimately, criticism after the fact for situations where you have run into major risks usually focuses more on your overall competence as a project leader than on your risk expertise.)

Determining how much effort is warranted and what specific risk management tactics to adopt involves judgment, as well as balancing the trade-offs between more thorough analysis and expected additional benefits. Chapter 2 provides ideas for justifying incremental investment for needed improvements in process maturity.

Effect of Risk Awareness on Team Motivation

Some project leaders avoid considering risks, citing the negative effects of exposing the team to a depressing, demoralizing wallow in pessimistic thinking. While focusing on project risks may seem demotivating, it can have the opposite effect. Before you articulate the specifics of project risks, situations may seem bleak, insurmountable, and confusing. Documenting and clarifying risks and their consequences allows you to uncover their root causes and develop both a deeper understanding of potential problems and tactics to deal with them. The "devil that you know" may well be less frightening than the vague general concerns that surround new projects.

When risk management is approached as a method for addressing past project problems and building resilience into plans, most team members will cooperate enthusiastically. Risk management work that helps to avoid or minimize catastrophes can be seen as a positive force that helps contributors see projects as realistic and doable. (And when the risk assessments reveal an overall project that is truly bleak, awareness of that up front—before investing a lot of money, time, and effort in a doomed undertaking—is invaluable and allows the focus to shift to better, more valuable projects.)

THE PROJECT RISK MANAGEMENT PROCESS

The overall structure of this book follows a long-established sequence of steps for project risk management similar to risk processes in many other fields. The topics are:

1. Plan Risk Management
2. Identify Risks

3. Perform Qualitative Risk Analysis
4. Perform Quantitative Risk Analysis
5. Plan Risk Responses
6. Implement Risk Responses
7. Monitor Risks

Chapter 2 covers the first topic, "Plan Risk Management," exploring the role of project risk management during project initiation. Chapters 3 through 6 address the topic "Identify Risks," focusing on scope risk, schedule risk, resource risk, and managing project constraints.

The next two topics, "Perform Qualitative Risk Analysis" and "Perform Quantitative Risk Analysis," relate to risk assessment. This is covered on two levels, for activity risks in chapter 7, and for overall project risk in chapter 9. The topics "Plan Risk Responses" and "Implement Risk Responses" are also discussed twice, in chapter 8 for activities and in chapter 10 for the project as a whole. Chapter 11 focuses on the topic "Monitor Risks," and chapter 12 covers the relationship between risk management and project closure.

These topics align with project management process categories as shown in figure 1-6. These categories are broadly representative of the phases in many project life cycles, and may be found described in PMI® publications such as *Process Groups: A Practice Guide*.

As in most project management literature, including many PMI® publications, most of this book aligns with project planning because this is where the "heavy lifting" of project risk management happens. The material here focuses on the how-to of effective risk management, from the practitioner's standpoint. This book places particular emphasis on ideas and tools that work well

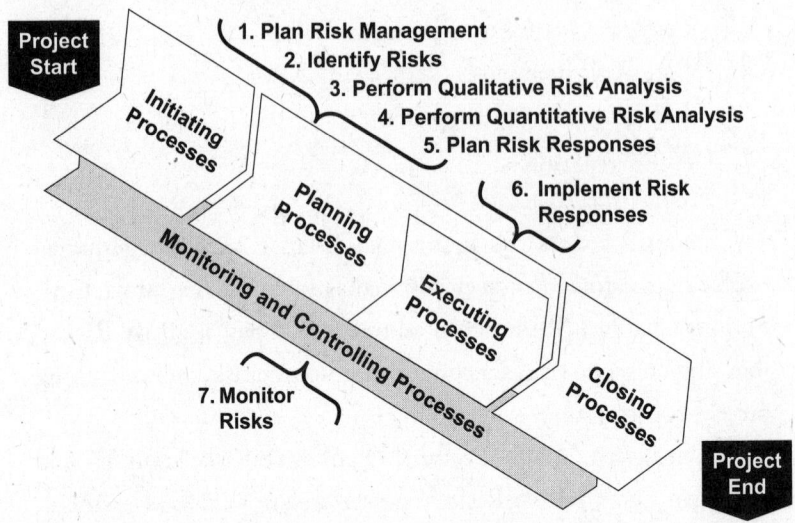

Project Start

Initiating Processes

1. Plan Risk Management
2. Identify Risks
   3. Perform Qualitative Risk Analysis
    4. Perform Quantitative Risk Analysis
    5. Plan Risk Responses

Planning Processes

    6. Implement Risk Responses

Executing Processes

Monitoring and Controlling Processes

7. Monitor Risks

Closing Processes

Project End

■ **Figure 1-6:** Project Risk Management Topic Links to Project Management Processes

in the real world and that can be easily adapted to complex and technical projects. Coverage of project risk management topics here is both broad and deep, and supports those who may be using this book to prepare to sit for the Project Management Professional (PMP®), Risk Management Professional (RMP®), or other certification tests.

ANATOMY OF A FAILED PROJECT: THE FIRST PANAMA CANAL PROJECT

Risk management is never just about looking forward. Heeding the lessons learned on projects of all types—even some distant examples—can help you avoid problems on new projects. One such example, illustrating that people have been making similar mistakes for a long, long time, is the initial effort by the French to construct a canal across Panama. Although this project is far from recent, it offers many lessons in managing risk that remain valuable to this day.

The construction of the Panama Canal over a hundred years ago faced unprecedented technical challenges and was the risky, high-tech project of its day. There were no earlier similar projects of its scale to learn from, and much of the engineering required extensive innovation. It was, for its time, breathtakingly expensive. The Panama Canal represents the single largest project investment anywhere on earth prior to the late twentieth century. The construction effort stretched over several decades, required a series of project leaders, and provides a wealth of project management examples, both positive and disastrous. (Examples cited throughout this book are drawn from a number of sources, but by far the best single source is historian David McCullough's first book: *The Path Between the Seas: The Creation of the Panama Canal, 1870–1914*.)

The story of the Panama Canal is especially instructive because it is actually the story of two projects that straddled the emergence of modern project management in the early twentieth century. The first project failed for many reasons, but lack of good project and risk management played a huge part. The second succeeded largely because of the rigorous and disciplined application of good project practices. The Panama Canal projects illustrate many of the points made in this book, and they demonstrate important concepts applicable to current projects.

First, successful project management practices are not new. They are well established and have worked effectively for over a century. Modern project management was developed in the late

1800s to deal with the increasingly enormous civil engineering projects of that era all over the world—the bridges, the transcontinental railroads, the dams, and other massive projects made possible by Machine Age technology. *Many basic lessons learned on earlier projects can be usefully applied to your high-tech projects today.*

Second, tools for managing projects have evolved significantly, but the fundamental principles have changed little. Henry Gantt, who developed the chart that bears his name, contributed to the planning of many projects. He did all of this with a ruler and a straight edge. Never in his whole life did he fire up Microsoft Project. *Having the very newest tool may or may not help your project, but understanding why management tools are important and how best to use them will always serve you well.*

Finally, the systematic application of good methods leads to successful outcomes in projects of all types. All projects are fundamentally dependent on people, and human beings are not very different today than we were hundreds, or even thousands, of years ago. *To motivate people and enhance performance on your project team, you can look to what has worked before—because by and large, it still does.*

The building of the Panama Canal was not an impossible project; it was, after all, ultimately completed. However, the initial undertaking was certainly premature. The first canal project, begun in the late 1800s, entailed massive risk. Negligible investment in project management contributed significantly to the decision to go forward in the first place and directly resulted in major project problems and its ultimate failure.

Although there was speculation far earlier, the first serious investigation of a canal in Central America was in the mid-1800s. Estimates were that such a canal would provide US$48 million a year in shipping savings and might be built for less than US$100 million. Further study onsite was less optimistic, but in 1850 construction of a railroad across the Isthmus of Panama started. The railroad was ultimately completed, but the US$1.5 million, two-year project swelled to US$8 million before it was finished, three years late in 1855. After a slow start, the railroad did prove to be a financial success, but its construction problems foreshadowed the canal efforts to come.

A few years later on the other side of the world, the Suez Canal was completed and opened in 1869. This project was sponsored and led successfully from Paris by Ferdinand de Lesseps. This triumph earned him the nickname "The Great Engineer," although he was actually a diplomat by training, not an engineer at all. He had no technical background and only modest skills as an administrator. However, he had completed a project many thought to be impossible and was now world famous. The Suez project was a huge financial success, and de Lesseps and his financial backers were eager to take on new challenges.

Examining the world map, de Lesseps decided that a canal at Panama would be his next triumph, so in the late 1870s a French syndicate negotiated the necessary agreements in Bogota, Colombia. (Panama was then the northernmost part of Colombia.) They were granted rights to build and operate a canal in exchange for a small percentage of the revenue to be generated over ninety-nine years.

Although it might seem curious today that these canal construction projects so far from France originated there, in the late 1800s Paris was the center of the engineering universe. The best schools in the world were there, and many engineering giants of the day lived in Paris, including Gustav Eiffel (then planning his tower). Such complex technical projects could hardly have arisen anywhere else.

The process of defining the Panama project started promisingly enough. In 1879, Ferdinand de Lesseps sponsored an International Congress to study the feasibility of a canal connecting the Atlantic and Pacific oceans through Central America. Over a hundred delegates gathered in Paris from a large number of nations, though most of the delegates were French. A number of routes were considered, and canals through Nicaragua and Panama both were recommended as possibilities. Construction ideas, including a realistic lock-and-dam concept (somewhat similar to the canal that was ultimately built), were also proposed. In the end, though, the Congress voted to support a sea-level canal project at Panama, even though nearly all the engineers present thought the idea infeasible and voted against it. Not listening to subject matter experts is a perilous way to start a project. The Panama Canal was neither the first nor the last project to suffer self-inflicted problems arising from insufficient technical input.

Planning for the project was also a low priority. De Lesseps paid little attention to technical problems. He believed need would result in innovation as it had at Suez, and the future would take care of itself. He valued his own opinions and ignored the views of those who disagreed with him, even recognized authorities. An inveterate optimist, he was convinced, based only on self-confidence, that he could not fail. These attitudes are not conducive to good risk management; few things are more dangerous to a project than an overly optimistic project leader. His primary risk management strategy seems to have been "hoping for the best."

The broad objective de Lesseps set for his Compagnie Universal du Canal Interoceanique was to build a sea-level canal in twelve years, to open in 1892. He raised US$60 million from investors through public offerings—a lot of money, but still less than one-third of the initial engineering cost estimate of more than US$200 million. In addition to this financial shortfall, there was little detailed planning done before work actually commenced, and most of that was done at the 1879 meeting in Paris. Even on the visits that de Lesseps made to Panama and New York to build support for the project, he failed to engage technical experts.

Eventually the engineers traveled to Panama, and digging started in 1882. Quickly, estimates of the volume of excavation required started to rise, to 120 million cubic meters—almost triple the estimates that were used for the decisions in 1879. As the magnitude of the effort rose, de Lesseps made no public changes to his cost estimates or to the completion date.

Management of risks on the project, inadequate at the start, improved little in the early stages of execution. There were many problems. Panama is in the tropics, and torrential rains for much of the year created floods that impeded the digging and made the work dangerous. The frequent rains turned Panama's clay into a flowing, sticky sludge that bogged down work, and the moist, tropical salt air combined with the viscous mud to destroy machinery. There was also the issue of elevation. The continental divide in Panama is not too high by North or South American standards, but it does rise to more than 130 meters. For a canal to cross Central America, it would be necessary to dig a trench more than fifteen kilometers long to this depth, an unprecedented amount of excavation. Digging the remainder of the eighty-kilometer transit across the isthmus was nearly as daunting.

Adequate funding for the work was also a problem because only a portion of the money that de Lesseps raised was allocated to construction. (Most of the money went for publicity, including an impressive periodic *Canal Bulletin*, used to build interest and support.) Worst of all, diseases, especially malaria and yellow fever, were lethal to many workers not native to the tropics, who died by the hundreds. As work progressed, the engineers, already dubious, increasingly believed the plan to dig a sea-level canal was doomed.

Intense interest in the project and a steady stream of new workers kept work going, and the *Canal Bulletin* reported good progress (regardless of what was actually happening). As the project progressed there were changes. Several years into the project, in 1885, the cost estimates were finally raised, and investors provided new funds that quadrupled the project budget to US$240 million. The expected opening of the canal was delayed "somewhat," but no specific date was offered. Claims were made at this time that the canal was half dug, but the truth was probably closer to 15 percent. Information on the project was far from trustworthy.

In 1887, costs were again revised upward, now exceeding US$330 million. The additional money was borrowed, as de Lesseps could find no new investors. Following years of struggle and frustration, the engineers finally won the debate over construction of a canal at sea level. Plans were shifted to construct dams on the rivers near each coast to create an enormous new lake that would serve as much of the transit. Sets of locks would be needed to bring ships up to, and down from, the manmade lake. Although this would slow the transit of ships somewhat, it significantly reduced the necessary excavation.

Even with these changes, problems continued to mount, and by 1889 more revisions and even more money were needed. After repeated failures to raise funding, de Lesseps liquidated the Compagnie Universal du Canal Interoceanique and shut the project down. This collapse caused complete financial losses for all the investors. By 1892 scandals were rampant, and the bad press and blame spread far and wide. Soon the lawyers and courts of France were busy dealing with the project's aftermath.

The French do not seem to have done a formal postproject analysis, but looking at the project in retrospect reveals over a decade of work, more than US$300 million spent, lots of digging, and no canal. Following the years of effort, the site was ugly and an ecological mess. The cost of this project also included at least 20,000 lives lost. (Many workers who came to Panama died so soon after their arrival that their deaths were never recorded; some estimates of the death toll run as high as 25,000.) As a direct result of this project failure, the French government fell in 1892, ending one of the messiest and most costly project failures in history.

The project leader did not fare well in the wake of the disaster. Lacking technical expertise, Ferdinand de Lesseps was misguided in his beliefs that equipment and medicines would appear when needed. He also chronically reported more progress than was real (through either poor analysis or deception; the records are not clear enough to tell). In 1894, he died a broken man, in poverty. Had he never undertaken the project at Panama, he would have been remembered as the heroic builder of the Suez Canal. Instead, his name is primarily linked to the failure at Panama.

The failed attempt provided clear evidence of the immense challenges building a sea-level canal at Panama faced from rains, flooding, geology, disease, and more. Many of these problems persist to this day, even with modern technology.

Although we can't know whether a canal at Panama could have been constructed in the 1880s, better project and risk management practices, widely available at the time, would have helped substantially. Setting a more appropriate initial objective, or at least modifying it sooner, would have improved the likelihood of success. Honest, more frequent communication—the foundation of well-run projects—would almost certainly have either forced these changes or led to the earlier abandonment of the work, saving thousands of lives and a great deal of money.

PLANNING FOR RISK MANAGEMENT

"You can observe a lot just by watching."

—YOGI BERRA

Planning for risk involves paying attention. When we don't watch, projects fail.

How many? One frequently quoted statistic is 75 percent. One prominent source for this assertion goes back to studies starting in the 1990s by the Connecticut-based Standish Group and documented in the 1994 *CHAOS Report*. This is what the Standish Group actually reported:

- About a quarter of the projects in the study delivered results on time and on budget.
- Approximately another quarter were canceled or they failed to deliver anything.
- The remaining roughly one half of the projects were in between. They were categorized as "challenged," because although they successfully produced deliverables they did so late, over budget, or both.

More recent Standish Group research reporting shows slightly better results (more than a third "successful," with less than two-thirds "challenged" or "failed"), but the overall picture they paint still appears bleak.

There are reasons to be skeptical of these numbers, starting with the fact that if three out of four projects actually failed, there would probably be a lot fewer projects. The Standish Group statistics focus on very large IT projects, which historically tend to be problematic. And project risk increases significantly with the kind of scale and complexity these projects represent. (Their 2015 *CHAOS* update reported, unsurprisingly, much better statistics for small- and medium-sized projects.)

And what about all those "challenged" projects? It is fair to ask what was being compared in these assessments. Some of these projects may have been saddled with unrealistic expectations at their start—making outright success unattainable—and many (as reported by Standish in 2015) did ultimately deliver significant value.

Whatever the true numbers for "failed" projects may be, however, it seems fair to say that too many projects unnecessarily get into trouble. Better project risk management can help.

Although unanticipated "acts of God" doom some projects, most fail for one of three reasons:

- The project is actually impossible.
- The project is overconstrained ("challenged," using the Standish Group model).
- The project is poorly managed.

A project is **impossible** when its objective lies beyond the technical capabilities currently available. "Design an antigravity device" is an example. Other projects are entirely possible, but **overconstrained**—not feasible to complete within the time and resource goals. "Rewrite all the corporate accounting software so that it can use a different database package in two weeks using two part-time university students" is an overconstrained project. And unfortunately, projects also fail despite having a feasible deliverable and plausible time and budget expectations. These projects fail because of **poor management**—simply because too little thought is put into the work to ensure successful project results.

Risk management and project planning enable you to distinguish among and deal with all three of these situations. For projects that are demonstrably beyond the state of the art, planning and other analysis will generally provide information needed to terminate the project or at least to redirect the objective (buy a helicopter, for example, instead of developing the antigravity device). Chapter 3, on identifying project scope risks, discusses these situations. For projects with unrealistic timing, resource, or other constraints, risk and planning data provide you with a compelling basis for project negotiation, shifting to more credible project goals (or, in some cases, abandoning projects that lack business justification). Chapters 4, 5, and 6, on schedule, resource, and other risk identification, discuss issues common for overconstrained projects. Dealing with "challenged" projects through negotiating a realistic project baseline is covered in chapter 10.

The third situation, a credible project that fails because of faulty execution, is definitely avoidable. With adequate attention to project and risk planning, these projects can succeed. Well-planned projects begin quickly, limiting unproductive chaos. Rework and defects are minimized, and people remain busy performing activities that efficiently move the project forward. A solid foundation of project analysis also reveals problems that might lead to failure and prepares the project team to take corrective action promptly. In addition to making project execution more efficient, risk planning also provides insight for faster, better project decisions. And although changes are required to succeed with the first two types of projects mentioned earlier, this third type depends only on you, your project team, and application of the solid project management concepts you will find throughout this book.

PROJECT SELECTION

Project risk is a significant factor even before there is a project. Projects begin as a result of an organization's business decision to create something new or change something old. Projects make up a large portion of the overall work done in most organizations today, and at any given time there are always many more attractive project ideas than can be funded or adequately staffed. Assumptions about embryonic projects may be wildly unrealistic, complicating the task of selecting appropriate projects. The process for choosing projects both creates project risk and relies on project risk analysis, so project portfolio management is tightly linked to project risk management.

Project selection affects project risk in several ways. Poor project portfolio management exacerbates a number of common project risks:

- Excessively rosy expectations for project results and benefits
- Too many projects competing for limited resources
- Project priorities that are misaligned with overall strategies
- Inadequately funded projects

- Unrealistic project deadlines
- Excessive organizational capability assumptions

Project risk management data is also a critical input to the project selection process. Project portfolio management uses project risk assessment as a key criterion for determining which projects to put into plan at any given time. Without high-quality risk data and credible estimates for candidate projects, excessive numbers of projects, many unrealistic, will be undertaken, and many of them will fail. Chapter 13 explores the topic of project portfolio risk management in some detail.

OVERALL PROJECT PLANNING PROCESSES

The project selection process is a major source of risk for all projects, but the overall project management approach is even more significant. In organizations lacking adequate project management processes, risks will be unknown and probably unacceptably high for most projects. Without adequate project analysis, no one has much idea of what "going right" looks like, so it is not possible to identify and manage the risks—the things that may go wrong. Project management processes provide the magnifying glass you need to inspect your project to discover its possible failure modes.

Good risk management depends on a regular review of the overall methods and processes used to manage projects. If most of the projects undertaken are successful, then control is probably sufficient across the organization. Too often for high-tech projects, however, this is not the case.

Exactly what process you employ matters less than that you have one and use it. If elaborate, formal, heavyweight project management works for you, great. If agile, more informal adaptive methodologies provide what you need, that's fine too. What's important for risk management is that you adopt and consistently use an effective process to manage your projects.

In too many environments there is indifference or even hostility to project planning. This may originate in organizations at several levels. At the project level, other types of work may carry higher priority, or planning may seem a waste of time. Above the project level, project management processes can be seen as unnecessary overhead, or they may even be discouraged to deprive project teams of the data needed to win arguments with their managers. Whatever the rationalizations, there can be little effective risk management without planning. Without at least a basic plan, most potential project problems and failure modes will remain undetected.

The next several pages provide support for the investment in project processes. If you or your management need convincing that project management is worthwhile, read on. If project planning and related management processes are adequate in your organization, skip ahead.

At the Project Level

A number of reasons are frequently cited by project leaders for avoiding project planning. Some projects are not thoroughly planned because the changes are so frequent that planning seems futile. Quite a few leaders know that project management methodology is beneficial, but because their time is limited they feel they must do only "real work." An increasingly common reason offered is the belief that in "internet time," thinking and planning are no longer affordable luxuries. There is a response for each of these assertions.

Inevitable project change is a poor reason not to plan. In fact, frequent change is one of the most damaging risk factors (and volatility supplies the first letter of VUCA). Managing project work in the face of change requires good project information. Project teams that have solid planning data are better able to resist inappropriate change, rejecting or deferring proposed shifts by demonstrating adverse consequences using the project plan data. Even when changes are necessary it is much more straightforward to carry on with a modified existing plan than to start over in a vacuum. In addition, many mid-project changes result directly from faulty project assumptions that persist because of inadequate or incomplete planning data. Better understanding leads to clearer definition of project deliverables and fewer reasons for change.

The time it takes to develop plans for at least the next phase or iteration of work is also not a good reason to avoid planning. Although it is universally true that no project has enough time, a belief that there is "no time for planning" is difficult to defend. Every bit of the work in any project must always be planned. The only choice to be made is when to do it. You can develop plans in focused, early-project efforts or as periodic iterative exercises, or you can identify upcoming work one activity at a time, day-by-day, all through the project. All the work must be identified by someone, sooner or later. An ad hoc approach requires comparable, if not more, overall effort, and it carries a number of disadvantages. First, there can be few, if any, meaningful metrics, and tracking project progress will at best be guesswork. Second, most project risks, even those that should be easily identified, will come as unexpected surprises when they occur. Early, more thorough planning provides other advantages, including better balancing of staffing resources. Why not invest in planning when the benefits are greatest?

Assertions about "internet time" are also difficult to accept. Projects that must execute as quickly as possible need more, not less, project planning. Delivering a result that maximizes value requires sequencing the work for efficiency and ensuring that the activities undertaken are truly necessary and of high priority. There is no time for rework, excessive defect correction, or unnecessary activity on fast-track projects. Project planning, particularly on time-constrained projects, *is* real work.

Above the Project Level

Organizations undertake projects assuming that they will create value, but there may be little consideration given to how they are managed. Little or no formal project process may be mandatory, particularly in high-tech environments, and it may even be discouraged.

If your organization has weak current standards and project management practices, it will be to your benefit to improve them. There are two ways to do this. Your best option is to convince the managers and other stakeholders that more formal project definition, planning, and tracking will deliver increased value to the business. When this is successful, all projects benefit. For situations where this does not work, you can still adopt greater formality on your own—if necessary in secret to avoid criticism and comments like "Why are you wasting time with all that planning stuff? Why aren't you working?"

In organizations where expenses and overhead are tightly controlled, it can be difficult to convince managers to adopt greater project formalism. Building a case for this takes time and requires metrics and examples, and you may find that some upper-level managers are highly resistant even to credible data. The benefits are substantial, though, so it is well worth trying; anything you can do to build support over time for effective project processes will help.

If you have credible, local data demonstrating the value of project management or the costs associated with inadequate process, assemble it. Most organizations that have such data also have good processes. If you have a problem that is related to inadequate project management, you may have little information available. For projects lacking a structured methodology—whether agile or traditional plan based—there may be few metrics in place. Mounting a compelling case for better overall project processes using new data may require both time and effort.

Typical metrics that may be useful in supporting your case relate to achieving specifications, managing budgets, meeting schedules, and delivering business value. Project processes directly impact the first three but may only indirectly influence the last one. The ultimate value of a project deliverable is determined by a large number of factors, many outside of your project and out of your control. Business value data may be the best information you have available, though, so make effective use of what you have.

Even if you can find or create only modest evidence supporting better project management processes, it is not hopeless. There are other approaches that may suffice, using anecdotal information, models, and case studies. How best to mount a convincing case depends on specific circumstances, because beliefs about project management among upper-level managers vary widely. Managers who naturally favor organized processes should require only minimal convincing, and any approach you use is likely to succeed.

Other managers are highly skeptical about project processes and will heavily focus on the visible costs (which are unquestionably real) and be dubious about benefits. The best approach in these cases is to gather copious information that shows the substantial penalties of informal processes as clearly as possible. Some extreme skeptics may ultimately be unpersuadable, leaving you only with the "below the radar" option.

Fortunately, most managers are somewhere in the middle, neither "true believers" in project management nor chronic process adversaries. The greatest potential for process improvement is with this ambivalent group. Using anecdotal information, models, case studies, and other information can be effective.

Anecdotal information: Building a case for more project process with stories depends on contrasting benefits with costs and demonstrating overall value. Project management lore is filled with stated benefits, among them:

- Better communication
- Less rework
- Lowered costs, reduced durations
- Earlier detection of requirement gaps and inadequate specifications
- Fewer surprises
- Less chaos, firefighting, and stress

In most organizations finding cases where better project management delivered on these benefits (or where lack of process created problems) is not difficult.

You must also address costs, and for project management some are direct and some are more subtle. The most obvious cost is the "overhead" project formality represents: meetings, documentation, and effort invested in other project management activities. Another is the initial cost of establishing good practices in an organization, such as training, job aids, and new process documentation. Assess and summarize these required investments.

There is a more subtle cost to managers in organizations that establish high project management standards: the shift that occurs in the balance of power in an organization. Without project management processes, all the power in an organization is in the hands of management; all negotiations tend to be resolved using political and emotional tactics. Having little or no data, project teams are fairly easily backed into whatever corners their management may choose. With data, the discussion shifts; future negotiations and discussions will focus more on fact-based information and less on biases and opinions. Even if you choose not to directly address this "cost," be aware of it in your discussions.

Successfully addressing the question "Is project management worth it?" using anecdotal information depends on credibly showing that the benefits outweigh the costs. Your case will be most effective if you find the best examples you can, using projects from environments as similar to yours as possible.

Models: Another possible approach for establishing the value of process relies on logical models. The need for process increases with scale and complexity, and managing projects is no exception to this. Scaling projects may be done in a variety of ways, but one common technique segregates them into three categories: small, medium, and large.

Small projects are universal; everyone does them. There is usually no particular process or formality applied, and more often than not these simple projects are successful. Nike-style ("Just Do It") project management is good enough, and although there may well be any number of slightly better ways to approach the work (apparent in hindsight, more often than not), the penalties associated with simply diving into the work are modest enough that it doesn't matter much. Project management processes are rarely applied with much rigor, even by project management zealots, because the overhead involved may double the work required to do the project.

Medium-size projects last longer and are more complex. The benefits of thinking about the work, at least a little, are obvious to most people. At a minimum, there is a "to do" list. Rolling up your sleeves and beginning work with no advance thought often costs significant additional time and money. As the "to do" list spills over a single page, project management processes start to look useful. The level of complexity where this occurs has a lot to do with experience, background, and individual disposition. Many midsize projects succeed, but the possibility of falling short of some key goal (or complete project failure) increases.

For large projects, the case for defined project processes should never be in doubt. Beyond a certain scale, all projects with no process for managing the work will fail to meet at least part of their stated objectives. For the largest projects, success rates are low even with program management and systems engineering processes in addition to thorough project management practices.

For projects of different sizes, costs of execution with and without well-established project management practices will vary. figure 2-1 shows the cost of a "best effort," or brute force, approach to a project contrasted with a more proactive project management approach. The assumption for this graph is that costs will vary linearly with project scale if project management is applied, and they will vary geometrically with scale if it is not. This figure, though not based on empirical data, is solidly rooted in a large amount of anecdotal information.

The figure has no units because the point at which the crossover occurs (in total project size and cost) is highly situational. If

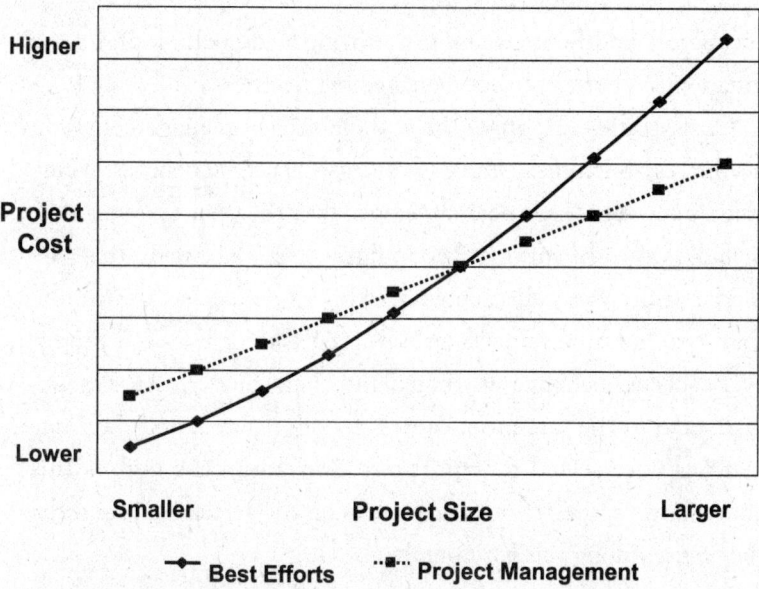

Figure 2-1: Cost Benefit for Project Management

project size is measured in effort-months, a common metric, a typical crossover might be about five total effort-months.

One motivation for adopting agile, iterative methods on complex project undertakings is to convert larger, longer projects into a succession of shorter ones—making the work of each "mini-project" iteration more straightforward to plan and manage.

Wherever the crossover point is, the cost benefit is minor near this point, and negative below it. For these smaller projects, project management is a net cost or has small financial benefit. (Cost may not be the only, or even the most important, consideration, though. Project management methodologies may serve other purposes, including legal requirements, better risk visibility, and improved coordination among interdependent projects.)

A model similar to this, especially if it is accompanied by project success and failure data, can provide a compelling argument for adopting better project management practices.

Case studies: To offset the costs of project management, you need to establish measurable (or at least plausible) benefits. Many studies and cases have been developed over the years to assess this, including the one summarized in figure 2-2. The data in this particular study was collected over a three-year period from more than two hundred projects at Hewlett-Packard. For each project every schedule change was noted and characterized. All changes attributed to the same root cause were aggregated, and the summations were sorted for the Pareto diagram in the figure. This chart shows aggregated consequences on the vertical axis and the root causes along the horizontal axis.

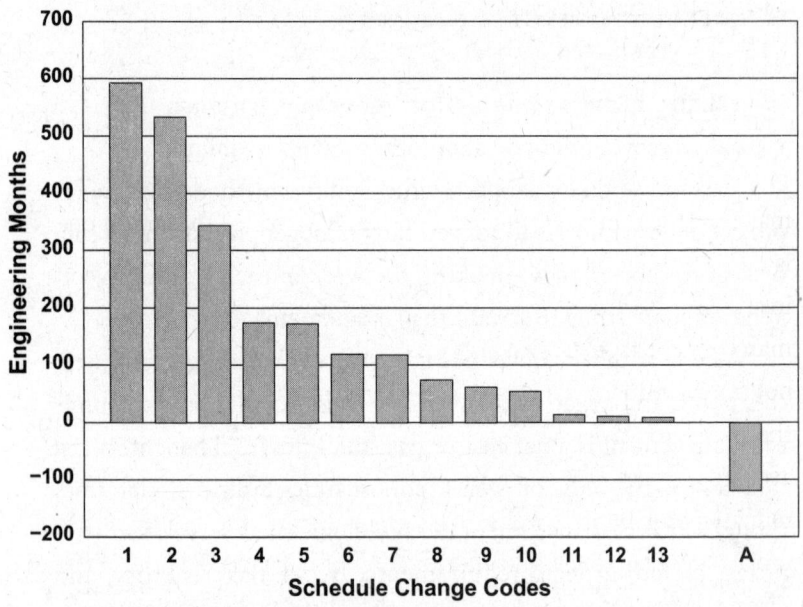

■ **Figure 2-2:** Schedule Change Pareto Diagram

Additional project work—hundreds of engineer months—was associated with the most common root causes. The codes for the root causes, sorted by severity, were:

1. Unforeseen technical problems
2. Poor estimation of effort/top-down schedules
3. Poor product/system design or integration problems
4. Changing product definition
5. Other
6. Unforeseen activities/too many unrelated activities
7. Understaffed, or resources not on time
8. Software development system/process problems
9. Related project slip (also internal vendor slip)
10. Insufficient support from service areas
11. Hardware development system/process problems
12. Financial constraints (tooling, capital, prototypes)
13. Project placed on hold
A. Acceleration

Not every one of these root causes directly correlates with project management principles, but most of them clearly do. The largest one is unforeseen technical problems, which are often a consequence of insufficient planning. The second, faulty estimation, is also a project management factor. Although better project management would not have eliminated all these slippages, it surely would have reduced them. The top two reasons in the study by themselves represent an average of roughly five unanticipated engineer-months per project; reducing this by half would have saved thousands of dollars per project. Similar conclusions may be drawn from the analysis of the Project Experience Risk Information Library (PERIL) database later in this chapter and elsewhere this book.

Case study data such as these examples can be compelling, particularly when directly related to your project work. You likely have access to data similar to this, or could easily pull together high-level recent project estimates for rework, firefighting, crisis management, missing work, and the cost of defects.

Other reasons for project management: Reducing uncertainty is a key motivator for organizations adopting project methodologies and standards. Many technical managers will go to great lengths to minimize nasty surprises. One manager who strongly supports project management practices uses the metaphor of going down whitewater rapids. Without project management, you are down flailing in the water—you have no visibility, it is cold, it is hard to breathe, and you are bouncing off rocks. With project management, you are up on a raft. It is still a wild ride, but you can see a few dozen feet ahead and steer around the worst obstacles. You can breathe more easily, you are not freezing and are less wet, and you have some confidence that you will survive the trip. In this manager's group, minimizing uncertainty is important and planning is never optional.

Another motivator is a desire (or requirement) to become more process oriented. Current standards and legal requirements for enterprise risk management in the United States and worldwide make adoption of formal processes for risk management obligatory. (The direct connection of this to project risk management is explored in chapter 13.) In firms that provide solutions to customers, using a defined methodology can be a strong competitive advantage that can help win business. In some organizations, evidence of process maturity is deemed important, so they aspire to standards for higher maturity using structures such as the Capability Maturity Models defined by the Software Engineering Institute. In other instances, specific process requirements may be tied to the work, as with many government contracts. Many industries and disciplines have strict regulations mandating specific processes, such as finance, biotech, and pharmaceuticals. In all of these cases, aspects of formal project management are mandatory, regardless of the opinions of individuals and managers.

The Project Management Methodology

Project risk management depends on thorough, sustained application of effective project management principles. While the precise nature of project management methodologies varies widely, managing risk tends to be most successful with consistent organization-wide processes. Common practices provide both additional useful data to work with and more durable support for the ongoing effort required. If you find it impossible to gain support for more effective project management principles broadly, at least resolve to apply them with sufficient rigor to your projects to help you manage your risks.

DEFINING RISK MANAGEMENT FOR THE PROJECT

In addition to basic project planning, effective risk management also involves its own specific planning. Risk planning begins by reviewing the initial project assumptions. Project charters, data-sheets, or other documents used to initiate a project often include information concerning risk, as well as overall goals, staffing assumptions, and other information. Any risk information included in these early project descriptions is worth noting; sometimes projects believed to be risky are described as such, or there may be other evidence of project risk. Projects believed to be low risk often involve assumptions leading to unrealistically low staffing and funding. Take note of any differences in your perception of project risk and the stated (or implied) risks perceived by the project sponsors and other initiators. In particular, work to understand the expectations of the project stakeholders, and adopt an approach to risk management consistent with their expectations.

Stakeholder Risk Tolerance and Quantification

Organizations in different businesses deal with risk in their own ways. Startups and speculative endeavors such as oil exploration must have a high tolerance for risk; in these environments most projects undertaken can be expected to fail, compensated by the small number that are extremely successful. More conservative organizations, such as governments and enterprises that provide solutions to customers for a fee, are generally risk averse and expect consistent success but more modest returns on each project. Organizational risk tolerance is reflected in the organizational policies, one example of which might be a pre-established prohibition on pursuing fixed-price contract projects.

In addition, project stakeholders may have strong individual opinions on project risk. Although some stakeholders may seek risks (and their associated opportunities) or be generally risk tolerant, others may wish to avoid risks through actions that minimize extreme outcomes. Technical contributors tend to prefer low risk. One often-repeated example of stakeholder risk preference is attributed to the NASA astronauts, who observed that they were perched on the launch pad atop hundreds of systems, each constructed by the lowest bidder. Risk tolerance often depends on where you are sitting.

Work to characterize the appetite for risk for your key stakeholders, especially your sponsor. In your interactions with them, ask questions to uncover clues to their risk tolerance, such as:

- Worst case, how much overall would they be willing to invest?
- What is the minimum result that they would find acceptable?
- What are the most significant concerns they have about the project?

Risk Management Strategy

Integrate what you learn about your stakeholder's risk tolerance into your overall project planning. If your key project stakeholders prefer to avoid risks, integrate processes for clearly defining requirements, detailed schedules with precise estimates, and quantitative analysis of uncertainties and worst cases. Include a thorough risk analysis in your planning and other project documents, and schedule periodic reviews to update your risk data as your project proceeds.

Even if your project is highly speculative, novel, or revolutionary, incorporate risk identification into all your planning and analysis processes and provide for thorough evaluation of all significant risks you uncover. Tolerance for risks is not a license to take them. Your goal after all is to run a successful project that delivers good value.

Planning Data

A major theme of this book is that risk management is not something that a project leader does only toward the end of project planning, if there is time. Risk permeates all projects, so risk identification processes work best when integrated into project planning and related processes. This approach offers two significant benefits. By focusing on risks as a fundamental part of project analysis, you will find more risks and unknowns. You will also expend less effort overall, because managing risks becomes a small part of work that you are doing anyway, instead of an incremental step in planning (which may appear to be optional or unnecessary overhead).

Risk identification is a fundamental part of defining and ana-lyzing scope, schedules, costs, and other project plans. As you develop planning documents, be alert to unknowns, such as work where you lack expertise, uncertain estimates, analysis depending on incomplete or unreliable-looking data, and other knowledge gaps. Develop "error bars" around quantitative estimates to assess uncertainty and probe for worst cases. Collect specific information about gaps, holes, and potential problems as you progress, and maintain a list of them as you initiate and plan your work. Chapters 3 through 6 will explore doing this in detail.

Risk Processes and Tools

To document specific project risks, establish a project risk register (as described in chapter 6, and including information such as that in figure 7-2). Throughout the project, use your risk register as the foundation for your risk management efforts and to keep identified risks for your project visible. Ensure that it includes the informa-tion you will need to analyze, prioritize, and respond to risks. You will find guidance for employing your risk register to assess and respond to risks in chapters 7 and 8. Use your register to populate a "Top Ten" risk list to keep significant current risks visible throughout your project.

Software tools for overall risk management include applications for project simulations and Monte Carlo assessments based on statistical modeling techniques. Chapter 9 explores selection and use of these techniques.

In general, as you set up processes and tools for tracking, communicating, and managing your project, ensure that they are consistent with your efforts to monitor and manage risks.

Priorities and Risk Assessment Criteria

Use your discussions with your sponsor to refine how you will prioritize risks (such as in defining qualitative assessment categories like "high, "moderate," and "low"), and ensure that your descriptions are consistent with organizational practices and your stakeholder's risk attitudes. Establish category descriptions for impact, probability, and any other parameters you plan to use in qualitative risk evaluations.

Risk Breakdown Structures, Templates, Statistics, and Metrics

Risk management is easier and more thorough when you have access to predefined templates for planning, project information gathering, and risk assessment. A "risk breakdown structure" (RBS) provides a useful template that can be customized to specific project types. An RBS defines a preestablished hierarchy of typical categories of risk. If your organization lacks such a template, the PERIL database, which will be discussed later in this chapter and throughout this book, is a very general RBS that could be a good starting point for organizing your risk data.

Templates that are preloaded with information common to most projects make planning faster and decrease the likelihood that necessary work will be overlooked. Consistent templates created for use with project scheduling applications organization-wide make sharing information easier and improve communication. If such templates exist, use them. If there are none, create and share proposed versions of common documents with others who do similar project work, and begin to establish standards.

What you collect and measure is also central to risk management. Define thresholds for project parameters such as schedule slippage, cost variances, deliverable performance, and any other status data you plan to collect. Determine in advance what actions to take whenever your project data exceeds the defined thresholds. Chapter 7 provides guidance on setting ranges and limits, and chapter 9 offers examples of metrics useful for risk management.

Project Data Archives

Long-term risk management requires a solid base of historical data. Archived project data supports project estimating, quantitative project risk analysis, and project tracking and control. Creating a shared repository of project metrics, experiences, and risks can provide trend data valuable for better risk management and process improvement in general. Chapter 12 addresses using project data to enhance overall project risk management.

Risk Management Plan

For small projects, risk planning may be informal, but for large, complex projects, you need a written risk management plan. A formal risk management plan includes information on stakeholders, planning processes, project tools, and metrics, and it states the standards and objectives for risk management on your project. While much of the information in a risk plan may apply generally to all projects in an organization, each specific project will have at least some unique risk elements.

A risk plan usually starts by summarizing your overall risk management approach, including the planning information discussed previously. In your risk plan, list the methodologies and processes that you plan to use, defining the roles for contributors responsible for them. Also include definitions and standards for any risk management tools you expect to use; the frequency and agenda for periodic risk review meetings; formats for risk management reports; and risk-related requirements for project status collection and other tracking.

In addition, for major projects and programs, define any specific activities for risk identification, analysis, control, and review, and secure the staffing and funding to support these efforts. Incorporate any budgets dedicated to risk analysis, contingency planning, and risk monitoring into your overall plans.

Another aspect of risk planning is ensuring that risk management plans include adequate attention to opportunities. Uncertainty in projects can swing both ways, and some project aspects may go better than expected. Allocate at least some of your risk management efforts to consider project efforts that could deliver better outcomes in addition to managing potential threats. Chapter 6 describes managing uncertain project opportunities.

RISK MANAGEMENT INFRASTRUCTURE FOR THE ORGANIZATION

Risk management at the project level is much more effective in organizations that take risk seriously. If you have access to available risk management assistance, use it. If there is little structured support for managing risk in your organization, encourage sharing of effective risk practices and data among your peers and managers. The discussion here briefly covers several organizational aspects of project risk management. Chapter 13 explores program, portfolio, and enterprise risk management in more detail.

Education and Coaching

Plan to participate in workshops, classes, or other formal development offerings on risk management in your organization. If there are none, propose bringing in consultants or educators to facilitate workshops aimed at building skills to improve your process maturity and more thoroughly deal with project risks.

If formal education seems not to be an option, at least organize periodic informal gatherings of your peer project leaders to network and share experiences. "Brown bag" lunchtime or similar gatherings can be a very effective tactic for exchanging ideas, sharing risks and tactics for managing them, and generally communicating practices that are effective in your environment.

If your organization has a Project Management Office (PMO) or similar centralized function dedicated to supporting project management efforts, work with the staff when setting up networking sessions. Encourage PMO team members to provide help, both formally, through consulting and similar interactions, and informally.

Whether or not you have access to a PMO or other established project resources, seek out the advice of seasoned project professionals in your organization who manage difficult projects well. Establishing mentoring relationships between novice and experienced project managers is a good way to improve overall project process maturity throughout an organization.

Process Review and Improvement

After each project, conduct a retrospective analysis to capture lessons learned, recognize effective practices, and identify processes you need to improve. Use the opportunity to collect information on any risks that occurred and what, in hindsight, you could have done differently to avoid or better manage the situation. In your postproject analysis, review your risk management approach, and initiate efforts to address deficiencies before the next projects begin. Share your findings and process updates with your peer project leaders, and review reports from other completing projects so you can also benefit from what they have learned.

Communication and Archives

During, and especially following, each project, document what you uncover about risks identified, experiences (both effective and ineffective) in managing them, and practices that you found useful in managing risks. Document and archive what you learn and share your results with other project leaders, your PMO or other support teams, key stakeholders, and others who might benefit from the information.

One way to gain a better understanding of organizational challenges and risks throughout an organization is to offer to help facilitate analysis and planning meetings (such as startup workshops, project reviews, and postproject retrospectives) for other project leaders. In addition to seeing what other projects similar to yours are facing, you will also build up goodwill and encourage other leaders to return the favor and help in facilitating your meetings. Broadening the perspectives of project analysis will uncover more risks, build a more thorough understanding of organizational challenges, and provide a foundation for better overall risk management.

Managing Organizational Biases

There are many sources of bias in most organizations that interfere with effective risk management. These include, but are hardly limited to, denial, optimism, recent experiences, poor understanding of probability and randomness, and faulty information. At the organization level, things can be done to minimize bias, but because much of it is hardwired in the human brain, it cannot be eliminated.

The most pervasive organizational source of bias affecting risk management is denial. No one wants to encounter risks, so most stakeholders put on their blinders and pretend that many sources of project risk do not exist. "Return on investment" analysis all too often assumes that all value and benefits can be realized in full, and that costs will be free of any efforts to deal with difficulties or unforeseen obstacles. In some organizations this bias runs so deep that sponsors and management actively discourage identifying and documenting risks, even accusing anyone who dares to mention them having bad attitudes. All projects have risks. Denial does not make them disappear, it just makes them bigger (and more damaging) surprises.

Optimism, recent experience, and understanding of probability also make managing risk more difficult. Most types of risk are, in fact, fairly unlikely. For risks that do not happen very often it may seem safe to ignore them, or at least to characterize them as extremely unlikely. It is human nature to underestimate the chances of encountering unlikely events with unfavorable outcomes (like most project risks) and to overestimate likelihoods for improbable events with beneficial outcomes. People often discount risks of a type that have not happened lately (or may not have happened yet). We tend to have short memories, and wishful thinking may convince us that something that has not happened for a while will never recur. We may also think that a low-probability risk that has occurred recently cannot happen again anytime soon. Establishing a broader base of risk data at the organization level makes most of these erroneous assumptions less likely. Optimism in the face of visible data showing otherwise is hard to justify. The human brain is not wired very well to think about probabilities, but even here an organization can invest in education to help people do more appropriate job assessing uncertainty.

Overall, the biggest biases in most organizations persist due to a lack of useful information. The more an organization invests in collecting, organizing, and understanding the data they have, the less "ignorance" bias they will encounter. The following section and much of the rest of this book explores typical risks encountered by actual projects. Data like this also provide a foundation to help with managing bias in the risk management process. Chapter 7 covers the topic of bias in more detail—particularly as it relates to precision and risk assessment.

THE PERIL DATABASE

Good project management is based on experience. Where does experience come from? Often, experience is won as a consequence of not-so-good project management. Fortunately, not all the expensive and painful experience has to be personal. We can also learn from the experience of others, avoiding the aggravation of seeing everything firsthand. The Project Experience Risk Information Library (PERIL) database provides a step in that direction.

In conducting workshops and classes on project risk management over decades, I have collected a great deal of anonymous data from hundreds of project leaders on their past project problems. Their descriptions included both what went wrong and the amount of impact it had on their projects. I have compiled this data in the PERIL database, which serves as a foundation for this book. The database describes a wide spectrum of things that have gone wrong with past projects, and it provides a sobering perspective on what future projects will face. The size of the PERIL database has grown with each edition of this book, and it presently includes slightly more than 1,300 cases.

Some project risks are easy to identify because they are associated with familiar work. Other project risks are more insidious because they arise from new, unusual, or otherwise unique requirements. The PERIL database is valuable in helping to identify at least some of these otherwise invisible risks. In addition, the PERIL database summarizes the magnitude of the consequences associated with key types of project risk. Realistic impact information can effectively counteract the overly optimistic assessments typically assumed for project risks. Although some of the specific cases in the PERIL database relate only to certain types of projects or may seem unlikely to recur, the majority of these situations will be applicable to most technical projects.

Sources for the PERIL Database

The information in the PERIL database comes primarily from participants in classes and workshops on project risk management, representing a wide range of project types. Slightly under half the projects are product development projects, having tangible deliverables. The remainder are information technology, customer solution, or process improvement projects. The projects in the PERIL database are worldwide, with a majority from the Americas (primarily the United States, Canada, and Mexico). The rest of the cases are from Asia (predominantly from Singapore and India) and from Europe and the Middle East (from about a dozen countries, but largely from Germany and the United Kingdom). As with most modern projects, the projects in the PERIL database, whatever their type or location, share a strong dependence on new or relatively new technology. The majority of these projects also involve software development. There are both longer and shorter projects represented here, but the typical project in the database had a planned duration between six months and one year. Although there are some large programs in PERIL, typical staffing on these projects was rarely larger than about twenty people.

The raw project numbers in the PERIL database are presented in the following table.

2022	AMERICAS	ASIA	EUR/ME	TOTAL
IT/Solution	575	98	43	716
Product Development	447	95	50	592
Total	1,022	193	93	1,308

Although the PERIL database represents many projects and their risks, even with 1,300 examples, it is far from comprehensive. The database contains only a small fraction of the many thousands of projects undertaken by the project leaders from whom the data were collected, and it does not even represent all the problems encountered on the projects that are included. Because of this, analysis of the data in the PERIL database is more suggestive of potential project risks than definitive. Despite this, as the PERIL database has grown, the overall patterns have persisted.

As with any data based on nonrandom samples, there are inevitable sources of bias. The database contains a bias for major project risks. Because the project leaders were asked to provide information on significant problems, trivial problems are excluded from this analysis by design. There is also potential bias because all cases are self-reported. Although all the information included is anonymous, some embarrassing details or impact assessment may well have been omitted or minimized. In addition, nearly all of the information was reported by people who were interested enough in project and risk management to invest their time participating in a class or workshop for skilled practitioners, so they are at least modestly skilled in project management. This probably means that problems related to poor project management will be underrepresented.

Even considering these various limitations and biases, the PERIL database does reveal a wide range of risks typical of today's projects. It is filled with constructive (and stable) patterns, and the biggest source of bias—looking only at major problems— accurately mirrors accepted strategies for risk management (focus on the "big stuff"). Nonetheless, before blindly extending the following analysis to any particular situation, be aware that your mileage may vary.

Measuring Impact in the PERIL Database

The problem situations that make up the PERIL database resulted in a wide range of adverse consequences, including forced overtime, significant overspending, scope reductions, and a long list of other undesirable outcomes that can be difficult to compare quantitatively. Although such an extensive assortment of misery may be fascinating, it is difficult to pummel into a structure for meaningful analysis. Because of this, I chose to normalize all the quantitative data in the database using only one consistent measure of impact: time, measured in weeks of project slippage. This tactic makes sense in light of today's obsession with meeting deadlines, and it was an easy choice because by far the most prevalent serious impact reported in the data was deadline slip. Focusing on time is also appropriate because among the project triple constraints of scope, time, and cost, time is the only one that's completely out of our control—when it's gone, it's gone.

For cases where the impact reported was primarily something other than time, I either worked with the project leader to estimate an equivalent project slippage or excluded the case from the database. For example, when a project met its deadline through use of substantial overtime, we estimated the slippage equivalent to working all those nights, weekends, and holidays. If a project found it necessary to make significant cuts to the project scope, we estimated the additional duration that would have been required to deliver the original scope. Where such transformations are included in the PERIL database, we were consistently conservative in estimating the adjustments.

To better reflect the reality of typical projects, the time data in the PERIL database also excludes extremes. In keeping with the theme of focus on major risk, projects that reported a time slippage of less than a week were omitted. On the assumption that there are probably better options for projects that overshoot their deadlines by six months or more, the cases included that reported longer slips are all capped at twenty-six weeks. This prevented a single case or two from inordinately skewing the analysis, while retaining the root causes for the problems.

The average impact for all records was roughly seven weeks, representing almost a 20 percent slip for a typical nine-month project. The averages by project type were consistently close to the average for all of the data, with product development projects averaging a bit more than seven weeks and IT and solution projects slightly less than seven weeks. By region, projects in the Americas averaged slightly more than seven weeks. Projects in

Asia and in Europe and the Middle East were slightly better, but still saw more than six weeks of slippage. This data by region and project type includes average impact, in weeks.

2022	AMERICAS	ASIA	EUR/ME	TOTAL
IT/Solution	6.8	6.6	6.8	6.8
Product Development	7.7	6.0	6.7	7.4
Total	7.2	6.3	6.7	7.1

Risk Causes in the PERIL Database

Although the consequences of the risks in the PERIL database are consistently reported in terms of time, the risk causes were varied and abundant. One approach to organizing this sort of data uses a risk breakdown structure (RBS) to categorize risks based on risk type. The categories and subcategories I have used to structure the database form an example of an RBS. Each reported problem in the database is characterized in the hierarchy based on its principal root cause. The top level of the hierarchy is organized similarly to the first half of this book, around the triple constraints of scope, schedule (time), and resource (cost). The database subdivides these types of risks based on further breakdown of the root causes of the risks. For most of the risks, determining the principal root cause was fairly straightforward. For others, the reported problem may have been caused by several factors, but in each case the risk was assigned to the project parameter that appeared to be the most significant.

Across the board, risks related to resource issues were dominant. They were both most frequent and, on average, most damaging. Schedule-related risks were next most numerous, followed by scope risks. Both of these categories were somewhat less consequential than the resource risks. The typical slippage for risks within each major type represented between six to eight weeks.

2022	COUNT	CUMULATIVE IMPACT (WEEKS)	AVERAGE IMPACT (WEEKS)
Resource	507	3,986	7.9
Schedule	437	2,682	6.1
Scope	364	2,557	7.0
Total	1,308	9,225	7.1

The total impact of all the risks is a bit more than 9,200 weeks—about 180 years—of slippage. A Pareto chart summarizing total impact by category is shown in figure 2-3.

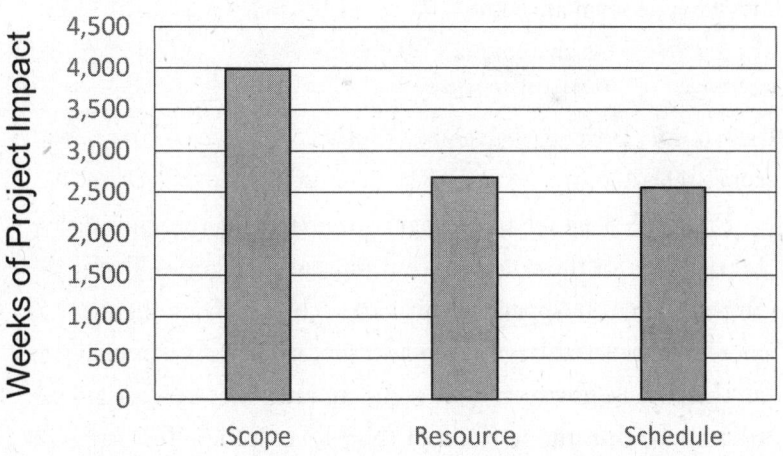

Figure 2-3: Total Project Impact by Root-Cause Category

The following table shows root-cause subcategories within scope, resource, and schedule:

2022 ROOT-CAUSE SUBCATEGORIES	DEFINITION	COUNT	CUMULATIVE IMPACT (WEEKS)	AVERAGE IMPACT (WEEKS)
Scope: Changes	Revisions made to scope during the project	367	2,972	8.1
Resource: People	Issues arising from internal staffing	270	1,436	5.3
Schedule: Delays	Project slippage due to factors under the control of the project	199	1,236	6.2
Scope: Defects	Failure to meet deliverable requirements	140	1,014	7.2
Resource: Outsourcing	Issues arising from external staffing	123	789	6.4
Schedule: Estimates	Inadequate durations allocated to project activities	95	757	8.0
Schedule: Dependencies	Project slippage due to factors outside the project	70	564	8.1
Resource: Money	Insufficient project funding	44	457	10.4

Figure 2-4 is a Pareto chart summarizing the cumulative impact data for these defined root-cause subcategories. By far the largest source of slippage in this Pareto chart is scope change; it is more than twice as large as the next subcategory. As depressing as all this data is, however, most of the subcategories here are at least partially within the purview of the project leader. This suggests that more focus on the things that you can control as a project leader can significantly reduce the number and magnitude of unpleasant surprises you'll encounter during your projects. The next three chapters will explore this idea in some detail.

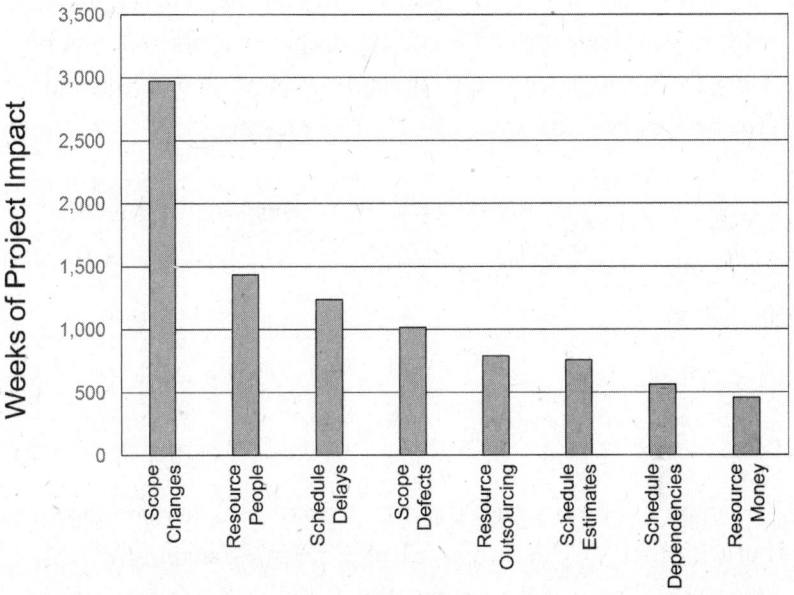

Figure 2-4: Total Project Impact by Subcategory

Risk and VUCA

Most books on project risk management spend a lot of time on theory and statistics. This book departs from that tradition by focusing instead on what actually happens to real projects, using the PERIL database as the foundation. The point is to illuminate significant sources of actual project risk, with specific suggestions about what to do about the most serious problems. Examining the PERIL data using the lens of VUCA (volatility, uncertainty, complexity, and ambiguity), we can see how the data align with these challenges.

Although the boundaries in the data for these factors can be a bit fuzzy, of the four VUCA factors uncertainty is dominant, causing close to half of the total slippage in the PERIL database. Uncertainty underpins all the root causes for resource risk. It is responsible for most of the schedule-driven risk impact, along with some complexity and volatility effects. For scope risk, ambiguity looms large, with volatility and complexity not far behind. The data in this table show where the factors align:

	UNCERTAINTY	COMPLEXITY	AMBIGUITY	VOLATILITY
Resource	2,682			
Schedule	1,693	746		• 118
Scope		1,129	1,639	1,218
Total	4,375	1,875	1,639	1,336

Figure 2-5 summarizes the data, with uncertainty dominant, but the other VUCA factors still significant. Managing VUCA requires attention at the project level, which will be addressed in chapter 10.

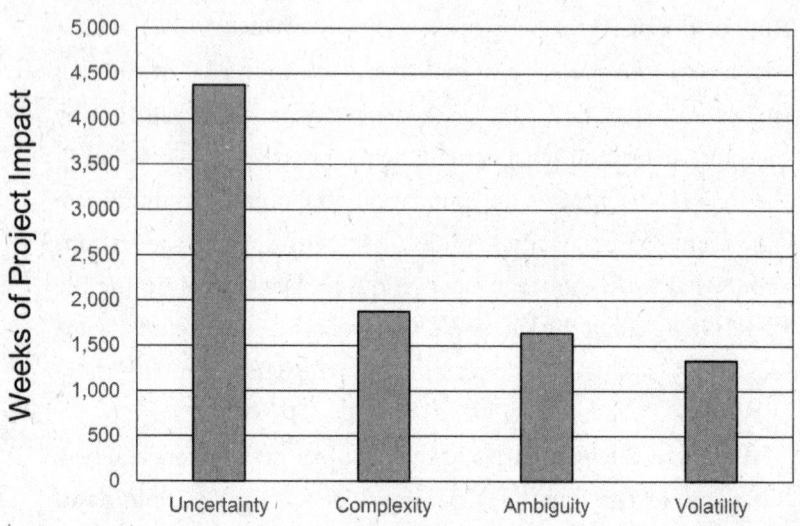

■ **Figure 2-5:** VUCA Impact in the PERIL Database

Dealing with project risks begins with identifying them. Whatever their type or cause, one of the most effective ways to pull risks into the open is to pay close attention as you proceed with project analysis and planning. The next several chapters will explore the root causes of the risks in the PERIL database in more detail and demonstrate how to use project planning processes to find and document specific project risks. Chapter 3 focuses on scope risks and identifying sources of uncertainty associated with developing requirements and work breakdown structures. Chapter 4 explores scheduling risks and using project estimating and workflow analysis to identify issues and worst cases. Resource risks including staffing issues and funding problems represented many incidents in the PERIL database, and chapter 5 digs into using resource planning processes to reveal staffing, outsourcing, cost estimating, and funding risks. Chapter 6 will discuss managing opportunities and project constraints, and additional ideas for making risks visible. To also aid you in identifying risks on your projects, the appendix lists many specific risks from the PERIL database.

Key Ideas for Project Risk Planning

- Project selection affects risk management and depends upon it.
- Project risk management builds on the foundation provided by your project definition and planning.
- A project risk plan summarizes your risk management approach.
- We can learn much from mistakes and errors (aka "experience").

A SECOND PANAMA CANAL PROJECT: SPONSORSHIP AND INITIATION (1902–1904)

"A man, a plan, a canal. Panama."

—FAMOUS PALINDROME

Successful projects are often not the first attempt to do something. Often, there is a recognized opportunity that triggers a project. If the first attempted project fails, it discourages people for a time. Soon, however, if the opportunity remains attractive, another project will begin, building on the work and the experiences of the first project. A canal at Panama remained an attractive opportunity. When Theodore Roosevelt became president of the United States in 1901, he decided to make successful completion of a Central American canal part of his presidential legacy. (And so it is. He is the "man" in the famous palindrome.)

As much as the earlier French project failed because of lapses in project management, the US project ultimately succeeded as a direct result of applying good project principles. In fact, the work of Fred Taylor, Henry Gantt, and other business thought leaders of the early twentieth century strongly influenced work on the new canal project in Panama. The results of better project and risk management on this second project will unfold throughout the remainder of this book.

Unlike the initial attempt to build a canal, the US effort was not a commercial venture. Maintaining separate US navies on the East and West coasts had become increasingly costly and inefficient. Cohesive management of a single larger navy required easy transit between the Atlantic and Pacific, so Theodore Roosevelt saw the Panama Canal as a strategic military project, not a commercial one. The US venture considered several routes, but as the French had done, they settled on Panama.

Theodore Roosevelt was a more typical project sponsor than Ferdinand de Lesseps. He delegated the management of the project to others. His greatest direct contribution to the project was in "engineering" the independence of Panama from Colombia. (This "revolution" was accomplished by a pair of gunboats, one at Colon on the Gulf of Mexico and another at Panama City on the Pacific. Without the firing of a single shot, Roosevelt created the independent nation of Panama in 1902. (The repercussions of this US foreign policy decision persist in Central America, more than a century later.) To get the project started quickly, Roosevelt also moved to acquire the assets of the Nouvelle Compagnie (which was of some value to shareholders of the original company, but not much).

"I took the isthmus!" Roosevelt said. He then went to the US Congress to get approval to go forward with the building of the canal. Following all this activity and the public support it generated, Congress had little choice but to support the project. Although the specifics for the project were still vague, the intention of the United States was clear: to build a canal at Panama capable of transporting even the largest US warships, and to build it as quickly as was practical.

Insight into Roosevelt's thinking concerning the project is found in this quote from 1899, two years before his presidency:

> Far better it is to dare mighty things, to win glorious triumphs, even though checkered by failure, than to take rank with those poor spirits who neither enjoy much nor suffer much, because they live in the gray twilight that knows not victory nor defeat.

Project sponsors often aspire to "dare mighty things." They are much more risk tolerant than most project leaders and teams. Good risk management planning serves to balance the process of setting project objectives, so we undertake projects that are not only worthwhile and challenging but also possible.

CHAPTER 3

IDENTIFYING PROJECT SCOPE RISK

"Well begun is half done."

—ARISTOTLE

Although beginning well will never actually complete half of a project, beginning poorly will lead to disappointment, rework, stress, and potential failure. A great deal of project risk can be discovered at the earliest stages of project work, when defining the scope of the project.

For risks associated with the elements of the project management triple constraint (scope, schedule, and resources), scope risk generally will be considered first. Of the three types of projects that will fail—those that are beyond your capabilities, those that are overconstrained, and those that are ineffectively executed—the first type is the most significant, because this type of project is literally impossible. Identifying scope risks will help show either that your project is feasible or that it lies beyond the state of your art. For impossible projects, identifying scope risks early will support good business decisions to either change the deliverables or abandon the project altogether.

There is a lack of consensus in project management circles on a precise definition of "scope." Broad definitions use scope to refer to everything in the project, and narrow definitions limit project scope to focus on project deliverables. For the purposes of this chapter, scope will be related primarily to the project output(s). This is consistent with the most common current definitions, including those found in PMI documents such as the *Guide to the Project Management Body of Knowledge*. We will explore other types of project risk in later chapters.

SOURCES OF SCOPE RISK

Scope risks are quite common in the PERIL database, representing almost 40 percent of the data. Even more important, risks related to scope accounted for well over 40 percent of the total schedule impact. The two broad categories of scope risk in PERIL relate to changes and defects. By far the most damage was due to poorly managed change (about three-quarters of the overall scope impact and roughly one-third of all the impact in the entire database), but all the scope risks represented significant project exposure. While some of the risk situations, particularly in the category of defects, were legitimately "unknown" risks, quite a few of the problems could have been identified in advance and managed as risks. In this table the two major root-cause categories for scope risk are separated into more detailed subcategories.

SCOPE ROOT-CAUSE SUBCATEGORIES	DEFINITION	COUNT	CUMULATIVE IMPACT (WEEKS)	AVERAGE IMPACT (WEEKS)
Changes: Creep	Any nonmandatory scope change	141	1,218	8.6
Changes: Gap	Legitimate scope requirements discovered late in project	203	1,639	8.1
Defects: Software	System or intangible deliverable problems that must be fixed	67	524	7.8
Defects: Integration	Program-level defects that require scope shifts in projects	15	101	6.7
Defects: Hardware	Tangible deliverable problems that must be fixed	58	389	6.7
Changes: Dependency	Scope changes necessary because of external dependencies	23	115	5.0

Scope changes due to gaps were the most frequent, but scope creep changes were the most damaging on average. A Pareto chart of overall impact by type of risk is summarized in figure 3-1, and a more detailed analysis follows.

Change Risks

As they say, "shift happens." Few if any projects end with the original scope intact. Managing scope risk related to change relies on tying up loose ends on requirements at project initiation and having (and using) a robust process for controlling changes throughout the work. In the PERIL database, there are three categories of scope change risks: scope gaps, scope creep, and dependencies.

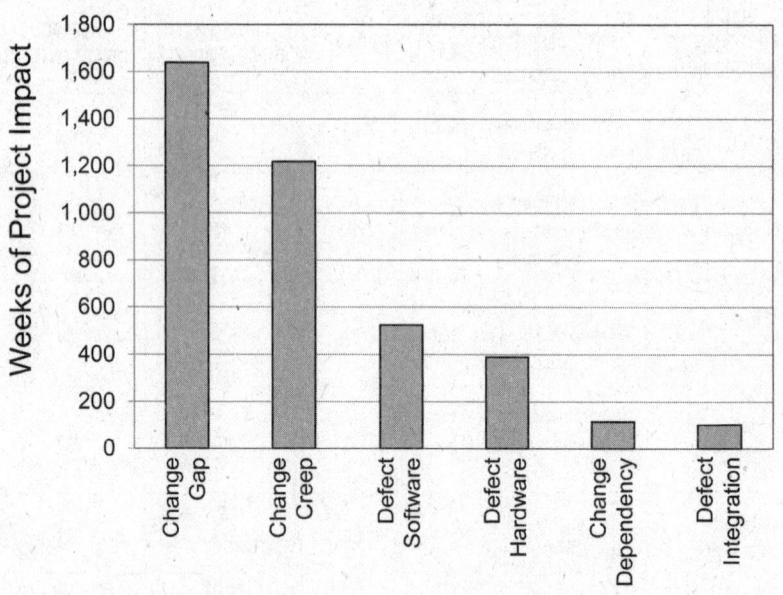

Figure 3-1: Total Project Impact by Scope Root-Cause Subcategories

Scope creep was the most damaging type of change risk, resulting in an average schedule slip of well over eight weeks. Scope gaps were only slightly less damaging, and these gaps were both more common and represented greater total impact. These two subcategories alone account for nearly a third of all the reported impact across the PERIL database.

Scope gaps are the result of committing to a project before the project requirements are well understood. When legitimate needs are uncovered later in the project, change is unavoidable. Some of the overlooked requirements are a consequence of the novelty of the project, and some are because customers, managers, team members, or other project stakeholders were not available (or not consulted) at project start. Although some scope gaps are hard to avoid, most of these cases are due to incomplete or rushed analysis. A more thorough scope definition, backlog inventory, or project work breakdown would have revealed the missing or poorly defined portions of the project scope. In the VUCA model, most scope gaps are a result of ambiguity.

Scope creep plagues all projects, especially technical projects. New opportunities, interesting ideas, undiscovered alternatives, and a wealth of other information emerges as the project progresses, providing a perpetual temptation to redefine the project and to make it "better." While some project evolution of this sort may be justified by clear-eyed business analysis, far too much non-mandatory change sneaks into projects because no analysis is done or because the consequences are drastically underestimated. The damage done by scope creep is often increased because the assumed benefits of the change are never fully realized. In retrospect, much of scope creep delivers little actual added value, and in extreme cases it can result in enough delay that the ultimate deliverable has no value at all. Scope creep requires unanticipated additional investment of time and money, generally demanding new effort and redoing already completed work. To manage scope creep, you need an initial requirements definition process that thoroughly considers potential alternatives, as well as an effective process for managing specification changes throughout a project.

Scope creep can come from any direction, but one of the most insidious is from inside the project. Every day a project progresses you learn something new, so it's inevitable that project team members will see things that were not apparent earlier. This can lead to well-intentioned proposals to "improve" the deliverable. Sometimes, scope creep of this sort may become part of the project without much broad awareness and within a portion of the project where the shift seems harmless. Only later may real, and sometimes catastrophic, unintended consequences emerge. Particularly on larger, more complicated projects, all changes deserve a thorough analysis and public discussion, with a particularly skeptical analysis of all alleged benefits. Scope creep is a good example of the first element of VUCA—volatility. Both scope creep and scope gaps are universal and pervasive issues for technical projects.

Scope dependencies make up the third subcategory of change risk. These scope risks are due to factors external to the project that affect scope. (Dependency risks that are primarily due to timing rather than requirements issues are defined as schedule risks in the database and will be explored in the next chapter.) Although less frequent in the PERIL database, scope dependencies did represent an average slippage of well over a month. Admittedly, some of the cases in the database involved situations that no amount of realistic analysis would have uncovered in advance. Most examples, though, resulted from factors that should not have come as complete surprises. Although legal and regulatory changes do sometimes happen without notice, a little research will generally provide advance warning. Projects also depend on infrastructure stability, and periodic review of installation and maintenance schedules will reveal plans for new versions of application software, databases, telecommunications, hardware upgrades, or other changes that the project may need to anticipate and accommodate. From a VUCA perspective, most scope dependencies are a result of complexity.

Defect Risks

Most projects rely on many complicated things to work as expected. Unfortunately, new things do not always operate as promised or as required. Even normally reliable things may break down or fail to perform as desired in a novel application. Defects represent over a quarter of the scope risks and almost one-eighth of all the risks in the PERIL database. The three categories of defect risks are software, hardware, and integration. From a VUCA perspective, all relate to complexity.

Software problems and **hardware** failures are the most common types of defect risk in the PERIL database, roughly equal in frequency. As to impact, software defects resulted in almost eight weeks of delay, and hardware problems were a bit under seven weeks. In several cases, the root cause was new, untried technology that lacked needed functionality or reliability. In other cases, a component created by the project (such as a circuit board or a software module) did not work initially and had to be fixed. In still others, critical items such as purchased components or custom integrated circuits failed and had to be replaced. Nearly all of these risks are visible in advance, at least as possibilities, through adequate analysis and planning.

Some hardware and software functional failures related to quality or performance shortfalls. Hardware may be too slow, require too much power, emit excessive electromagnetic interference, or exhibit other unacceptable behavior. Software may be too difficult to operate, have inadequate throughput, or fail to work in specific circumstances. As with other defects, the definition, planning, and analysis of project work will help in anticipating many of these potential performance issues.

Integration defects are the third type of defect risk in the PERIL database. These defects relate to system problems above the component level. Although they are not as numerous in the database, they are quite damaging. Integration defects caused an average of about seven weeks of project slip. For large programs, work is typically decomposed into smaller, related subprojects that can progress in parallel. Successful integration of the deliverables from each of the subprojects into a single system deliverable requires not only that each of the components delivered operates as specified but also that the combination of all these parts functions as a system. All computer users are familiar with this failure mode. Whenever all the software in use fails to play nicely together, our systems lock up, crash, or report some exotic "illegal operation." Integration risks, though relatively less common than other defect risks in the PERIL database, are particularly problematic, as they generally occur near the project deadline and are never easy to diagnose and correct. Again, thorough analysis relying on disciplines such as software architecture and systems engineering can ensure timely identification and management of possible integration risks.

Scope Risk and VUCA

Although nearly half of the impact in the PERIL database overall relates to uncertainty, scope risks mainly originate with the other three VUCA factors. Ambiguity (a lack of clarity in objectives) leads the way with about 40 percent. Not far behind, and causing approximately equal damage, are volatility (shifting goals) and complexity (insufficient understanding of problem characteristics). Being aware of these VUCA considerations can help in finding and documenting scope risks. You can minimize the effects of VUCA through better definition of requirements, disciplined assessment of potential alternatives and options, feasibility studies and iterative development techniques, and thorough analysis of project complications. Reviewing the example scope risks from the PERIL database listed in the appendix can be a good starting point for uncovering possible scope-related problems on your next project.

DEFINING DELIVERABLES

Scoping gaps are the top category of risk in the PERIL database. Defining deliverables thoroughly is a powerful tool for uncovering these potential project risks. The process for specifying deliverables for a project varies greatly depending on the type and the scale of the project.

While informal methods can work well for small projects, effective project risk management requires a more rigorous approach for most projects. Defining deliverables is typically your earliest opportunity to begin uncovering risks. Whatever process you may use, your goal in defining deliverables will be to develop specific, written requirements that are clear, unambiguous, and agreed to by all project stakeholders and contributors. Some projects do this thoroughly at the start, and anticipate only small, managed adjustments as the work proceeds. Projects using agile methods scope the overall work provisionally and select a well-defined prioritized subset for the first development iteration. Subsequent delivery cycles use a disciplined process to manage periodic adjustments using feedback from the results of earlier iterations. In all cases, stakeholder agreement on clear requirements is essential for managing scope.

A good, thorough process for defining project deliverables begins with identifying the people who should participate, especially those who must agree. Project scope risk increases when key project stakeholders are not involved in the project early enough. Many scope gaps only become visible late in the project, after these people do finally get involved. Should you be unable to involve some of the specific people who will participate later, at least involve individuals who can represent all the needed perspectives and functional areas. Vagueness, ambiguity, and gaps are expensive and damaging; if you need to, call in favors, beg, plead, or do whatever you need to do to get the right people involved.

Deliverable definition includes all of your core project team, but it rarely ends there. You will also need others from outside your team, from other functions such as marketing, finance, sales, and support. You are also likely to need input from people who may even be outside your organization: from customers, users, other related project teams, and potential subcontractors. Consider the project over its entire development life cycle. Think about who will be involved with all stages of design, development, manufacturing or assembly, testing, documentation, marketing, sales, installation, distribution, support, and other aspects of the work.

Even when the right people are available and involved early in the initial project definition activities, it is difficult to be thorough. The answers to many questions may not yet be available, and some of your data may be ranges or even guesses. Specifics concerning new methods or technologies add more uncertainty. Three useful techniques for uncovering with scope risk are using a rigorous requirements management process, developing a straw-man definition document, and adopting disciplined evolutionary methods.

Requirements Management

Processes for defining deliverables vary depending on the nature of the project. For product development projects, the following guidelines are a typical starting point for requirements management. By reviewing such a list and documenting both what you know and especially what you don't know, you set the foundation for identifying project scope risks so you can begin to identify activities needed to fill in and manage the gaps.

Topics for a typical deliverable definition process are:

1. **Alignment with business strategy:** How does this project contribute to stated high-level business objectives?

2. **User and customer needs:** Has the project team captured the ultimate end-user requirements that must be met by the deliverable?

3. **Compliance:** Has the team identified all relevant regulatory, environmental, and manufacturing requirements, as well as any relevant industry standards?

4. **Competition:** Has the team identified both current and projected alternatives to the proposed deliverable, including not undertaking the project?

5. **Positioning:** Is there a clear and compelling benefit-oriented project objective that supports the business case for the project?

6. **Decision criteria:** Does this project team have an agreed-upon hierarchy of measurable priorities for cost, time, and scope?

7. **Delivery:** Are logistical requirements understood and manageable? These include, but are not limited to, sales, distribution, installation, sign-off, and support.

8. **Sponsorship:** Does the management hierarchy collectively support the project and will they provide timely decisions and ongoing resources?

9. **Resources:** Does the project have, and will it continue to have, the staffing and funding needed to meet the project goals within the allotted time?

10. **Technical risk:** Has the team assessed the overall level of risk it is taking? Are technical and other exposures well documented?

(This list traces back to the 1972 SAPPHO Project at the University of Sussex, England.)

Although this list is hardly exhaustive, examining each criterion and documenting the information you already have provides solid initial data for scoping and helps you see what is missing. Determining the degree to which you understand each element (on a scale ranging from "clueless" on one extreme to "omniscient" on the other) reveals the biggest gaps. Although some level of uncertainty is inevitable, this analysis clarifies where the exposures are and helps you understand the level of risk. The last item on the list, technical risk, is most central to scope risk identification. High-level project risk assessment techniques are discussed in detail later in this chapter.

As the requirements come into focus, compile a written list. A list will not only provide a dependable, common source of data for subsequent project planning, it also will help you identify aspects that are in conflict and stimulate useful stakeholder feedback.

Straw-Man Definition Document

Many books on project management prattle on about identifying and documenting all the known project requirements. This is much easier said than done in the real world. It can be nearly impossible to get users and stakeholders of technical projects to cooperate with this strategy. When too little about a project is clear, many people see only two options: accept the risks associated with incomplete definition (including inevitable scope creep), or give up and abandon the project. Between these, however, lies a third option. Instead of simply accepting a lack of data, the project team can create a straw-man definition, generating a plausible list of specific requirements. These requirements may come from earlier projects, assumptions, or guesses, or they can come from your team's concept of a potential solution to the problem that the project is expected to solve. Any definition constructed this way is certain to be incomplete and at best only partially accurate, but clearly documenting even inadequate requirements leads to one of two beneficial results.

The first possibility is that these made-up requirements will be accepted and approved, giving you a solid foundation for planning. Once sign-off has occurred, anything that is not quite right or deemed incomplete can still be changed, but only through a disciplined project change process. (Some contracting firms get quite rich using this technique. They win business by quoting fixed fees that are below the cost of delivering all the stated requirements, knowing full well that there will be changes. They then make their profits by charging for the inevitable changes as they occur, generating large incremental project billings.) Even for projects where the sponsors and project team are in the same organization, the sign-off process gives the project team a great deal of leverage when changes are proposed later in the project. (This whole process brings to mind the old riddle: How do you make a statue of an elephant? Answer: You get an enormous chunk of marble and chip off anything that does not look like an elephant.)

The second possible outcome is a flood of criticism, corrections, edits, and "improvements." Where most people are intimidated by a blank piece of paper or an open-ended question, everyone, deep down, is a born critic. Once a straw-man requirements document is created, the project leader can circulate it far and wide as "pretty close, but not exactly right yet." Using such a document to gather comments (and providing big, red pens to get things rolling) is an excellent way to generate scoping information, although it may be humbling to the original authors. Embarrassing or not, it is far better to identify scoping issues early than to discover that you missed something during acceptance testing at the end. As the feedback accumulates, you can collect data on gaps, inconsistencies, and unknowns.

Agile and Iterative Methods

From a VUCA perspective, many projects face significant ambiguity. When the end deliverable is truly novel or intangible, or cannot be initially specified with much certainty, agile (or evolutionary, or cyclic) methodologies may be more effective. Rather than defining a system as a whole, these more organic approaches define the problem to be addressed and set out general overall objectives. These goals are laid out in a sequence of incremental stages, each producing a functional deliverable. Generally the first cycles will focus on the portions of the work that are most clear, using the feedback and learnings to adjust the scope for subsequent iterations. Software development projects have employed these step-by-step techniques for decades, with increasingly wide application since the creation of the "Agile Manifesto" in 2001.

Such techniques are effective for innovative development projects undertaken by small project teams that have ready access to their end users.

The deliverables released at the end of each development cycle add additional value and functionality, and each iteration brings the project closer to its final destination. As the work continues, specific scope is defined for the next cycles using user feedback from testing of the previous cycle's deliverables. Typical development iterations vary from about two to six weeks, depending on the specific methodology. (Scrum, the most prevalent, generally uses development sprints of thirty days.) Deliverables are scoped in detail one cycle at a time, with future cycles defined only in general terms. This allows scoping to evolve using results to make course corrections.

Although this approach can be useful in managing revolutionary projects where definition is not initially possible, it may encourage scope creep. It can also result in "gold plating," or delivering additional functionality because it's possible, not because it's necessary.

Evolutionary methodologies may also carry higher costs than other project approaches. Whenever a project can define project deliverables with good precision early using a more traditional "plan-based" approach, it will result in a faster, less costly project. By avoiding a meandering definition process and eliminating the need to deliver to users every cycle and then evaluate feedback multiple times, comparative costs for more traditionally run projects may be as little as a third, and timelines can be cut in half. From a risk standpoint, evolutionary methodologies focus primarily on managing scope risk, defining no certain end date or budget. Without disciplined management, such projects might never end.

Risk management on such multicycle projects requires frequent reevaluation of the current risks as well as carefully focused scope management. To manage overall risk using agile methodologies, establish firm limits for both time and money, not only for the project as a whole but also for checkpoints no more than a few months apart. Also, set stringent standards for value delivered whenever setting or adjusting scope in each succeeding iteration.

Current thinking on evolutionary software development includes a number of methodologies that adopt robust scope control and incorporate project management practices intended to avoid the "license to hack" nature of some of the earlier evolutionary development models. Concepts such as "Minimum Viable Product" (MVP) and related ideas guard against scope creep and nonessential scope expansion. "Disciplined agile" and other metric-oriented iterative methods adopt effective project management principles for estimating, managing scope, setting acceptance criteria, planning, and communicating. Modern agile practices work closely with end users to prioritize the scope, but the amount of scope delivered in each cycle is determined exclusively by the programmers. Within an iteration, revision of scope is rare, and only as a zero-sum game—any additions cause something to be removed.

Scope Documentation

However you go about defining requirements, once they are defined you need to document them. Managing scope risk requires a scope definition that clearly defines both what you expect to accomplish and what you intend to exclude. One problematic type of scope definition characterizes project requirements as "musts" and "wants." (Sometimes this is expanded to "MoSCoW" lists:

Must haves, Should haves, Could haves, and Want to haves.) Although it may be fine to have some flexibility during early project analysis, carrying uncertainty into development work exacerbates scope risk. Retaining discretionary scope remains common on many high-tech projects. This makes planning chaotic, estimates inexact, and ultimately results in late (often expensive) scope changes. From a risk management standpoint, the "is/is not" technique is far superior to "musts and wants." The "is" list is equivalent to the "musts," but the "is not" list serves to establish a limit for scope. Determining what is not in the project specification is never easy, but if you fail to do it early many scope risks will remain hidden behind a moving target. An "is not" list does not cover every possible thing the project might include. It is generally a list of completely plausible, desirable features that could be included, and in fact might well be in scope for some future project—just not this one.

The "is/is not" technique is particularly important for projects that have fixed deadlines and constrained resources, because it defines a boundary for scope consistent with the timing and budget limits. It is always preferable to deliver the minimum requirements on time than to carry superfluous scoping objectives that either make you miss your deadline or must be dropped near the end of the project. As you document your project scope, establish limits that define what the project will not include, to minimize scope creep.

There are dozens of formats for a document that defines scope. In product development, it may be a reference specification or a product data sheet. In a custom solution project (and for many other types of projects), it may be a key portion of the project proposal, contract, or statement of work. For information technology projects, it may be part of the project charter document. In other types of projects, it may be included in a plan of record. For agile software methodologies, it may be a brief summary on a webpage and a collection of index cards tacked to a wall or forms taped to a whiteboard. Whatever it may be called or be a part of, an effective definition for project requirements must be in writing. Specific information typically includes:

- A description of the project (what are you doing?)
- Project purpose (why are you doing it?)
- Measurable acceptance and completion criteria (what does "done" look like?)
- Planned project start
- Expected deadline and any other timing constraints
- Cost expectations (at least a rough order-of-magnitude) and budget constraints
- Intended customer(s) or users
- What the project will and will not include ("is/is not")
- Dependencies (both internal and external)
- Staffing requirements (including skills and experience)
- High-level risks
- Technology required
- Hardware, software, or other infrastructure required
- Detailed requirements, outlining functionality, usability, reliability, performance, supportability, and any other significant issues
- Other data customary and appropriate to your project

The third item on the list, acceptance criteria, is particularly important for identifying defect risks. When the requirements to be used at the end of the project are unclear or not defined, there is little chance that you will avoid problems, rework, and late project delay. The key for identifying scope risk is to capture what you know and, even more important, to recognize what you still need to find out. As you define your scope, make note of uncertainties, requirements that exceed those of past projects, and any gaps or other unknowns.

HIGH-LEVEL RISK ASSESSMENT TOOLS

Technical project risk assessment is central to project initiation. Even though there may be little concrete information for such an early project risk assessment, there are several techniques that provide useful insight into project risk even in the beginning stages. These tools are:

- Risk framework
- Risk complexity index
- Risk assessment grid

The first two are useful in any project that creates a tangible, physical deliverable through technical development processes. The third is appropriate for projects that have less tangible results, such as software modules, new processes, commercial applications, network architectures, or internet service offerings. These tools all start with answering the same question: How much experience do you have with the work the project requires? The tools use this information differently, and each builds on the assessment of technical risk in different directions. These tools are not mutually exclusive, so more than one may provide insight into overall risk.

Any of these tools may be used at the start of a project to get an indication of project risk, but none of the three is precise. The purpose of each is to provide insight into the risk for a new project. Although these three techniques are not foolproof, their results provide a reasonable basis for deciding whether to go beyond initial investigation into further project work. (You may also use these three tools to reassess project risk later in the project. Chapter 9 discusses reusing these tools, as well as several additional project risk analysis methods that rely on planning details to refine overall project risk assessment.)

Risk Framework

This is the simplest of the three high-level techniques. To assess risk, consider the following three project factors:

- Technology (the work)
- Marketing (the user)
- Manufacturing (the production and delivery)

For each of these factors, assess the amount of change required by the project. For technology, does the project use only well-understood methods and skills, or will new skills be required (or developed)? For marketing, will the deliverable be used by someone (or by a class of users) you know well, or does this project address a need for someone unknown to you? For manufacturing, consider what is required to provide the intended end user with your project deliverable: are there any unresolved or changing manufacturing or delivery channel issues?

For each factor, the assessment is binary: change is either trivial (small) or significant (large). Assess conservatively; if the change required seems somewhere between these choices, it is safest to assume that it will be significant.

Nearly all projects will require significant change to at least one of these three factors. Projects representing no (or little) change may not even be worth doing. Some projects, however, may require large changes in two or even all three factors. For technical projects, large required shifts correlate with risk. The more change inherent in a project, and the more different types of change, the higher the risk.

In general, if your project has significant changes in only one factor, it probably has an acceptable, manageable level of risk. Evolutionary-type projects, where existing products or solutions are upgraded, leveraged, or improved, often fall into this category. If your project changes two factors simultaneously, it has higher relative risk, and the management decision to proceed, even into further investigation and planning, should reflect this. Projects that develop new platforms intended as the foundation for future project work frequently depend upon new methods for both technical development and producing the deliverable. For projects in this category, balance the higher risks against the potential benefits.

If your project requires large shifts in all three categories, the risks are greatest of all. Many, if not most, projects in this risk category are unsuccessful. Projects representing this much change are revolutionary and a decision to go forward must be justified by substantial financial or other benefits expected from successful completion. Often the risks seem so great—or so unknowable—that a truly revolutionary project requires the backing of a high-level sponsor with a vision.

A commonly heard story around Hewlett-Packard from the early 1970s involved a proposed project pitched to Bill Hewlett, the more technical of the two HP founders. The team brought a mockup of a handheld device capable of scientific calculations with ten significant digits of accuracy. The model was made out of wood, but it had all the buttons labeled and was weighted to feel like the completed device. Bill Hewlett examined the functions and display, lifted the device, slipped it in his shirt pocket, and smiled. The HP-35 calculator represented massive change in all three factors; the market was unknown, manufacturing for it was unlike anything HP had done before, and it was debatable whether the electronics could even be developed on the small number of chips that could be crammed into such a tiny device. The HP-35 was developed primarily because Bill Hewlett wanted one. It was ultimately a hugely successful product, selling more units in a month than had been projected for the entire year. It generated spectacular profits. The HP-35 also fundamentally changed the direction of the calculator market worldwide, and it wiped out the market for slide rules and mechanical computing devices forever.

This story is known because the project was successful. Similar stories surround other revolutionary offerings, like the Apple Macintosh and iPhone products, the Google search engine, and many other market-defining products. Stories around the risky projects that fail (or fall far short of their objectives) are harder to uncover; most people and companies would prefer to forget them. The percentage of revolutionary ideas that "crash and burn," based on the rate of Silicon Valley startup company failures, is historically around 90 percent. The higher risks of such projects should always be balanced against sufficiently large plausible benefits.

Risk Complexity Index

The risk complexity index is the second technique for assessing risk on technical projects. As in the risk framework tool, technology is the starting point. This tool looks more deeply at the technology being employed, separating it into three parts and assigning to each an assessment of difficulty. In addition to the technical complexity, the index looks at another source of project risk: the risk arising from larger project teams, or scale. The following formula combines these four factors:

Index = (Technology + Architecture + System) * Scale

For this index, *Technology* is defined as new, custom development unique to this project. *Architecture* refers to the high-level functional components and any external interfaces, and *System* is the internal software and hardware that will be used in the product. Assess each of these three against your experience and capabilities, assigning each a value from 0 to 5:

- 0—Only existing technology required
- 1—Minor extensions to existing technology needed in a few areas
- 2—Significant extensions to existing technology needed in a few areas
- 3—Almost certainly possible, but innovation needed in some areas
- 4—Probably feasible, but innovation required in many areas
- 5—Completely new, technological feasibility in doubt

The three technology factors will generally correlate, but some variation is common. Add these three factors, to a sum between 0 and 15.

For *Scale*, assign a value based on the number of people (including all full-time contributors, both internal and external) expected on the project:

- 0.8—Up to 12 people
- 2.4—13 to 40 people
- 4.3—41 to 100 people
- 6.6—More than 100 people

The calculation for the index yields a result between 0 and 99. Projects with an index below 20 are generally low-risk projects with durations of well under a year. Projects assessed between 20 and 40 are medium risk. These projects are more likely to get into trouble, and often take a year or longer. Most projects with an index above 40 are high risk, and many will finish long past their stated deadline, if they complete at all.

Risk Assessment Grid

The first two high-level risk tools are appropriate for physical deliverables. Projects with intangible deliverables may not easily fit these models, so the risk assessment grid can be a better approach for early risk assessment.

This technique examines three project factors, similar to the risk framework. Assessment here is based on two choices for each factor, and technology is again the first. The other factors are different, and here the three factors carry different weights. The factors, in order of priority, are *Technology*, *Structure*, and *Size*.

The highest weight factor, *Technology*, is based on required change, and it is rated either low or high, depending on whether the project team has experience using the required technology and whether it is well established in situations similar to the current project.

The second factor, *Structure*, is also rated either low or high, based on factors such as solid formal specifications, project sponsorship, and organizational practices appropriate to the project.

Structure is rated low when there are significant unknowns in staffing, responsibilities, infrastructure issues, objectives, or decision processes. Good up-front definition indicates high structure.

The third factor, *Size*, is similar to the Scale factor in the risk complexity index. A project is rated either large or small. For this tool, size is not an absolute assessment. It is measured relative to the size of teams that the project leader has successfully led in the past. Teams that are as little as 20 percent larger than the size a project leader has successfully led should be considered large. Other considerations in assessing size are the expected duration of the project, the overall project budget, and the number of separate locations where project work will be performed.

Low	Medium	High
LOW Technology HIGH Structure SMALL Size **A**	LOW Technology LOW Structure LARGE Size **D**	HIGH Technology LOW Structure SMALL Size
LOW Technology HIGH Structure LARGE Size **B**	HIGH Technology HIGH Structure SMALL Size **E**	**G**
LOW Technology LOW Structure SMALL Size **C**	HIGH Technology HIGH Structure LARGE Size **F**	HIGH Technology LOW Structure LARGE Size **H**

A = Lowest Risk; H = Highest Risk

Figure 3-2: Risk Assessment Grid

After you have assessed each of the three factors, the project will fall into one of the sections of the grid, A through H (see figure 3-2). Projects in the right column are most risky; those to the left will be more easily managed.

Beyond risk assessment, these tools may also guide early project risk management, indicating ways to lower project risk by using alternative technologies, making changes to staffing, decomposing longer projects into a sequence of shorter projects with less aggressive or incremental goals (agile methods), or improving the proposed structure. Chapter 10 will revisit using these techniques, along with others, to manage overall project risk.

SETTING LIMITS

Although many scope risks come from specifics of the deliverable and the overall technology, scope risk also arises from failure to establish firm, early limits for the project.

In workshops on risk management, I demonstrate another aspect of scope risk using an exercise that begins with a single US one-dollar bill. I show it to the group, setting two rules:

- The dollar bill will go to the highest bidder, who will pay the amount bid. All bids must be for a real amount—no fractional cents. The first bid must be at least a penny, and each succeeding bid must be higher than earlier bids. (This is the same as with any auction.)
- The second-highest bidder also pays the amount he or she bid (the bid just prior to the winning bid), but gets nothing in return. (This is unlike a normal auction.)

As the auctioneer, I start by asking if anyone wants to buy the dollar for one cent. Following the first bid, I solicit a second low bid, "Does anyone think the dollar is worth five cents?" After two low bids are made, the auction is off and running. The bidding is allowed to proceed to (and nearly always past) $1.00, until it ends. If $1.00 is bid and things slow down, a reminder to the person who has the next highest bid that he or she will spend almost one dollar to buy nothing usually gets things moving again. The auction ends when no new bids are made. The two final bids nearly always total well over $2.00.

By now everything is quite exciting. Someone has bought a dollar for more than a dollar. A second person has nothing to show for a bid almost as high. To calm things down, I put the dollar away, explain that this is a lesson in risk management (not a swindle), and apologize to people who seem upset.

So, what does the dollar auction have to do with risk management? This game's outcome is similar to what happens when a project that hits its deadline (or budget), creeps past, and just keeps going. "But we're so close. It's almost done; we can't stop now . . ." The auction effectively models any case where people have, or think they have, too much invested in an undertaking to quit.

Dollar auction losses can be minimized by anticipating the possibility of an uncompensated investment, setting limits in advance, and then enforcing them. Rationally, the dollar auction has an expected return of half a dollar (the total return, one dollar, spread between the two final bidders). If each participant set a bid limit of fifty cents, the auctioneer would always lose. For projects, clearly defining limits and then monitoring intermediate results will provide an early indication of trouble. Using ideas like "minimum viable product" to clearly set deliverable goals can also reduce scope risk associated with extraneous features and requirements.

Project metrics such as earned value (described in chapter 9), can also be useful in minimizing unproductive investments by detecting project overrun early enough to abort or modify questionable projects. Defining project scope with sufficient detail and explicit limits is essential for risk management.

WORK BREAKDOWN STRUCTURE (WBS)

Scope definition reveals some risks, but scope planning digs deeper into the project and uncovers even more. Product definition documents, scope statements, and other written materials provide the basis for decomposing of project work into increasingly finer detail, so it can be understood, delegated, estimated, and tracked. The process used to do this—to create the project work breakdown structure (WBS)—reveals potential defect risks.

One common approach to developing a WBS starts at the scope or objective statement and proceeds to carve the project into smaller parts, working "top down" from the overall project concept. Decomposition of work that is well understood is straightforward and quickly done. Whenever it is confusing or difficult to decompose project work into smaller, more manageable pieces, there is scope risk. Whenever any part of your project resists breakdown, it reveals a lack of understanding, which is inherently risky.

Work Packages

The ultimate goal of the WBS process is to describe the entire project in much smaller pieces, often called "work packages." Each work package should be deliverable-oriented and have a clearly defined output. General guidelines for the size of the work represented by the work packages at the lowest level of a WBS are usually in terms of duration (between two and twenty workdays) or effort (no more than roughly eighty person-hours). When breakdown to this level of granularity is difficult, it is generally because of gaps in project understanding. If you cannot resolve such gaps as part of project scoping, you should document the unknowns as scope risks. (The relationship between processes for estimation and risk are explored in chapters 4 and 5.)

Work defined at the lowest level of a WBS may also be called "activities," "tasks," "stories," "use cases," or use other descriptions for project work. The precise name does not really matter much, but for each you need a solid understanding of how you will get it done. Note as risks all cases where you cannot decompose the work into small, understandable pieces.

Aggregation

A WBS is a hierarchy of increasingly detailed effort descriptions, so it provides a useful method for detecting missing work. The principle of "aggregation" for a WBS ensures that the defined work at each level plausibly includes everything included in the summary level above it. If the listed items under a higher-level work package do not represent its complete "to do" list, your WBS is incomplete. Either complete it by adding the missing work to the WBS, or note the WBS gaps as project scope risks. Any work in the WBS that you cannot adequately describe contributes to your growing accumulation of identified risks.

Parts of a project WBS that resist easy decomposition are rarely visible until you systematically seek them out. The WBS development process provides a tool for separating the parts of the project where you have a solid grasp on the work from those where you are clueless. Before proceeding into a project with significant unknowns, you also must identify these risks and determine whether the worst-case costs or other consequences can be justified.

Ownership

There are many reasons why some project work is difficult to break into smaller parts, but the root cause is often a lack of experience. One typical way to detect this is through delegation of ownership. A key objective in completing the project WBS is to associate each lowest-level work package (or whatever you may choose to call it) with a named individual who will be responsible for that part of the project.

Delegation is most effective when it's voluntarily. It is fairly common on projects to allow people to assume ownership of project activities in the WBS by signing up for them, at least on the first pass. Delegating work to volunteers for most tasks is generally straightforward, and can be sorted out as you associate names of contributors having relevant experience with activities and balance the workload. For activities where no one wants to be the owner, however, there are project risks to be identified. A lack of enthusiastic volunteers can be a result of several root causes. One discussed earlier is that no one understands the work, because the description is unclear. Other possibilities are that no one currently on the project has developed key skills that the work requires, or the work is technically so uncertain that no one believes it can be done at all. Or the work may be feasible, but no one believes that it can be completed in the "roughly two weeks" expected for activities defined at the lowest level of the WBS. It is also possible that no one has any time to do the work. If everyone on the project is already working beyond full capacity on other things, no one will volunteer.

There are many other possible reasons, and these are also risks. It may be that the activity requires working with people no one likes, or perhaps are viewed as untrustworthy. Some activities may depend on outside support or require external inputs that the project team is skeptical about. Few people willingly assume responsibility for work that is likely to fail because of issues beyond their control.

In addition, the work itself might be the problem. Even easy work can be risky, if people see it as thankless or unnecessary. All projects have at least some required work that no one likes to do. It may involve documentation or some other dull, routine aspect of the work. If work such as this is completed successfully, no one notices; this is simply expected. If anything goes wrong, though, there is a lot of attention. A contributor who turns a supposedly easy part of the project into a disaster can at least expect to be yelled at. Most people avoid these activities.

Another situation is the "unnecessary" activity. Projects are full of these too, at least from the perspective of the team. Life cycles, phase gate processes, and other project methodologies carry requirements that may seem to be (and in some cases, may actually be) unnecessary overhead. Some project work may be scheduled primarily because it is part of a planning template or because "That's the way we always do it." If the work is actually not needed, good project managers strive to eliminate it.

To the project risk list, add clear descriptions of each risk identified while developing the WBS, including your best understanding of the root cause for each. A typical risk listed might be: "The project requires conversion of an existing database to a new platform, and no one on the current project staff has the needed experience."

WBS Size

Project risk correlates with size; when projects get too large, risk becomes overwhelming. Scope risk rises with complexity, and one measure of complexity is the size of the WBS. Once you have decomposed the project work, count the number of items at the lowest level. Whenever the number is much above 100, project risk is high.

The more separate bits of work that a single project leader must understand, the more likely it becomes that something crucial to the project will be overlooked. As the volume of work and project complexity expand, the tools and practices of basic project management become more and more inadequate.

At high levels of complexity, the overall effort is best managed in one of two ways: as a series of shorter projects in sequence delivering what is required in stages, or as a program made up of a collection of smaller projects. In both cases, the process of decomposing the total project into sequential or parallel parts starts with a decomposition very like a WBS. In the case of sequential execution, the process may involve agile methods such as those discussed earlier in this chapter. For programs involving teams working in parallel, the resulting decomposition creates a number of projects. Each project will be managed by a separate project leader using project management principles, and the overall effort will be the responsibility of a program manager. Project risk is managed by the project leaders, and overall program risk is the responsibility of the program leader. The relationship between managing project and program risk is discussed in chapter 13.

When scale is excessive and must be managed as a single project managed by one project leader to plan, manage risk, and execute, from a VUCA perspective complexity is high and the probability of successful completion is low.

OTHER SCOPE-RELATED RISKS

Not all scope risks are strictly within the practice of project management. Examples are market risk and confidentiality risk. These risks are related, and although they may not show up in all projects, they are fairly common. Ignoring these risks is dangerous.

A business balance sheet has two sides: assets and liabilities. Project management primarily focuses on "liabilities," the expense and execution side, using measures related to the triple constraint of scope, schedule, and resources. Market and confidentiality risks tend to be on the asset, or value, side of the business ledger, where project techniques and teams may be involved indirectly, if at all. Project management is primarily about delivering what you have been asked to deliver, but this does not always equate to "success" in the marketplace. Although it is obvious that "on time, on budget, within scope" will not necessarily make a project an unqualified success, managing these aspects alone is a big job and is really about all that a project leader should reasonably be expected to deliver. The primary owners for market and confidentiality risks may be stakeholders who are not active project contributors, although many kinds of technical projects now engage cross-functional business teams—making these risks more central to the project. In any case, the risks are real, and they relate to scope. Unless you identify and manage them, these risks can result in project failure.

Market Risk

This first type of risk is about getting the definition wrong. Market risk can relate to features, timing, cost, or almost any facet of the deliverable. When long development efforts are involved, the problem to be solved may change, go away, or be better addressed by an emerging new technology. A satisfactory deliverable may be brought to market shortly after an essentially identical offering from a competitor. Even when a project produces exactly what was requested by a sponsor or economic buyer, it may be rejected by the intended end user. Sometimes the people responsible for promoting and selling a good product fail to follow through. Even though your deliverables may meet required specifications and be delivered on time and on budget, there is a chance that they will fail to meet user expectations or will never be used.

The longer and the more complicated the project is, the greater the market risk tends to be. Project leaders can help manage these risks through active, continuing participation in any market research and customer interaction, and by frequently communicating with stakeholders who are involved with deployment of the deliverable.

Some of the techniques already discussed can help in managing this. A thorough process for deliverable definition probes for many of the sources of market risk, and the high-level risk tools outlined previously also provide perspective on the environment surrounding the project.

In addition, ongoing contact with the intended users, through interviews, surveys, market research, and other techniques, will help to uncover problems and shifts in project assumptions. Agile methodologies employ ongoing user involvement in the definition of short, sequential project cycles, minimizing the "wrong" deliverable risk greatly for project teams working closely with their end users through a succession of evolving deliverables.

If the project is developing a product that will compete with similar offerings from competitors, ongoing competitive analysis to predict what others are planning can be useful (but, of course, competitors will not make this straightforward or easy—confidentiality risks are addressed next). Responsibility for such ongoing effort may be fully within the project, but if it is not, the project team should still periodically review what is going on, and if necessary, encourage the marketing staff (or other stakeholders) to keep the information current.

The project team should always probe beyond the specific requirements (the stated needs) to understand where the specifications come from (the real needs). Understanding what is actually needed is generally much more important than simply understanding what was requested, and it is a key part of opportunity management. Early use of models, prototypes, mockups, and other simulations of the deliverable will help you learn whether the requested specifications are in fact likely to provide what is needed. Short cycles of development with periodic releases of meaningful functionality (and value) throughout the project also minimize this category of risk. It is useful to establish standards, testing requirements, and acceptance criteria in clear, specific terms, and periodically review them with those who will evaluate your deliverables.

Confidentiality Risk

A second type of risk that is generally not exclusively in the hands of the project team relates to secrecy. Although some projects are done in an open and relatively unconstrained environment, confidentiality is crucial to many high-tech projects, particularly long ones. If information about the project is made public, its value might decrease or even vanish. Better-funded competitors with more staff might learn of what you are working on and build it first, making your work irrelevant. Of course, managing this risk well will potentially increase the market risk, as you will be less free to gather information from end users. You will need to avoid using prototypes, models, mockups, or even detailed descriptions to keep your competitors in the dark. On some technical projects, the need for secrecy may also be a specific contractual obligation, as with government projects. Even if the deliverable is not a secret, you may be using techniques or methodologies that are proprietary competitive advantages, and loss of this sort of intellectual property also represents a confidentiality risk.

Within the project team, several techniques may help. Some projects work on a "need to know" basis and provide to team members only the information required to do their current work. Although this will usually hurt teamwork and motivation, and may even lead to substandard results (people will optimize only for what they know, not for the overall project), it is one way to protect confidential information.

Emphasizing the importance of confidentiality also helps. Periodically reinforce the need for confidentiality with all team members, and especially with contractors or other outsiders. Be specific about the requirements for confidentiality in contract terms when you bring in outside help, and make sure all nondisclosure terms and conditions are clearly understood. Any external market research or customer contact also requires effective nondisclosure agreements, again with enough discussion to make the need for secrecy clear.

In addition to all of this, project documents and other communication must be appropriately marked "confidential" (or according to the requirements set by your organization). Restrict distribution of project information, particularly electronic versions, to people who need it and who understand, and agree with, the reasons for secrecy. Protect information stored on computer networks or in the cloud with passwords that are changed frequently enough to limit inappropriate access. Use legal protections such as copyright registrations and patents as appropriate to establish ownership of intellectual property. (Timing on this can be tricky. On the one hand, legal protections can establish your rights. On the other hand, they are public and may reveal to competitors what you are working on.)

Although the confidentiality risks are partially the responsibility of the project team, many lapses are out of their control. Managers, sponsors, marketing staffs, and favorite customers are the sources for many leaks. Project management tools principally address execution of the work, not secrecy. Effective project management relies heavily on good, frequent communication, so projects with substantial confidentiality requirements can be difficult and quite frustrating to lead. Managing confidentiality risk requires discipline, frequent reminders of the need for secrecy to all involved (especially those involved indirectly), limiting the number of people involved, and more than a little luck.

DOCUMENTING THE RISKS

As the requirements, scope definition documents, WBS, and other project data start to take shape, you can begin to develop a list of specific issues, concerns, and risks related to the scope and deliverables of the project. When the definitions are complete, review the risk list and inspect it for missing or unclear information. If some portion of the project scope seems likely to change, note this as well. Typical scope risks involve performance, reliability, untested methods or technology, or combinations of deliverable requirements that are beyond your experiences. Make clear why each item listed is an exposure for the project; cite any relevant specifications and measures that go beyond those successfully achieved in the past in the risk description, using explicitly quantified criteria. An example might be, "The system delivered must execute at double the fastest speed achieved in the prior generation."

Sources of specific scope risks include:

- Requirements that seem likely to change
- Mandatory use of new technology
- Requirements to invent or discover new capabilities
- Unfamiliar or untried development tools or methods
- Extreme reliability or quality requirements
- External sourcing for a key subcomponent or tool
- Incomplete or poorly defined acceptance tests or criteria
- Technical complexity
- Conflicting or inconsistent specifications
- Incomplete product definitions
- Large WBS

Using the processes for scope planning and definition will reveal many specific technical and other potential risks. List these risks for your project, with information about causes and consequences. The list of risks will expand throughout the project planning process. Your risk list will serve as your foundation for a risk register, which you will use to analyze and manage for project risk.

Key Ideas for Identifying Scope Risks

- Clearly define all project deliverables, and note challenges.
- Set limits on the project based on the value of the deliverables.
- Decompose all project work into small pieces, and identify work not well understood.

- Assign ownership for all project work and probe for reasons behind any reluctance.
- Note risk arising from expected project duration or complexity.

PANAMA CANAL: SETTING THE OBJECTIVE (1905–1906)

One of the principal differences between the earlier unsuccessful attempt to build the Panama Canal and the later project was the application of good project management practices. However, the second project had a shaky beginning. It was conceived as a military project and funded by the US government, so the scope and objectives for the revived Panama Canal project should have been clear, even at the start. They were not.

The initial manager for the project when work commenced in 1904 was John Findlay Wallace, formerly the general manager of the Illinois Central Railroad. Wallace was visionary; he did a lot of investigating and experimenting but he accomplished little in Panama. His background included no similar project experience. In addition to these difficulties, Wallace could do almost nothing without the consent of a seven-man commission set up back in the United States, a commission that rarely agreed on anything. Also, nearly every decision, regardless of size, required massive amounts of paperwork. A year later, in 1905, US$128 million had been spent but still there was no final plan, and most of the workers were still waiting for something to do. The project had in many ways picked up just where the earlier French project had left off, problems and all. Even after a year, it was still not clear whether the canal would be at sea level or constructed with locks and dams.

In 1905, mired in red tape, Wallace announced the canal was a mistake, and he resigned.

John Wallace was promptly replaced by John Stevens, who was also from the railroad business but whose experience was on the building side, not the operating side. He built a reputation as one of the best engineers in the United States by constructing railroads throughout the Pacific frontier. Before appointing Stevens, Theodore Roosevelt eliminated the problematic seven-man commission, and he significantly reduced the red tape, complication, and delay. As chief engineer, Stevens, unlike Wallace, effectively had full control of the work. Arriving in Panama, Stevens took stock and immediately stopped all work on the canal, stating, "I was determined to prepare well before construction, regardless of clamor of criticism. I am confident that if this policy is adhered to, the future will show its wisdom." And so it did.

With the arrival of John Stevens, managing project scope became the highest priority. He directed all his initial efforts at preparation for the work. He built dormitories for workers to live in, dining halls to feed them, warehouses for equipment and materials, and other infrastructure for the project. The doctor responsible for health of the workers on the project, William Crawford Gorgas, had been trying for over a year to gain support from John Wallace for measures needed to deal with the mosquitoes, by then known to spread both yellow fever and malaria. Stevens quickly gave this work his full support, and Dr. Gorgas proceeded to eradicate these diseases. Yellow fever was conquered in Panama just six months after Dr. Gorgas received Stevens's support, and he made good progress combating malaria as well.

Under the guidance of Stevens, all the work was defined and planned employing well-established, modern project management principles. He said, "Intelligent management must be based on exact knowledge of facts. Guesswork will not do." He did not talk much, but he asked lots of questions. People commented, "He turned me inside out and shook out the last drop of information." His meticulous documentation served as the basis for work throughout the project.

Stevens also determined exactly how the canal should be built, to the smallest detail. The objective for the project was ultimately set in 1907 according to his recommendations: The United States would build an eighty-kilometer (fifty-mile) lock-and-dam canal at Panama connecting the Atlantic and Pacific oceans, with a budget of US$375 million, to open in 1915. With the scope defined, the path forward became clear.

CHAPTER 4

IDENTIFYING PROJECT SCHEDULE RISK

"Work expands so as to fill the time available for its completion."

—C. NORTHCOTE PARKINSON, "Parkinson's Law"

Although Parkinson's observation was not backed up with any empirical data, its truth is rarely questioned. It seems particularly appropriate for technical projects, because besides all the obvious reasons that people have for using up the time available to complete their work, on technical projects there is another reason. Most people who are drawn to technical projects are analytical, and they like to be precise, accurate, and thorough. If there is time available to attempt to make something perfect, most engineers will try.

Projects, however, are rarely about perfection. They are about pragmatism, delivering a result that is "good enough." Practicality is not particularly motivating, and it is rarely much fun, so technical projects often diverge from the direct path and out into the weeds. Thoroughly identifying schedule risks requires awareness of this and disciplined use of project management planning tools to create appropriate schedules that avoid overengineering.

In the previous chapter, we considered factors that can make projects literally impossible. In this chapter, and in chapter 5 on resource risks, our focus is on constraints—factors that transform otherwise reasonable projects into ones that are doomed to fail. Project processes for scheduling and resource planning provide a fertile source for discovery of project risks that arise from these constraints.

SOURCES OF SCHEDULE RISK

Schedule risk cases make up well over a quarter of the records in the PERIL database. These risks have an average impact of about seven weeks, a bit less than scope risks and somewhat higher than the average for resource risks. They represent more than a quarter of the overall impact in the PERIL database. Schedule risks fall into three categories: delays, estimates, and dependencies. Delay risks were most numerous; these are defined as schedule slips due to factors that are at least nominally under the control of the project team. Estimate risks were next most numerous and were caused by inaccurate duration assessment of project activities. Schedule dependency risks, also significant, relate to project slippage due to factors outside the project, and on average caused the most harm—over eight weeks of slippage. (These schedule dependencies all relate to timing—dependency problems primarily caused by deliverable requirements are grouped with the scope change risks.) Each of the three root-cause categories is further divided into subcategories, shown in the following table.

SCHEDULE ROOT-CAUSE SUBCATEGORIES	DEFINITION	COUNT	CUMULATIVE IMPACT (WEEKS)	AVERAGE IMPACT (WEEKS)
Dependency Legal	A shift in legal, regulatory, or standards	11	121	11.0
Estimates Learning	New work assumed to be easier than it turned out to be	47	431	9.2
Dependency Project	Project interdependency delay in programs	31	250	8.1
Estimates Deadline	Top-down, imposed deadlines that are unrealistic	15	118	7.9
Dependency Infrastructure	Infrastructure not ready or support not available (printing, IT, shipping, etc.)	28	193	6.9
Delay Information	Slip due to unavailability of specification or other needed data	41	270	6.6
Delay Parts	Delay waiting for needed deliverable component	84	552	6.6
Estimates Judgment	Poor estimating process or inadequate analysis	33	208	6.3
Delay Hardware	Needed equipment arrives late or fails	41	232	5.7
Delay Decision	Slip due to untimely decision for escalation, approval, phase exit	33	182	5.5

The overall impact of these schedule risk subcategories is summarized in figure 4-1. The subcategory with the largest total impact is waiting for a needed component (particularly common during recent supply-chain problems), with estimating novel work not far behind.

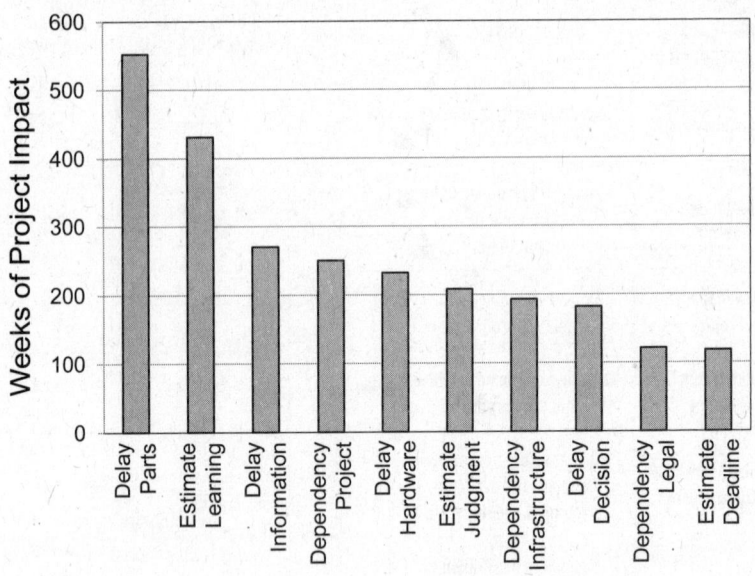

■ **Figure 4-1:** Total Project Impact by Schedule Root-Cause Subcategories

Delay Risks

Delay risks represent almost half of the schedule risks and about one-sixth of all the risks in the PERIL database. Impact from delays averaged about a month and a half. Types of delay risk in the PERIL database include parts, hardware, information, and decisions.

Parts that were required to complete the project deliverable were the most frequently reported source of delay, with an average schedule impact of over five weeks. Delivery problems and supply chain disruptions were common sources for this delay, but there were also quite a few issues involving customs and paperwork for international shipping. Delays also resulted from parts that arrived on time but were found to be defective.

More than 20 percent of the delay risks were caused when **hardware** needed to perform project work was late, including systems and other equipment. Risks in this subcategory averaged almost a month and a half of delay. Over the recent past supply chain issues have spiked, resulting in an increase compared with earlier PERIL database statistics in delays due to both late parts and hardware.

Information needed by the project represented another fifth of the cases in the delay category. These and parts delays were also the most damaging on average, representing an average of over six weeks of project slip. Some of the information delay was due to time differences between parts of distributed global teams. Losing one or more days on a regular basis due to communication time lags and misunderstandings was common. In other cases, access to information was inadequate, or delivery of needed reports was interrupted.

Slow **decisions** also caused project slippage. Roughly one-sixth of the delay examples were due to managers or other stakeholders who did not act as quickly as necessary to keep the project on schedule. Sometimes the cause was poor access to the decision-makers, or their lack of interest in the project. For other projects, delays were the result of extended debates, discussions, or indecision. Projects facing these issues lost over five weeks on average.

Potential delay risks in general are often difficult to anticipate, and many of the examples in the PERIL database can legitimately be categorized as "unknown" risks. Thorough analysis of the input requirements at each stage of the project plan, however, will highlight many of them.

Estimating Risks

Of all the types of schedule risk found in technical projects, estimating is the most visible. When you ask project managers what their biggest difficulties are, estimating is high on, if not at the top of, the list. Despite this, the number of incidents in the PERIL database is not too large, under 8 percent of the records, and only about a quarter of the total schedule risks. The average impact of estimating risks is only slightly above that of the PERIL database as a whole, at roughly two months of slippage. One frequently cited issue with estimating in technical projects is the relatively rapid change in the work. Good estimates rely on history. When the environment is in constant flux, history may not seem all that useful (more on this later in the chapter). The estimating risk subcategories relate to learning curves, judgment, and imposed deadlines.

Learning curve issues were the most common type of estimating risk. Their impact was well above the average for the database, in excess of nine weeks. The quality of the estimates when new technology or new people (or even worse, both) are involved is not good. The portions of project work that require staff to do things they have never done before are always risky, and although thorough analysis of the work can show which parts of the project plan are most exposed, precise estimating is difficult.

Judgment in estimating was the next most common estimating problem in the PERIL database. For most of these cases, the estimates were simply overoptimistic—one of the most common sources of project bias. Some of these estimates were too short by factors of three or four. Dealing with this source of estimating risk requires thorough planning, with appropriate understanding and decomposition of the work, so that the effort and steps required are known. It also requires good recordkeeping. Metrics and project data archives are invaluable in creating future estimates that are more consistent with reality than past estimates have been (even for projects where things change rapidly). Having some data always beats having to guess. Another powerful tool in revealing and combating optimistic estimates is worst-case analysis. The answer to the question "What might go wrong?" will not only reveal something about the likely duration, it will also uncover new potential sources of risk.

Imposed **deadlines** were the third subcategory of estimating risks. These inaccurate estimates caused a typical two months of slippage, and there the root cause lies outside the project team. Technical projects frequently have aggressive deadlines set by stakeholders in advance, with little or no input from the project team. Even when the project plan shows the deadline to be unrealistic, these unattainable timing objectives are often retained. Such projects are doomed from the start.

Dependency Risks

Dependency risks make up about a sixth of the schedule risks. The impact from schedule dependency risks averaged just over eight weeks of slip per incident. There are three dependency risk subcategories: other projects, infrastructure factors, and legal issues.

Other **projects** with shared dependencies not only are the most numerous of the dependency risks, they also are quite damaging, with an average of about two months. In larger projects (often classified as programs), a number of smaller projects interact and link to each other. In addition to providing each other with information and deliverables that meet well-defined specifications (also a scope risk exposure), each project within a larger program must also synchronize the timing of schedule dependencies to avoid being slowed down by (or slowing down) other projects. Managing all these interface connections is difficult in complex programs, and the amount of damage increases with time; many of these risks in the PERIL database were noticed only near the end of the projects. Even for the interfaces that were defined in advance, delay was fairly common due to the uncertainty in each project and the high likelihood that at least one of the interconnected projects would encounter some sort of difficulty. With so many possible failure modes, it is all but certain that something will go wrong. Analysis of the dependencies and interfaces between projects is a key aspect of program management, and many of the risks faced by the projects become visible through interface management techniques (detailed in chapter 13).

Infrastructure dependencies also interfered with project schedules in the PERIL database. The frequency of these problems was somewhat lower than those due to project interdependencies; their impact was less on average, but still almost seven weeks. These situations included interruption of technical services, such as computer systems or networks required by the project, and inadequate access to resources such as help desks, system support, and people who understood older but necessary applications. Several projects were delayed by maintenance outages that were unknown to the project team, even though they had been scheduled in advance.

Legal and regulatory dependencies are also problematic. Though the number of cases is well under 20 percent of the dependency risks, the average impact was highest for any subcategory in the PERIL database at about eleven weeks. Legal and paperwork requirements can cause problems when they change abruptly. Monitoring for planned or possible changes to laws and mandatory standards can provide early warning for many types of potential regulatory problems.

Schedule Risk and VUCA

As with the PERIL database as a whole, schedule risks are dominated by uncertainty, with two-thirds of the impact. These predictability issues arose from inaccuracies in estimates and scheduling dependencies. Complexity was the next most significant VUCA factor, causing most of the remaining third of the harm due to inadequate understanding of interactions with other projects and legal and organizational dependencies. Volatility also contributed some damage, primarily through imposed (and unrealistic) deadlines. You can minimize the schedule risk effects of VUCA through more thorough analysis, honest assessment of worse cases, better analysis of project complications, and documenting and carefully reviewing project information. Additional examples of schedule risks from the PERIL database are found in the appendix.

ACTIVITY DEFINITION

Building a project schedule starts with defining project work at an appropriate level of detail. Estimating and sequencing of project work is much more accurate and realistic when based on smaller parts of the project, and is therefore less risky. Although the entire project may be big, complicated, and confusing, the principle of "divide and conquer" allows for the project team to bring order out of chaos. The starting point for schedule development (as well as for resource planning) is the project work breakdown structure (WBS) or some similar collection of smaller efforts, as discussed in chapter 3. If the work described at the lowest level for your project is consistent with the guidelines of "2 to 20 days duration" or "80 hours of effort," those items can provide a solid foundation for scheduling. If your WBS decomposition is not yet to that level of granularity, hidden risks and questionable estimates will remain until you have done further analysis and decomposition. Managing risk depends upon knowing what "going right" looks like, so it's best to work with small, deliverable-oriented bits of your project that you understand, and can competently estimate, schedule, and monitor.

The lowest level of a WBS hierarchy provides the basis for developing a schedule, but the terminology used varies. Some people call the items "work packages," scheduling tools often use the term "tasks," and agile software methodologies refer to "stories" or "use cases." The most common term for these pieces of work is "**activities**," so that is the term used here.

Creating a project schedule requires both duration estimating and activity sequencing. Which of these planning tasks you undertake first is largely a matter of personal preference, and most of the time the two processes proceed in parallel. Both estimating and activity sequencing are iterative processes, and there is a good deal of interaction between the two when building a project plan. If starting to sequence project activities prior to estimating them seems more natural for your projects, use the material in this chapter in that order. What is essential for risk management is that you do both thoroughly, as each reveals unique schedule risks.

ESTIMATING ACTIVITY DURATION

Project estimates are often treated as facts—in charts, planning reports, and other project documentation. Estimates are not facts; they are forecasts. All project work estimates are uncertain: some trivially, others representing wild inaccuracy. Estimating risk provides a substantial number of the entries in the PERIL database and represents on average about two months of impact. A good estimating process is a powerful tool for minimizing this type of schedule risk. If you can identify the most uncertain estimates, the risky parts of the project will be more visible.

In the dictionary, an estimate is "a rough or approximate calculation." Project plans require approximations of both time and cost. The focus of this section is on the risks associated with duration estimates. All project estimates are related, though, and we will expand the concepts introduced here in chapter 5 to discuss using estimates of effort and cost to identify resource risks. Estimates of varying accuracy are derived throughout a project, from the "rough-order-of-magnitude" estimates used to initiate projects to the more precise estimates that are refined as the project runs to monitor and control project work. The single-point estimates commonly used mask the uncertainty in complex projects. Estimates that make risk visible use range information, plus-or-minus percentages, or even probability distributions.

Estimation Pitfalls

Estimating project work is challenging, and most project leaders will admit that they don't do it as well as they would like. Understanding why accurate estimating is hard provides insight into project risks and helps us improve future estimating. Four key impediments to estimating well are:

- Avoidance
- Optimism
- Lack of information
- Granularity

Probably the most significant problem with estimating is that project contributors do not like to estimate, so they avoid it. Much of the appeal for projects is the work—designing, programming, engineering, building, and other activities that those drawn to such work enjoy. People avoid estimating (and planning in general) because it is seen as overhead, or boring "administrivia." Estimates are often done quickly and only grudgingly. Most technical people have little estimating experience or training for estimating, so their skill level is low. People hate doing things they do poorly. To make matters worse, because the estimates provided are so often inaccurate, most of the feedback estimators get is negative. It is human nature to avoid activities that are likely to result in criticism and punishment.

Too much optimism is another enemy of good estimates. In the PERIL database, the most common causes for poor estimating are learning curves and judgment, both of which may be symptoms of the very common human bias for optimism. Estimates that are too short create many additional project problems including severe increases in late-project work and deadline slippage. Optimistic estimates are often based on best-case scenario analysis (each activity is planned assuming that nothing will go wrong), excessively generous assumptions about the amount of time that people will have available to do project work, and overconfidence in the talent and speed of the project team. The third kind of estimating risk in the PERIL database is top-down deadline pressure. When sponsors and stakeholders are inappropriately optimistic, they impose unrealistic time constraints on the project, forcing the project team to accept estimates in their plans based on the time available ("schedule to fit"), not based on the reality of the work.

A third issue is a lack of information. Initial project estimates are the product of early analysis, when the amount and quality of available project information is still low. Often, scope definition is still changing and incomplete, and significant portions of the work are poorly understood when these estimates are made. Compounding this, for many projects there is little (sometimes no) historical information to use in estimating, and there are no defined estimating processes used. Far too often estimates are based on guesses.

A fourth factor contributing to poor estimates is the granularity of the work. Early estimates are often done for projects based on descriptions of the work and deliverables that lack much detail. Estimates are chronically inaccurate when they are based on high-level project deliverables with vague acceptance criteria. The quality of estimates for long-duration project activities is also poor. Guidelines for project activities at the lowest level of the WBS—roughly two weeks' duration, or eighty hours of effort— enable better estimating. When an activity duration extends beyond a month, duration assessments tend to be wildly inaccurate.

All of these factors contribute to estimating risk. Building more realistic understanding of timing requires capturing metrics, using well-defined estimating procedures, clearly defining deliverables, and breaking the project into understandable pieces.

Estimation Techniques

Most of the estimating risks in the PERIL database are catego- rized as judgment and learning curve problems. The projects affected by these risks all had significant delays due to unrealisti- cally short estimates. Many projects failed to account properly for the increasing complexity or new technologies in their work. Other projects chronically underestimated time needed for com- monplace project activities. Better processes and more attention to performance data will help to identify many of these risks, if not eliminate them.

Effective estimating techniques all rely on history. The best predictor for work duration (or effort) on a project will be a past measurement made when doing the same (or similar) earlier work. All effective estimating processes either use historical data directly or rely on history as a foundation. Good estimating is based on:

- Historical data
- Experts and expert judgment
- Heuristics and parametric formulas
- Relative size or scale assessment
- Delphi group estimating
- Further decomposition

For cases where none of these methods are effective, there will be estimating risk.

Historical data: The simplest estimating technique is to "look up the answer." The most useful historical information, for projects of all types, is solid empirical data, collected with discipline and care during earlier work. Unfortunately, such project metric databases are rare for many types of project work, so useful information is sparse. If you lack a formal repository of actual performance data, effort and duration information may be found by reviewing data from:

- Postproject analysis and "lessons learned" reports
- Personal notes and status reports from recent projects
- Documents provided by team members
- Published technical data (either inside your organization or public)
- Reference materials and engineering or other standards
- The web (offering data of wildly varying reliability)

Anecdotal historical information is often plentiful. Discuss the project with others and probe their memories. Written historical data tends to be more reliable, but anecdotal information is easier to find. While memories may not be very trustworthy, they can still serve as a good starting point for preliminary estimating, especially if the data is recent, relevant, and credible.

A lack of documented history is a problem that is easy to fix. Measurement and productivity analysis are essential to ongoing management of estimation risk, so resolve to begin, or to continue, collecting actual activity data at least for your own projects. Chapter 9 addresses metrics useful for risk management.

Experts and expert judgment: Historical information need not be personal to be useful. Even when no one on the project has relevant experience or data, there may be others outside of your project who do. Look to peers, managers, and technical talent elsewhere in your organization. Seek out the opinions of colleagues in professional societies who do similar work for other companies. Outside consultants in technical or management fields may have useful information that they will share for a fee. Even quotations and proposals from service suppliers may contain useful data that you can use for estimating project work.

Heuristics and parametric formulas: When a type of work is repeated often, the data collected over time may evolve into useful formulas for duration or for effort. These formulas may be informal "rule of thumb" heuristics that provide approximate estimates related to measurable aspects of activity output, or they may be elaborate, precise (or at least precise-looking) analytical equations derived by regression analysis using data from past projects. One often-referenced parametric formula in the software development world is the Constructive Cost Model (COCOMO), initially introduced several decades ago by Barry Boehm at TRW, with refinements over the years based on work at the University of Southern California and by many others. If your organization supports such size-based estimation methods, use them, and contribute data from your projects to improve their accuracy and keep them current.

Relative size or scale assessment: Parametric estimating techniques such as COCOMO use quantitative metrics to derive estimates of duration and cost, but size-based estimates can be useful even if they are based on more qualitative assessments. For small projects (or the short iterations used by agile projects), "T-shirt" estimation techniques can be useful for planning. Activities are defined and then sorted into categories such as "small," "medium," "large," or "extra large." Within the categories, defined work can be compared and some adjustments made for work that does not appear sufficiently similar. Relative estimating works best when standards are defined (for example, "small" might equal one to three person-days) and the team has sufficient experience with the technique to ensure reasonable correlation between the number of activities in each category that can be completed in a month (or some other fixed amount of time). Relative size estimating can also be a low-anxiety way to introduce analytical estimating methods.

Delphi group estimating: What individuals can't tell you, the wisdom of a crowd sometimes can. The Delphi process uses inputs from several people (a minimum of four or five) to establish numerical estimate ranges and stimulate discussion. This method relies on the fact that although no one person may be able to confidently provide reliable estimates, a population of stakeholders can frequently provide a realistic prediction (as well as range information useful in assessing uncertainty). Delphi is a "group intelligence" process to tap into anecdotal historical data that would otherwise remain hidden, and because it is collaborative, it contributes to group buy-in, ownership, and motivation.

Further decomposition: Another approach you can use when you lack historical data is to create some. Begin by breaking the activity to be estimated into even smaller pieces of work, and choose a representative portion. Perform this part of the work and measure the duration (or effort) required to complete it. Use your actual measurements for the portion of the work completed to extrapolate to an estimate for the rest of the activity. Some activities can also be better estimated if thought of as small projects, with phases such as investigation, analysis, development, documentation, and testing. Further breakdown also helps by enabling you to distinguish between the portions of the work you understand well (and presumably can estimate accurately), and work that is risky.

For activity estimates where none of these methods prove useful, you will face estimating risk.

The Overall Estimating Process

Good project estimating requires many inputs, starting with a comprehensive list of project activities. Another is a resource plan, information about the people and other resources available to the project. (The resource plan is a major topic in chapter 5, focusing on resource risks.) One key reason for the resource information was mentioned in chapter 3: You need to know the owners for activities at the lowest level of the project WBS. Activity owners are generally responsible for initial activity duration estimates. Whether the owner is the only contributor, or leads a team, or serves as a liaison to another group where the work will be done, work estimates ultimately are part of the owner's responsibilities.

Accurate estimates require clear, specific information about each activity. Document any constraints on activity durations or project assumptions that might affect the estimates. Activities with more than one deliverable may be easier to manage and have less risk if they are broken down further, creating new, smaller activities for each deliverable. Acceptance criteria and unambiguous, measurable requirements also contribute to accurate estimates. If specifications are unclear, clarify them or note the project risks.

There are three distinct types of project estimates:

- Duration estimates, measured in active work time (usually workdays)
- Effort estimates, measured using a combination of people and time (person-days or something similar)
- Calendar estimates, measured in elapsed time (calendar days)

Each type of estimate has its place in the planning process. Duration estimates are used as input to computer scheduling tools and for schedule analysis. Effort estimates are based on resource analysis and relate to project costs. Calendar duration estimates underpin project deadlines and support accurate tracking. Project planning requires all three estimate types, and either starts with duration estimates or effort estimates. The other estimates follow, ultimately generating calendar estimates that are used to ascertain the project timeline. Whatever estimating sequence you prefer, good planning and risk management depends on estimates derived from bottom-up project analysis. Avoid "pegged-date" or arbitrary, politically specified estimates. Building a plan with unrealistic estimates creates risk and undermines your ability to negotiate necessary project changes.

Some project leaders prefer to derive duration estimates first, and then develop the effort estimates when other planning data, such as activity sequencing information, is available. Effort estimates may then be used to validate and adjust the duration estimates. This process is summarized in figure 4-2. You may prefer to begin with effort estimating, but whatever sequence you employ must consider the same issues, factors, and risks.

■ **Figure 4-2:** Estimation Process

Project-specific factors and duration estimates: Project estimating methods (including guessing) start with information derived in some way from history and experience. Beginning with the best available historical data for each activity, develop duration estimates. Use project-specific information to adjust these initial assessments, based on differences between the current project and earlier work. Project-specific factors include:

- Clarity of the project specifications
- Likelihood of significant specification change
- New resource requirements
- Longer overall project duration
- Unusual technical complexity

- New required technology
- Extreme requirements for reliability
- Geographic separation and cultural diversity on the project team
- Infrastructure and environment differences
- Training requirements

Every lowest-level activity in your WBS requires a duration estimate, measured in workdays (or some suitable units). In addition to providing input for adjusting historical data, these project-specific factors may also reveal significant project risks. If so, list them.

The estimates themselves may reveal risks. Any activities with uncertain estimates are risky. However, lack of confidence in an estimate is a symptom of risk, not the risk itself. Whenever any of your project estimates seem untrustworthy, probe for why, and note the root cause as the risk. Two common sources of low-confidence estimates are lack of experience with the work and activities that may have several different outcomes, such as an investigation.

Resource factors and effort estimates: Duration estimates, combined with project information on people and teams, provide the basis for effort estimates. Initial resource plans provide information on resource factors, such as:

- The amount of time each day each team member has for project work
- The number of people contributing to each activity
- The skills, experience, and productivity of each team member
- Training and mentoring requirements
- Nonproject responsibilities for each person

- Communication lags and other consequences of distributed teams
- Expected turnover or attrition of staff during the project
- The number and duration of project (and other) meetings
- The amount of project communication and reporting
- Travel requirements
- The number of required people not yet assigned to the project

The first factor in the list, the number of project hours in a day, is a common cause of underestimation. Not every hour that people work is available for project activities. Meetings, communication (both formal and informal), breaks, meals, and other interruptions take time. Even the common assumption of "five to six" hours per day for project activities may be significantly higher than the reality available to many projects. Productivity is also a source of variation, and for individual team members it can vary wildly. Any estimates of effort or duration made in advance of assigning the specific people who will do the work are risky. Chapter 5 will address these and other resource-related risks in greater detail.

By considering these resource factors, you can develop more accurate activity estimates (in person-hours, contributor-days, or some other combination of staffing and time).

Nonproject factors and calendar estimates: The final stage of estimation is to translate duration estimates into calendar estimates. To translate workday duration estimates into elapsed-time estimates, you need to account for all the days that are not available for project work. Computer scheduling tools simplify this process; many of the following factors can be entered into the calendar database, allowing the software to do the calculations. Some nonproject factors include:

- Weekends
- Holidays
- Vacations and other paid time off
- Other projects
- Other nonproject work
- Lengthy nonproject meetings
- Equipment and system downtime
- Interruptions and shutdowns
- Scheduled or anticipated medical leave

Calendar estimates account for all the days between the start and end of each activity. Specific dates for each activity are derived by combining duration estimates, nonproject factors, and the activity sequencing process that is a main focus later in this chapter. One particular risk common for global projects is a result of differences in scheduled time off for geographically separate parts of the project team. Frequent loss of some of the project team to various national and religious holidays is disruptive enough, but all too often these interruptions come as a surprise to the project leader, who may not know about all the relevant holidays.

Applying Estimating Techniques

Figure 4-3 summarizes estimation techniques that are applicable in various situations. For each project activity, the team either has experience or does not. For the type of work involved, relevant metrics may or may not exist.

The highest estimating risk is found in the worst case, lower right quadrant: no experience and no data. This case is far from unusual; on modern projects, it may be true for many activities you need to estimate. Project estimating methods frequently involve guessing, and in these situations guesses may be your best option. You can

	Relevant metrics exist	No data is available
Prior activity experience	• **Retrospectives** • **Databases** • **Parametric formulas** • **Experiential rules and "Size" methods** • **Notes and status reports**	• **Task owner input** • **Peer inputs** • **Inspections** • **Delphi analysis** • **Short tasks (20-day maximum) in WBS** • **Further decomposition**
No activity experience	• **Published information** • **Vendor quotes** • **Expert consultation**	• **Guesses** • **Outside help** • **Older technology**

■ **Figure 4-3:** Estimating Techniques

also consider alternatives such as getting someone who does have experience to consult on your project or even replanning the work to use an approach where your team does have experience.

Only slightly better than this is the case where you have no experience, but you have found some external information. Estimates based on someone else's measurements are better than nothing, but unless your project, environment, and team expertise are similar to the project where the measurements were made, the data may not be relevant. In all cases that lack relevant experience, estimation risk is high and the potential for damaging inaccuracy of timing information belongs on your project risk list.

The upper right quadrant is for activities that have been done before but for which no data exists. Although this should not happen, it is fairly common on technical projects. Thorough analysis and estimating methods such as Delphi may provide adequate estimates, but the results of these processes still contain estimation risk. Over time, more disciplined data collection can help you better manage these risks.

The best case is the upper left quadrant. The existence of both experience and measurements should provide credible, reliable estimates for project activities. Eventually, proactive risk management and disciplined application of other project processes will move many, if not most, activities here, even on high-tech projects.

One other significant source of estimation risk arises from the people who are assigned to do the work. "Good" estimates need to be believable, which means that they are derived from data and methods that make sense. This is a good foundation, but even the best estimating techniques yield unreliable estimates if they lack the project team buy-in. To be accurate, estimates also must be believed. No matter how much data goes into creating estimates, if the people who will do the work do not agree with them, they are risky. Good estimates are both *believable* and *believed*. Be on the alert for skepticism of duration estimates, particularly from contributors who are responsible for the work in question.

Duration Estimates Adjusted for Uncertainty

All the techniques just discussed generate deterministic, single-point estimates for project activities. This type of estimate implies a precision that is far from realistic. To better deal with uncertainty and risk, the U.S. military developed the Program Evaluation and Review Technique (PERT) methodology in the late 1950s. The earliest forms of PERT used three-point range estimates for each activity: an **optimistic** estimate, a **most likely** estimate, and a **pessimistic** estimate. (PERT may be used for both time and cost analysis. This discussion focuses on time analysis; chapter 5 will explore PERT for cost estimating.) Traditionally, PERT mapped a bell-type distribution that could skew either toward the optimistic or pessimistic estimate, usually using a Beta distribution such as the one in figure 4-4. The three estimates defined the range and peak of the distribution as in the figure, and an "expected" activity duration (the 50-percent point for the curve) could be derived using the formula:

$t_e = (t_o + 4t_m + t_p)/6$, where

t_e is the calculated "expected" duration—the mean

t_o is the "optimistic" duration (the "best case")

t_m is the "most likely" duration (the peak of the distribution)

t_p is the "pessimistic" duration (the "worst case")

In addition to the "expected" estimate, PERT is also used to quantitatively assess estimation risk. For PERT, the range of possible outcomes allows you to approximate the standard deviation for each activity duration estimate, where:

One standard deviation = $(t_p - t_o)/6$

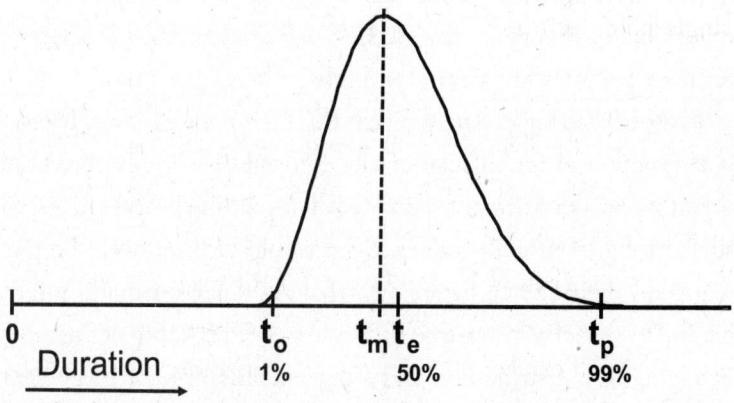

Figure 4-4: Duration Estimates for PERT Analysis

The theory behind PERT was a step in the right direction, but in practice PERT analysis may be problematic. The three most common issues people have with PERT are the time and effort required for the analysis, the quality of the data, and misuse of the information.

PERT requires more data—three estimates. This requires more time to collect, enter, and analyze. The collection process is annoying to the project team, and the three estimates are not easily incorporated using common project management tools. Because of this, the effort and cost of PERT analysis may exceed the apparent value of the results.

Also, as discussed earlier, the quality of even a single-point estimate can be suspect. The accuracy of the two additional estimates is usually worse. Definitions of optimistic and pessimistic can be inconsistent, arbitrary, and confusing. PERT initially defined the range limits as "1-percent tails." It was suggested that people imagine doing an activity 100 times and select estimates so that only once would the duration fall below the optimistic estimate and only once would it lie above the pessimistic estimate. For most activities, these estimates were generally wild guesses, or fixed plus/minus percentages. Because of this, PERT analysis results were often the victim of "garbage in, garbage out."

Probably the biggest reason that PERT is not more widely used is the potential for misuse of the information involved. Many organizations experiment with PERT for a time before this issue surfaces, but eventually it does. Everything starts out well. Project teams do their best to figure out what the three estimates might be for each activity, using difficult-to-understand definitions involving Beta distributions and 1-percent tails (or 5- or 10-percent tails—there are many variants). Project PERT analysis proceeds for a time, and some insight into project uncertainty begins to emerge. This continues until some bright midlevel manager notices the optimistic estimates. Because the project teams have at least implied that these estimates are not actually impossible, managers begin to insist that schedules be based only on these most aggressive estimates. When these unlikely estimates are used to set project deadlines, the statistical underpinnings of PERT ensure that there is essentially no chance of success. The results are invariably disastrous. If any interest in PERT remains after this, the battered project teams start to use different definitions for optimistic estimates in self-defense.

Although PERT methodology can be troublesome, especially in its traditional form, three-point estimates can be useful. Optimistic estimate analysis is an important tool for managing opportunities, and in chapter 6 we will explore using this "best-case" analysis to explore project options.

Even more important, pessimistic (or worst-case) estimates are a particularly fertile source of project risk information. After collecting activity estimates, investigate worst cases using questions such as:

- What might go wrong?
- What are the likely consequences should any issues arise?
- Is the staff involved experienced in this area?
- Have we had problems with this kind of work before?
- Does this activity depend on inputs, resources, or other factors we don't control?
- Are there aspects of this work that we don't understand well?
- If you were betting money on the estimates, would they change?

Probing for responses to these and related questions will provide two important pieces of project risk data. The potential consequences you uncover, including slippage, additional costs, and other information, will be useful for assessing project risk impact. Even more revealing, the sources or root causes for any potential slip (or other significant consequences) are project risks that belong on your risk list.

Schedule impact information can also be used for a simplified variation on PERT to provide insight into schedule risk. This variation on PERT uses the initial activity estimates as both the optimistic and most likely estimates (which Parkinson's Law, the quotation that opened this chapter, predicts anyway). The worst-case information that you collect for activity durations provides data for your pessimistic estimates. The distribution this implies will be essentially triangular and similar to figure 4-5. The formula approximating the expected duration is $t_e = (5t_m + t_p)/6$.

■ **Figure 4-5:** "PERT-Like" Estimating

Although PERT techniques such as three-point estimating relate to activity estimating, PERT analysis and more sophisticated simulation techniques are really tools for project risk assessment. Chapters 7 and 9 will more deeply explore this use of PERT and related tools for understanding project risk.

Estimation Risks

Estimating is a forecasting process, and it is one that you can improve. Better estimating starts with doubt. Be skeptical of all project estimates until you have considered experiences with past similar work and probed to uncover worst cases and reveal details about the required work. Be especially skeptical of estimates for any project activities where you have little prior experience. As you develop estimates for project activities, note any situations where your assessments are mostly guesswork. Ask questions and involve others with different perspectives in planning discussions to broaden your understanding and uncover things you have missed, particularly for unfamiliar project work.

Errors in judgment and unexpectedly long learning curves caused a lot of harm to projects in the PERIL database, so add risks to your list for all large worst-case estimates, cases where your realistic estimates substantially exceed a constrained task duration, novel work, and other uncertain estimates.

ACTIVITY SEQUENCING

Additional scheduling risks become visible as you build your understanding of project workflow by combining sequencing information with the activity estimates. Activity sequencing requires you to determine the dependencies for each project activity, and these linkages reveal many potential sources of project delay. Delay and other dependency risks were responsible for almost three quarters of the scheduling risks in the PERIL database.

One effective method for minimizing schedule risk related to sequencing is to break long, complex projects into a series of much shorter ones. This principle is fundamental to agile (evolutionary, cyclic) software development methodologies. If the cycles are sufficiently short—about four weeks is a common cycle in methodologies such as scrum—the dependencies either become irrelevant or are sufficiently simple that managing them becomes trivial. For the most part, scrum ignores workflow dependencies except as special cases within each iteration cycle, or sprint. The same principle applies generally; the shorter the overall arc of a project is, the fewer complications and risks there will be arising from activity dependencies.

In more complex projects, there are many possible types of dependencies that may connect project activities, but most are linked by finish-to-start relationships—once one activity or a collection of activities is complete, other project activities can begin. Occasionally, some activities might need to be synchronized by either starting or finishing at the same time, and the logic of project work may also require interruptions and lags of various kinds. Although project plans may include some of these more exotic dependencies, the majority of the dependencies in a typical project workflow network will be finish-to-start linkages. It is these sequential-activity dependencies that are most likely to result in disruptions and delays.

Discovering risks arising from schedule dependencies requires each project activity to be linked both to predecessor work done earlier and successor activities that follow it. Schedule development depends on a logical network of project activities (and milestones) with no gaps. Establish a logical flow of work for your project so that each project activity, without exception, has an uninterrupted path backward to your initial project milestone and a continuous path forward to the final project deadline. Project analysis and risk identification will be incomplete (and possibly worthless) if there are gaps or dangling connections.

For project planning using a computer tool, avoid the use of features such as "must start on" and "must end on" pegged-date logic. The software will generate a Gantt chart that looks a lot like a project plan, but you will be unable to do any "what if" schedule analysis, effectively track project work, or thoroughly identify schedule-related risks.

Critical Path Methodology

Critical path methodology (CPM) analysis combines duration estimates with dependency information to calculate the minimum project duration. For larger projects, the analysis is best done using a computer scheduling tool. Once all your activities, duration estimates, and dependencies are entered into the database of a scheduling tool, the software automatically analyzes the project network. The set (or sets) of activities that make up the longest sequence is the project critical path, which is generally highlighted using an appropriately scary red color. Each of the red activities carries schedule risk, because if it exceeds its duration estimate, everything that follows in the project will also slip, including the project deadline.

CPM also calculates "float" or "slack" for "noncritical" activities, revealing any flexibility available. If the float is small, even though a given activity might be colored a soothing blue, it's also risky. Even project activities that have a large amount of float can be risky when their worst-case estimates exceed the calculated float. The other noncritical activities, those with significant float and reliable-looking estimates, are also relevant to risk management. They may represent replanning opportunities you may need to keep your project on track.

Computer scheduling tools make it is easy to do "what if" analysis and reveal risky activities in addition to those on the project's critical path. The first step is to make a copy of the database for the project (so you can manipulate the copy to identify additional schedule risks while leaving your foundation schedule intact). By deleting all the critical activities in your copy (relinking any resulting broken dependencies as you go), you can see what the resulting project looks like and generate a list of the next tier of risky activities to keep an eye on.

It's even more illuminating to replace all your initial estimates with worst-case estimates to see what happens. When you do this one activity at a time, you discover how sensitive the overall project is to each potential problem. If you enter all of your worst-case estimates, you get a version of the plan that shows a far longer schedule than is probable, but the end point displays just how bad things might get if everything goes wrong. (And remember, your analysis is based only on known risks; there may be significant *unknown* project risks, so even your worst-case schedule may be optimistic.)

In reality, every activity in the project represents at least a small level of schedule risk. Any piece of work in the plan could be the one that causes your project to fail. CPM analysis is a useful technique for determining which schedule risks belong on your risk list.

Multiple Critical Paths and Timing Uncertainty

Projects can and often do have more than one critical path. Multiple critical paths further increase schedule risk. To see why, consider the simple network in figure 4-6. Both paths "A-D-J" and "C-H-L" are marked as critical, and for this analysis we will assume "expected" durations where the probability of an activity finishing early (or on time) is the same as the chance of the activity finishing late. For a project with a single critical path, the project as a whole has identical probabilities—50/50. (This assumes all events and activities are independent—more on this later.) What can we say about the project in figure 4-6, with two critical paths?

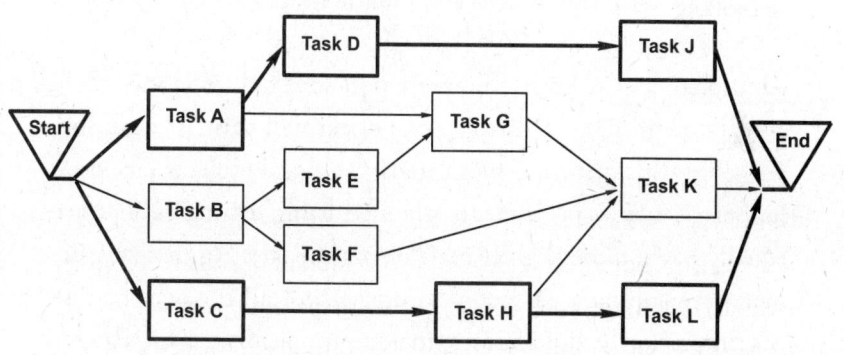

■ **Figure 4-6:** Project with Two Critical Paths

The expectation for each path being on time or early is the same as for the activities, 50 percent, but there are two of them. If the risks associated with the two paths are independent, the matrix in figure 4-7 shows the probabilities for each possible outcome. The project has only one chance in four of finishing early or on time because this requires both paths to be early or on time, which is expected 25 percent of the time.

If there are more than two critical paths, the situation gets worse. With three critical paths, the chances of success fall to one in eight, and this fraction shrinks by a factor of two with each

		Early/ on time	Late
C H L	**Early/ on time**	25%	25%
	Late	25%	25%

■ **Figure 4-7:** Result Matrix for a Project with Two Critical Paths

additional critical path. The more potential failure modes there are, the more likely it is that the project will miss its deadline. Although this picture is bleak, most technical projects face even higher risk. Few projects are planned using estimates that are equally likely to be slightly early or slightly late. Aggressive estimates are common on technical projects for all the reasons discussed earlier in the chapter, including optimism bias, lack of experience, and political pressure. If the estimates are actually 10 percent likely to be early or on time versus 90 percent likely to be late, a matrix similar to figure 4-7 for two critical paths will calculate only a 1 percent chance of success.

In addition, this analysis assumes statistical independence for all events. Although the assumption of independence may be valid for some project work, on most projects the work is all done by one small team of people, so all of the work tends to be related. Assuming that the outcome of a given activity will have no effect on succeeding activities is unrealistic. Project problems tend to cascade, and there is often significant positive correlation among project activities. The upshot of all this is that schedule risk and timing uncertainty increase significantly whenever there are multiple parallel failure modes.

Scheduling Risky Work

The timing of activities may also increase project risk. Whenever an activity has high uncertainty, it is human nature to schedule it late in the project. If an activity requires the invention of something new, or the specifics of the work are far from obvious, you may be tempted to defer the work until later in the project, reasoning that the delay might give you a chance to figure it out. Also, scheduling risky work toward the end of your project will allow you to write at least a few weekly status reports that are not filled with bad news about delays and troubled activities.

Tempting though this is, it is a bad idea. Deferring riskier activities until the end of a project can lead to both increased project risk and cost. By scheduling risky activities earlier, you can learn faster, and frequently with less effort, whether there are any show-stoppers—activities that make your whole project impossible. When you discover the problems earlier, project decision-makers have more options, including modifying objectives, using the time still available to seek alternate ways to proceed with the project, or even abandoning the work altogether before a lot of time, effort, and money has been invested. If a risky activity is deferred until late in the project, changes may be impossible or much more costly, and there will be little or no time left to seek another approach. Perhaps the worst case of all is discovering that the project is not feasible and canceling it after months (or even years) have elapsed. When risky work is scheduled earlier, decisions to abort the effort can be made before wasting a lot of money. In addition to being expensive, late cancellation is demotivating for the project team and can make it difficult to find enthusiastic staff for future projects.

Schedule Path Convergence

Another project risk arises from "fan-in." Most places in a project network where there are a lot of predecessor dependencies tend to be milestones, but any point of convergence in a project network represents schedule risk. Because project work stops at a milestone or activity if any of the preceding activities are incomplete, each additional path in represents an additional failure mode and increases the probability of delay. Milestones, phase exits, stage gates, and other life cycle checkpoints are often delayed for large programs because of a single missing requirement. Even when most other work is satisfactorily done, the project halts until the final predecessor dependency completes.

The largest fan-in exposure for many projects is the final milestone, which often has many predecessor activities. Even in the simple project network in figure 4-6, there are three predecessor dependencies for the finish milestone.

Interfaces

Dependency risks outside the project are also common in the PERIL database. Dependencies of all kinds may represent schedule risks, but interfaces—dependencies that connect one or more projects—are particularly problematic; the impact of these risks is among the highest for all schedule risks in the PERIL database, averaging over eight weeks per project. Connections between projects are most common for projects that are part of a larger program. As each project team plans its work, interdependencies with other projects will surface and must be planned and managed.

Dependencies that are wholly within a project carry schedule risk, but interfaces between projects are even riskier. For a schedule interconnection, each project contains only half of the linkage, either the predecessor or the successor activity. The deliverables can be components, services, information, software, or almost anything that one project creates that is required as an input by a separate project. The project that expects to receive the deliverable potentially faces both schedule and scope risk. If the hand off is late, the dependent project may slip. Even when it is on time, if the deliverable is not acceptable, the project (and perhaps the entire program) may be in trouble. Interfaces are particularly important to identify and manage because of the limited visibility of progress across separately managed projects.

The process for managing these interfaces and the risks related to them is best managed at the program level. The section of chapter 13 on program risk management explores this process in detail.

Interface management requires agreement and commitments in writing between each involved project, and even then it's risky. Add each interface dependency for your project to your list of project risks.

Planning Horizon

Yet another source of schedule risk relates to project duration. When you drive an automobile at night on a dark road with no illumination other than your headlights, you can see only a limited distance ahead. The reach of the headlights is several hundred meters, so you must stay alert and frequently reexamine the road ahead to see things as they come into view.

Projects also have visibility constraints. Projects vary a good deal in how much accurate planning is possible, but all project planning has a limit. For some projects, planning even three months in advance is difficult. From a VUCA standpoint, highly volatile project environments are difficult to plan very far in advance, making agile, iterative methods attractive. In more stable project environments, the planning horizon might be longer, but even here project planning is rarely accurate more than about six months or so into the future. Uncertainty inherent in work planned too far in advance is a source of significant schedule risk for any long-duration project. Make specific note of any unusual, novel, or unstaffed activities more than three months out. On a regular basis, include explicit activities in the project plan to review estimates, risks, assumptions, and other project data. Risk management relies on periodic recommendations for project plan adjustments based on the results of these reviews.

Project reviews are most useful at natural project transitions. The most common of these are major milestones, such as at the end of a life cycle phase, a development iteration, a stage gate, or other checkpoint. It is also useful to conduct a review after any significant change to the project objective, whenever key contributors leave or are added to the project team, or following organizational changes. At a minimum, schedule reviews for longer projects at least every three to six months. Chapter 11 outlines a process for conducting effective project reviews.

Workflow Risks

In the PERIL database there are a wide variety of inputs and other dependencies, both from within and external to a project, that caused disruptive delays. Review what will be required for all activities that are critical to your project's schedule and note any situations where you have doubts or concerns as risks. In particular, add dependencies on other projects and any components, equipment, or information coming from new sources to your risk list.

DOCUMENTING THE RISKS

Schedule risks become visible throughout the planning and scheduling processes. The specific instances discussed in this chapter are all project risks:

- Long-duration activities
- Significant worst-case (or pessimistic PERT) estimates
- High uncertainty estimates
- Overly optimistic estimates
- All critical path (and near-critical path) activities
- Multiple critical paths
- Convergence points in the logical network
- External dependencies and interfaces
- Cross-functional and subcontracted work
- Deadlines beyond the planning horizon

Augment the list of project scope risks, adding each schedule risk identified with a clear description of the risk situation. The list of risks continues to expand throughout the project planning process and serves as the foundation for project risk analysis and management.

Key Ideas for Identifying Schedule Risks

- Determine the root causes of all uncertain duration estimates.
- Identify uncertain activity estimates, especially significant worst cases.
- Identify all estimates not based on historical data.
- Note dependencies that pose delay risks, including all interfaces.
- Identify risky activities and schedule them early in the project.
- Ascertain risks associated with multiple critical (or near-critical) paths.
- Recognize the riskiest dependencies at fan-in points in the project schedule.
- Note risks associated with lengthy projects.

PANAMA CANAL: PLANNING (1905-1907)

Early in his work in Panama, John Stevens spent virtually all of his time among the workers, asking questions. His single-minded pursuit was thorough project planning. Stevens put all he learned into his plans, establishing the foundation he needed to move the project forward.

The primary tool for construction was one Stevens was familiar with: the railroad. He recognized that digging enormous trenches was only part of the job. Excavated soil had to be moved out of the cut in central Panama where someday ships would pass, and it had to be deposited near the coasts to construct the required massive earthen dams. In the rainforests of Panama at the turn of the twentieth century, the railroad was not only the best way to do this, it was the only practical way. Much of the planning that Stevens did centered on using the railroad as a tool, and by early

1906, he had documented exactly how this was to be done. When excavation resumed, his elaborate, "ingeniously elastic" use of the railroad enabled progress at a vigorous pace, and it continued virtually nonstop until the work was complete.

Once Stevens had broken the work down into smaller, easily understood activities, the canal project began to look possible. Each part of the job was now understood to be something that had been done, somewhere, before. It became a matter of getting it all done, one activity at a time.

For all his talents and capabilities, John Stevens never considered himself fully qualified to manage the entire project. His experience was with surveying and building railroads. The canal project involved construction of massive concrete locks (like enormous bathtubs with doors on each end) that would raise ships nearly 30 meters from sea level and lower them back again at the end of the transit—twelve structures in total. The project also required a great deal of knowledge of hydraulics; moving enormous amounts of water quickly was essential to efficient canal operation. Stevens had no experience with either of these types of engineering. These gaps in his background, coupled with his dislike of the hot, humid climate and the omnipresent (and still dangerous) insects, led him to resign as chief engineer after two years, in 1907.

This did not sit well with Theodore Roosevelt. Losing such a competent project leader was a huge risk to the schedule. Both of his project leaders had now resigned before completing his most important project, and Roosevelt was determined that this would not happen again. To replace John Stevens, Roosevelt chose George Washington Goethals, an immensely qualified engineer. Goethals had been seriously considered for the job twice previously and was ideally qualified to complete the Panama Canal. He had built a number of similar, smaller projects, and he had a great deal of experience with nearly all the work required at Panama.

Theodore Roosevelt wanted more than competence, however. For this project, he wanted "men who will stay on the job until I get tired of having them there, or until I say they may abandon it." He was safe in his choice of a new chief engineer and project leader: George Goethals was a major (soon to be lieutenant colonel) in the US Army Corps of Engineers. If Goethals tried to resign, it might have resulted in his court-martial.

CHAPTER 5

IDENTIFYING PROJECT RESOURCE RISK

"If you want a track team to win the high jump, you find one person who can jump seven feet, not several people who can jump six feet."

—FREDERICK TERMAN,
Stanford University dean and professor of engineering

F red Terman is probably best known as the "father of Silicon Valley." He encouraged Bill Hewlett and Dave Packard, the Varian brothers, and hundreds of others to start businesses near Stanford University, just south of San Francisco. Starting in the 1930s, alarmed at the paucity of job opportunities in the area, he helped his students start companies, set up the Stanford Industrial Park, and generally was responsible for the establishment of the world's largest high-tech center. He was good at identifying and nurturing technical talent, and he understood how critical it is in any undertaking.

A lack of technical skills or access to appropriate staff is a large source of project risk for complex, technical projects. Risk management on these projects requires careful assessment of needed skills and commitment of capable staff.

SOURCES OF RESOURCE RISK

Resource risks represent about one-third of the records in the PERIL database and nearly 30 percent of the overall impact. They caused an average project slip of over six weeks. There are three categories of resource risk: people, outsourcing, and money. People risks arise within the project team. Outsourcing risks are a consequence of using people and services outside the project team for required project work. The third category, money, is the rarest risk subcategory for the PERIL database, as few of the problems reported were primarily about funding. Money, however, has the highest average impact of any of the eight PERIL risk categories, and the effect of insufficient funding has substantial impact on projects in many other ways. The root causes of people and outsourcing risk are further characterized by type, shown in the following summary.

RESOURCE ROOT-CAUSE SUBCATEGORIES	DEFINITION	COUNT	CUMULATIVE IMPACT (WEEKS)	AVERAGE IMPACT (WEEKS)
Money Limitation	Slip due to funding limits	44	457	10.4
People Motivation	Loss of team cohesion and interest; common on long projects	16	142	8.9
People Late Start	Staff available late; often due to delayed finish of earlier projects	27	185	6.9
Outsourcing Late or Poor Output	Deliverable late from vendor. Includes queuing, turnover	96	656	6.8
People Loss	Permanent staff member loss due to resignation, promotion, reassignment, health, etc.	83	566	6.8

RESOURCE ROOT-CAUSE SUBCATEGORIES	DEFINITION	COUNT	CUMULATIVE IMPACT (WEEKS)	AVERAGE IMPACT (WEEKS)
Outsourcing Delayed Start	Contracting-related delays	27	133	4.9
People Queuing	Slip due to bottleneck (includes specialized equipment)	54	224	4.1
People Temp Loss	Temporary staff loss due to illness, hot site, support, etc.	90	319	3.5

A Pareto chart of overall impact by type of risk is in figure 5-1. Although risks related to internal staffing were most numerous, both outsourcing and money risks are in the top three for impact.

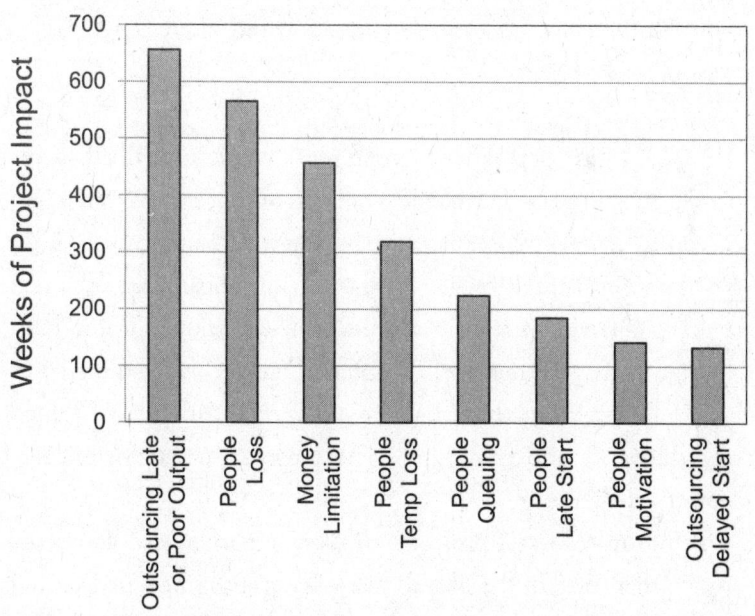

Figure 5-1: Total Project Impact by Resource Root-Cause Subcategories

People Risks

Risks related to internal project staff represent the most numerous resource risks, constituting nearly 20 percent of the entire database and over 60 percent of the resource category. People risks are subdivided into five subcategories:

- **Loss:** Permanent staff member loss to the project due to resignation, promotion, reassignment, health, or other reasons
- **Temporary loss:** Short-term staff loss due to illness, hot site, support priorities, or other reasons
- **Queuing:** Slip due to other commitments for needed resources or expertise
- **Late start:** Staff not available at the project start, often because of late finish of previous projects
- **Motivation:** Loss of team cohesion and interest; typical of long projects

Loss of staff permanently represents nearly one-third of the people-related risks. Permanent staff loss of project team members caused an average slip of just under seven weeks and resulted in by far the highest total impact for the people subcategory. The reasons for permanent staff loss included resignations, promotions, reassignments to other work or different projects, and staffing cutbacks. Discovering these risks in advance is difficult, but good recordkeeping and trend analysis are useful in setting realistic project expectations.

Temporary loss of project staff is the common people-related risk, with a third of the overall cases. Its overall impact was lower than for permanent staff loss, causing an average slip of less than four weeks. A typical reason for short-term staff loss was a customer problem (a "hot site") related to the deliverable from an earlier project. Other reasons for short-term staff loss included illness, travel problems, and organizational reorganizations.

Queuing problems represent 20 percent of the people-related risks in the PERIL database. The average schedule impact due to queuing was roughly four weeks. Most organizations optimize operations by investing the bare minimum in specialized (and expensive) expertise, and in costly facilities and equipment. This leads to a potential scarcity of these individuals or facilities, and contention between projects for access. Most technical projects rely on at least some special expertise that they share with other projects, such as system architects needed at the start, testing personnel needed at the end, and other specialists needed throughout the project. If an expert happens to be free when a project is ready for the work to start, there is no problem, but if he or she has five other projects queued up already when your project needs attention, you will come to a screeching halt while you wait in line. Queuing analysis is well understood, and it is relevant to a wide variety of manufacturing, engineering, computer networks, and many other business systems. Any system subject to queues requires some excess capacity to maximize throughput. Optimizing organizational resources needed for projects based only on cost drives out necessary capacity and results in project delay.

Late starts when key staff are unavailable at the beginning of a project also cause a good deal of project delay. Although only 10 percent of the people-related resource risks, their average impact was almost seven weeks. Staff joining the project late had a number of root causes, but the most common was a situation aptly described by one project leader as the "rolling sledgehammer." Whenever a prior project is late, some, perhaps even all, of the staff for the new project is still busy working to get it done. As a consequence, any following project gets a slow and ragged start, with key people beginning their contributions to the new project only when they can break free of the earlier one. Even when these people become available, there may be additional delay, because the staff members coming from a late project are often burned out from the stress and long hours typical of an overdue project. The "rolling sledgehammer" creates a cycle that self-perpetuates and is hard to break. Each late project causes the projects that follow also to be late.

Motivation issues are the smallest subcategory, at only a bit more than 5 percent of the people-related resource risks. However, these risks had an average impact of nearly nine weeks, among the highest for any of the subcategories in the PERIL database, and motivation issues are certainly contributing factors in several of the other categories. Motivation issues are generally a consequence of diminishing interest on long-duration projects, or due to interpersonal conflicts.

Thorough planning and credible scheduling of the work well in advance will reveal some of the most serious potential exposures regarding people. Histogram analysis of resource requirements may also provide insight into staffing exposures a project will face, but unless analysis of project resources is credibly integrated with comprehensive resource data for other projects and all the non-project demands within the business, the results may not provide sufficient insight. Aligning staffing capacity with project requirements requires ongoing attention. One significant root cause for understaffed projects is little or no use of project planning information to make or revise project selection decisions at the organization level, triggering the "too many projects" problem. (Managing such portfolio risks is explored in chapter 13.)

Retrospective analysis of projects over time is also an effective way to detect and measure the consequences of inadequate staffing, especially for chronic problems.

Outsourcing Risks

Outsourcing risks account for nearly 30 percent of the resource risks. Although the frequency in the PERIL database is lower than for people risks, the impact of outsourcing risk was higher, in excess of six weeks. Risks related to outsourcing are separated into two subcategories: late or poor outputs and delayed start.

Late or poor output from outsource partners is a problem that is well represented in the PERIL database. The recent growth of outsourcing has been driven primarily by a desire to save money, and often it does. However, there is generally a trade-off between economy and predictability. Work done at a distance is out of sight, and problems that might easily be detected with efforts within the organization may not surface as an issue until it is too late. Roughly 80 percent of the outsourcing risks involved receiving a late or unsatisfactory deliverable from an external supplier, and the average impact for these incidents was almost seven weeks. These delays result from many of the same root causes as other people risks—turnover, queuing problems, staff availability, and other issues—but a precise cause may not be known. Receiving anything the project needs late is a risk, but these cases are compounded by the added element of surprise; the problem may be invisible until the day of the default (after weeks of reports saying, "Things are going just fine . . ."), when it is too late to do much about it. Lateness was often exacerbated in cases in the PERIL database because work that did not meet specifications caused further delay (and cascades of additional problems) as a result of unanticipated work reassigned to the project team.

Delayed starts are also fairly common with outsourced work, causing about a fifth of the outsourcing problems. Before any external work can begin, contracts must be negotiated, approved, and signed. All these steps are time-consuming. Beginning a new, complex relationship with people outside your organization can require more time than expected. For projects with unusual needs, just finding an appropriate supplier may cause significant delays. The average impact from these delayed starts in the database was about five weeks.

Outsourcing risks can be detected through planning processes, and by careful analysis and thorough understanding of the contract. Both the project team and the outsourcing partner must understand the terms and conditions of the contract, especially the scope of work and timing requirements.

Money Risks

The third category of resource risks was rare in the PERIL database, representing a little over 10 percent of the resource risks and about 3 percent of the whole. It is significant, however, because when funding is a problem, it is often a big problem. The average impact was the highest for any subcategory, at well over 10 weeks. Insufficient funding can significantly stretch out the duration of a project, and it is a contributing root cause in many other subcategories (people turnover due to layoffs and outsourcing of work primarily motivated by cost-cutting, as examples).

Resource Risk and VUCA

From a VUCA perspective, about half of the impact in the PERIL database was caused by uncertainty, including all of the resource risks. The cases reported were all the result of predictability issues associated with staffing or funding. You can minimize the uncertainty from resource risk effects of VUCA through better data archives and metrics showing recent trends and performance, more reliable staffing and budget commitments, and disciplined and thorough planning. You will find many examples of typical resource risks listed in the appendix.

RESOURCE PLANNING

Resource risks account for a third of the incidents in the PERIL database. Resource planning processes provide insight into the people, outsourcing, and money risks faced by modern projects. Inputs to resource planning include the project work breakdown structure (WBS), scope definition, activity descriptions, duration estimates, and the project schedule. Resource planning begins with assessing resource requirements, which can be done through informal manual methods, histogram analysis, or using computer tools.

Resource Requirements

As project plans come into focus you will need to determine the skills and staffing required for each activity, based on assumptions about the work. It is increasingly common, even for relatively small projects, to use a computer tool to organize your scheduling information. For each identified task, begin to list the team members who will contribute by name. Although preliminary resource planning can start using functions or roles, effort estimates done without staffing information are imprecise, and there is significant resource risk until the project staff has been named and committed. Identify as a risk any work depending on contributors who remain "to be assigned" throughout project planning.

For the project as a whole, also identify all holidays, scheduled time off, significant nonproject meetings, and other time that will not be available to the project. Do this for each team member as well, and identify any scheduling differences for different regions, countries, and companies involved in the project. A computer scheduling tool can provide a useful location to store calendar information, such as holidays, vacations, and any other important dates. If you do use a computer tool, enter all the calendar data into the database before you begin resource analysis.

You also need to determine the amount of effort available from each contributor. Even for "full-time" contributors, it is difficult to get more than five to six hours of dedicated project activity work per day, and "part-time" staff will contribute much less.

Particularly for project activities that are already identified as potential risks (such as those on the critical path), determine the total effort required and verify who will do the necessary work. Knowing the resources your project will need and comparing this with what is available will reveal project staffing risks.

Whether you do this analysis manually by inspection of the project plans, through a tabular or spreadsheet approach, or by using resource analysis functionality in project management software, focus on detecting resource shortfalls that could hurt your project. Work to uncover any resource overcommitments and undercommitments. Even if you do use a computer tool (and there are many), remember that scheduling tools are only a database with specialized output reports. The quality of the information the tool provides can never be any better than the quality of the data that you put in. You and the project team must still do the thinking; a computer cannot plan your project or identify its risks.

Histogram Analysis Using Computer Tools

For more complicated projects, graphical resource analysis is useful. Resource histograms can reveal where project staffing is inadequate graphically on an individual-by-individual or an over-all project basis. The graphical format provides a visible way to identify places in the preliminary schedule where project staffing fails to support the planned workflow, as shown in figure 5-2. In this case, the effort profile for a project team member expected to contribute to all these activities shows when this person would need to work a double shift to support the schedule because of the activity overlaps.

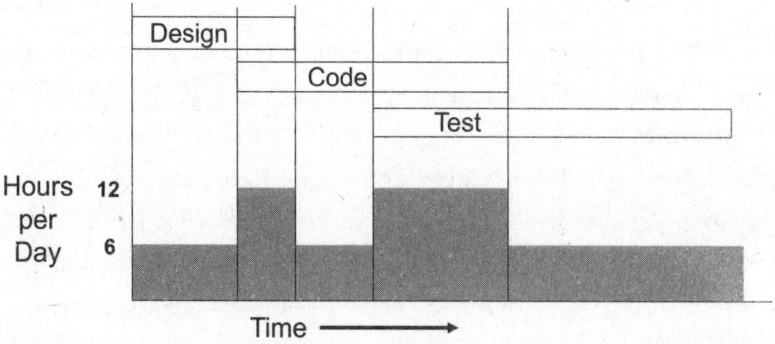

■ **Figure 5-2:** Histogram Analysis for an Individual

The benefits of entering resource data into a scheduling tool include:

- Identifying resource overcommitment risks
- Improving the precision of the schedule
- Building compelling evidence for negotiating budgets and schedules
- Focusing more attention on project estimates

These benefits require some investment on your part. Histogram analysis adds complexity to the planning process, so it increases the planning effort. In your resource analysis, allocate sufficient time for this into your overall project workload.

Be particularly wary of assumptions that contribute to project risk, such as the dependability of committed start dates for project contributors. Both late starts (people tied up completing earlier work expected to be finished) and queuing delays waiting for availability of contributors with specialized skills are significant sources of risk in the PERIL database.

Resource shortfalls are not limited to staffing. Early in your project, assess your project infrastructure: the equipment, software, and any other project assets. If required computers, software applications, test gear, instruments, communications and networking equipment, or other available hardware elements are inadequate or not up to date, either plan to replace, update, or augment them, or document the shortfalls as risks. Effort and money to upgrade facilities and infrastructure tend to be easiest to obtain during the planning and startup phases of a new project, so the earlier you can make issues visible, the more likely you will successfully secure the resources to address them. Also, getting familiar with new hardware and software is less disruptive early than it will be in the middle of the project, when it could disrupt high-priority project activities.

STAFF ACQUISITION

Histograms and other project analysis are necessary, but they are rarely sufficient for determining if a project has the staffing and skills required to do the work. Particularly for the riskiest project activities, revalidate both the skills needed and your effort estimates.

Skill Requirements

As part of project scope definition and preliminary planning, identify specific skills and other needs that will be required by the work. Your initial project staffing will often include adequate coverage for some or perhaps even most of these, but on many projects there will inevitably be substantial gaps. These gaps will remain project resource risks unless they can be resolved.

Specific skills that are not available on the project team might be acquired by negotiating for additional staff, or through training or mentoring. In some cases, needed skills can be added through outsourcing. These options are most possible when the needs are identified early and supported with credible planning data. You may also be able to replan the parts of the project that require unavailable skills to use alternative methods based on skills the project team already has. If there are knowledge gaps that can be filled through training, schedule the training early in the project. Postponing training until just before you need it increases two risks: that the time or money required for it may no longer be available, and the ramp-up time to competence may exceed what you expect. (Learning curve issues are a major source of schedule risk in the PERIL database.) Building desirable new skills can also be a powerful motivator and team builder—both of which can reduce risk for any project.

The ultimate goal of staff acquisition is to ensure that all project activities are aligned with specific, named people who are competent and can be depended upon to get the work done. Two significant resource risks related to staff acquisition are unnamed staff members and contributors with unique skills. Every identified staffing need on your project roster that remains blank, identified only with a function, or marked "to be hired" is a risk. Even if these people are later named, their productivity may not be consistent with your estimates and assumptions. It is not uncommon for some names to remain missing even after work is scheduled to begin—and some staffing requirements may never be filled. Plans based upon unassigned staffing are unreliable, and every project staffing requirement that lacks a credible commitment by an actual person represents a project risk.

Unique skills also pose a problem. When project work can be assigned to one of several competent contributors, there is a good chance that it can be done adequately and on schedule. When only a single person knows how to do the work, the project faces risk. There are many reasons why a necessary person may be unavailable to the project when needed, including illness, resignation, injury, or reassignment to higher-priority work. When a key contributor is missing, project work will halt. If a crucial part of your project depends on access to a single specific individual, note it as a risk.

Revisiting Estimates

As noted in chapter 4, resource planning and activity estimating are interrelated. As the staffing plan for the project takes shape, you will uncover new resource risks as you review assumptions around your estimates. Project resource risks are usually most significant for activities that will affect the project schedule—activities that are on the critical path, have little float, or have worst-case estimates that would put them on the critical path. Reviewing the effort estimates for these activities will reveal resource risks related to staff ability, staff availability, and the work environment.

Staff ability: Individual productivity varies a great deal, so it matters which team members are involved with each project activity. Even for very simple tasks, there can be great differences in performance. Cooks often encounter the requirement for "one onion, chopped." The amount of time this task will take depends greatly on the person undertaking it. For a home cook, it might take two or three minutes. A professional chef, as watchers of television cooking shows know, dispatches this task in seconds. On the other extreme one finds the perfectionist, who could make an evening out of ensuring that each fragment of onion is identical in size and shape.

Productivity measurements for "knowledge" work of most kinds show a similar wide spectrum. Research on productivity shows that people who are among the best at what they do typically work two to three times as fast as the average, and they are more than ten times as productive as the slowest. In addition to being faster, the best performers also make fewer errors and seldom have to do rework.

Differences due to variations in productivity are a frequent source of inaccurate project estimates. Project leaders often plan the project using data from their own experience, and then delegate the work to others who may not be as skilled or experienced as they are. When there are historical metrics that draw on a large population, you can accurately predict how quickly an average person will be able to accomplish similar work. If your project contributors are significantly more (or less) productive than the average, however, your effort and duration estimates will be accurate only after they are adjusted accordingly. In cases where you do not yet have a named person associated with the work, risks can be significant.

Staff availability: No one can ever actually work on project activities "full time." Every project contributor has commitments even within the project that are above and beyond the scheduled project work, such as communication activities (email or texts, meetings, conversations). Further, some team members will inevitably be responsible for significant work outside the project.

Studying computer and medical electronics firms, Steven Wheelwright and Kim Clark (in *Revolutionizing Product Development*) reported the effect of assigning work on parallel projects to engineers. For engineers assigned to a single project or two projects, about 70 percent of the time spent went into project activities, roughly equivalent to the often-quoted "five or six" hours of project work per day. With three or more projects, useful time plummeted precipitously. In this study, the overhead burden on engineers dealing with five projects left only 30 percent of their time for project activities. Not all projects are equal, so when you are faced with this situation, find out how your overcommitted contributors prioritize their activities. Ask each part-time contributor about both the **importance** and the **urgency** of the work on your project. Both matter, but it's a lack of urgency that will hurt your project the most. When contributors see your project's work as low priority, it is a risk. If you are unable to adjust it, you may even need to consider alternative resources or other methods for your project's work.

The "too many projects" problem takes a heavy toll on project progress, and estimates of duration or effort that fail to account for the impact of competing priorities can be absurdly optimistic.

Project environment: The project environment is yet another factor that has an impact on the quality of project estimates. Noise, interruptions, the workspace, and other factors may erode productivity significantly. When people can work undistracted, a lot gets done.

This is not typical, though. Frequent disturbances are commonplace, particularly with work done in an "open office" environment. The background noise level, nearby conversations, colleagues who drop by to chat, and other interruptions are actually much more disruptive than generally assumed when compiling project estimates. People can't shift from one activity to a different one instantaneously. Studies of knowledge workers indicate that it takes twenty minutes, typically, for the human brain to come back to full concentration following an interruption as short as a few seconds. A contributor who gets several telephone calls, a few tweets, or quick questions from a peer each hour will not get much work done.

Once the staffing for your project is set, consider all these factors, particularly the talent, proportion of time dedicated to your project, and the effect of the environment on the estimates in your project plan. Ensure that the effort and duration assessments for planned work are consistent with your committed staffing assumptions. Always ask questions about effort estimates and discuss them with activity owners, stakeholders, and others who have relevant perspectives to better understand what the effort estimates are based on. Review the amount of work actually required to complete similar tasks on earlier projects.

As noted in the discussion on duration estimating in chapter 4, all estimates are just forecasts. They are intrinsically uncertain. Probe for worst cases and note any effort estimates that are mostly guesses. Adjust your efforts assessments as necessary, and identify and add any resource risks to your project risk list.

Staffing Risks

Delays documented in the PERIL database related to people represent well over half of the total damage described. Loss of staff, either permanently or for a substantial time, were the most frequently reported, with significant recent increases in the data due to viruses, quarantines, and other staffing disruptions. Capture as risks any situations where staffing seems minimal, has historically been less than dependable, or relies on skills that are scarce due to high demand or other factors.

OUTSOURCING

Outsourcing is a significant source of resource risk in the PERIL database, causing an average project slip of over six weeks. Better management of outsourcing and managing external staff can uncover many of these problems in advance. (The focus of this section is from the perspective of a project leader who acquires staffing and other services procuring external services. Risks for leaders managing fee-for-service projects on a contract basis largely parallel those for projects in general.)

Not all project staffing needs can be met with internal people. More and more work today on typical projects uses outside services. It is increasingly difficult (and expensive) to maintain competence in all the fields of expertise that might be required, especially for skills needed only infrequently. A growing need for specialization underlies the trend toward increased dependence on project contributors outside the organization. Other reasons for this trend are attempts to lower costs and a desire in many organizations to reduce permanent staffing.

Outsourcing Process

The process for managing external contract project resources has four main components:

- Plan for outsourced services.
- Identify a provider and negotiate a contract.

- Manage outsourced services.
- Complete work and close the contract.

This section explores significant opportunities for risk identification in the first two steps. Chapter 8 includes ideas for responding and managing outsourcing risks. Chapter 12 addresses contract closure and minimizing future outsourcing risks.

Outsourcing project work is most successful when appropriate legal and other documentation is detailed and integral to project planning. The risks of outsourced work can be minimized by thorough definition both in the initial request and in the ultimate contract, providing everyone involved with a clear understanding of the work required and how it will be evaluated. It is difficult to do this well, and it generally takes more effort and attention to detail than other project planning.

Specific risks permeate all aspects of the outsourcing process, starting before any work directly related to the contracting process formally starts. The process generally begins with identification of any work that cannot be done using existing staff. Planning to employ outside services involves investigation of possible options, and requires a "make-or-buy" analysis to determine whether there are any reasons why using outside services may be undesirable or inappropriate. From the perspective of project risk, delegating work to dedicated staff whenever possible is almost always preferable. Communication, visibility, continuity, motivation, and project control are all easier for "in-house" work. Other reasons to avoid outsourcing may include higher costs, potential loss of confidential information, a desire to maintain core skills (on future projects or for required support), and lack of confidence in the available service providers. Some outsourcing decisions are made because all the current staff is busy and there is no one available to do necessary project work. These decisions seem to be based on the erroneous assumption that project outsourcing can be done successfully without incremental work. Ignoring the substantial effort required to find, evaluate, negotiate and contract with, routinely communicate with, monitor, and pay a supplier is a serious risk.

Even though it may be desirable to avoid outsourcing, project realities may require it. Whenever the make-versus-buy decision comes out "buy," there will be risks to manage.

The next step in the outsourcing process is to develop a request for proposal (RFP), also known as request for bid, invitation to bid, and request for quotation. In organizations that outsource project work on a regular basis, there are usually standard forms and procedures to be used for this, so the steps in assembling, distributing, and later analyzing the RFP responses are generally not up to the project team. This is fortunate, because using well-established processes, preprinted forms, and professionals in your organization who do this work regularly are all useful in minimizing risk. If you lack templates and processes for this, consult colleagues who are experienced with outsourcing and borrow theirs, customizing as necessary. Outsourcing is one aspect of project management where figuring things out as you proceed will waste a lot of time and money and massively increase overall project risk.

Risk management also requires that at least one member of the project team be involved with planning and contracting for outside services, so that the interests of the project are represented throughout the outsourcing process.

Ensure that each RFP includes a clear, unambiguous definition of the scope of work involved, including the terms and conditions for evaluation and payment. Although it is always risky for any project work to remain poorly defined, outsourced work deserves particular attention. Inadequate definition of outsourced work leads to all the usual project problems, but it often results in even more schedule and resource risk. Problems with outsourced deliverables usually surface late in a project and with no advance warning (generally, following a long series of "we are doing just fine" status reports). Occurring late, these problems frequently will delay the project deadline, as is evident in the PERIL database where late delivery or inadequate deliverables resulted in an average of almost seven weeks of project slippage. There are also increased project costs when the issues cause required changes and late-project expedited work. Minimize outsourcing risks through scrupulous definition of all deliverables involved, including all measurements and performance criteria you will use for their evaluation.

As part of planning for outsourced services, define how you plan to evaluate submitted proposals. Determine what is most important to your project and ensure that these aspects are clearly spelled out in the RFP, with guidance for the responders on how to supply the information that you require. Because the work on modern projects tends to change over time, there is a good chance that criteria used for past supplier selection will, sooner or later, need updating. Before sending out the RFP, review any proposed criteria in light of your emerging project plans to ensure that they remain appropriate. Establish priorities and relative weights for each evaluation criterion, as well as how you will assess the responses you receive. Communicating your priorities and expectations clearly in the RFP will help responders to self-qualify (or disqualify) themselves and will better provide the data you need to make a sound outsourcing decision.

Relevant experience is also important to avoiding outsourcing risk. In the RFP, request specifics from responders on similar prior efforts that were successful, and ask for contact information so you can follow up and verify. Even for work that is novel, ask for reference information from potential suppliers that will at least allow you to investigate past working relationships. Although it may be difficult to get useful reference information, it is always prudent to request it.

Once you have established the specifics of the work to be outsourced, as well as the processes and documents you plan to use, the next step is to find potential suppliers and encourage them to respond. One of the biggest risks in this step is failure to contact enough suppliers. For some project work, networking and informal communications may be sufficient, but sending the RFP to lists of known suppliers, putting information on public websites, and even advertising may be useful in letting potential responders know of your needs. If too few responses are generated, the quality and cost of the choices available may not serve the project well.

Bringing the RFP process to closure is also a substantial source of risk. There are potential risks in decision-making, negotiation, and the contracting process.

Decision-making risks include not doing adequate analysis to assess each potential supplier and making a selection based on something other than the needs of the project.

Inadequate analysis can be a significant source of risk. It is fairly common for demands related to outsourcing to conflict with other project work. Constructing and getting responses to an RFP often requires more time than expected, and there may be little time available to evaluate the technical merit of proposals. Judging proposals by weight, appearance, or some other superficial criteria may save time, but is not likely to result in the best selection. Evaluating and comparing multiple complex proposals thoroughly takes time and effort. Allocate sufficient time to ensure a thorough evaluation of potential suppliers before you make a decision. Remember the old saying, "Act in haste; repent at leisure." (Except in your case you will be repenting when you are very busy.)

Another potential risk in the selection process is outside pressure to make a choice for reasons unrelated to your project. Influences from other parts of the organization may come to bear during the decision process—to favor friends, to avoid some suppliers, to align with "strategic" partners of some other internal group, or to use a global (or a local) supplier. Because the decision will normally be signed and approved by someone higher in the organization, sometimes the project team may not even be aware of such factors until late in the process. Documenting the process and validating your criteria for supplier selection with your stakeholders can reduce this problem, but use of outside suppliers not selected by the project team can pose significant, and sometimes disastrous, project risk. Overall, you must diligently stay on top of the process to ensure that the selections made for each RFP are as consistent with your project requirements as possible.

The next step in the process is to negotiate a contract, to finalize finances and the details for the work. After you select a service provider, the balance of power begins to shift from the purchaser to the supplier, raising additional risks. As work proceeds, your project will depend on the supplier for crucial, time-sensitive project deliverables. The supplier is primarily dependent on the project for money, which in the short run is neither crucial nor urgent. To a lesser extent, suppliers are also dependent on future recommendations from you (which often provides substantial leverage for ongoing risk management), but from the supplier's perspective, the relationship is based mainly on cash.

Effective and thorough negotiation is the last opportunity for the project to identify (and manage) risks without high potential costs. All relevant details of the work and deliverables need to be thoroughly discussed and clearly understood by all parties. The ultimate contract should unambiguously define the scope of work so everyone involved will be in sync. In your contract discussions, clarify details concerning tests, inspections, prototypes, and other interim deliverables. Specifics concerning partial and final payments, as well as the process and cost for any required changes or modifications, are also essential aspects of the negotiation process. Failure to conduct thorough, principled negotiation with a future supplier is a potential source of massive risk. Shortening a negotiation process to save time is never a good idea.

Because the primary consideration on the supplier side is financial, the best tactic for risk management in negotiation is to strongly align payments with achievement of specific results. Payment for time, effort, or other less tangible criteria may allow suppliers to bill the project even while failing to produce what your project requires. When negotiating the work and payment terms, the least risky option for you as the purchaser is to establish a "payment for result" contract.

Outsourcing risk can also be lowered by negotiating contract terms that align with specific project goals. Although a contract must include consequences for supplier nonperformance, such as nonpayment, legal action, or other remedies, these terms may do little to ensure project success. If a supplier fails to perform, your project will be in trouble and financial or other penalties will not change this. Lack of a key deliverable will lead to project failure, so it is also useful to negotiate terms that more directly support your project objectives. If there is value in getting work done early, incentive payments are worth considering. If there are specific additional costs associated with late delivery, establish penalties that reduce payments proportionate to the delay. For some projects, more complex financial arrangements than the simple "fee for result" may be appropriate, where percentages of favorable variances in time or cost are shared with the supplier and portions of unfavorable ones may be deducted from the fees. Negotiating terms that more directly support the project objectives and increase supplier engagement in the project can significantly reduce outsourcing risks.

If the negotiation process, despite your best efforts, results in terms that represent potential project problems, note these as risks. In extreme cases, you may want to reconsider your selection decision, or even the decision to outsource the project work at all.

Once you have consensus on the terms and conditions for the work, you must finalize the contract. All agreed-upon terms must be documented in a signed contract and put into force. One effective way to minimize risk is to use a well-established, preprinted contract format to document the relationship. This should include all of the information that a complete, prudent contract must contain, so the chances of leaving out something critical, such as protection of confidential information or proprietary intellectual property, will be reduced. In addition, using standard formats with no significant modifications or deletions will reduce the time and effort required for contract approval. In large companies, contracts that vary from standard formats can take an additional month (or even more) for review, approval, and processing. Adding data to a contract is also generally a poor idea, with one big exception. Every contract needs to include a clear, unambiguous definition of the scope of work that specifies measurable deliverables and payment terms. A good contract also provides an explicit description of the process to be used if any changes are necessary.

One other source of risk in contracting is also fairly common for technical projects. The statement of work must be clear not only in defining the results expected but also in specifying who will be responsible. It turns out that this is quite a challenge for engineers and other analytical people. Most engineering and other technical writing is filled with passive-voice sentences, such as, "It is important that the device be tested using an input voltage varying between 105 and 250 volts AC, down to a temperature of minus 40 degrees Celsius." In a contract, there is no place for the passive voice. If the responsible party is not clearly specified, the sentence has no legal meaning. It fails to make clear who will do the testing and what, if any, consequences there may be should the testing fail. To minimize risks in contracts, write requirements in the active voice, spelling out all responsibilities in clear terms and by name.

Finally, when setting up a contract, minimize the resource risk by establishing a "not to exceed" limitation to avoid runaway costs. Set this limit somewhat higher than the expected cost, to provide some reserve for changes and unforeseen problems, but not much higher. Many technical projects provide a reserve of about 10 percent to handle small adjustments. If problems or changes arise that require more than this, they will trigger review of the project, which is prudent risk management.

Outsourcing Risks

There are a variety of other risks that arise from outsourcing. One of the largest is cost, even if the work seems to be thoroughly defined. Unforeseen aspects of the work, which are never possible to eliminate completely, may trigger expensive change fees.

Continuity and turnover of contract staff is a risk. Although people who work for another company may be loyal to your project and stay with it through the end, the probabilities are lower than for the permanent staff on your project. Particularly with longer projects, turnover and retraining can represent major risks.

Outsourcing may also increase the likelihood of turnover and demotivation of your permanent staff. If it becomes standard procedure to outsource all the new, "bleeding-edge" project work, your permanent staff gets stuck doing the same old things, project after project, never learning anything new. It becomes harder to motivate and hold on to people who have no opportunity for development.

There may also be hidden effort for the project due to outsourcing, not visible in the plan. Someone must maintain the relationship, communicate regularly, deal with payments and other paperwork, and carry the other overhead of outsourcing. Although this may all run smoothly, if there are any problems it can become a major time sink. The time and effort this overhead requires is routinely overlooked or underestimated. And much, perhaps all, of this will likely fall on you.

Finally, the nature of work at a distance requires significant additional effort. Getting useful status information is a lot of work. You will not get responses to initial requests every time, and verifying what is reported may be difficult. You can expect to provide much more information than you receive, and interpreting what you do get can be difficult. Even if the information is timely, it may not be completely accurate, and you may get little or no advance warning for project problems. Working to establish and maintain a solid working relationship with outsourcing partners can be a major undertaking, but it is prudent risk management.

In the PERIL database, just under a third of the resource-related delays are a result of outsourcing problems. Late or unusable deliverables are the most common problem, so note any important project deliverables created by external suppliers as risks. Also add any cases where contracts with new parties will need to be negotiated to your risk list.

EFFORT ESTIMATES ADJUSTED FOR RISK

Once you have validated the effort estimates for each activity in the project WBS, you can calculate the effort required in each project phase and total project effort. The "shape" of projects generally remains consistent over time, so the percentages of effort for each project phase derived from your planning process ought to be consistent with the measured results from earlier projects. Whatever the names for project phases or life cycle stages may be, any significant deviation in the current plan compared with historical norms is good reason for skepticism. It's also evidence of risk; any plan that shows a lower percentage of effort associated with a portion of a project than is typical has probably either failed to identify some work or underestimated it.

Published industry norms may be useful, but the best information to use for comparison is local. How projects run in different environments varies a great deal, even for projects using a common life cycle or methodology. Historical data from peers can be helpful, but data directly from projects that you have run is better. Disciplined collection of project metrics is essential for accurate estimation, better planning, and effective risk management. If you have personal data, use it. If you lack data from past projects, improving your estimating is a good reason to start collecting it.

Not all project phases are as accurately planned as others, because some project work is more familiar and receives more attention. The middle phases of most project life cycles contain most of the work that defines "what we do." Programmers program; hardware engineers build things; tech writers write; and in general, people do what it says on their business card. Whatever the "middle" phases are called (development, implementation, execution, and so forth), it is during this portion of the work where project contributors use the skills where they have the most background and experience. These phases of project work are generally planned in detail, and activity estimates are often quite accurate. The phases that are earlier (such as investigation, planning, analysis, and proposal generation) and later (test, rollout, integration, and ramp-up) are generally less accurate. Using the life cycle norm data, and assuming the "development" portion of the plan is fairly accurate, it is possible to detect whether project work may be missing or underestimated in the other phases. If this analysis shows inadequate effort allocated to the early (or late) phases based on historical profiles for effort, it is a good idea to find out why.

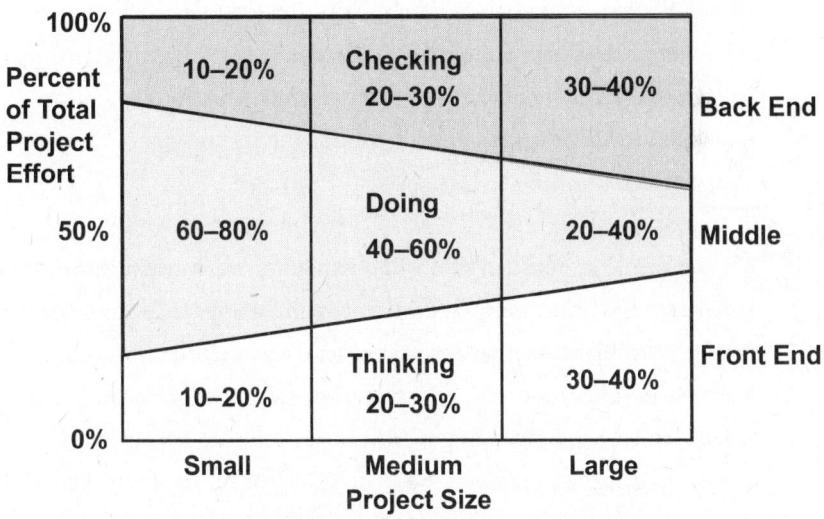

Figure 5-3: Effort by Project Phase

Effort profiles for projects also vary with project size. By mapping the data from a large number of projects with various life cycles into a simple, generic life cycle, a significant trend emerges. The simplified project life cycle in figure 5-3 is far less detailed than any you are likely to use, but all life cycles and methodologies define phases or stages that map into these three broad categories:

- **Thinking:** All the initial work on a project, such as planning, analysis, investigation, charter establishment, initial design, proposal generation, requirements analysis, specification, and preparation for the business decision to commit to the project.
- **Doing:** The work that generally defines the project, including development. This is where the team rolls up their sleeves and digs into the creation of the project deliverable.
- **Checking:** Evaluating the results created by the project, conducting acceptance tests, searching for defects in the deliverable(s), correcting problems and omissions, obtaining approvals and sign-offs, and closing the project.

As projects increase in size and complexity, the amount of work grows rapidly. Project effort tends to expand geometrically as projects increase in time, staffing, specifications, or other factors. In addition to this overall rise in effort, the effort spent in each phase of the project, as a percentage, shifts. As projects become larger, longer, and more complex, the percentage of total project effort increases for both early front-end project work and for back-end activities at the end of the project. The graphical summary in figure 5-3 shows this shift, based on data from a wide range of projects.

Small projects (fewer than six months, most work done with a small collocated team) spend nearly all their effort in "doing"—creating the deliverable. Medium projects (six to twelve months long, with a sizable team of people contributing) might spend about half of their effort in other work. Projects that are still larger (one year or longer, with several distributed or global teams) will spend only about a third of the total effort developing project deliverables. This rise in effort both in the early and late stages of project work stems from the increased amount of information and coordination required, and the significantly larger number of possible (and, therefore, statistically expected) failure modes in these more difficult projects. Fixing defects in complex systems requires substantial time and effort. Software consultant Fred Brooks (author of *The Mythical Man-Month*) states that a typical software project is one-third analysis, one-sixth coding, and one-half testing.

All this bears on project risk for at least two reasons. The first is chronic underestimation of late project effort. If a complex project is planned with the expectation that 10 percent of the effort will be in up-front work, followed by 80 percent in development, the final phase will rarely be the expected 10 percent. It will balloon to another 80 percent (or more). This is a primary cause of the all-too-common "late project work bulge." Many entirely possible projects fail to meet their deadline (or fail altogether) because early underinvestment in analysis and planning results in substantial late project chaos and loose ends to tie up.

The second reason that life cycle norms are valuable is found in the symmetry of figure 5-3. The total effort required for a project tends to be lower when the initial and final phases of the work are roughly in balance. If the life cycle norms for typical projects reveal that little effort is invested up front and a massive (often unexpected) amount of effort is necessary at the end, then all projects are taking longer and costing more than necessary. Better up-front analysis and planning can be an antidote for end-of-project problems. And overall risk increases with scale, so you may be able to minimize this "late work bulge" exposure by approaching your goals using a series of shorter, less ambitious projects.

COST ESTIMATES, BUDGETS, AND RISK

Inadequate overall funding was a major problem for nearly all the projects in the PERIL database with money risks, causing well over ten weeks of average slippage. Total project expense is generally dominated by staffing and outsourcing costs, but also includes estimates for equipment, services, travel, communications, and other project needs. Uncertainty can originate from any of these sources.

Cost Estimates Adjusted for Uncertainty

PERT is one way to explicitly analyze cost risk. Chapter 4 discussed using PERT for time, based on three-point duration estimates for each activity (an *optimistic* estimate, a *most likely* estimate, and a *pessimistic* estimate). This range information could be used to calculate the "expected estimate," that would lie at the midpoint of the distribution. PERT for cost also employs the same three estimates to derive an expected cost for each activity, using essentially the same formula:

$c_e = (c_o + 4c_m + c_p)/6$, where
    c_e is the "expected" cost

c_o is the "optimistic" (lowest realistic) cost

c_m is the "most likely" cost

c_p is the "pessimistic" (highest realistic) cost

As with PERT for time, the standard deviation is estimated to be $(c_p - c_o)/6$. A distribution showing this graphically is in figure 5-4.

Figure 5-4: Cost Estimates for PERT Analysis

Cost-based PERT estimates are generally done in monetary units (pesos, rupees, euros), but they may also be evaluated in effort (person-hours, engineer-days) instead of, or in addition to, the financial estimates.

Whether for time or cost, PERT concepts are useful in gathering risk information about project activities, particularly when considering the worst-case (pessimistic) estimates. Use of PERT and three-point estimates for overall project risk management goes well beyond adjusting cost and duration estimates for uncertainty. Chapters 7 and 9 will explore this in detail.

Staffing and Outsourcing Costs

Staffing costs can be calculated using the activity effort estimates, based on your histograms, spreadsheets, or other resource planning information. Using standard staffing cost rates (including overhead) and your effort estimates, you can convert effort into project costs. For longer projects, you may also need to consider factors such as salary changes and the effect of inflation. Consider three-point effort estimates and worst-case analysis when assessing the credibility of all cost estimates.

Estimate any outsourcing costs using the contracts negotiated for the services, working with figures about halfway between the baseline contract fees and the "not to exceed" amounts.

Equipment and Software Costs

The best time on a project to request new equipment or upgrade older hardware, systems, and applications for a project is at the outset. You should assess the project's needs, and research the options that are available. Inspect all equipment and software applications already in place to determine any opportunities for replacement or upgrade. Document the project's needs and assemble a proposal including all potential purchases. As discussed earlier in the chapter, proposing the purchase and installation of new equipment at the start of the project has two benefits: getting approval from management when it is most likely, and allowing for installation when there is little other project work to conflict with it. Propose buying the best equipment available, so if purchase is approved you will be able to work as fast and efficiently as possible. If you propose the best options and only some of the budget is approved, you still may be able to find alternative hardware or systems that will enable you to complete your project. Estimate the overall project equipment expense by summing the cost of any approved proposals with other expected hardware and software costs.

Travel

The best time to request travel money for your project is also at the beginning; midproject travel requests are often denied. ("Sorry, that's not in the budget.") As you plan the project work, determine when travel will be necessary and decide who will need to be involved. Travel planned and approved in advance is easier to arrange, less costly, and less disruptive for the project and the team members than last-minute, emergency trips. Request and justify face-to-face meetings with distant team members. Plan to get team members from each site together at the project start—and for longer projects, at least every six months thereafter. Also budget for appropriate travel to interact with users, customers, and other stakeholders.

There are no guarantees that travel requested at the beginning of the project will be approved, or that it might not be cut back later. If you do not estimate and request travel funds early, however, the probability of approval may be zero.

Other Costs

Communication is essential on technical projects, and for distributed teams, it may be quite costly. Although it has become much more commonplace and affordable, establishing high-quality conferencing technology may require up-front expense and ongoing usage fees. Schedule and budget for frequent status meetings, using the most appropriate technology you can find.

Projects that include team members outside of a single company may need to budget for setup and maintenance of a secure public-domain website outside of corporate firewalls for project information that will be available to everyone. Other services such as shipping, couriers, and photocopying may also represent significant expenses for your project.

Cost Budgeting and Project-Level Estimates

Cost budgeting is the accumulation of all the cost estimates for the project. For many modern projects, the main costs are for people, either permanent staff or workers under some kind of contract. The project cost baseline also includes estimated expenses for equipment, software and services, travel, communications, and other requirements. Whenever your preliminary project budget analysis exceeds the project cost objectives, the difference represents a significant project risk. Unless you are able to devise a credible lower-cost plan or negotiate a larger project budget, your project may prove to be impossible because of inadequate resources.

Funding Risks

The cases in the PERIL database representing financial limitations are not numerous, but they are painful, representing more than two months of slippage on average and often resulting in project cancellation. As you review the resource requirements for the work needed for your project, determine if the overall budget will cover the efforts needed, with at least a small contingency reserve. For projects that are inadequately funded, chapter 6 explores the process of negotiating changes to project goals, including adjustments to overall budgets.

If you anticipate significant reductions in funding, such as are common for projects that start in one fiscal year and continue into the next (or beyond), add this as a risk to your documented list.

DOCUMENTING THE RISKS

Resource risks become visible throughout the planning and scheduling processes. Resource risks discussed in this chapter include:

- Activities with unknown staffing
- Understaffed activities
- Activities requiring a unique resource
- Part-time team members
- Remote team members
- The impact of the work environment
- Activities with uncertain costs or high worst-case (or pessimistic PERT) resource estimates
- Work that is outsourced
- Contracting risks
- Budget requirements that exceed committed project funding

Add each specific risk discovered to the list of scope and schedule risks, with a clear description of the risk situation. This growing risk list provides the foundation for project risk analysis and management.

Key Ideas for Identifying Resource Risks

- Identify all required skills you need for which you lack named, committed staffing.
- Determine all situations in the project plan where people or other resources are overcommitted.
- Identify all activities with insufficient resources.

- Identify uncertain activity effort and cost estimates, especially worst cases.
- Note outsourcing risks.
- Gain funding approval early for needed training, equipment purchases, and travel.
- Determine and document all expected project costs.

PANAMA CANAL: RESOURCES (1905–1907)

Project resource risk arises primarily from people factors, as demonstrated in the PERIL database, and this was certainly true on the Panama Canal project. Based on the experiences of the French during the first attempt, John Stevens realized project success required a healthy, productive, motivated workforce. For his project, money was never an issue, but retaining people to do difficult and dangerous work in the hot, humid tropics certainly was. Stevens invested heavily, through Dr. Gorgas, in insect control and other public health measures. He also built an infrastructure at Panama that supported the productive, efficient progress he required. At the time of his departure from the project, Stevens had established a well-fed, well-equipped, well-housed, well-organized workforce with an excellent plan of attack.

This boosted productivity, but George Goethals realized that success also relied on continuity and motivation. He wanted loyalty, not to him, but to the project. The work was important, and Goethals used any opportunity he had to point this out. He worked hard to keep the workers engaged, and much of what he did remains good resource management practice today.

Goethals took a number of important steps to build morale. He started a weekly newspaper, the *Canal Record*. The paper gave an accurate, up-to-date picture of progress, unlike the *Canal Bulletin* periodically issued during the earlier French project. In many ways, it served as the project's status report, making note of significant accomplishments and naming those involved to build morale. The paper also provided feedback on productivity. Publishing these statistics led to healthy rivalries, as workers strived to better last week's record for various types of work, so they could see their names in print.

It was crucial, Goethals believed, to recognize and reward service. Medals were struck at the Philadelphia Mint, using metal salvaged from the abandoned French equipment. Everyone who worked on the project for at least two years was publicly recognized and presented with a medal in a formal ceremony. People wore these proudly. In a documentary made many years after the project, Robert Dill, a former canal worker interviewed at age 104, was still wearing his medal, number 6726.

Goethals also sponsored weekly open-door sessions on Sundays when anyone could come with their questions. Some weeks over a hundred people would queue up to see him. If he could quickly answer a question or solve a problem, he did it then. If a request or suggestion was not something that would work, he explained why. If there were any open questions or issues, he committed to getting an answer, and he followed up. Goethals treated workers like humans, not brutes, and this engendered fierce loyalty.

Although all this contributed to ensuring a loyal, motivated, productive workforce, the most significant morale builder came early on, from the project sponsor. In 1906, Theodore Roosevelt sailed to Panama to visit his project. His trip was without precedent; never before had a sitting US president left the country. The results of the trip were so noteworthy that one newspaper at the time conjectured that someday, a president "might undertake European journeys."

Roosevelt chose to travel in the rainy season, and the conditions in Panama were dreadful. This hardly slowed him down at all; he was in the swamps, walking the railroad ties, charging up the slopes, even operating one of the huge, ninety-seven-ton Bucyrus steam shovels. He went everywhere the workers were. The reporters who came along were exhausted, but the workers were hugely excited and motivated to see him.

On Roosevelt's return to Washington, so much was written about the magnitude and importance of the project that interest and support for the canal spread quickly throughout the United States. People believed: "With Teddy Roosevelt, anything is possible."

CHAPTER 6

MANAGING PROJECT CONSTRAINTS AND DOCUMENTING RISKS

"A good plan, violently executed right now, is better than the perfect plan executed next week."

—GENERAL GEORGE S. PATTON

Reviewing a plan to deal with constraints—detecting problems and making improvements—ought to be a brief exercise done toward the end of initial project planning. This chapter is not about obsessive application of every single project management practice in an endless quest for the flawless plan (sometimes called "analysis-paralysis"). The topic here is realistic, commonsense project analysis. You have a plan. Now the objective is to review it, quickly, to find defects, omissions, and unrealistic constraints. You are not after a perfect plan, just the best one possible using what you currently know about your project.

This part of the planning process relates to risk management in two important ways. First, the process of replanning to deal with constraints nearly always creates project risk because minimizing one parameter of a project (changes to reduce a schedule, for example) often requires trade-offs that put more pressure on other aspects of the work (such as more work in parallel and new failure modes). Any additional exposures and potential problems must be recognized, documented, and added to the project risk list. A second type of project risk is that of taking on an "inferior" project. All projects have alternatives, and examining at least some of these options is central to opportunity management, which we will also explore in this chapter.

ANALYZING CONSTRAINTS

As you proceed through preliminary project definition and planning, a coherent picture of your project starts to emerge. Although your project plan is unfinished, your work breakdown structure, preliminary schedule, and resource analysis will provide insight into whether the project objective is possible or not. Often, it shows the unpleasant fact that, based on your current plans, your project is impossible, or at least overconstrained; the result of initial bottom-up planning frequently fails to meet at least part of the stated project objectives. Your preliminary analysis might reveal a schedule that extends beyond the deadline, resource requirements that exceed initial budgets, or other significant issues. Your bottom-up plans reveal just how much trouble you are in.

Failure of your initial draft plans to meet overall project objectives is not the only issue that emerges at this stage. Above and beyond the high-level constraints, most projects also have other constraints to be managed. Timing requirements for intermediate documents, prototypes, and other midproject deliverables may mandate fixed-date milestones within the project plan. The profile of available resources may be interrupted at specific times by the business cycle, by holidays and vacations, or by higher-priority projects. In addition, projects undertaken in lean organizations (where keeping everyone busy all the time in the name of efficiency is a top priority) will frequently run into a queue when access to a critical, unique resource is required. Delays for contract approvals, management sign-off, and other decisions are common. Identifying and managing risks from these other constraints is also part of project risk management.

Your primary goal in managing project constraints is to eliminate, or at least minimize, the differences between the project objective and your project plans, in terms of scope, schedule, and resources. The standard triangle diagram for examining project trade-offs is one way to show these differences, as in figure 6-1. The plan, represented by the gray triangle, is quite a bit larger than the objective, shown as the darker triangle.

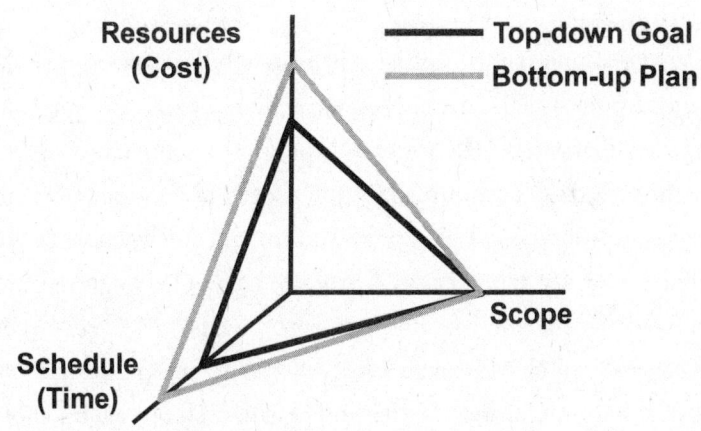

Figure 6-1: Objective Versus Plan

For this project, the initial plan suggests that the deliverable is probably feasible, so this project is not literally impossible—its scope appears within your capabilities. However, as shown, the project will require both more time and more resources (people, money, etc.) than envisioned in the project objective. So based on your current plan, the project looks infeasible. For projects where the scope is achievable, the situation in figure 6-1 is fairly common. Bottom-up project planning begins with a WBS that is consistent with the desired scope, but the initial schedule and resource plans fall wherever the WBS leads them—often with significant variance compared with the project objective.

For some projects, the objective is firm, based on hard limits that cannot be modified. For other projects, the objective may be based on softer constraints, goals that are desirable but not absolutely necessary. Each project is unique, so determining how to approach trade-off analysis for your project requires you to understand what the constraints and priorities are, and how they were determined.

In the simplest form, project priorities boil down to the old saying, "Good, fast, cheap: Pick two." Every project requires at least one degree of freedom. Any of the three parameters could be the most flexible, but for planning purposes, at least one of them must be unconstrained. Although you can get a deliverable out of a project quickly and cheaply, it may not be good enough to meet the need. This lesson was illustrated in the late 1990s by NASA on several failed Mars missions. Working under the mantra "Faster, Better, Cheaper," faster and cheaper fell quite a bit short of better. Similarly, excellent results are often possible in short time frames, but the cost of this compression is high and may not be justified by the result. (We will cover "crashing" project activities in a project schedule later in this chapter.) And you may even be able to deliver good results at low cost in projects where time is not limited (although unlimited time is not always your friend—think "analysis-paralysis").

A slightly more sophisticated analysis rests on prioritizing the triple constraint. Rank-ordering scope, schedule, and resources shows which of the three is most important for your project. A simple three-by-three grid is often used for this, as in figure 6-2.

	Schedule	Scope	Resources
Constrain Least Flexible	●		
Optimize Somewhat Flexible			●
Accept Most Flexible		●	

Figure 6-2: Project Priority Matrix

The project priorities shown here are common for current projects, as timing dominates more and more of the work. In contract work, deadlines with financial penalties are often looming. In product development, pressure from competitors, trade show schedules, and other real constraints on timing are often at issue. Even in application development, delivery must synchronize with fiscal accounting periods. Schedule in all these cases is the dominant priority, and failure to meet the project deadline will have significant, possibly dire consequences. Schedule is the parameter such projects constrain.

In figure 6-2, the second priority is resources. This is also common, as the desire to minimize resources and execute as efficiently as possible is a key goal for many projects. In fact, many projects face inflexible limits on competent, available staff. In the time frame of most projects, the number of available people who are familiar with the relevant technologies is fixed and can only increase gradually over time through training, mentoring, and other methods for hauling people up the learning curve. Modern projects tend to optimize their resources.

The largest degree of freedom for the project in figure 6-2 is for scope, indicating that there may be aspects or specifications in the objective that, although desirable, may be discretionary. The project may be able to accept small changes to the expected deliverable, especially if failing to make the changes would require time, resources, or both that exceed what is available. The prioritization in figure 6-2 is one of six possibilities, and good examples for each of the other five can be easily imagined. Though all prioritizations are possible, today's projects frequently converge on the "schedule/resources/scope" of figure 6-2.

For the example in figure 6-1, the initial plan failed to meet the deadline and also was over budget. Doing some "what if" analysis, you may discover a way to use a top-notch group of consultants

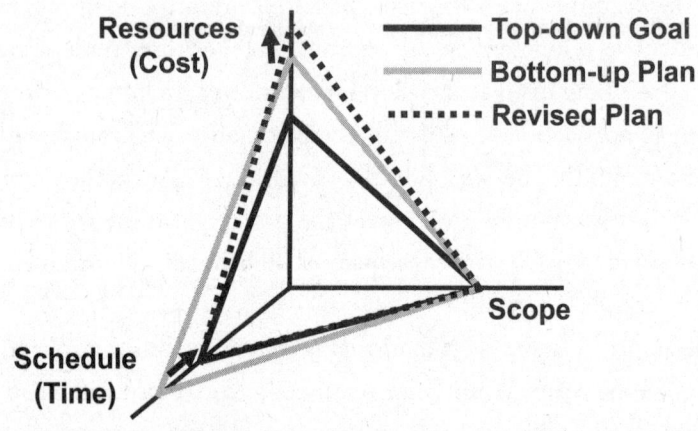

■ **Figure 6-3:** Plan Trade-offs

with a credible track record to perform more work in parallel, shortening the overall project. This approach will not be inexpensive; it makes the budget problem even bigger, and results in the shift shown in figure 6-3. In this figure, the schedule has been compressed, bringing it in line with the objective, but the resources required for the project, which already exceeded the objective, are even farther out of line with the project expectations.

For projects where resources are the lowest priority, this tactic may be a good alternative. For projects with the priorities in figure 6-2, however, this is not likely to be the best plan. It may be better to reevaluate the specifications and propose a plan that achieves its deadline within budget but falls slightly short on scope. For some projects, portions of the initially requested requirements may not be essential. In other situations, you might propose delivering the most valuable functionality on time, and then delivering the rest in a follow-on project later. The analysis for such a scope reduction might result in a shift similar to figure 6-4.

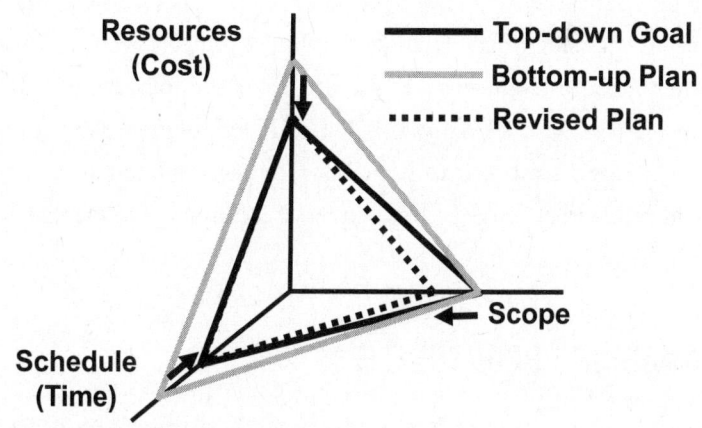

■ **Figure 6-4:** Seeking the "Best" Plan

In this case, changes proposed to the initial plan affect all three of the project parameters, with the most significant difference between the objective and the plan being a reduction in the deliverable's feature set.

The overall objective of the plan review and "what if" analysis is to discover the options available as alternatives to the initial plan, and to investigate whether it might be desirable, or even necessary, to revise the project's overall objective. This triangle model allows you to explore trade-offs in the project "state space," seeking plan alternatives that represent realistic, feasible projects. For particularly ill-conceived projects, this analysis may fail to turn up any options close to the original objective. For such projects, you need to negotiate a major change to the objective, abandon the project, or at least consider updating your résumé.

In most cases, though, reasonable alternatives for your project are not difficult to find. Start your analysis of the project plan with the parameter that has the lowest priority, and explore possible changes related to that aspect of the project. These modifications are generally the easiest to negotiate, so it makes sense to focus first on that side of the triangle. For most projects, you will also want to examine alternatives for the other two parameters. The next sections describe using this "what if" technique for exploring project opportunities, and then for options related to scope, resources, and schedule. (This sequence follows the prioritization of figure 6-2.)

MANAGING OPPORTUNITIES

In cases where your preliminary plan falls short of the project objective, it may seem inappropriate to revisit opportunities, because doing so will probably make things worse. There are a number of good reasons for exploring these project options, though, and they relate directly to risk management. Where risk management seeks to understand what might go badly in a project, opportunity management looks for what might go better. In particular, opportunity management asks what similar, but superior, projects might be possible. Realizing halfway through the work that you could have achieved a more valuable result is not useful. It's too late at that point to do anything about it. As discussed in chapter 1, projects are driven by opportunity, and many times a project's sponsors and stakeholders may not know enough to identify the best opportunity. As planning proceeds, the project team may be well-positioned to discover new technologies, methods, or other possibilities that would result in a superior project. Adopting a better opportunity in such a case might also result in a more interesting, more motivating project that can enhance teamwork and provide opportunities to develop new skills valued by contributors. Mostly, however, it helps to ensure that you are not working on the wrong project. As with risks, a good starting point for opportunity management is the triple constraint of scope, schedule, and resources.

Scope

Project deliverables are set using two kinds of input: user/market demand and technological possibilities. Most project work relies primarily on the first. The sponsors, economic buyers, managers, and others who get projects started are generally doing so to meet a need, solve a problem, or respond to some specific request. Although this may be sufficient, for technical projects the requested deliverables may fall well short of what is possible. Technology moves fairly quickly, so user requests may represent continued use of an older technology even after emerging new ideas and approaches become available. If you were collecting specifications for a project deliverable from people sitting on a riverbank washing their clothes with two large stones, their requirements would probably involve developing lighter rocks. The concept of a washing machine will not occur to them if the technology is outside their experience. Similarly, the project team may be able to see possibilities based on technology unknown to the users that would solve the problem or meet the need much more effectively than the original request. Opportunity management is about merging a deep understanding of user needs with the technical capabilities available to create the best deliverable—and not necessarily the one initially envisioned. A "what if" project with a slightly longer schedule and higher budget compared with the original objective, but with a superior deliverable such as depicted in figure 6-5, might represent a much better project alternative.

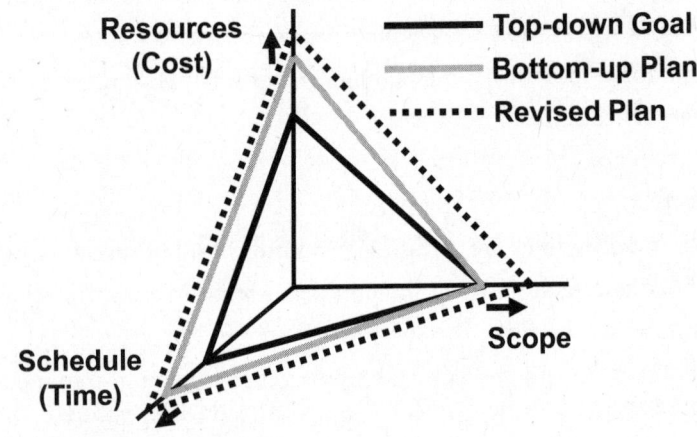

■ **Figure 6-5:** An Opportunistic Plan

Scope opportunity management often requires a counter-proposal to the original objective, and may involve negotiation. Some project leaders actively avoid this sort of confrontation, viewing it as unpleasant and possibly futile. This is unfortunate because this process represents one of the real sources of power and influence available to the project leader. There is a saying, "If you are going to lose an argument, change the subject." Proposing an alternative that is demonstrably superior to the requested deliverable can effectively "change the subject," avoiding an otherwise doomed project by substituting a better, more realistic one.

The main motivation for opportunity management, however, is to increase the business value of the project. There are a number of ways to approach this. Surveying the current state of relevant and closely related technologies is a typical starting point. It may be that a new generation of hardware has become available. New technologies or methods may provide greater performance or reliability. Emerging standards may be applicable to your work, which could extend the possible uses of the deliverable, both for the current project and in future applications. It might be possible to develop a deliverable with capabilities that solve a whole class of problems instead of the single one that triggered the project. Conversely, it may be possible to break up an ambitious project into shorter stages, developing something that provides tangible value (perhaps most of what is actually needed) in a fraction of the time and for a smaller cost than the originally proposed project.

Resources

Explore options for efficiency or schedule reduction through the use of additional, more highly skilled, or outside contributors. If improvements to your tools, systems, or other aspects of your infrastructure will help performance, propose upgrades. Gain access to and use the best available facilities and methods for communications. Bringing distributed teams together and arranging other closer collaboration may significantly boost progress and teamwork. Bringing people face-to-face generally improves productivity, so make the case for necessary travel. If additional training for contributors will help the project, schedule it.

If there are team members who have open time during portions of the project, consider replanning to more effectively use the effort available (though this will reduce resource reserve and may increase potential failure modes).

Schedule

Schedule opportunities include revising the schedule to exploit float, revising logical dependencies, devising ways to exploit the "optimistic" end of a three-point estimate range, and "crashing" activities. Seek valid shortcuts and better, newer methods for the work. Although any of these ideas can reduce the schedule, each also tends to increase overall risk. Later in this chapter we will explore the effects of schedule modification techniques such as these.

Opportunities in General

Some project leaders list opportunities with risks and assess them together. Although opportunities and risks are related, they are not symmetric. While the project team will generally be responsible for managing most harmful risks, most opportunities are out of their hands. Aggressive opportunities ("stretch goals," as discussed in chapter 1) are choices made at project inception by key stakeholders, and are embedded in the project assumptions. These opportunities are fundamental to the project business case and are often the source of many project risks, particularly scope-related risks. New opportunities uncovered during planning may originate with the project team, but adopting them, particularly if they involve significant scope or other overall changes, is never a project team decision. Proposals are needed before consideration, and a commitment to modify the project deliverable will require stakeholder approval.

The consequences represented by risks and opportunities are also not symmetric. It's often said, "Success has many fathers, while failure is an orphan." Whenever things work out better than expected, everyone takes credit—especially the managers. When things go badly, the project team will be left standing alone.

Opportunities that significantly change the project require sponsor support, and accepting them is nearly always more complex than the risk assessment process described in chapter 7. Opportunities that do not represent substantial shifts to the overall project objective (including much of what follows in this chapter) mostly fall into the category of "good project planning." Some of the opportunities and alternative plans you consider may reduce project risk, while others may increase it. Explicitly note the consequences of any project alternatives that you may adopt in your risk list.

SCOPE MODIFICATION

Proposed project deliverable changes may be easily accepted, absolutely nonnegotiable, or anything in between. This depends on the project, the sponsors and users, and the type and magnitude of the change. Whatever the circumstances, a conscientious project team will spend at least a little time considering adjustments and alternatives to the project deliverable. This "what if" exercise helps your team understand the work better and provides you with valuable information for decision-making.

To meet project constraints, many projects will ultimately trim the requested scope. Before deciding what features or aspects of the project deliverable to drop or change, determine which requirements are absolute "must haves" and which are lower priorities. There are several techniques for prioritizing requirements. The simplest is to list the requirements and sort them into a sequence where the most essential ones are at the top and the least important ones are at the bottom. "Is/is not" analysis, described in chapter 3, is another possible starting point. You will need to revisit the list of items on the "is" list to validate that each requirement is in fact essential. Determining what portions of scope can be demoted to the "is not" list effectively limits scope. This is particularly useful for projects that have hard limits on timing and budget; the "is/is not" technique establishes a firm boundary for scope that is consistent with the other limits.

The purpose of the exercise, however you approach it, is to capture and document the specifications that you must deliver, separating them from the portions of the requested deliverable that may be desirable but are not absolutely necessary. Accepting small decreases in reliability or performance may cause a significant reduction in project time and cost, and such trade-offs may result in a project that is a much better business opportunity.

Dropping project scope requirements is far easier when done early. Late changes are often painful and expensive, especially following work that would have been unnecessary had the change been made earlier. Freezing scope early does not mean that project scope will never shift; it just means that any modifications will be subject to analysis and change control before being accepted. Determining the lowest-value features and requirements allows you to intelligently determine what to exclude (either permanently or as part of a follow-on project or future iteration).

RESOURCE MODIFICATION

Revisiting your resource assessments also can result in an overall plan that better fits the objective. Alternative approaches to staffing, cross-training, outsourcing, and other elements of the resource plan are all potentially useful tactics.

Resource Analysis

For some projects, there may be ways to get work done faster without increasing the overall required resources. One possibility is to rearrange the work assignments to use available staffing more fully and effectively. Schedules may be too long because of nonproject commitments. If the external work can be postponed or eliminated, it could have a significant impact on your schedule. You may also be able to find ways to improve the effectiveness of the project team by asking individuals what they need to work faster and finding a way to make it available. Many people get more work done through telecommuting, working at off hours, or being in a different work environment. Until you ask, these possibilities will remain hidden.

You may even be able to minimize distractions and noise during some or most of the project through moving work off-site, collocating the team in a closed-off area, or relocating to space that is out of normal foot-traffic areas. One project team I worked with attributed much of their on-schedule performance to their location in a trailer (while new buildings were being completed). It was quiet there, and no one dropped by to visit.

Training Additional Staff

Another tactic that can potentially help the schedule as well as mitigate a source of project risk is mentoring and cross-training. Project timelines are often longer than theoretically necessary because only one person understands some part of the work. These activities must be scheduled in sequence, queued up for the expert. Work can speed up if others on the staff have an interest in this area of expertise and can be trained to take on activities in parallel. Of course, people new to a discipline will rarely work as fast as experienced staff. Duration estimates for activities assigned to them will generally be longer, due to learning curves and training requirements. Activities assigned to the current expert may also take somewhat longer if he or she will provide mentoring support. Despite this, the benefits to the schedule in getting the work done concurrently can be substantial. In addition, the project risk profile will improve, as the project will no longer be dependent on a single individual. If the expert becomes unavailable to your project (because of illness, higher priority work, resignation, or whatever), your project will not grind to a halt but can continue (although more slowly) using the newly trained staff.

Staffing Alternatives

For projects where schedule is much more important than budget, subcontracting work to outside service providers may speed things up, providing that it is possible for more people to work in parallel on activities that were planned to be done in sequence. If the project priority is high, more staff from within the organization may also be an option. Some projects cannot run as quickly as theoretically possible because the experience and talent available on the current project team is low, so exploring the possibility of securing staff who are more productive may be useful. Additional resources of other types, such as better systems, newer equipment for test and other work, or hardware to automate manual activities, can also potentially help to compress the project. New work methods require training and practice, but nonetheless may save time. All these options will likely increase the project cost, but for some projects this trade-off may be justified.

SCHEDULE MODIFICATION

Reexamining the schedule also provides alternative project strategies. Some ideas to consider include using float, revising activity dependencies, and crashing the schedule.

Using Float

One simple approach for shortening your project involves reducing the amount of float associated with noncritical activities. Float is derived from the critical path analysis of the schedule (discussed in chapter 4), and it measures how much an activity can slip without impact to the project deadline.

To shorten your project using float, you shift some of the work on critical path activities to staff assigned to noncritical activities. These staffing shifts will cause changes to noncritical activities (such as delaying the start, interrupting the activity, or reducing productivity), but the additional effort on the critical activities could shorten the overall project. Bear in mind that schedule compression that removes schedule flexibility comes at a price. Using all (or nearly all) of the float for an activity increases project risk and creates new failure modes.

Revising Workflow Dependencies

A second, more elaborate idea involves revising activity workflow dependencies. Here, the schedule is shortened through rearranging or redefining the work. The simplest possibility is to inspect the dependencies linking critical path activities, seeking opportunities to shorten the schedule using a more compact logical workflow.

You might also reexamine longer activities on the critical path to look for alternate breakdowns or a completely new approach. This technique may involve breaking critical path activities down further, to create smaller activities that can be executed in parallel, as in figure 6-6.

■ **Figure 6-6:** Converting Activities to Parallel Execution

This concept has a variety of names, including concurrent engineering, "fast tracking," and simultaneous development. For parallel execution to be effective, there are at least two requirements. First, you need to allow integration time in the estimates for the parallel activities or define a new activity (as in figure 6-5) during which all the separately developed components are assembled. The second requirement is often less visible but even more important. Detailed up-front analysis is essential to ensure that the integration works. All the connections, interfaces, and relationships between the independently developed activity deliverables must be defined and thoroughly documented. Whatever this work is called—architecting, systems engineering, or something else—doing it well will be the difference between components that mesh properly and integration efforts that fail. When the system decomposition is done poorly, integration activities can consume all the time you expected to save, and more. Even worse, it may fail utterly, resulting in components that are completely unusable. Before committing to a plan that uses independent parallel development, explicitly identify when and by whom the system analysis will be done, and note the integration risks on your project risk list.

Another approach for schedule compression through revising activity dependencies involves overlapping the work. In the plan, there may be finish-to-start dependencies on the critical path that can be converted to start-to-start dependencies with lags.

In figure 6-7, the preliminary project plan includes a design activity scheduled for three weeks followed by a coding activity scheduled for four weeks. After thinking about it, the project team may decide that it would be possible to begin coding after only two weeks of design, because there will be enough information to start programming for some of the modules at that point, and staffing will be available to get going. Although it may seem that converting a finish-to-start dependency to start-to-start dependency with an overlap of a week would save that week on the schedule, this is overly optimistic. There is an increased likelihood of rework or discovery of something unexpected in the final week of design, so when you elect to make this sort of change, increase your duration estimates for any activities that you choose to begin early (in this case, about two days have been added to the coding activity), and also explicitly note the new risk.

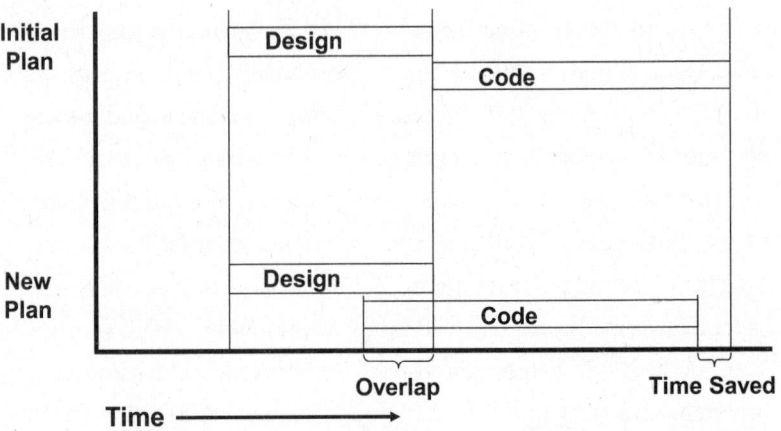

"Optimistic" Estimates

"Best case" estimates are mostly wishful thinking. Few will actually happen due to Parkinson's Law and other factors. Some, however, will be based on effective ideas for working more efficiently or productively, and represent ways to credibly shorten the schedule. If there are ways to modify the approach taken, the project environment, or other factors that would support shortening a duration estimate, consider incorporating the changes into your project. Whenever compressing a schedule using "best case" analysis data, however, be aware that this is a choice that may have unintended consequences, and it does carry at least some risk because you can never completely wipe out the "worst-case" scenarios.

"Crashing" the Schedule

An additional scheduling technique, common on projects with extreme schedule pressure, is "crashing." In this sense, crashing means applying additional resources to gain speed—as in a crash program. Not all activities can be crashed. It is not possible to crash activities where one person must do all the work, where activities cannot be partitioned, or where activities have time constraints you do not control. A good example of an uncrashable activity is sailing a ship from New York to London. With one ship, it takes five days. With five ships, it still takes five days.

Even when crashing helps, it adds both additional cost and new risks to projects. If an activity is efficiently executed by a team of three people, a team of six will rarely be able to do it in half the time. Involving more people requires extra communication, overhead, and complexity, so resources and time never trade off in a linear way. This has been observed and documented for all types of projects for a long time, but the best discussion of this for technical projects remains *The Mythical Man-Month*, by Fred Brooks. Brooks covers in detail how people get in each other's way and how inefficiencies grow as the number of people working on a project increases. As productivity drops, project risk increases because of the larger staff, potential confusion, work methods, and general complexity.

For all this, when time is critical to your project, these trade-offs may be justified. Crashing a project schedule requires you to locate the activities that can be shortened, and to estimate for each what the impact of compression will be, particularly regarding incremental cost. Experienced project leaders usually have a good sense of how to do project work efficiently, so initial plans are generally built using assumptions for staffing and work methods that minimize overall effort and cost. For any given activity, though, other combinations of staffing and duration may be possible. One person working alone on an activity might take a long time; two working together could take quite a bit less. Adding more people will, for some activities, continue to reduce the activity duration even more. Eventually, though, you reach a point of diminishing returns, where adding more staff makes a negligible difference in the activity duration. A curve describing the relationship between staffing and time has a bend in it at that point, giving it an L shape, similar to the curve in figure 6-8.

Figure 6-8: Trade-off Between Effort and Time

For any given activity, there is also a minimum possible duration; no amount of additional staffing, money, or other tactics will allow you to do the work in less time.

Because the initial estimates tend to be near the bend in the curve (where the total cost is minimized), shortening projects by crashing can be quite expensive. Strategies for compressing projects by crashing begin by seeking a number of ideas, more than may be needed to meet the project deadline. Examine the schedule for activities that could be crashed, expedited, or otherwise changed in ways that could shorten the project, initially focusing on the critical path(s). Ideas for each activity can then be considered in turn and assessed for both effectiveness and cost.

If the next priority after schedule is cost, you will first adopt the strategies that have the least impact to the project budget. This will require you to estimate the "cost penalty" for each idea. The usual way to do this is to calculate the cost per time (usually per day) associated with the schedule reduction. For example, one idea might be to shorten a development activity, initially estimated to take fifteen workdays and consume $4,000 of effort. You believe that this could be reduced to eleven days if you bring in an outside contractor to help for a week at a rate of $6,000. Both the initial and compressed approaches to this activity are indicated in figure 6-9, and the slope of the dotted line connecting them, $1,500 per day, defines the cost penalty for schedule compression.

Ideas for schedule compression can come from a variety of sources. The project team can brainstorm, you can consult peers or experts, or you can research what similar past projects did when they ran into trouble and were forced to work faster. In addition to providing a potentially rich source of ideas, successful past project recovery efforts also offer data for costs and describe the work that will be required.

Typical methods that may prove effective in shortening project activity durations (for a price) include:

- Adding staff
- Paying for overtime

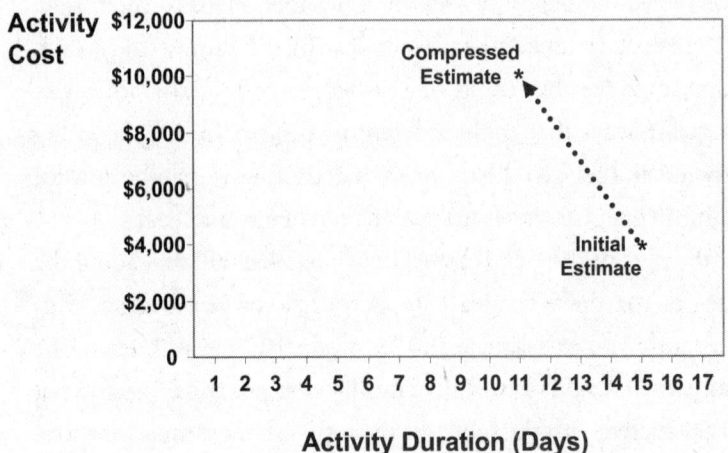

■ **Figure 6-9:** Estimates for Crashed Activity

- Hiring outside staff to help or outsourcing whole project activities
- Paying to expedite shipping or other services
- Upgrading or replacing slower equipment
- Spreading work over more shifts

For each crashable activity idea you develop, estimate the total cost involved and assess the cost penalty—the expense for each day of schedule improvement—so you can arrange the ideas from least costly to most expensive, per day. Starting with the least costly strategies, make schedule changes affecting critical activities and note the cost for the incremental resources. For each modification considered, check that the change does in fact provide a schedule improvement, and monitor for noncritical path activities that become critical. You can continue the process, crashing activities until you reach your compression goals, or it is not possible.

Any schedule compression ideas that you do not use can be held in reserve as possible contingency plans for your project. (Chapter 8 will cover contingency planning in detail.)

An alternative to adopting tactics for shortening the project based on cost takes this concept an additional step. Ideas for crashing can be useful as contingency plans only if they relate to future portions of the project. To maximize the potential utility of any crashing tactics you have developed, you might choose to apply them based on timing. If you start with the ideas that shorten the project by acting on the earliest activities, any leftover tactics will remain available as contingency plans. Although this will generally cost more, it will result in a more resilient plan.

Before leaving the topic of schedule changes, it's worth noting that as you compress a schedule you create additional failure modes and generate a good deal more stress for the project leader and team. The trade-offs between time and cost and time and scope are visible throughout the process of managing project constraints. The trade-off between time and risk is more subtle, but nonetheless real. At the conclusion of this process, document any changes you made and list all the new risks introduced to your project plan, including the new critical and near-critical activities. Also be aware of the increased overall project risk contributed by the added complexity and stress.

ASSESSING OPTIONS AND UPDATING PLANS

Armed with potential scope, resource, and schedule changes, you are prepared to assess your options and seek the plan that best meets the project objective. Your analysis may yield a credible project plan (including a detailed project schedule, resource plan, and description of major project deliverables) that supports the project objective and any other significant constraints. If so, your next step is risk analysis.

If the best plan you can develop is still far from the objective, you almost certainly have an overconstrained project. In such a case, use your "what if" analysis of scope, schedule, and resource combinations to develop at least two additional plans that achieve slightly different project objectives, such as:

- A plan that uses fewer resources, but has a longer schedule or reduced scope
- A plan that increases scope (with higher demonstrable value), but requires more time or resources
- A plan with a compressed schedule, but that needs more resources (or reduces the scope)

For each option, document relative benefits and risks. These alternative plans can be used in discussions and negotiations. (Negotiating project objective changes is a key topic of chapter 10.)

Incorporate any plan changes that you are empowered to make into your preliminary schedule and other project documents. If you have developed alternative scenarios, document them as well, and note any proposed changes or opportunities that will require higher-level approval.

SEEKING MISSING RISKS

Although you will have collected risk data throughout the planning of project work, your risk list remains incomplete. Review your scope definition, preliminary schedule, and resource plan, using the ideas in chapters 3 through 5, seeking risks you have missed. You may also want to review the selected risks from the

PERIL database listed in the appendix to further stimulate your search for potential project problems. The processes that follow are also useful in detecting potential challenges and risks.

Brainstorming

Brainstorming is a powerful risk discovery tool. With the project team, review your current risk list. Work together to brainstorm additional potential project problems. Review the methods and processes you plan to use and consider any aspects that are new or that you expect to be particularly difficult. Think about risks that may arise as a consequence of any pending (or rumored) organizational changes. Finally, focus on outside factors that might have an impact on your project, such as natural disasters, weather, government or legal changes, and actions of competitors. Also, plan to spend at least some of your time focusing on uncertain events that could have a beneficial effect on your project—opportunities that could make your work easier.

Capture every suggested risk without comment or criticism. Limit questions to those that seek better clarity. Encourage people to suggest new risks that are triggered by the thoughts of others. List every risk that is mentioned, even those you think you can do nothing about. Keep the brainstorming going, striving to hear from every member of the project team, until the flow of ideas seems at an end. Conclude the process by reviewing the risks, and work to clarify any risks that are vague or ambiguous. Combine risks where you find redundancy, and add the results of the brainstorming to your project risk list.

Retrospective Analysis

Another useful technique for finding risks in new projects is reviewing what went wrong in earlier projects. The adage

"Lightning never strikes twice in the same place" is demonstrably false; lightning strikes the same spot hundreds of times, always the highest place with the best electrical connection to the ground. (If this were not the case, lightning rods would not work.) On projects, the analogous statement "Well, *that* can never happen again!" is equally untrue. Risks tend to recur in project after project, unless you overtly change what you are doing to avoid them. Postproject analyses from earlier work (in the form of project retrospectives, lessons learned, postmortems, or closeout reports) are a rich source of risk information.

These reports generally contain two types of data useful for risk management: effective practices worth repeating and areas where improvement is warranted. In the area of good practices, seek specific ideas from what was done well, practices to repeat or extend, and specific significant accomplishments. Examine your plan to see whether you are incorporating opportunities to take full advantage of known good practices. In the realm of things that did not go well, review previous project data for problems, assumptions, poor estimates, significant schedule variances and delays, underestimated activity complexity, late mandatory changes, undetected dependencies, and other issues. Identify any aspects that impacted progress, and list as risks any that could affect your current work as planned.

Scenario Analysis

Additional risks may come to light through scenario analysis. Discuss situations expected along the project timeline, step-by-step, asking questions such as, "What might go wrong here?" and "What will be keeping me up at night during this portion of the work?" You can close your eyes and "play a movie in your head" to gain insight into the project's work and the problems it may be exposed to. Techniques such as inspections and structured walk-throughs can also reveal weaknesses, omissions, and risks in the project plans.

Assumptions Analysis

Risks also come to light when you review your project assumptions. As you think through project scenarios, consider the project assumptions. Identify any that seem inappropriate or that could change. As you proceed through your project planning, assumptions analysis can reveal where initial expectations may shift, resulting in possible project failure modes.

SWOT Analysis

A similar approach to scenario analysis is "strengths, weaknesses, opportunities, and threats" (SWOT) analysis. SWOT analysis is commonly done as part of project initiation. As the project planning process approaches closure, revisit both the identified weaknesses and threats for the project to ensure that you have included as risks any that are not adequately addressed in your planning.

Expert Interviews

Interviews with experienced people both inside and outside of your organization can be a potentially rich source of information on risks that your project may encounter. Particularly when embarking on work that is novel to you and your team, tapping into the perspectives of those who have broader knowledge can be a potent technique for identifying and managing risks.

Root-Cause Analysis

Root-cause analysis or "cause-and-effect" exercises are effective tools for risk discovery. Risk management requires knowledge of the root causes that lead to project problems. There are a number of useful techniques for uncovering the sources of problems, and although they are most often applied retrospectively, they can also be used to examine future problems. These techniques include failure mode and effect analysis, fishbone diagrams, root-cause analysis, K-J analysis, or other varieties of cause-and-effect analysis. Using these processes to look for potential risks begins by stating an outcome the project intends to avoid—such as losing a key resource, delay in getting an important input, or significant increases in the cost of some portion of the project. The next step is to challenge the project team to work backward to expose plausible sources that could cause the problem. In addition to uncovering specific risks that might not otherwise be detected, this exercise will often raise the perception of how probable specific problems might be. When the causes of potential trouble are not visible, most projects look fairly straightforward. After documenting specific events or situations that can lead to project difficulty, people develop a much more realistic view of the work. This is a good way to balance the frequently excessive optimism that is common early in a new project. Chapter 8 further explores using root-cause analysis as a tool developing risk responses.

Bow-Tie Analysis

Like root-cause exploration, bow-tie analysis facilitates discovery of antecedents to project problems. Bow-tie analysis is often used to help provide a clear picture for catastrophic failure modes involving public health and safety. The overall process incorporates both sides of the risk picture—what comes before it and what follows it. Bow-tie analysis is named for the overall shape of a typical diagram, as shown in figure 6-10.

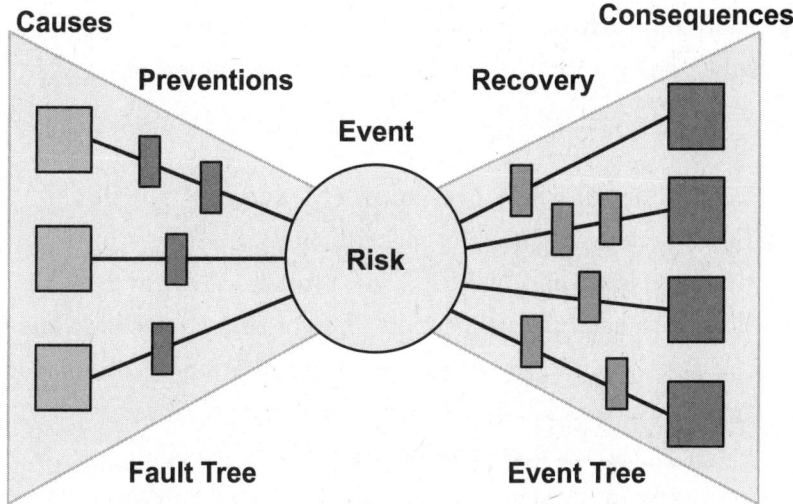

Causes

Consequences

Preventions

Recovery

Event

Risk

Fault Tree

Event Tree

■ **Figure 6-10:** Generic Bow-Tie Diagram

The "Fault Tree" portion on the left side of the diagram is most relevant to risk identification. It focuses on the causes of known risks, and like root-cause fishbone diagrams it provides insight into the underlying sources of potential trouble.

Bow-tie analysis is a robust technique for documenting not only risks but also the actions that are planned for both prevention and risk recovery. You will find an example and more details on using the bow-tie technique for planning risk responses in chapter 8.

Value Analysis and ROI Risk

Projects are undertaken based on a belief that investing in them will be justified by the benefits generated. It's prudent to spend at least some time during your planning to test the assumptions about the expected value of your project. Consider potential problems that might undermine the business case, such as scoping shortfalls, delays, competitor actions or other external changes, or other possible outcomes. Add any significant exposures you uncover to your risk list.

Other Risks and Risk Breakdown Structure Analysis

Finally, categorize the items included on your risk list using classifications based on a "risk breakdown structure." Many organizations have defined detailed hierarchies of risks. If you have one that is relevant for your project, use it. If you lack one, the generic structure of the PERIL database with its subcategories for scope, schedule, and resources provides a good starting point.

Review what you have listed and pay particular attention to any categories of risk where your list has few or no entries. Add any risks to your list that arise from this examination. Also focus your review on identifying uncertainties in risk categories that fall outside your overall planning processes and control, such as those involving safety, legal, environmental, market shifts, and other factors outside project management.

CREATING A RISK REGISTER

Risk management depends on making risks visible, and documenting them. Every time you uncover a risk, write it down. For each listed risk, check that the description is clear and includes a summary of the consequences. Use a consistent format to describe each risk, such as: "If [cause], [risk] could occur, resulting in [consequence]." For example, "If our lead designer Sara leaves, we will have insufficient experienced staff to complete the design, resulting in a delay of at least four weeks."

Once you have listed and clearly defined all the risks you have identified, begin to assemble a risk register to support the next steps of analysis and assessment. Your risk register may be a table, spreadsheet, database, or even a specialized risk tracking application. Completeness matters more than the specific format you choose, so ensure that your risk register provides space for entering (at least):

- Clear risk description
- Probability assessment
- Impact estimate
- Overall rating
- Impact description, including when the risk would most likely occur
- Risk owner
- Triggers or other indicators that signal risk occurrence
- Response summary
- Contingency or recovery summary

Create your project risk register using your risk list, and begin adding the additional details.

Key Ideas for Constraint Management and Risk Discovery

- Minimize differences between project plans and objectives.
- Understand and clearly document project priorities.
- Explore project opportunities.
- Use priorities to identify project alternatives.
- Identify and explicitly remove unnecessary project scope.

- Determine benefits and costs of plans for alternate projects.
- Minimize unknown risk through brainstorming, analysis, and research.
- Thoroughly document known project risks.

PANAMA CANAL: IMPROVING THE PLAN (1906)

Many projects, viewed in retrospect, failed because they could not manage the work within mandated constraints. In reviving the Panama Canal project, a great deal of effort went into rethinking the approach to the work so the project would avoid the most significant issues that plagued the earlier project.

For projects of all types, it is beneficial to invest effort early, investigating whether there are better, faster, more efficient ways to do what is required. New technologies, methodologies, and approaches are born this way. Several key innovations were introduced in the US canal project. Avoiding schedule and cost problems required new equipment and new methods for the work.

On the equipment side, twentieth-century technology made possible the huge, powerful steam shovels that gave the US effort a big advantage over the nineteenth-century project. New technology also provided equipment capable of standing up to the warm, damp, machine-destroying environment of Panama.

As important as the hardware was, how the work was done made an even bigger difference. John Stevens, as a railroad engineer, saw the canal project as a railroad problem. To him, the canal was "the greatest of all triumphs in American railroad engineering." To keep the huge shovels digging continuously, Stevens developed a system so that as excavations proceeded, shovel loads of soil and rock could be dropped onto railroad flatcars that ran along track adjacent to the shovels. The flatcars circulated in large loops out to the dams and other places where these loads could be deposited. Once there, huge fixed scoops (similar to the fronts of enormous snowplows) cleaned off the flatcars for their return to the shovels. There was never a need to stop or pause at any point with this enormous conveyor belt. Using this arrangement and the much larger steam shovels, the US project was soon moving more earth in one day than the earlier French project had accomplished in a month.

This system would have been sufficient for the project if the shovels had been simply digging deep holes in one place, but they were not. As the digging proceeded, the shovels had to move, and so did the railroad tracks that carried the flatcars. For this, John Stevens developed an elaborate, elastic method for moving the track, providing a constant, steady stream of empty flatcars flowing by the steam shovels. With his system, twelve men could move almost two kilometers of track in a single day. Using conventional track-laying methods, six hundred men would have had difficulty equaling this performance. As the construction continued and excavation in the Culebra Cut widened and deepened, these methods were used at multiple levels. Each level had its own railroad loop, shovels, and crews. The total track moved in one year approached 2,000 kilometers. Without these innovations, the canal project would have taken years longer to complete and cost far more, and it might well have been abandoned before completion, like the earlier project.

CHAPTER 7

QUANTIFYING AND ANALYZING ACTIVITY RISKS

"When you know a thing, to hold that you know it, and when you do not know a thing, to allow that you do not know it—this is knowledge."

—CONFUCIUS

P roject planning processes serve several purposes, but probably the most important for risk management is to differentiate the parts of the work that are well understood, and therefore less risky, from the parts where you are clueless. Often, what separates an impossible project from a possible one is isolating the most difficult work early, so it receives the attention and effort required to deal with it. Risk assessment techniques are central to gaining an understanding of what is most uncertain about a project, and they are the foundation for managing risk. The focus of this chapter is analysis and prioritization of the specific project risks listed in your project risk register. Chapter 9 will focus on assessing overall project risk.

QUALITATIVE AND QUANTITATIVE RISK ANALYSIS

Risk analysis strives for deeper understanding of potential project problems. Techniques for doing this are based on either qualitative information (used to prioritize risks) or quantitative risk estimates (used to measure them).

Uses for Qualitative Assessment

Qualitative techniques are easier to apply and generally require less effort. Qualitative assessment considers ranges for probability and categories of impact when analyzing "loss times likelihood." While qualitative methods lack precision, they do provide a way to consider risk consequences that cannot be easily measured. Qualitative risk assessment is generally the basis for rank-ordering risks, allowing you to select the most significant ones to manage using the techniques discussed in chapter 8.

Uses for Quantitative Assessment

Quantitative methods strive for greater precision, and they can reveal more about each risk. These methods require more work, but quantitative analysis also provides insight into the absolute magnitude of risk impacts and supplies data necessary for sizing schedule and/or budget reserves based on project risk.

Precision and Bias

Although quantitative and qualitative risk analysis seems to be a dichotomy, in reality risk analysis methods fall into a continuum of possibilities. They range from qualitative assessment using a small number of categories, through methods that use progressively more and finer distinctions, to the extreme of providing specific numerical estimates for each risk. If the primary goal of risk analysis is to prioritize risks to determine which ones are important enough to warrant further analysis and response, straightforward qualitative methods generally suffice. If you wish to assess significant risks with more precision, then you can use quantitative assessment methods to refine your analysis (although the nature of the data available—much of it based on guesswork—generally puts a rather modest limit on your accuracy).

Accurately estimating and assessing risks is challenging even for the most experienced project professionals. Difficulty with precise assessment of risks suffers from all the factors that make any project estimating difficult: lack of relevant experience, a paucity of useful data, and bias. In addition to optimism bias, which results in underestimation for both probability and impact assessment, other biases are also in play, including recency bias ("That has not happened lately") and judgment bias, where people tend to "cherry pick" the data they prefer to pay attention to.

Bias is a significant issue for project risk management, and may even result in failure to list significant risks that we choose to ignore. (Just because a risk seems unlikely or has not happened recently does not mean you can assume it will *never* happen.) Effective risk management depends on understanding these and other sources of bias, and working to overcome them throughout the risk identification and assessment processes. To do this well, you need to ask a lot of questions and maintain a high level of skepticism. Work to ensure that estimates and analysis are based on reality rather than wishful thinking, and that you understand the reasoning behind the assessments.

PROBABILITY AND IMPACT

Both qualitative and quantitative assessment methods have the same foundation. They rest on the simple definition of risk discussed in chapter 1: "loss" multiplied by "likelihood." The realm of likelihood is statistics and probability. Loss in projects is measured in impact, including time, money, and other project factors (some that may be difficult to quantify). These two parameters characterize risk, either qualitatively using categories, or quantitatively using estimates.

Risk Probability

All project risks involve uncertainty. The likelihood, or probability, for any specific risk will always be somewhere between zero (no chance of occurrence) and one (inevitable occurrence). Qualitative risk assessment methods divide the choices into probability ranges and require project team members to assign each risk to one of the defined ranges. Quantitative risk assessment assigns each risk a specific fraction between zero and one (or between zero and 100 percent).

Risk probability must always fall between zero and one, but picking a credible value is hard. There are only three ways to estimate probabilities. For some situations, such as flipping coins and throwing dice, you can construct a **mathematical model** and calculate an expected probability. In other situations, a simple model does not exist, but there may be many comparable past events. In these cases, **statistical analysis of empirical data** may be used to estimate probabilities. Actuaries are employed in the insurance industry to crunch the numbers and determine historical probabilities. In all other cases, probability estimates are based on **guesses**. For complex events that have seldom or perhaps never occurred, you can neither calculate nor measure to determine a probability. Ideas such as referencing analogous situations, scenario analysis, and "gut feel" come into play. For most project risks, probabilities tend to be guesses not based on much objective data, so they tend to be imprecise.

In fact, assessing likelihood in general is problematic for a number of reasons. One of the most fundamental is that the human brain is not equipped to deal well with the concept of probabilities. Our optimism bias is a consequence of this. We tend to see desirable outcomes as much more likely than they actually are. ("This lottery ticket is sure to win.") Conversely, we estimate undesirable outcomes as far less likely. ("That risk could never happen.") Another bias concerns recency, a tendency to base predictions mostly on the immediate past. Instead of thinking in terms of randomness and probability, we tend to discount both risks that have not happened lately ("We are on a lucky streak that will continue") and risks that have ("We just had that unlikely problem on the last project, so it surely can't occur again for a while"). Randomness does not follow patterns and rules. The likelihood of flipping "heads" is always 50 percent, even after a run of heads (or tails). Judgment bias is also a large impediment, particularly when dealing with small percentages. It is common to think in terms of "likely" and "unlikely," without much consideration of degree. Inability to think clearly about relative probability leads to lumping risks together that have significantly different likelihoods. Effective probability assessment requires us to manage our biases, and to remain wary of them.

Assessing probability with qualitative methods requires less precision because it does not require specific numerical values. Qualitative assessment divides the complete range of possibilities into two or more non-overlapping ranges of probability. The simplest qualitative assessment uses two ranges: "more likely than not" (between 0.5 and 1) and "less likely than not" (between 0 and 0.4999)." Project teams may be able to pick one of these choices for each risk with little difficulty, but the coarse granularity of the analysis makes prioritizing significant risks for further attention fairly arbitrary.

A more common method for qualitative assessment uses three ranges, assigning a value of high, medium, or low to each risk. The definitions for these categories vary, but these are typical:

- **High:** 50 percent or higher (likely)
- **Medium:** Between 10 and 50 percent (unlikely)
- **Low:** 10 percent or lower (very unlikely)

These three levels of probability are generally easy to determine for project risks without much debate, and the resulting characterization of risk allows you to discriminate adequately between likely and unlikely risks. It can help people in managing their biases (and muddled thinking about chance) to align these categories with events for which people have experience. High probability is similar to the flipping of a two-sided coin (heads or tails). Medium probability is about the same as rolling a specific number using a six-sided die (or perhaps having your birthday fall on a Saturday in a given year). Low probability might be likened to rolling snake eyes (a pair of ones) or boxcars (a pair of sixes) using a pair of six-sided dice. Whatever you can do to help people better associate risks with a realistic probability range will improve your analysis.

Qualitative probability assessment may also use four, five, or even more categories. These methods tend to use linear ranges for the probabilities: quartiles for four, quintiles for five, and so forth.

(The names assigned to five categories are typically: Very high, High, Moderate, Low, and Very low.) The more ranges there are, the better the characterization of risk, at least in theory. More ranges do make it harder for the project team to achieve consensus, though, and people may perceive little meaningful difference between some of the intermediate categories. The apparent additional precision that comes from more categories may mask bias and imply accuracy that is unwarranted.

The logical extension of this continues through increasingly quantitative assessments using integer percentages (100 categories) to continuous estimates allowing fractional percentages. Although it may look like the accuracy is improved, the process for determining numerical probabilities can require a lot of overhead, and you must remember that most probability estimates are at least partly guesses, based on little, perhaps no objective data. The illusion of precision can be a source of risk itself. It can make subjective information look objective, generating unwarranted confidence that may result in questionable decisions.

Depending on the project, the quality of data available, and the planned uses of the risk data, there are a number of ways to estimate probability. For qualitative assessment methods using five or fewer categories, experience, polling, interviewing, and analysis of the risk situation may be sufficient. Describing events that people have some experience with (games of chance using dice or decks of playing cards can be effective) and aligning them with probability categories may enhance the quality of your assessments. For cases where people are unsure, probe with worst-case questions ("Could this sort of thing happen once a year?") and select the category based on what people consider the upper range of what is possible.

For quantitative methods, a solid base of historical performance data is always the best data source, as it provides an empirical foundation for probability assessment and is less subject to bias. Estimating probabilities using methods such as the Delphi technique (discussed in chapter 4), computer modeling (which we will explore later in this chapter), and employing knowledgeable experts (who may have access to more and better data than you do) can also potentially improve the quality of quantitative probabilities.

Measurement-based probabilities, when available, serve an additional purpose in project risk management: trend analysis. In hardware projects, statistics for component failure support decisions to retain or replace suppliers for future projects. If custom circuit boards, specialized integrated circuits, or other hardware components are routinely required on projects, quarter-by-quarter or year-by-year data across many similar projects can provide statistical information on faulty components, and provide guidance for making process changes that may improve yields and success rates. Managing risk over the long term relies heavily on metrics, which are discussed in chapter 9.

Risk Impact

The loss, or project impact, for an individual risk is more complicated to define than the probability. Although the minimum is again zero, both the units and the maximum value for impact vary with the risk. The impact of a given risk may be relatively easy to ascertain and have a single, predictable value, or it may be best expressed as a distribution or histogram of possibilities. Qualitative risk assessment methods for impact again divide the choices into ranges. The project team assigns each risk to one of the ranges, based on the magnitude of the risk consequences. For quantitative risk assessment, impact may be estimated using units such as days of project slip, money, or some other project metric.

Qualitative impact assessment assigns each risk to one of two or more non-overlapping options that include all the possible risk consequences. A two-option version uses categories such as "low severity" and "high severity," with suitable definitions of these terms related to how the risk affects the project objective. As with probability analysis, the usefulness of only two categories is limited.

There will be better discrimination using three ranges, where each risk is assigned a value of high, medium, or low. There are many ways to define the three categories, but one useful technique relates each to the project objective and plan as follows:

- **High:** Project objective is at risk (mandatory change to one or more of scope, schedule, or resources).
- **Medium:** Project objectives can be met, but significant replanning will be required.
- **Low:** No major plan changes; the risk is an inconvenience or it will be handled through overtime or other minor adjustments.

These three levels of project impact are not difficult to assess for most risks and provide useful data for sequencing risks according to severity.

Other methods use additional categories, and some partition impact further into specific project factors, related to schedule, cost, and scope or other parameters. Impact measurement is open-ended; there is no theoretical maximum for any of these factors (in a literally impossible project, both time and cost may be considered infinite). Because the scale is not bounded, the categories used for impact are often geometric, with small ranges at the low end and progressively larger ranges for the upper categories. For an impact assessment using five categories, definitions might be:

- **Very low:** Less than 1 percent impact on scope, schedule, cost, or quality
- **Low:** Less than 5 percent impact on scope, schedule, cost, or quality
- **Moderate:** Less than 10 percent impact on scope, schedule, cost, or quality
- **High:** Less than 20 percent impact on scope, schedule, cost, or quality
- **Very high:** 20 percent or more impact on scope, schedule, cost, or quality

Risks are assigned to one of these categories based on the most significant predicted variance, so a risk that represents a 10 percent schedule slip and negligible change to other project parameters would be categorized as "moderate." As with probability assessment, the more ranges there are, the better the characterization of risk, but the harder it will be to achieve project team consensus.

Similar assessment may also be devised to look at specific kinds of risk separately, such as cost risk or schedule risk, to determine which are most likely to affect the highest project priorities.

The most precise assessment of impact requires quantitative estimates for each risk. Few risks relate only to a single aspect of the project, so there may be a collection of measurement estimates, generally including at least cost and schedule impact. Cost is conceptually the simplest, because it is unambiguously measured in dollars, yen, euros, or some other monetary unit, and any adverse variance will directly affect the project budget. Schedule impact is not as simple, because not every activity delay will necessarily represent an impact to the schedule. Activities off the critical path will generate schedule impact only for adverse variances that exceed the available float.

As with other project estimating, determining cost and schedule variances attributable to risks is neither easy nor necessarily accurate. Quantitative assessments of risk impact may look precise, but the accuracy of such estimates is often questionable, due to optimism and other bias. Optimism bias leads to general underestimation of risk impact, similar to the effect it has on project estimates in general. As with probability, most people tend to align their expectations with their preferences (overestimating beneficial outcomes and discounting adverse ones), so underestimating potential damage from risks can be substantial. Other sources of bias can also lead to underestimation of impact, including availability (when you lack data you need, using other information that happens to be handy), representativeness (excessive reliance on expectations and stereotypes) and even anchoring (aligning estimates with recently encountered numbers, even when they are irrelevant)—all of which tend to result in faulty estimates.

The discussion of risk impact here so far has focused on measurable project information—even the qualitative categories tend to be based on numerical ranges or percentage changes. Limiting impact assessment to such factors overlooks risk impact that may be difficult to quantify. For some risks this approach may ignore factors that may be highly significant. Because the impact resulting from these other factors can be hard to determine with precision, it is often ignored or assumed to be irrelevant for project risk assessment. Categories for these more "qualitative" types of impact, listed in sequence from the most narrow perspective to the broadest, include:

- Personal consequences
- Career penalties
- Loss of team productivity
- Team discord
- Organizational impact
- Business and financial consequences

Measurable consequences for some of these factors may be roughly quantified, at least in the short term. The last two listed types of impact, which are the most severe, can likely be estimated by someone in your organization, although probably not by you or your team. And even estimates made by others who have a wider perspective may vastly underestimate true long-term overall effects.

It is difficult to include the possible consequences for each of these categories of impact into your risk assessment. But despite the challenges, it is worthwhile to carefully consider and describe the potential impact from these factors, because the true overall impact for many project risks may well be dominated by them. Here are some suggestions about how to include these factors when prioritizing your risks. Although not exhaustive, the lists provide guidance and a starting point.

Many risks faced by projects include potential **personal consequences** that can be quite severe, ranging from inconveniences and aggravations to major impositions. These include:

- Personal relationship troubles, marital problems, and divorce
- Canceled vacations
- Missed family activities
- Excessive unpaid overtime

- Fatigue and exhaustion
- Deterioration of health
- Exposure to unsafe conditions, poisonous or volatile chemicals, dangerous environments, or undesirable modes of travel
- Loss of face, embarrassment, lowered prestige, bruised ego, and reduced self-esteem
- Required apologies and "groveling"

Major project difficulties can lead to a variety of **career penalties**, and personal reputations may suffer, leading to:

- Job loss
- A bad performance appraisal
- Demotion
- Lowered job security, diminished prospects for promotion

Both during and following a major risk, team members may work less efficiently. **Loss of team productivity** may lead to:

- Additional meetings, reporting, reviews, and interruptions
- Individuals assuming responsibility for work assigned to others
- Exhaustion of project reserves and contingency funds
- Increased communication overhead, especially if across multiple time zones
- Added stress, tension, and pressure
- More errors and inaccuracies
- Burnout

- Chaos, confusion
- Rework

Even if productivity is unaffected, **team discord** may rise. The success of a project relies on maintaining good teamwork among your project contributors. When things start to unravel, the consequences can include:

- Conflict, hostility, resentment, and short tempers
- Lack of cooperation and strained relationships
- Low morale
- Frustration, disappointment, and discouragement
- Demoralization and disgruntlement

Project risk consequences may lead to **organizational impact** that extends well beyond your current project's prospects for success. Some of these include:

- Delayed concurrent projects
- Late starts for following projects
- Resignations and staff turnover
- Loss of sponsor (and stakeholder) confidence, trust, and goodwill
- Questioning of methods and processes
- Ruined team reputations
- Micromanagement and mistrust by supervisors
- Required escalations and expediting of work
- The need to get lawyers involved

Finally, some risks will have significant **business and financial consequences**. Although these effects can theoretically be estimated and quantified, the true costs may only be clear after—and often well after—the project. Some examples are:

- Loss of business to competitors and competitive disadvantage
- Bad press, poor public relations, and loss of organizational reputation
- Customer dissatisfaction and unhappy clients
- Loss of future business and lowered revenues
- Reduced margins and profits
- Loss of client trust and confidence
- Complications resulting from failure to meet legal, regulatory, industry standards, or other compliance requirements
- Damaged partner relationships
- Reduced performance of the project deliverable
- Compromised quality or reliability
- Rushed, inadequate testing
- Missed windows of opportunity
- Continued cost of obsolete systems or facilities
- Inefficient, unpleasant manual work-arounds
- Service outages and missed service level agreements
- Bankruptcy and business failure (if the project is big enough)

Although for some risks the short-term quantifiable impact on your project's schedule or budget may be modest, the overall consequences, particularly some of the items on the last two lists, will have major impact on the organization. Even though these potential impacts may be primarily qualitative, it is desirable to integrate them into your risk assessment and prioritization. One way to do this is to apply impact criteria such as in the five-level assessment demonstrated in the following table.

RISK IMPACT	CRITERIA
Very Low	Any impact that can be handled within a single status cycle and would likely not be visible outside the project team
Low	Any impact that can be dealt with within the project team and has no anticipated long-term effects
Moderate	Any impact that would result in significant project replanning or that could lead to a noticeable and inconvenient effect on the organization
High	Any impact that would threaten the project's objective (failure to meet one or more of the project's triple constraint parameters) or might lead to significant, measurable longer-term business impact for the organization
Very High	A project "showstopper" that would result in cancellation, or a risk that has potential for overall long-term business impact in excess of the project's budget

Analysis based on these criteria remains subjective, but it provides a practical way to assess the relative importance of project risks—even risks where measurable impact is difficult to pin down.

Qualitative impact assessment using three to five categories is usually relatively easy, and it is sufficient for prioritizing risks based on severity. Techniques such as polling, interviewing, team discussions, and reviews of planning data are effective for assigning risks to impact categories. As with probability assessment for each risk, the best foundation for quantitative estimates of impact is history, along with techniques such as Delphi, computer modeling, and consulting peers and experts.

For quantitative assessments of impact in situations that frequently repeat, statistics may be available. A good way to provide credible quantitative impact data is to select the mean of the distribution for initial estimates of duration or cost and use the difference between that estimate and the measured "90 percent" point. This principle is the basis for PERT analysis. (The PERT estimating techniques were discussed in chapters 4 and 5. Other aspects of PERT and related techniques for dealing with project uncertainty are covered later in this chapter and in chapter 9.)

QUALITATIVE RISK ASSESSMENT

The starting point for risk assessment is a sequenced list of risks, rank-ordered by perceived severity. It is most common to sort the listed risks from most to least significant using your assessment of loss times likelihood. If your list of risks is short enough, you can quickly arrange the list based on a few passes of pair-wise comparisons, switching any adjacent risks where the more severe of the two is lower on the list. The most serious risks will bubble to the top and the more trivial ones will sink to the bottom. This technique is generally done by a single individual.

A similar technique, related to Delphi, combines data from lists sorted individually by each member of a team. The risks on each list are assigned a score equal to their position on the list, and all the scores for each risk are summed. The risk with the lowest total score heads the composite list, and the rest of the list can be arranged based on the aggregate scores. If there are significant variances in some of the lists, further discussion and an additional iteration may provide better consensus. A list based on multiple perspectives is generally more objective than a sequence created by an individual, and it will be credible to most because the result represents input from the whole team.

Although these sorting techniques produce an ordered risk list, such a list shows only relative risk severity, without indication of the project exposure that each risk represents.

Risk Assessment Tables

Qualitative risk assessment based on explicit categorization of both probability and impact provides greater insight into the absolute risk severity. A risk assessment table or spreadsheet where risks are listed with category assignments for both probability and impact, as in figure 7-1, is one approach for this. (This data is also part of a typical project risk register.)

Risks	Probability	Impact	Overall Risk

Figure 7-1: Risk Assessment Table

After listing each risk, assign a qualitative rating (such as High/Moderate/Low) for both probability and impact. Consider all potential impact, not just that which is easily measured, and be skeptical about probabilities. The last column, "Overall Risk," is based on "loss times likelihood." Although any number of rating categories may be used, the quickest method that results in a meaningful sort uses three categories (defined as in the earlier discussions of probability and impact) and assigns either combinations of the categories or weights such as 1, 3, and 9 for low, moderate, and high, respectively. An example of a sorted qualitative assessment for five risks might look like figure 7-2.

Risks	Probability (H/M/L)	Impact (H/M/L)	Overall Risk
Software Guru Is Not Available	M	H	HM
Consultant Is Incompetent	M	M	M
Purchased Component Comes Late	L	H	M
Software Development Is Too Slow	L	M	ML
Needed Test Gear Is Not Available	L	L	L

■ **Figure 7-2:** Qualitative Risk Assessment Example

For the data in the last column, categories may be combined (as shown), factors multiplied (the numbers would be 27, 9, 9, 3, and 1), or "stoplight" icons displayed to indicate risk (red for high, yellow for moderate, and green for low). From a table such as figure 7-2, you can select risks above a certain level, such as moderate, for further attention.

Risk Assessment Matrices

An alternative method for qualitative risk assessment involves placing risks on a two-dimensional matrix, where the rows and columns represent the categories of probability and impact. The matrices may be two-by-two, three-by-three, or larger. Risk matrices are generally square, but they may have different numbers of categories for probability and impact. Figure 7-3 is a typical example of a five-by-five matrix.

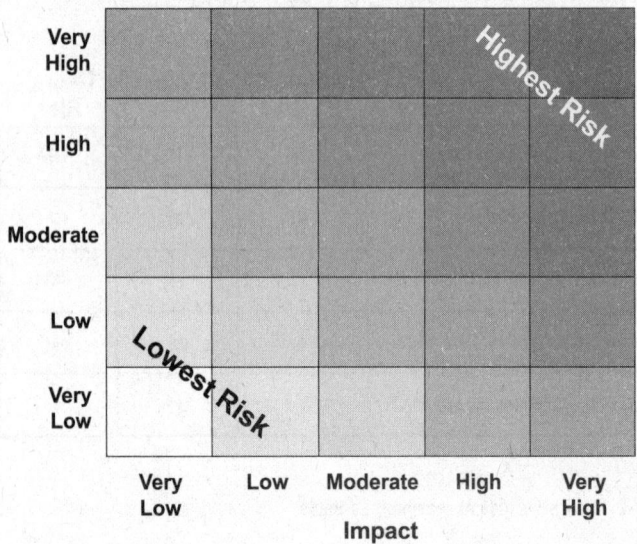

Figure 7-3: Risk Assessment Matrix

Such matrices are often displayed in color, with green cells in the lower left, yellow ones in the middle, and red cells in the upper right. Versions like this are also called "heat maps." The farther up and to the right a risk is assessed to be, the higher the overall risk severity. Risks are selected for management based on whether the cell in the matrix represents a risk above some predetermined level of exposure. An organization's risk tolerance (or appetite) is generally bounded by one of the sets of lighter gray cells in the matrix. Two-dimensional assessment matrices can be useful for displaying modest numbers of risks, but they do have some shortcomings. One is the implied equivalence of risks along the central diagonal connecting low-probability, high-impact risks and high-probability, low-impact risks. In fact, there is a big difference between "frequently encountered trivial impact risks" and "low probability showstopper risks." The first may mostly be annoyances and warrant little or no consideration, but you ignore the latter only at your peril. A second issue with the heat map is the quality of the data in it. Especially for five-by-five matrices, placement within the middle categories for both probability and impact may imply more precise analysis than is realistic.

A matrix such as figure 7-3 is usually applied to the analysis of risks having negative consequences (threats). This type of diagram may also be used to assess uncertain project opportunities. Some of the opportunities discussed in chapter 6 relate to events that might or might not happen. For these opportunities assessment is based on likelihood and gain (rather than loss). An example of this type of opportunity might be buying something needed by the project that occasionally goes on sale. If you believe that there may be an opportunity to purchase the item at a reduced price, managing this "risk" could involve delaying the purchase hoping to take advantage of the sale price. For most projects, there are not many uncertain opportunities of this sort compared with risks having adverse consequences.

For analysis of uncertain opportunities, the definition of probability is unchanged. The impact is also similar, but for opportunities the categories relate to beneficial variances, not harmful ones. Using the same matrix, you can assess potentially positive events to determine those that deserve further attention—again by focusing near the corner representing the combination of highest impact and probability. Another variant on this matrix technique joins together the threat matrix and a mirror-image opportunity matrix into a single matrix (for this case, five cells high and ten cells wide). You find the highest impact in the middle of such a hybrid matrix, so the uncertain events most deserving your attention will be those in the cells near the top and center of the combined matrix.

Assessing Options

Standard project scheduling software and workflow analysis methods do not generally support the use of conditional branching. Because it is not uncommon to have places in a project schedule where one of several possible alternatives, outcomes, or decisions could be chosen, you need some method for analyzing the situation. One qualitative way around this limitation is to construct a baseline plan using the assumption that seems most likely and deal with the other possible outcomes as risks. If it is not possible to determine which outcome may be most likely, a prudent risk manager will usually select the one with the longest duration (or highest cost) to include in the project baseline, but any one option may be selected. Assessing the risk associated with choosing incorrectly involves determining the estimated impact to the project when something different occurs, weighted by the probability of this happening (loss times likelihood once again). List all significant workflow alternatives in your risk register and assess them along with your other project risks and uncertainties.

Data Quality Assessment

Not all risks are equally well understood. Some risks happen regularly, so for these data may be plentiful. Other project risks arise from work that is unique compared with past projects. Assessment of probability and impact for these risks tends to be based on inadequate information, so it's common to underestimate overall risk.

Even with qualitative risk assessment, these poorly understood risks can be identified and singled out for special treatment. For each assessment, consider the quality, reliability, and integrity of the data used to categorize probability and impact. Where the information seems weak, seek out experts or other sources of better information. You can also err on the side of caution and raise your probability and impact estimates to elevate the visibility of the risk.

Other Impact Dimensions for Qualitative Assessment

Although a risk that has high probability and impact will require your attention, those that relate to work well into the future may not need it immediately. Other aspects of risk that may enter into qualitative assessment are urgency and surprise. The impact of even a modest risk can cause harm to your project overall if it happens early and affects the perception of your competence or the teamwork of your contributors. Risks tend to cascade, so early problems may result in more trouble later in the project. If a risk relates to work that is imminent, factor this into your impact assessment, increasing impact estimates where justified.

Some risks are relatively easy to see coming. Other risks, such as the examples from the PERIL database describing faulty late deliverables from an outsourcing partner, are harder to anticipate. Consider the trigger events for each risk when estimating consequences, and increase your impact assessment of risks where the harm could be amplified by the surprise factor.

Risks Requiring Further Attention

The main objective of qualitative risk assessment is to identify major risks by prioritizing the known project risks and rank-ordering them from most significant to least. You can populate a sequenced list using any of the methods described, but the use of three categories (low, moderate, and high) for both probability and impact generally provides a good balance of adequate analysis and minimal effort and debate. However you analyze and sort the list, you need to determine which risks deserve further consideration.

The first several risks on your risk register sorted by severity nearly always warrant your attention, but the question of how far down the list to go is not necessarily simple. One idea is to read down the list, focusing on the consequences and the likelihood of each risk until you reach the first one that won't keep you awake at night. The "gut feel" test is not a bad way to initially set the boundary for your sorted risk register. A similar idea using consensus has team members individually select the cut-off point, and then discuss as a team where the line should be, based on individual and group experiences. You can also set an absolute limit, such as moderate overall risk, or you can use a diagonal stair-step boundary from the upper left to the lower right in a matrix. Whatever method you choose, review each of the risks that is not selected to ensure that there are none below the line that deserve your attention, carefully considering any risks that could result in severe consequences.

Following this examination, you are ready to prepare an abridged list of risks for potential further quantitative analysis and management.

QUANTITATIVE RISK ASSESSMENT

Quantitative risk assessment involves more effort than qualitative techniques, so qualitative methods are generally applied first to sort and select significant risks. This is not absolutely necessary, though, because qualitative methods using tables and matrices have quantitative analogues that you may use to prioritize your risk register. Additional techniques for quantitative project risk assessment include sensitivity analysis, statistical methods, risk decision trees, and computer simulations.

Quantitative Risk Assessment Tables

For quantitative assessment, tables similar to figures 7-1 and 7-2 may be used by replacing the categories for probability and impact with absolute numerical estimates. For each risk, estimate the impact in cost, effort, time (considering only time in excess of any available scheduling flexibility or "float"), or other factors, and then assess overall risk as the product of the impact estimates and the selected probability. One drawback of using this method for sequencing risks is that for some risks it may be difficult to develop consensus estimates for both the impact and probability. A second, more serious issue is that impact may be measured in more than one way (for example, time or money), making it difficult to determine a single uniform quantitative assessment of overall risk.

Although you could certainly list impacts of various kinds, weighted using the estimated probabilities, you may find it difficult to rank order your list based on this data. One way to overcome this is to focus on only one type of impact, such as time, and convert impact of other kinds into an equivalent project duration slip (as was done for the PERIL database). You could also develop parallel tables, one for cost, another for schedule, and others for scope, quality, safety, or any other type of impact for which you can develop meaningful numerical estimates. You can then sort each table on a consistent basis, and select risks from each for further attention. This multiple-table process also requires you to do a final check of unselected risks to detect any that are significant only when all potential consequences are considered in aggregate.

Two-Dimensional Risk Graphs for Quantitative Analysis

A qualitative matrix such as the one in figure 7-3 may be converted to a quantitative tool by replacing the row and column labels with perpendicular axes. Probability on the vertical axis runs from zero to 100 percent, with impact plotted on the horizontal axis from zero to some upper limit (perhaps using an exponential scale). Each risk identified represents a point in the two-dimensional space, and risks requiring further attention will again be found up and to the right, beyond some defined boundary for "risky." As with tables, this method is most useful when all risks can be normalized to some meaningful single measure of impact such as cost or time. Alternatively, you may employ several graphs, each based on a different impact measure.

A variation on this concept plots risks on a pair of axes that represent estimated project cost and project schedule variances, representing each risk using a "bubble" that is sized proportionately with estimated probability instead of a single point. Because impact is higher for bubbles farther from the origin, several boundaries are defined for the graph. A diagonal close to the origin defines significant risk for the large (very likely) bubbles, and other diagonals farther out define significant exposure for the smaller bubbles. In figure 7-4, there are several risks that are clearly significant. Risk F has the highest total impact, and Risk E is not far behind. Others would be selected based on their positions relative to the boundaries of the graph.

Sensitivity Analysis

The damage actually caused by a given risk involves more than just a simple assessment of impact. Schedule risks not affecting resources are significant only when the estimated slippage exceeds any available float. For simple projects, a quick inspection of the

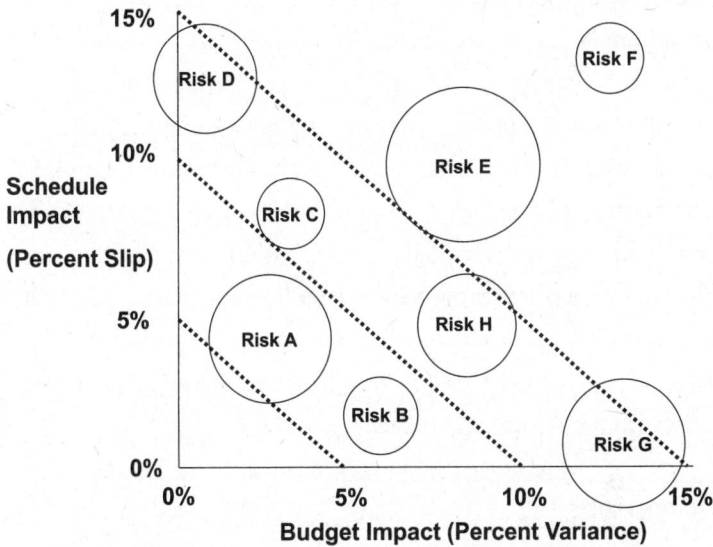

Figure 7-4: Risk Assessment Graph

plan using the risk list will distinguish the risks that are most likely to cause substantial damage. For more complex networks of activities, using a copy of the project data entered into a scheduling tool provides a fast way to detect risks (and combinations of risks) that are most likely to result in project delay. "What if" schedule analysis uses worst-case estimates to investigate the overall project impact for each risk. By sequentially entering your worst-case durations and then backing them out, you can see the quantitative schedule sensitivity to each schedule risk, or combinations of them.

Unlike activity slippage, all adverse cost variances contribute to budget overruns. However, for some projects not all cost impact is accounted for in the same way. If a risk results in an out-of-pocket expense for the project, then it impacts the budget directly. If the cost impact involves a capital purchase, then the project impact may be only a portion of the actual cost, and in some cases the entire expense may be accounted for elsewhere. An increase in overhead cost, such as a conference room commandeered as a "war room" for a troubled project, may or may not be charged back to the project directly. Increased costs for communications, duplication, shipping, and other services considered routine are frequently not borne directly by individual projects. Travel costs may also not be allocated directly. Although it is generally true that all cost and other resource impact is proportionate to the magnitude of the variance, it may be worthwhile to segregate potential direct cost variances from any that are indirect.

Decision Trees

When only a small number of options or potential outcomes are possible, decision trees can also be useful for quantitative risk assessment. Decision tree analysis is a quantitative version of the qualitative assessment process for "Assessing Options" discussed previously. Decision trees can be used to evaluate alternatives prior to selecting one of them to execute. The concept is applied to risk analysis in a project by using the weights and estimates to ascertain potential impact for specific alternatives.

Whenever there are points in the project where several options are possible, each can be planned and assigned a probability (the sum for all options totaling 100 percent). As with PERT, an "expected" estimate for either duration or cost may be derived by weighting the estimates for each option and summing these figures to get a "blended" result. Based on the data in figure 7-5, a project plan containing a generic activity (that might be any of the three options) with an estimate of sixteen days would result in a more realistic plan than simply using the twelve-day estimate of the "most likely" option. The schedule exposure of the risk situation here may be estimated by noting the maximum adverse variance (an additional four days, if the activity is schedule critical) and associating this with an expected probability of 35 percent. (An alternative treatment here would be to assume the worst and schedule twenty days, treating the other possibilities as opportunities to be managed.)

Weighted Duration

25% → Alternative A (17 days) — 4.2 days

Investigate Alternatives → 35% → Alternative B (20 days) — 7 days

40% → Alternative C (12 days) — 4.8 days

"Expected" Duration = 16 days

Figure 7-5: Decision Tree for Duration

Decision analysis may also be used to guide project choices that have varying costs. You can use decision trees to evaluate expected monetary value for alternatives to explore expected costs and potential cost variances. Decision analysis can help in minimizing project risks whenever there are several alternatives, such as either upgrading existing equipment or purchasing new hardware. The analysis of costs in figure 7-6 argues for replacement to minimize cost variance (none, instead of the $20,000 to $120,000 associated with the upgrade), and for the upgrade to minimize the expected cost. As is usual on projects, there is a trade-off between minimizing project parameters and minimizing risk—you must decide which is more important and balance the decisions with your eyes open.

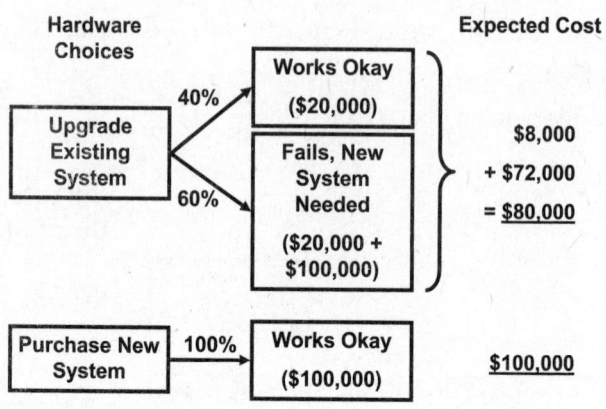

Figure 7-6: Decision Tree for Cost

Simulation and Modeling

Decision trees are useful for situations where you have discrete estimates. In more complex cases, options may be modeled or simulated using Monte Carlo or other computer-based techniques. If the range of possibilities for an activity's duration or cost are assumed to be a statistical distribution, the standard deviation (or variance) of the distribution provides a measure of risk. The larger the range selected for the distribution, the higher the risk for that activity. For single activities, modeling with a computer is rarely necessary, but when several activities (or all the project's activities) are considered together, computer-based simulations can be useful and effective. Use of both software tools and manual approximations for this are key topics in chapter 9.

PERT Methodology

The term "PERT" has assumed a number of meanings for project management. The most common usage, which actually has little to do with PERT methodology, is associated with the graphical network of activities used for project planning, often called a "PERT chart." Logical project networks are used for PERT analysis, but PERT methodology went beyond the deterministic, single-point estimates of duration to which a typical "PERT chart" is generally limited. A second, slightly less common meaning for PERT relates to three-point estimating (discussed in earlier chapters), but the original purpose of PERT methodology was actually much broader.

The principal reason PERT was originally developed in the late 1950s was to help the US military quantitatively manage risk for large defense projects. PERT was used on the development of the Polaris missile systems, on the NASA manned space projects, including the Apollo moon missions, and on countless other government-funded projects. The motivation behind all of this was the observation that as programs became larger, they were more likely to be late and to have significant cost overruns. PERT was created to provide a better basis for setting expectations on these massive, expensive endeavors.

PERT is a specific example of quantitative risk analysis, and it can be applied to exposures for both schedule (PERT Time, discussed in chapter 4) and budget (PERT Cost, discussed in chapter 5). PERT is based on some statistical assumptions about the project plan, requiring both estimates of likely outcomes (the estimates typically generated) and estimates of the uncertainty for these outcomes (which PERT methodology added). PERT techniques may be used to analyze all project activities or only those activities that represent high perceived risk. In either case, the purpose of PERT is to provide data on overall project risk, for schedule, cost, or both. PERT concepts for range estimates are useful in gathering risk information about project activities, particularly concerning the pessimistic (or worst-case) estimates. PERT, along with other methods such as computer-based Monte Carlo analysis, depends on the concept of range estimates to analyze risk for the project as a whole. Chapter 9 explores assessing overall project risk using PERT methodology and related techniques.

Statistical Concepts and Probability Distributions

The PERT methodology introduced the idea of using three-point range estimates to examine project uncertainty. Nearly all project analysis prior to the 1950s was based primarily on single-point, deterministic estimates. PERT methodology assumed a continuum of possibilities. It generally assumed that three-point activity estimates would define a Beta distribution, a type of bell-shaped probability density function that could skew to the right or left. Figure 7-5 is an example of a Beta distribution fitted to three estimates for activity duration. This example uses the traditional "1 percent tails" to bound the range of possibilities, but PERT analysis can also be based on 5 or 10 percent tails. The Beta distribution was used initially because it was flexible enough to accommodate different "shapes," was not hard to understand (or draw), and was simple enough to be used for the relatively primitive computer analysis available for projects at the time.

Probability distribution functions, or even discrete data values defined by a histogram, may better describe the range of potential impact for a given risk. Some additional distribution types commonly used today include:

- **Triangular:** a linear rise from optimistic estimate to the most likely, followed by a linear decline to the pessimistic estimate.
- **Normal:** the Gaussian bell-shaped curve, with the most likely and expected values both at the center of a symmetric distribution.
- **Uniform:** all values in the range are assumed equally likely, also with the most likely and expected values both at the midpoint.

There are many other more exotic statistical distributions available for modeling, along with limitless possible histograms. Triangular (a skewed example is in figure 7-8), uniform (figure 7-9), and other bounded types of distributions are "closed," in that all expected data points are confined within defined numerical bounds. Beta (figure 7-7), normal (figure 7-10), and other similar distributions are "open," with no theoretical upper (or lower) limit on possible values.

The precise shape of the distribution you choose, and even whether it is bounded or not, will generally have only a small

■ **Figure 7-7:** Typical "Beta-Type" Distribution

■ **Figure 7-8:** A Triangular Distribution

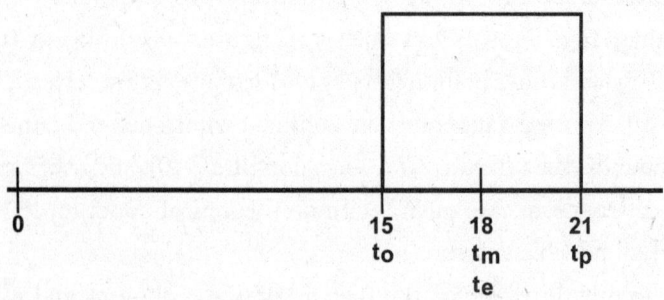

■ **Figure 7-9:** A Uniform Distribution

■ **Figure 7-10:** A Normal, Gaussian Distribution

effect on the two parameters that matter the most for risk analysis: the mean and the standard deviation of the distribution. Assessment of risk is based primarily on these two parameters, and they vary little among the distribution types available. In addition, although it is theoretically possible to carry out a detailed risk analysis mathematically, it is impractical. Project risk analysis using probability distributions is most commonly done by computer simulation or by rough manual methods that approximate the results. From a practical standpoint, the choice of a specific distribution for each activity has only minimal effect on quantitative assessment of risk for activities. For project risk analysis, the choice of a particular density function for activity data is not crucial.

To illustrate this, figures 7-8, 7-9, and 7-10 show expected duration estimates calculated using the weighted average PERT formula discussed in chapter 4 with upper and lower bounds of fifteen and twenty-one days. The expected durations, t_e, vary somewhat between the distributions, but for quantitative risk assessment you would select some value above the mean. A "90 percent" point is not uncommon for this, and for each of the distributions in the examples, all will be quite close to the upper (t_p) estimate. Because t_p is twenty-one days, the 90 percent point for each of these distributions will be roughly twenty days (rounded off to the nearest whole day), regardless of the distribution selected. There are ways to calculate all of this with very high precision, displaying many (seemingly) significant digits in the results. Considering the precision and expected accuracy of the input data, though, the results are at best accurate only to the nearest whole day. Arguments over the "best" distribution to use and endless fretting over how to proceed are not a fruitful investment of your time. Assessment of uncertainty will rely on the estimated variance for the chosen distribution, which for all these examples will be similar because the range limits are the same.

As you can see, almost any reasonable choice of distribution will provide comparable results for activity risk analysis, so use whichever concepts you find most appropriate and easiest to work with.

At the project level, where uncertainty data for all the work is combined, the distributions chosen for specific activities become even less relevant. When there are many uncertain activities in the model for a project, the aggregate project-level cost and duration distributions depend almost not at all on the specific distribution shapes selected. Chapter 9, on project-level risk assessment, will explore this topic in some detail.

Setting Estimate Ranges

While it generally matters little what distribution you select for your range estimates, the "error bars" you define matter a great deal. Setting the range that is too narrow (a common bias) will materially diminish the quantitative perception of risk. Risk, assessed using PERT or similar techniques, is based on the total anticipated range of possible outcomes, which varies directly with the estimation uncertainty.

Arriving at credible upper and lower limits for cost and duration estimates is never easy. One way to develop this data is through further analysis of potential root causes of each activity that has substantial perceived risk. As discussed in chapter 4, reviewing worst-case scenarios is a powerful tool for estimating the upper limits. Be realistic about potential consequences; it is human nature to minimize or overlook the potential impact of risks.

When there is sufficient historical information available, the limits (and possibly even the shape) of the distribution may be inferred from the data. Discussions and interviews with experts, project stakeholders, and contributors may also provide information useful in setting credible range boundaries.

In any event, quantitative assessment of risk impact depends on credible three-point (or at least expected and worst-case) project estimates.

Key Ideas for Activity Risk Analysis

- Assess probability and impact for each project risk.
- Understand and work to minimize biases.
- Use qualitative risk analysis to prioritize risks.
- Apply quantitative risk analysis techniques to better understand significant risks.
- When using PERT or related techniques, keep things simple.

PANAMA CANAL: RISKS (1906–1914)

As with any project of the canal's size and duration, risks were everywhere. Based on assessment of cost and probability, the most severe were diseases, mudslides, the constant use of explosives, and the technical challenges of constructing the locks.

Diseases were less of a problem on the US project, but health remained a concern. The first two managers both cited tropical disease among their reasons for resigning from the project. Life in the tropics in the early 1900s was neither comfortable nor safe. The enormous death toll from the earlier project made this exposure a top priority.

Mudslides were common for both the French and the US projects, as the soil of Panama is not stable, and earthquakes made things worse. Whenever the sloping sides of the cut collapsed, there was danger to the working crews and potential serious damage to the digging and railroad equipment. In addition to this, it was demoralizing to face the repair and rework following each slide, and the predicted additional effort required to excavate repeatedly in the same location multiplied the cost of construction. This risk affected both schedule and budget; despite precautions, major setbacks were frequent.

Explosives were in use everywhere. In the Culebra Cut, massive boulders were common, and workers set off dynamite charges to reduce them to movable fragments. The planned transit for ships through the manmade lakes was a rainforest filled with large, old trees, and these, too, had to be removed with explosives. The dynamite of that era was not stable, especially in the tropics. It exploded in storage, in transit to the worksites, while being set in place for use, and in many other unintended situations. The probability of premature detonation was high, and the risk to human life was extreme.

Beyond these daunting risks, the largest technical challenge on the project was the locks. They were gigantic mechanisms, among the largest and most complex construction ever attempted. Although locks had been used on canals for a long time, virtually all of them had been built for smaller boats navigating freshwater rivers and lakes. Locks had never before been constructed for large oceangoing ships. (The canal at Suez has no locks; as with the original plan for Panama, it is entirely at sea level.) The doors for the locks were to be huge, and therefore heavy. The volume of water held by the locks when filled was so great that the pressure on the doors would be immense, and the precision required for the seams where the doors closed to hold in the water was also unprecedented for manmade objects so large. The locks would be enormous boxes with sides and bottoms formed of concrete, which also was a challenge, particularly in an earthquake zone. For all this, the biggest technological hurdle was the requirement that all operations be electric. Because earlier canals were much smaller, usually the lock doors were cranked open and shut and the boats were pulled in and out by animals. (To this day, the trains used to guide ships into and out of the locks at Panama are called "electric mules.") The design, implementation, and control of a canal using the new technology of electric power—and the hydroelectric installations required to supply enough electricity—all involved emerging, poorly understood technology. Without the locks, the canal would be useless, and the risks associated with resolving all of these technical problems were enormous.

These severe risks were but a few of the many challenges faced on the canal project. Each was singled out for substantial continuing attention. At the end of chapter 8 we will explore how these challenges were managed.

MANAGING ACTIVITY RISKS

"Statistics are no substitute for judgment."

—HENRY CLAY, US Senator

R isk assessment provides a prioritized risk register. When you review this list, it becomes clear just how much trouble your project is in. An accumulation of significant scope risks may indicate that your project is literally impossible. Too many schedule or resource risks may indicate that your project is unlikely to complete within its constraints. Project risk management can be a potent tool for transforming a seemingly doomed project into a merely challenging one.

Managing risk begins with your prioritized risk register. Based on your sorted list, you can set the boundary that defines your most significant risks. Risk response planning uses this boundary as a guide; all the risks above the line deserve at least some attention. In addition, a prudent project leader reviews the whole list, at least briefly, to reconsider any risks that have significant consequences. When the potential impact for a risk exceeds acceptable limits, a response may be in order even if the probability is estimated to be very small. There may also be low-rated risks for which there are simple, cheap responses. It makes little sense to ignore risks for which there are trivial cures.

For each risk you deem significant, you can begin to consider root causes to help you determine your best management strategy. For risks where the project team has influence over the root cause, you can develop ideas to reduce or eliminate the risk, and then modify the project plans to incorporate these ideas wherever it is feasible. For risks that cannot be avoided or that remain significant, you can also develop contingency plans for recovery should the risk occur.

ROOT-CAUSE ANALYSIS

What, if anything, can be done about a risk depends a great deal on its causes. For each identified risk that is assessed as significant, your response planning begins by determining the source and the type of the risk.

The process for cause-and-effect analysis is straightforward. For risk analysis, begin by reviewing the listed risks and their descriptions. The next step is to brainstorm possible sources for the risk. Any brainstorming process will be effective as long as it is successful in determining conditions or events that may lead to the risk. You can begin with major cause categories (such as scope, schedule, and resource) or simply think about specific factors that may lead to the risk. However you begin the analysis, complete it by organizing the information into categories of root cause. Some redundancy between items listed in various categories is common.

Cause-and-effect analysis using fishbone diagrams, so called because of their appearance, was popularized by Japanese quality movement guru Dr. Kaoru Ishikawa. (They are also sometimes called Ishikawa diagrams.) These diagrams may be used to display root causes of risk visually, allowing deeper understanding of the source and likelihood of potential problems. Organize the possible causes into a branching diagram similar to the one in figure 8-1. Note that some causes may themselves have multiple potential sources. Continue the root-cause analysis process for each significant risk in the project.

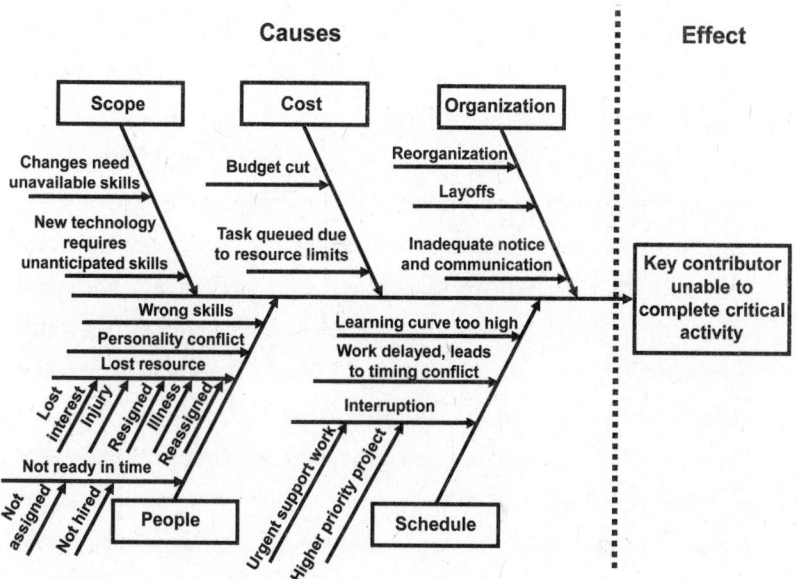

Figure 8-1: Fishbone Diagram Example

Fishbone-type diagrams are useful for displaying sources of risk. This type of "fault tree" structure is also used for bow-tie analysis. The initial portion of a bow-tie diagram is based on a root-cause hierarchy, and it includes information about prevention strategies. The remainder of a bow-tie diagram focuses on the consequences of the risk event, including your plans for recovery. You will find more on bow-tie analysis and an example at the end of this chapter.

CATEGORIES OF RISK

In dealing with risk, there are really only two options. In an advertisement some years ago, the options were demonstrated pictorially using an egg. On the left side of the picture was an egg falling toward a pillow held in a person's hand. On the right side was a broken egg oozing over the flat, hard surface it had smashed into, with a second hand swooping in with a paper towel. The left side was titled "Prevention" and the right side "Recovery." Management of risk in projects always involves these tactics—prevention to deal with causes, and recovery to deal with effects.

The three categories of project risk are controllable known risks, uncontrollable known risks, and unknown risks. All the risks cataloged in your risk register are known risks, and each of them are either under your control or not. It is possible to plan for response for any listed risk, at least in theory. The third category, unknown risks, is hidden, so specific planning is not generally possible. The best method for managing unknown risk involves setting project reserves, in schedule or budget (or both), based on the measured consequences of unanticipated problems on similar past projects. Keeping track of specific past problems also converts your past unknown risks into known risks. Managing unknown project risk is addressed in chapter 10.

Root-cause analysis not only makes known project risks more understandable, it also shows you how to best manage each risk. Based on the root cause or causes, some risks arise from factors you can control and may therefore be preventable. Other risks are out of your hands, and these risks are generally managed through recovery. These strategies are summarized in figure 8-2.

Known controllable risks are at least partially under the control of the project team. Risks such as the use of a new technology,

■ **Figure 8-2:** Risk Management Strategies

small increases in complexity or performance of a deliverable, or pressure to establish aggressive deadlines are examples of this. Working from an understanding of the root causes for these problems, you may be able to modify your project plans to avoid or minimize the risk.

For known uncontrollable risks, the project team may have essentially no influence on the source of the risk. Loss of key project staff members, business reorganizations, and external project factors such as weather are examples. When these problems are significant, your best tactic is to deal with effects after the risk (if it occurs), using a contingency plan you have prepared in advance.

It is common for a root-cause analysis to uncover some causes that you can control as well as some that you cannot for the same risk. Responding to risks with several possible sources may require both rethinking your plans and preparing for recovery.

Although the dichotomy between controllable and uncontrollable may seem simple, it often is not. The perceived root causes of a risk vary depending on the description of the risk. To take the example of the fishbone diagram in figure 8-1, many of the root causes seem out of the control of the project team, as the risk is described as the loss of a particular person. If the exposure were redefined to be the loss of a particular skill set, which is probably more accurate, then the root causes would shift to ones that the project might influence through cross-training, negotiating for additional staff, or other actions.

Review your risk register, considering options for reframing risks that might provide you with more control and risk response alternatives. Even when a risk seems to be uncontrollable, the venerable idea from quality analysis of "Ask why five times" may open up the perspective on the risk and reveal additional options for response. If weather, earthquakes, or other natural disasters are listed as risks for particular activities, probe deeper into the situation to ask why and how that particular problem would affect the project. The risk may be a consequence of a project assumption or a choice made in planning that could be changed, resulting in a better, less problematic project. Shifting the time, venue, infrastructure, or other parameters of risky activities may remove uncontrollable risks from your project, or at least diminish their potential for harm.

SELECTING RISKS TO ADDRESS

One of the main purposes of qualitative risk assessment is to help you decide which risks to focus on and how to deal with potential problems you identify. Qualitative methods are useful for this, but they rarely provide as clear a picture as you need. The heat map view of risks (as in figure 7-5 in the previous chapter) often comes with a crisp-sounding set of high-risk cells in the grid that deserve attention, with the rest of the map considered low risk. Even without considering the inherent lack of precision and symmetry problems discussed in the last chapter, it is never that simple.

What appears at first to be a simple decision is actually often quite complicated. One way to dealing with this starts with a simpler grid than the standard risk assessment matrix. The grid in figure 8-3 recognizes that even your uncertainty may be uncertain. This three-by-three matrix begins with a defined threshold for high probability based on stakeholder risk tolerance. The threshold is typically in the vicinity of 30 percent or so, high enough that disregarding threats of this sort would result in frequent unpleasant surprises. Low would be below this and considered unlikely by key stakeholders. In between high and low, the grid has provision for "Uncertain" probability, reflecting that some events are infrequent enough that assessing their likelihood is mostly guesswork.

Similarly, you define a threshold for high impact that aligns with significant and visible damage to the project or organization in the eyes of your stakeholders (for example, inevitable changes to project objective, or consequences that would significantly exceed the project's budget, deadline, or other major goals). Low impact will generally be effects that are not visible outside the project, and "Uncertain" catches cases where there is no reliable basis (at least within the project) for assessing the results.

The corner cells with labels in figure 8-3 are the easy cases.

Where the impact and probability assessments are "**High-High**," you need to take the risks seriously. The safest course is to treat these risks the same way you would issues or problems. Plan to develop a response in advance whenever possible. Accept these risks only where there is no credible or cost-effective response possible. For any of these significant risks where prevention is not feasible, develop detailed contingency and recovery options.

Where you have a credible impact and probability assessments of "**Low-Low**," most risks can be safely accepted. For these demonstrably minor risks, ad hoc responses will likely be sufficient.

Probability:

	Low	Uncertain	High
High			Manage
Uncertain			
Low	Accept (Most)		

Impact: Low   Uncertain   High

Figure 8-3: Risk Assessment Considering Uncertainty (the Easy Cases)

But what about all the other cases:

- Low probability risks with high impact estimates?
- Risks with "nonquantitative," but possibly significant impact?
- Any risks where the prevention (avoid/mitigate/transfer) costs are well below the "loss times likelihood."
- Risks with moderate (or low) probability/impact assessments?
- Risks where your best probability estimates are wild guesses?
- Risks where your best impact estimates are unknown or there is a wide spectrum of potential significance?

One case here is the right-hand column of the grid, where impact is estimated to be high. When the probability is also high, as already noted, you need to consider options for dealing with them. But what do you do about the other cases, where your best probability assessment is either low or unknown? However unlikely a risk may seem, it is never safe to assume it will not occur. The entire world had a chance to deal with an example of this, starting in spring 2020. As COVID-19 emerged, while the probability of a single individual getting the virus was low, the consequences—particularly for some subgroups—were serious illness or death. And in sufficiently large populations, even low-probability events add up to a lot of aggregate impact. Whenever the impact of a risk you are examining will be significant, it is best to **manage most** of them. This includes both perceived low-likelihood events and any consequential risks where you are unsure of the probability. Taking all risks seriously whenever potential impact exceeds what you (or your organization) can afford is always prudent, and it's always best to be skeptical of any low-probability risk estimates, because many may be based more on wishful thinking than any realistic analysis. For COVID-19, there have been endless debates about responses that were adopted. What is hard to deny, however, is that based on what was happening and known in mid-2020, not responding at all would have been irresponsible. Some responses had high cost and consequences, and in retrospect have been criticized. Other responses, such as distancing, mask-wearing, and avoiding large, crowded places, required mostly minor inconveniences. Determining how best to respond to a risk is always a judgment call, but when the worst-case consequences of a risk are large it is foolish to do nothing. Plan to accept high-impact risks only when the cost of any response appears high compared with the expected risk, or in cases where you can devise no effective response (and when the project would still make business sense even if the risk occurs).

Regardless of how you plan to respond, retain any risks you choose to accept in your risk register, and plan to explore contingency and recovery plans.

Essentially the same strategy may be applied to the top center column of the grid, where the probability is high and impact is unclear. You should **manage most** of these risks as well, because they are likely to occur and you do not know how much damage they could potentially cause for your project.

The remainder of the center column, where probability is unknown or low, is dangerous to ignore for the same reason. Probabilities aside, the effects of such risks could be project-threatening. In determining your response, **consider worst-case impact**. If you can determine the potential range for impact, document what the worst outcome might be. Manage most of the risks where the consequences could exceed what you and your stakeholders would tolerate. Generally, accept these risks only if the cost of a response seems expensive compared with the worst-case cost of the risk.

The remaining cases on the grid contain low-impact risks with either high or uncertain probabilities. Because the impact for these cases is small and can be contained within your project, you will probably **accept most** of these cases. Recovery from such risks does require revisions to plans and staff assignments, and will tax whatever reserves you have established for your project, but all this generally falls within the purview of competent project management. You should always consider managing any risks in these (and any other) categories where you can devise an effective response that involves only trivial project changes. (Many contract-related risks can be mitigated with a thorough review of all the documents, which although not much fun is not very difficult. Effective project communication is a good preventative for many kinds of risk, and this is really just the project leader's job.) Also consider responses for any risks that could recur frequently and represent an aggregate impact from all the instances that might prove significant. Figure 8-4 shows the earlier figure with the remaining cells populated.

Over time, risks may evolve so strategies for managing them should shift accordingly. To consider the longer-term aspects of the COVID-19 example, vaccines, effective treatments, improved air filtration, and better understanding of transmission rates have over time significantly reduced the risk impact. Even with this, however, many will continue situationally to respond to the residual risk by avoiding large indoor crowds, wearing masks, and bearing other minor inconveniences, particularly during colder weather when threats from this and other diseases tend to increase.

Probability:

	Low	Uncertain	High
High	Accept Most	Manage Most	Manage
Uncertain	Accept Most	Consider Worst-case Impact	Manage Most
Low	Accept Most	Consider Worst-case Impact	Manage Most
Impact:	Low	Uncertain	High

Figure 8-4: Risk Strategies Based on Assessment

Retain all identified risks, even those you choose to accept in your risk register. Plan to monitor and reassess their impact periodically, especially on longer projects. To summarize, develop a response for risks in your risk register for any of the following reasons:

- They are significant risks for which you have a cost-effective response.
- They are risks with high or unknown impact where a response is justified, regardless of assessed probability. (Unless something is literally impossible, you should assume that it will eventually happen.)
- They are minor risks that have simple, low-cost, effective responses.

Other risks in your risk register you will accept without adopting a specific response for any of the following reasons:

- They are significant risks where you could devise no response.
- They are significant risks where the response you developed has a cost too high to justify.
- They are minor risks that do not warrant attention in advance.

RISK RESPONSE PLANNING

Two basic options are available for risk response planning: dealing with causes and dealing with effects. There are, however, variations on both of these themes.

Risk Response Techniques

Dealing with the causes of project threats involves risk prevention—eliminating the risk (**avoidance**), lowering its probability or potential impact (**mitigation**), or making it someone else's problem (**transfer** or **escalation**). Avoidance of risks requires revising your project plans or approach to remove the root cause of the risk from your project. One way to avoid falling off a cliff is to avoid cliffs. Mitigating actions do not remove a risk completely, but they do serve to lower their significance. Some mitigating actions reduce the probability of a risk event, such as inspecting your automobile tires before a long trip. Other mitigations reduce the risk consequences, such as wearing a seat belt when driving to minimize injury. Neither of these actions prevents automobile problems, but they do serve to reduce the overall risk by lowering the "loss" and/or the "likelihood."

Similarly, some damaging risks may be transferred to others, or escalated. Many kinds of financial risks may be transferred to insurance companies; you can purchase coverage that will compensate your losses in the event of a casualty that is covered by the policy. Another tactic for some risks is to delegate their management to others, generally by escalating responsibility to stakeholders who may be in a better position to deal with the risks. Neither of these tactics will entirely remove a risk, however. Transfer can reduce the financial impact should the risk occur, so it can help in cases where the impact of the risk is primarily financial. Escalation broadens the foundation for possible responses and adds high-level attention and visibility to significant risks. Transfer tactics like insurance, and involvement of stakeholders who have significant authority, also provide resources that can be effective in responding to risk effects and aiding in recovery.

Throughout most of this chapter, the term "risk" will be used to describe an uncertain event that could harm the project—a threat. Not all uncertain project events are threats, however. There may also be uncertain *opportunities* where risk management strives to increase the probability or impact. Benefiting from uncertain project opportunities involves embracing these "positive risk" situations. Similar tactics are applied to these potential opportunities, analogous (though reversed) to those just outlined for prevention of threats. Where you might avoid threats by replanning to remove the potential for harm, you would replan the project to **exploit** or to capture the opportunity. You work to make it a certain part of the project. If a required item might go on sale, for example, you might determine the timing of the sale and schedule the purchase around that date. Mitigation serves to reduce the probability or impact of a threat, and the corresponding tactic is to **enhance** the plan to pursue opportunity, making the potential benefits more likely or more helpful. In the case of the sale, you might be unable to determine when (or even if) it might occur, but you could time your purchases around the dates for a sale from last year on the theory that this is when such a sale would be most likely. As with threats, sometimes the strategy involves strength in numbers. Where threats may be transferred to limit their impact, opportunities may be improved when **shared** or in some cases **escalated**. Cost reductions for purchased items comparable to a sale might be available if you can find others with similar needs and make purchases together to take advantage of favorable quantity pricing. There may also be situations where involving high-level stakeholders through escalation can assist in achieving uncertain benefits.

As discussed in earlier chapters, managing opportunities generally involves choices. Choices and decisions, including those involving uncertain opportunities, may require trade-offs and affect other aspects of your project.

Dealing with the effect of a threat may either be done in advance (contingency planning) or after the fact (acceptance). Uncertain opportunities generally need no particular contingency planning; those you choose not to manage are generally ignored. Some trivial risks may be too insignificant to consider preventing. Prevention strategies for other risks may prove too costly or time-consuming. Acceptance can be appropriate for any of these situations; simply plan to deal with the consequences if and when the risk occurs. For more serious problems where avoidance, mitigation, transfer, or escalation are ineffective, impractical, too costly, or impossible, contingency planning is usually the best option.

For some risks, one of these response strategies will be sufficient; for others, you may want to consider several.

Timeline for Known Risks

As was discussed briefly in chapter 6, each activity risk will have a signal, and perhaps more than one, indicating that the risk has crossed over from a possibility to a certainty. This signal, or trigger event, may be in advance of the risk or coincident with it. Triggers may be visible to everyone involved in the project, or they may be subtle and hidden. For each risk, document how you will know the risk is imminent, seeking as much advance notification as possible. Consider the risk: "A key project team member quits." One possible trigger event might be the submission of a resignation letter. This is an obvious trigger, but it is a late one. There are earlier triggers to watch for, such as reduced motivation, erratic attendance, frequent distractions, or even an uncharacteristic improvement in grooming or dress. These triggers are not foolproof and they require effort to monitor, but some may foreshadow other problems even for staff members who are not planning to leave.

In addition to one or more trigger events, identify when in the project plan each risk is most probable, being as precise as possible. For some risks there may be a single exposure related to one specific activity. More general risks (such as loss of key staff members) may occur throughout the project.

Risk management decisions and plans are made in advance of the trigger event, and they include all actions related to avoidance, mitigation, escalation, or transfer, as well as preparation for any contingent actions. Risk management responses that relate to recovery fall on the project timeline after the risk trigger, but are used only if necessary. For each significant risk that you cannot remove from the project, assign an owner to monitor for the trigger event and to be responsible for implementing the contingency plan or otherwise working toward recovery. The risk management timeline is summarized in figure 8-5.

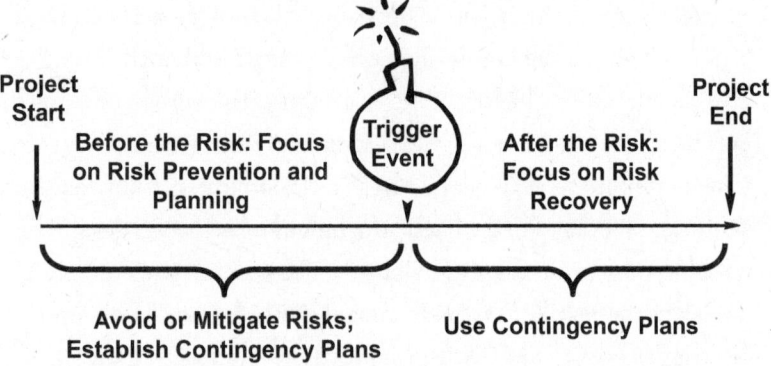

Figure 8-5: Risk Management Timeline

DEALING WITH RISK CAUSES

After you have categorized each risk and identified risks where you can influence some or all of the causes, you are ready to begin developing threat prevention responses. As described earlier, these include *avoid, mitigate, escalate,* and *transfer* (or for uncertain opportunities, *exploit, enhance, escalate,* and *share*). As you develop risk responses, consider both the cost of the ideas and their potential benefits. Your best ideas are potential revisions that can reduce risk and deal with specific potential problems, but they need to earn their way in. Even excellent ideas that completely remove a risk must be set aside if they come at too high a price. Also, you will need to review any tactics you are inclined to adopt to ensure that they do not create significant new risks or bring adverse unintended consequences.

Planning for risk responses begins with generating ideas. Brainstorming with your project team is a good way to generate a range of possible response strategies. When dealing with unfamiliar types of risk, it is also useful to discuss them with peers who have relevant experience and to consult experts and specialists.

Few known risks are completely novel, so it is quite possible that many of the risks in your risk register will have been addressed by earlier projects. A quick review of project retrospective analyses, final reports, "lessons learned," and other archived materials may provide information about how similar risk situations have been resolved in the past. You are likely to find useful ideas for effectively dealing with your current risks (and also valuable information about things that were tried that did not help).

There are also many ideas available in the public domain, in papers, books, and articles and on the web. References on project management, particularly those specific to projects like yours, are filled with practical advice. Life cycles and project management methodologies also provide direction and useful ideas for managing risks.

A number of possible preventative actions follow, including tactics for risk avoidance, mitigation, escalation, and transfer. These can be useful in seeding a brainstorming exercise and in planning for specific responses. These tactics include ideas for dealing with the sort of risks common in the PERIL database. The ideas listed here include some that may be appropriate only for particular kinds of projects, but many tactics will be useful on any type of project.

Risk Avoidance

Avoidance is the most thorough way to deal with risks, because it obliterates them. Unfortunately, avoidance is not possible for all project risks because some risks are tightly coupled to project requirements and goals. Avoiding risks in your project requires you to reconsider choices and decisions you made in defining and planning your project. Most of chapters 3, 4, and 5 concerned using project planning processes to identify risks. Although some of the risks you discovered may be unavoidable, a review of your current plans may turn up opportunities to rearrange the work to remove specific serious risks. Your review may even uncover risks where the problems arise from environmental or infrastructure aspects that could (and should) be changed.

Tactics for avoiding scope risks suggested by the material in chapter 3 include:

- Identify the minimum acceptable deliverable; avoid overdesign ("gold plating").
- Negotiate and clearly document all interface deliverables expected from other projects.

- Avoid untried, unfamiliar, or "bleeding edge" technology whenever practical.
- Plan to design using standard, modular, or well-understood procedures. Look for ways to achieve project specifications using older, tried-and-true methods.
- Buy instead of make.
- Avoid "not invented here" thinking; be willing to leverage work done by others.

Many of your schedule risks are consequences of planning. You may be able to remove sources of schedule risk using ideas covered in chapter 4:

- Reduce the number of critical paths.
- Look for ways to modify the workflow to have fewer activity dependencies.
- Schedule the highest uncertainty activities as early as possible.
- Avoid having the same staff members working on two successive or concurrent critical (or near-critical) activities.
- Decompose lengthy activities further.
- Reschedule work to provide greater flexibility.

Resource risks may also be a consequence of choices you made in resource planning. Explore opportunities to avoid these risks using the concepts of chapter 5:

- Assign a named owner for all required project work.
- Get explicit availability commitments from all project staff (and from their managers).

- Work to limit commitments by project staff to other projects, maintenance and support work, and other time conflicts. Explicitly quantify and document any that remain.
- Modify plans to reduce the load on excessively committed staff.
- Use the best people available for the most critical activities.
- Educate team members to use more efficient or faster methods, and do it early in the project.
- Use mentoring to build teamwork and establish redundancy for critical skills.
- Upgrade or replace older equipment to make work more efficient, and do it at the project start.
- Automate manual work whenever possible.
- Locate and gain access to experts to provide all required skills that are unavailable on the project team.
- Minimize dependence on single individuals or other scarce resources for project work.
- When you use outside services, use the same suppliers that you (or others that you trust) have used successfully in the past.
- Establish contract terms with all suppliers that are consistent with project objectives.

Avoidance tactics are not limited to these ideas by any means. Anything that you can realistically do to eliminate the root cause of a risk by modifying your plans or by successfully lobbying for changes outside your project can potentially avoid risks.

Risk Mitigation

Avoidance can never deal with every significant project risk, so most risk responses rely on mitigation strategies. Risk mitigation serves to reduce the probability and/or the impact of potential problems. Some generic ideas for risk mitigation include:

- Good communication and risk visibility
- Using specialists and generalists
- Strong sponsorship
- Continuing user involvement
- Clear decision priorities

One of the least expensive and strongest preventative actions a project leader can take is to communicate more—and more effectively. Risks and risk consequences that are visible always affect the way that people work. If all the team members are aware how painful the project will become following a risk, they are likely to work, to the best of their ability, in ways that will reduce the impact of known risks. Keeping significant risks visible can also reduce the likelihood that they will occur. Communicate. Communicate. Communicate.

Another broad strategy for managing risk relates to project staffing. Difficult projects benefit from having a mix of specialists and generalists. Specialists are essential on complicated projects because no one can know everything, and a specialist can usually complete assigned work in his or her area of expertise much faster and with fewer errors than a generalist. However, a project team composed only of specialists is not very robust and tends to run into frequent trouble. This happens because project planning on specialist-heavy projects can be very detailed for work involving the specialists' areas, but remarkably vague for other work. Also, such teams may lack broad problem-solving skills. Generalists on a project are needed to fill in the gaps and ensure that project work overall is visible and thoroughly planned. Generalists are also best for solving cross-disciplinary problems. As the head generalist, the project manager should always reserve at least a small percentage of his or her time for problem-solving, helping out on troubled activities, and general firefighting. Even when the project leader has a solid grasp of all the technical project issues, it is useful to have other generalists on the team in case several things on the project get in trouble at the same time. Generalists are often able to reduce the time to solution for problems of all kinds and minimize schedule impact.

Managing project risk is always easier with friends in high places. Establish and work to sustain strong sponsorship for your project. Although strong sponsorship does not ensure a risk-free project, weak (or no) upper-level sponsorship is a significant source of risk. Form a good working relationship with the project sponsor(s) and work to understand their expectations for project information. Reinforce the importance and value of the project regularly, and don't let sponsors forget about you. Validate project objectives with sponsors and customers and work to set realistic expectations. Using your budget and staffing plans, get commitments for adequate funding, staffing, and expertise. Plan to update your management frequently on project progress and challenges, and establish processes for prompt escalation whenever problem situations require authority you lack. (For some risks, escalation—discussed next—could provide your most effective response.) Strong sponsorship reduces timing problems and other risk impact and lowers the probability for many kinds of resource risks.

Project risk will increase, particularly on lengthy projects, whenever the project team is disconnected from the ultimate customers for the deliverable. Establish and maintain contact with the end users, or at least with people who can adequately represent them. Seek strong user buy-in, and work with users to avoid scope gaps by validating all acceptance and testing criteria. Establish measurable acceptance criteria for project deliverables, and determine what will be required for the users to deem the project a success. Identify the individual or individuals who will have the final word on this and keep in contact with them. Agile methods deeply involve users in the development process, reducing many types of deliverable-related risk. The probability of scope risk and the likelihood of late project schedule difficulties can both be reduced through ongoing user involvement.

A final general strategy for lowering project risk is setting clear decision priorities for the project. Validate the priorities with both your sponsors and the end users, and ensure that the project team clearly understands the project's priorities. Base project decisions on the priorities, and know the impact of failing to meet each priority established for the project. This not only helps manage scope risks, it also permits quick decisions within the project that minimize scope creep and other change-related impact.

MITIGATION STRATEGIES FOR SCOPE RISKS

Mitigating scope and technical risks involves shifts in approach and potential changes to the project objective. Ideas for mitigating scope risks include:

- Explicitly specify project scope and all intermediate deliverables, in measurable, unambiguous terms, including what *is not* in the deliverable. Eliminate "wants," "could haves," "should haves," and other scoping ambiguity early—make suggested requirements explicitly part of scope, or drop them.

- Gain acceptance for and use a clear and consistent specification change control process.
- Adopt iterative or agile methods to manage scope based on user feedback and current priorities.
- Build models, prototypes, and simulations, and use them to collect user and stakeholder feedback.
- Test with users, early and often.
- Schedule risk-prone, complex work early.
- Obtain funding for all required outside services.
- Translate, competently, all project documents into relevant languages.
- Minimize external dependency risks.
- Consider the impact of external and environmental problems.
- Keep all plans and documents current.

Changes are the cause of almost one-third of the total risk impact in the PERIL database. Minimizing change risk involves the first two tactics—scope definition and change management. Scope risk is high for projects with inadequate specifications. Although it is true that thorough, clear definition of the deliverable is often difficult on modern, complex projects, failure to define the results adequately leads to even greater difficulty. Closely inspect the list of features to be included to verify that all the requested requirements are in fact necessary. Employ iterative development techniques or other methods to refine uncertain requirements as early as possible.

The second necessary tactic for reducing change risk is to uniformly apply an effective process for managing all changes to project scope as a project proceeds. To manage risks on large, complex projects, the process is generally formal, using forms, committees, and extensive written reporting. For projects done under contract, risk management also requires that the process be described in detail in the contract signed by the two parties. On smaller projects, even if it is less formal, there still must be uniform treatment of all proposed changes, considering both their benefits and expected costs. For projects using agile methods, adopt a disciplined process to manage decisions and scope adjustments for future development cycles based on relevant priorities and frequent user feedback. For your project, adopt a process that rejects (or at least defers) all changes that fail the cost-justification test. It is not enough to have a change management process; mitigating scope risks requires its disciplined use.

Scope risks are often hard to evaluate at the beginning of complex projects. One way to gain better insight is to schedule work during planning to examine feasibility and functionality questions in parallel with early planning and other analysis. Use prototypes, simulations, and models to evaluate concepts with users. Schedule early tests and investigations to verify the feasibility of untried technology. Identify potential problems and defects early through walk-throughs and scenario discussions. Also consider scale risks. Even if there are no problems during small-scale, limited tests, scope risks may still remain that will surface only in full-scale production. Plan for at least some rudimentary tests of functionality in full-scale operation as early in the project as practical. Schedule work to uncover issues and problems near the beginning of the project or during early development iterations. Be prepared to modify your plan and assumptions, or even to abandon the project, based on what you learn.

Although it is risky to defer difficult or unknown activities until late in the project, it may be impractical to begin with them. To get started, you may need to complete some simpler activities first, and then move on to more complicated activities as you build expertise. Do your best to schedule the risk-prone activities as early in your project as you are able.

Lack of skills on the project team also increases scope risk, so define exactly how you intend to acquire all needed expertise. If you intend to use outside consultants, plan to spend both time and effort in their selection, and ensure that the necessary funding to pay for them is in the project budget. If you need to develop new skills on the project team, identify the individuals involved and plan so each contributor is trained, in advance, in all the needed competencies. If the project will use new tools or equipment, schedule installation and complete any necessary training as early in the project as practical.

Scope problems also arise from faulty communications. If the project depends on a distributed team that speaks several languages, identify all the languages needed for project definition and planning documents and provide for their translation and distribution. Confusion arising from project requirements that are misinterpreted or poorly translated can be expensive and damaging, so verify that the project information has been clearly understood in discussions, using interpreters if necessary. Also commit to providing written follow-up after meetings and telephone discussions.

Projects often depend on the quality and timely delivery of things received from others. Mitigating these scope risks requires clear, carefully constructed specifications that increase the possibility that what you receive will provide what you need. If you have little experience with a provider, finding and using a second source in addition to the first may be prudent, even though this will increase the cost. The cost of a redundant source could be small compared to the cost of a project delayed because "all the eggs were in the same basket."

External factors also lead to scope risks. Natural disasters such as floods, earthquakes, storms, global pandemics, supply chain disruptions. Even not-so-natural disasters like computer viruses may cause loss of critical information, software, or necessary components. You can't prevent these exposures, but you can minimize the impact through actions such as establishing some redundancy, providing for frequent backups of computer systems, and scheduling work to reduce dependency on singular locations.

Finally, managing scope risk also requires tracking of the initial definition and tracing all requirements and scoping changes approved or accepted during the project. You can significantly lower scope risk by adopting a process that tightly couples all accepted changes to the planning and requirements management processes, as well as by making the consequences of scope decisions visible throughout the project.

MITIGATION STRATEGIES FOR SCHEDULE RISKS

Schedule risks may be minimized by making additional investments in planning and revising your project approach. Some ideas to consider include:

- Use "expected" estimates when worst cases are significant.
- Schedule highest priority work early.
- Manage external dependencies proactively.

- Before adopting a new technology, explore possibilities for using older methods.
- Use parallel, redundant development.
- Send shipments early. Avoid reliance on "just in time."
- Know customs requirements and use reliable services for international shipments.
- Be conservative in estimates for training and new hardware.
- Break projects with large staffs into parallel efforts.
- Partition long projects into a sequence of shorter ones.
- Schedule project reviews.
- Reschedule work coincident with known holidays and other time conflicts.
- Track progress with rigor and discipline and report status frequently.

The riskiest activities in the project tend to be the ones that have significant worst-case estimates. For any activity where the most-likely duration estimate is significantly shorter than what might occur, calculate an "expected" duration using the PERT formula. Use these estimates in project planning to provide some reserve for particularly risky work, and to reduce the schedule impact.

Project risk is lower when you schedule activities related to the highest priorities for the project as early as possible, moving activities of lower priority later in the project. For each scheduled activity, review the deliverables and specify how and when each will be used. Wherever possible, schedule the work so there is a time buffer between when each deliverable is complete and the start of the activities that require them. If there are any activities that produce deliverables that seem to be unnecessary, confirm and document why the deliverables are needed with project stakeholders. Remove any nonmandatory work from your project plan.

Many schedule risks are caused by delays that may be avoided through more proactive communication. Whenever decisions are needed, plan to remind the decision-makers at least a week in advance and get commitment for a swift turnaround. If specialized equipment or access to limited services is required, put an activity in the plan to review your needs with the people involved somewhat before the scheduled work. If scarce equipment for some kinds of project work is a chronic problem, propose adding capacity to lower the risk on your project, as well as for all other parallel work. The preventive maintenance schedules for production systems are generally determined well in advance. Monitor availability schedules for needed services and synchronize your plans with them to reduce conflicts and delays.

New things—technology, hardware, systems, or software—are common sources of delay. Manage risk by seeking alternatives using older, known capabilities unless using the new technology is an absolute project requirement. A "lower-tech" alternative may in some cases be a better choice for the project anyway, or it could serve as a standby option if an emerging technology fails to meet your needs. Identify what you would need to do or change in the project to complete your work without the newer technology.

One cause of significant delay is developing a specific design and then sending it out to be built or created before it can be tested. It may take weeks to get the tangible result of the design back, and if it has problems the entire cycle will need to be repeated, doubling the duration (or worse—it may not work the second time either). In areas such as chip design, more than one chip will be made on each wafer anyway, and it might be useful to design a number of slightly different versions that can all be fabricated at the same time. Most of the chips will be of the primary design, but other variations created with it can also be tested, thus increasing the chances of having a component that can be used for continued project work. There are other situations where slightly different versions may be created in parallel, such as printed circuit boards, mechanical assemblies, or other newly designed hardware. Although creating multiple designs may increase the project cost, protecting the project schedule is often much more important. Varying the parameters of a design and evaluating the results may also be useful for understanding the principles involved more thoroughly, which may reduce risks on future projects.

Delays due to shipping problems are significant on many projects and in many cases can be avoided simply by ordering or shipping items earlier in the project. Just because it is generally thought to take a week to ship a piece of equipment from San Jose, California, to Bangalore, India, does not mean you should wait until a week before it is needed in India to ship it—as many learned the hard way when supply chain problems caused worldwide manufacturing disruptions. With shipping, there are only two ways to get something sooner—expedite it or order it earlier. Expediting may not always work (even if it is in your budget), so it is always prudent to request things that must be transported physically well ahead of the need, particularly when the process involves complex paperwork and international customs regulations. Use only shipping services with a good performance record, knowledge of legal requirements, and an ability to track shipments.

Similarly, delay may result from the need to have new equipment or new skills for the project. Hardware delay and learning curve issues are common in the PERIL database, and the time necessary to get new equipment installed and running or to master new skills may prove longer than you think. If you underestimate how long things will take, project work that depends on the new hardware or skills will have to wait. Planning proactively for these project requirements will remove many risks of this sort from your project (and, as mentioned earlier, it also lowers the chances that you might lose, or never get, the funding required). Estimate these activities conservatively, and schedule installations, upgrades, and training as early in your project as practical—well before you are planning to depend on them.

Large projects are intrinsically risky. If a project requires more than twenty full-time staff members, explore the possibility of partitioning it into smaller projects responsible for subsystems, modules, or components that can be developed in parallel. Doing this will rely on program management techniques to deal with the autonomous smaller projects, so ensure that all interfaces between the subprojects are clearly defined both in terms of specifications required and timing. Although the independent projects will be easier to manage and less risky, the overall program could be prone to late integration problems without adequate systems-level planning and strong interface controls.

Long projects are also risky. Work to break projects longer than a year into phases that produce measurable outputs. A series of short evolutionary projects will create value sooner than a more ambitious longer project, and the shorter projects are more likely to fall within a reasonable planning horizon of less than six months. This is a central principle for agile methodologies and evolutionary software development, used to deliver intermediate results sooner and to better manage both scope and schedule risk.

If a lengthy project must be undertaken as a whole, adopt a "rolling-wave" planning philosophy. At the end of each project phase, plan the next phase in detail and adjust plans for the remainder of the work at a summary level. Make adjustments to the project plans for future phases as you proceed to reflect what has been learned in the previous phases, including changes to the project deliverable, shifts in project staffing, and other parameters of the project objective. Rolling-wave planning requires that the project team conduct a thorough project review at the end of each phase and be prepared to continue as planned, continue with changes, or abort the project.

Schedule risk also arises from time conflicts outside the project. Check the plan for critical project work that may conflict with holidays, the end of financial reporting periods, times when people are likely to take vacations, or other distractions. Verify that intermediate project objectives and milestones are consistent with the personal plans of the staff members responsible for the work. On global projects, collect data for each region to minimize problems that may arise when part of the project team will be unavailable because of local holidays. Avoid known project time conflicts by accelerating or delaying the planned work around them.

Finally, commit to rigorous activity tracking throughout the project, and periodically schedule time to review your entire plan: the estimates, risks, workflow, project assumptions, and other data. Publish accurate schedule status regularly.

MITIGATION STRATEGIES FOR RESOURCE RISKS

Mitigating resource risks includes ideas such as:

- Avoid planned overtime.
- Build teamwork and trust on the project team.

- Use "expected" cost estimates where worst-case activity costs are high.
- Obtain firm commitments for funding and staff.
- Keep customers and users involved.
- Anticipate staffing gaps.
- Minimize safety and health issues.
- Encourage team members to plan for their own risks.
- Delegate risky work to successful problem-solvers.
- Rigorously manage outsourcing.
- Detect and address issues with the project objective promptly.
- Rigorously track project resource use.

One of the most common avoidable resource risks on technical projects is planned overtime. Starting a project with full knowledge that the deadline is not possible unless the team works overtime for much of the project's duration is a prescription for failure. Whenever the plan shows requirements for effort in excess of what is realistically available, strive to eliminate it. Even on well-planned projects there are always plenty of opportunities for people to stay late, work weekends and holidays, lose sleep, and otherwise devote time to the project from their side of the work/life balance. Projects that require substantial overtime from the outset also face significant risks due to low productivity, poor motivation, and potential turnover.

Resource risk is lower on projects whenever motivation is high. Motivation is a key factor in whether people will voluntarily work overtime, and low motivation is frequently a root cause of many resource-related risks. Today's projects are always difficult. When projects succeed, it is not because they are easy; it is because the project team cares about them. Project leaders who are good at building teamwork and getting contributors working on the project to trust and care about each other are much more successful than project leaders who work impersonally at a distance.

Teamwork across cross-functional project boundaries also matters. The more involvement in project planning, startup or launch activities, and other collaborative work you do early in the project, the more team cohesion you can count on. People who know and trust each other will back each other up and help to solve each other's problems. People who do not know each other well tend to mistrust each other, leading to conflict, arguments, and unnecessary project problems. Working together to plan and initiate project work transforms it from "the project leader's project" to "our project."

Financial risk is also significant for many projects. For activities in the project that have significant worst-case costs, estimate a realistic "expected cost" and use it to reflect the potential financial exposure and in determining the proposed project budget.

As with schedule risk, adequate sponsorship is essential to resource risk management. Get early commitment from the project's sponsor for staffing and for funding, based on planning data (a discussion of negotiating for this follows in chapter 10). The priority of the project is also under the control of the project sponsor, so work to understand the relative priority of the project in his or her mind. Strive to obtain the highest priority that is realistic for your project (and document this in writing). If the project has more than one sponsor, determine who has the most influence on the project. In particular, it is good to know who would be able to make a decision to cancel your project, so you can take good care of them and keep them aware of your progress. It is also useful to know who in the organization above you would suffer the most serious consequences if your project does not go well, because these managers have a personal stake in your project and are likely to be most useful whenever risk recovery requires escalation.

Too little involvement of customers and end users in definition, design, and testing is also a potential resource risk, so obtain commitments early for all activities that require it. Also, plan to remind them in advance of the project work that needs their participation.

Risks resulting from staffing gaps can be reduced or detected earlier through more effective communication. Assess the likelihood that project staff (including you) might join the project late because of ongoing responsibilities in prior projects that are delayed. Get credible status reports from these projects and determine how likely it is that the people working on them will be available to work on your project. If the earlier projects are ending with a lot of stress and overtime, reflect the need for some recovery time and less aggressive estimates in your project plans for the affected team members. Also plan to notify any contributors with part-time responsibilities on your project in advance of their scheduled work.

Loss of project staff due to safety or health problems is always possible, so a review of activities involving dangerous work (although uncommon for many projects, a source of significant risk on others) is a good idea. Modify plans for any activities that you suspect may have health or safety risks to minimize the exposure. You may be able to make changes to the environment, time, or place for the work or to mitigate the risk by modifying the practices used. Also consider the experience and skills of any contributor who might be exposed to risks, and work to replace or train any team members who have insufficient relevant background.

For any activity risk where the team members involved could contribute to the risk, involve the individuals in developing a response. In addition to potentially finding more, and better, ideas for prevention, this will tend to sensitize them to the impact of the problem and the visibility may greatly reduce the likelihood of the risk.

For new, challenging, or otherwise risky activities, strive to find experienced contributors who have a reputation for effective problem-solving. While you cannot plan creativity or innovation, you can always identify people who seem to be good at it.

Outsourcing is a large and growing source of resource risk on projects. The discussion in chapter 5 includes a number of exposures, and mitigating these risks requires discipline and effort. For each contract with a service provider that your project depends upon, designate a member of your project team who has relevant experience as liaison to manage the relationship. Also explicitly identify individuals who will serve as liaisons for other project teams in your own organization that you will need to work with. If you plan to be the liaison yourself, ensure that you have sufficient time allocated for this in addition to all your other responsibilities. Involve the owner of each contract relationship in selection, negotiation, and finalization of the agreement. Ensure that the agreement is sufficiently formal (a contract with an external supplier, a "memo of understanding" or similar document with an internal supplier or other project leaders) and that it clearly defines both time and technical requirements for the work that are consistent with your project plan. Provide incentives and penalties in external agreement when appropriate, and whenever possible schedule the work to complete earlier than your absolute need.

With any project work performed outside the view of the project team, establish a regular schedule for reviews and discussions.

Also, participate in inspections and interim tests, and examine prototypes. Identify and take full advantage of any early opportunities to verify tangible evidence of progress. Plan to collect status information regularly, and work to establish a relationship that will make it more likely that you will get credible status, including bad news, throughout your project.

A significant risk situation on fee-for-service projects is a lack of involvement of the project team during the proposal and selling phases. When a project is scoped and a contract commitment is made before those who will do the work have any involvement in the project, resource risks (not to mention schedule and scope risks) can be enormous. A "price to win the business" philosophy is far too common in proposals for fee-for-solution projects. This often results in fixed-price contracts with large and seemingly attractive revenues that are later discovered to require even larger and very unattractive expenses. Some projects sold this way may be impossible to deliver at all. Preventing this risk would be reasonably easy using time-travel technology, by turning back the clock and involving the project team in setting the terms and conditions for any agreement. Because that is impossible, and this risk may already be a certainty when the project team gets into project and risk planning, the only recourse is to mitigate the situation insofar as possible.

Minimizing the risks associated with committed projects based on insufficient analysis requires the project team to initiate the processes of basic project and risk planning as quickly as they can, doing bottom-up planning based on the committed scope. Using best-effort planning information, uncover any unrealistic expectations for timing and cost. Timing expectations are visible to all, so any shifts there must be dealt with internally as well as with the customer, and this may require contract modifications. Resource and cost problems can be hidden from the customer, but they still will require internal adjustment and commitment to a realistic budget for the project—even if it significantly exceeds the amount that can be recovered under the contract. If this is all done quickly enough, before everyone has mentally settled into expectations based on the price to win the contract, it may even be possible to adjust the fees in the contract. Although it may be tempting to adopt a "safe so far" attitude and hope for the miracle that would allow project delivery consistent with the flawed contract, delay nearly always makes things worse. The last best chance to set realistic expectations for such a project is within a few days of its start. After this, the situation becomes progressively uglier, more expensive, and more difficult to resolve.

Documenting and making such "price-to-win" situations visible will reduce future risk by minimizing the chances for future recurrence. (Organizations that chronically pursue business like this rarely last long.)

Finally, establish resource metrics for the project, and track them against realistic planning data. (Chapter 9 will explore using project metrics to improve overall project risk management.) Track progress, effort, and funding throughout the project, and plan to act quickly when the information shows that the trends show adverse variances against the plan. Establish effective processes to keep resource status information visible in regular reporting.

Risk Transfer and Escalation

Along with avoidance and mitigation, transfer and escalation provide two more potential options for risk prevention. Transfer is most effective for risks where the impact is primarily financial and escalation can be effective when the root causes for a risk can be removed by stakeholders who have the authority and power to do so.

The best-known form of transfer is insurance: For a fee, someone else will bear the financial consequences of your risk. Transfer
works to benefit both parties, because the purchaser of the insurance avoids the risk of a potentially catastrophic monetary loss in
exchange for paying a small (by comparison) premium, and the
seller of the insurance benefits by aggregating the fees collected to
manage the risk for a large population of policyholders who provide a reliable source of profit. As long as the premium payments
in aggregate exceed a stable and predictable "average" risk, there
will be more than sufficient funds to pay for the small percentage
of policyholders who submit claims. This sort of transfer is not
extremely common for projects, but it is used. Transfer does not
actually do anything to lower the probability of the risk event, and
it does not diminish any nonfinancial impact for risks. With transfer, the risk is accepted, and it will either occur or not. For example, if flooding would create major problems for a project, obtaining
flood insurance could be a very good idea. If a flood occurs, you
will still need to deal with its effects. The costs and budgetary
impact of your recovery efforts will be covered by insurance pay-
outs from outside the project, limiting the resource consequences,
but you will still need to deal with the time, effort, and other
impact.

Transfer of scope and technical risk is often one justification for
outsourcing, In some cases this can be effective, at least to a point.
If the project team lacks a needed skill, hiring an expert or experienced consultant to do the work transfers the activities to people
who may be better skilled to get it done. Unfortunately, the risk
does not actually transfer to the third party. The project still
belongs to you, so any risk of nonperformance is ultimately still
yours. Should things not go well, the fact that a bill for services
will not need to be paid will be of small consolation. Even the

possibility of eventual legal action is unlikely to help the project. Using outsourcing as a risk transfer strategy is very much a judgment call. In some cases the risks accepted may significantly exceed the risks managed, no matter how carefully you write the outsourcing contract.

Similarly, some risk situations may be escalated to managers or others who are responsible for factors that can either cause or avoid risks. Escalation as a risk prevention tactic works well in cases where you can assign ownership of a risk to a high-level stakeholder who is able to eliminate the root causes of a risk, for example by authorizing the addition of staff, budget, or other resources that will allow you to adjust your plans to avoid the potential problems. When escalation can remove a risk, it provides a thoroughly effective response. As with transfer, though, if escalation only serves to mitigate a risk (or you have legitimate concerns about how reliable the escalation response will be), your project still owns at least a portion—perhaps the major portion—of the risk.

IMPLEMENTING PREVENTIVE IDEAS

Avoidance, mitigation, and transfer nearly always have costs, sometimes significant costs. Escalation also can involve at least the cost involved with burdening (or annoying) high-level stakeholders that you work for. Before you adopt any ideas to avoid or reduce risks, some analysis is in order.

Comparing Costs and Benefits

For each risk to be managed, estimate the expected consequences in quantitative terms. For each proposed risk response, assess the incremental costs and timing impact involved. After comparing this data, consider business-justified preventive actions for inclusion in the project plan.

The expected cost of a risk, as usual, is based on "loss times likelihood." For this, you need the probability in numerical terms, as well as estimates of the risk impact in terms of financial, schedule, and possibly other factors.

For a risk that was assessed as "moderate" probability, the historical records may provide an estimated probability of about 15 percent. The impact of the risk must also be assessed quantitatively. For a risk that represents three weeks of schedule slip and $2 million in cost and a probability of 15 percent, the expected risk impact will be about one-half week (which is probably not too significant) and $300,000 (which would be, for most projects, very significant). In each case, this is 15 percent of the total impact, shown graphically in figure 8-6.

Figure 8-6: Expected Impact

The consequences of each idea for avoiding or mitigating the risk in time and money should be compared with the expected impact estimates to see whether they are cost-justified. If an idea only mitigates a risk—lowering the impact or probability of the problem—then the comparison is generally between the cost for mitigation and difference between the "before and after" estimates for the risk. (By how much will the impact be reduced? What is the value of any lower likelihood of occurrence?)

Determining whether a preventive is justified is always a judgment call, and it may be a difficult one. It is made more so because the data is often not very precise or dependable, making these comparisons fairly subjective. The exercise of comparing costs for risk prevention with the expected impact is important, though, because it is human nature to attempt to prevent problems whenever possible. You should not necessarily prevent a risk just because you can. Seeking a risk-free project is illogical for two reasons. First, it is impossible. All projects have some residual risk no matter what you do to avoid it. Second, a project with every possible risk prevention idea built into the plan will be far too expensive and time-consuming to justify.

For each potential idea that reduces or removes a project risk, contrast the expected costs of the risk with the cost of prevention before pulling it into the project plan. In the case mentioned previously, with the expected half week of delay and $300,000 in expense, an idea that requires a week of effort and costs $1.5 million would most likely not be adopted, as the "cure" is nearly as bad as the relatively unlikely risk. This situation would be similar to paying insurance premiums that exceed the cost of the expected loss. A preventive that costs less and requires little effort, though, may well represent a prudent plan modification.

Responding to some high-impact risks even though they seem to have low assessed probabilities can be prudent, as discussed earlier in this chapter. A decision to manage the example risk here should also consider whether a $2 million unanticipated expense could be absorbed by the organization. The cost of the risk will never be $300,000; it will either be nothing or $2 million. If the worst-case outlay is unacceptable, a "MiniMax" strategy would lead you to invest in a risk response, presuming you can identify a plausible one that does not invalidate your project's overall net value.

Even if some of the ideas you generate for risk prevention prove not to be cost-justified, those (or similar) ideas may still be useful in developing contingency plans.

Managing the "Right" Risks

The decision to respond to a given risk can be a complex one. The question posed in chapter 1, "Can you manage project risks?" is difficult to answer precisely because projects are always uncertain.

Risks, by definition, may or may not occur. There are no guarantees that actions you take to manage them will be beneficial, because some of the risks you may choose to address will probably never happen. (In fact, some may not happen precisely because of actions you took to manage them.) It is also true that risks you choose not to manage might work out fine, because at least some of those also will not occur. In statistics, the concepts of "Type 1" and "Type 2" errors are used to characterize false positives (such as when a medical test indicates a patient has a disease that is not present) and false negatives (such as the opposite, a medical test that indicates a patient is free of a disease that he or she has).

With risks, there are four possible outcomes for any given risk. It will either happen or not, and we will choose to respond to it or not. The following table summarizes these cases:

		CHOOSE TO RESPOND	
		YES	NO
RISK OCCURS	YES	Hooray for Us	Type 2 Errors (Rude Surprises)
	NO	Type 1 Errors (Oh, Well)	Lucky

Type 1 errors in risk management are the risks we manage that do not happen. They involve waste, because the investment made in responding will not appear in retrospect to be necessary. For projects, this is not good, but the other type of error, risks we accept that do befall us, is almost always much worse. Inevitably both kinds of error are likely to happen, and there is ample opportunity even on smaller projects for second-guessing.

Because the overall consequences are generally less severe for Type 1 errors, most experienced project leaders tend to have a bias toward responding to risks that minimize problems, particularly risks that carry substantial (or unknown) impact. This is reflected in the table in figure 8-4. As a practical matter, though, it is never that easy. Justifying action and obtaining resources in advance of risks that do not seem to be very likely can be very tough to sell. Key stakeholders may doubt your analysis and fail to support your proposals to manage risk efforts. Whenever you decide to manage a risk that fails to develop, there is high potential for at least some after-the-fact criticism: "You squandered resources taking unnecessary actions." For risks that never happen, you can never "prove" a risk-preventive action was justified, and in most cases you will not even be able to show with any precision that your estimates of potential harm were accurate. For these Type 1 cases, however, at least you were ready, and sometimes there are positive effects of your actions (contributors trained in new skills, backup equipment available, or other longer-term benefits) that may partially justify the work you did.

The Type 2 case involves failing to manage a risk that happens. From a planning perspective, this is easy. Accepting a risk does not require you to do anything other than list it in your risk register and monitor the work (which presumably you would do anyway). You may also be unable to respond to some risks even if you want to because of resource or other constraints that preclude any action, or because your proposal to respond was not approved by your sponsor or key stakeholders. Even low (or assumed to be low) probability risks do happen, however. The PERIL database is filled with examples of significant unexpected slippage that caused a lot of anguish to project teams. Criticism after such risks, especially if the effect is substantial, can be very harsh: "How could you fail to see and manage this (now, in retrospect) obvious problem?"

Overall, it is best to respond to most significant identified risks, and it will be easiest to do this if you identify thresholds for both probability and impact that align with your stakeholder's risk tolerance. If a risk representing a month of slip or a few hundred thousand dollars of unanticipated expense is unacceptable, use your risk assessment data to justify responding to risks that plausibly could result in this damage.

Risk Escalation

Escalating risks to influential stakeholders and upper-level managers may provide effective strategies for preventing specific risks, as discussed previously. As you proceed with any decisions to delegate ownership of risks to high-level stakeholders, also document your overall risk plans and share them with your project sponsors, decision-makers, and other key stakeholders. Use open, visible communications describing your response strategies to create broad awareness of what your project faces and how you are preparing to deal with potential problems.

For significant risks that you are planning to accept (and situations where your mitigation plans leave substantial residual impact), document your analysis clearly. This will help to defer (at least some) later criticism concerning risks you accept that your project later encounters. In particular, whenever the primary reason you did not respond to a major potential project problem was a lack of funding, support, or other approval, document the particulars. Misery may or may not love company, but it is always preferable not to be catching abuse all by yourself.

Updating Your Plans

Integrating your risk responses into your plans is the final step in risk response planning. Incorporate each cost-justified (or otherwise approved) risk avoidance, mitigation, transfer, or escalation idea into your project planning documents. (Uncertain opportunities may also entail changes related to exploiting, enhancing, and sharing of risks.) Most ideas will require additional or different work, so the project work breakdown structure (WBS) may shift, and there will likely be revisions to activity effort and duration estimates. Any added work will require staffing, so the profiles in your resource plan will also likely require updating. When updated plans create conflicts with existing project constraints, you will face more replanning, which may generate additional project risks.

Before adoption, each risk response idea must earn its way into the project by lowering, not increasing, project risk. Before any modifications, review the plan for unintended consequences and document the justification for all additional project work.

DEALING WITH RISK EFFECTS

For some risks, your best strategy may be to deal with risk effects rather than causes. Adding preventative actions to the project serves to make a project less risky, but risks will inevitably remain. For some of these risks, you may have no influence on the root causes or could devise no cost-effective preventative actions. For other risks, you may have mitigation strategies that help but still leave substantial residual risk. For most of the significant risks that remain, you either need to develop contingency plans or decide to accept the risk.

Contingency Planning

Contingency planning deals with risk effects by generating plans for recovery or "fall back." The process for contingency planning is exactly the same as for any other project planning. It is best conducted at the same level of detail and using the same methodologies and tools as other project planning.

Each contingency plan begins with the trigger event that signals the risk has occurred. The most effective risk triggers provide for lead time before the risk consequences occur. Early triggers increase the number of potential recovery options, and in some cases they may permit you to reduce the impact of the risk, so review your trigger events to ensure you have the best option available.

Each risk to be managed with a contingency plan also must have an owner. The risk owner should be involved with developing the initial contingency plans, will monitor for the trigger event, and will be responsible for maintaining the contingency plans. If the risk should occur, the risk owner will be responsible for beginning to execute the contingency plan and working toward project recovery. The owner of a project risk will most often be the same person who owns the project activity (or activities) related to the risk, but for risks with particularly severe, project-threatening consequences, the project leader may be a better choice.

GENERAL CONTINGENCY PLANNING STRATEGIES

Contingency planning for risks often starts with leftover ideas. Some ideas may have been considered for schedule compression (discussed in chapter 6), but not used. Others could be risk prevention strategies that were not adopted in the preliminary baseline plan for cost or other reasons. Although some of these ideas may be adopted as contingency plans without modification, in other cases they may need to be modified for "after-the-fact" use. Prevention strategies you considered but did not use, such as using an alternate source for components or schedule compression strategies for expediting outsourced activities, can be documented as contingency plans without much modification. Risk avoidance ideas you did not adopt can serve as contingencies after minor changes. Employing an older technology, for example, might require additional work to back out any dependencies on a newer technology that has failed.

Contingency planning in itself is a powerful risk prevention tool, as the process of planning for recovery vividly shows how difficult and time consuming it will be to recover from problems. This provides additional incentive for the project team to work in ways that will minimize risks. Always strive to make risks and risk planning as visible as possible in project communications. Your project team will only work to avoid potential problems if they know they are there.

CONTINGENCY PLANNING STRATEGIES FOR SCOPE RISKS

Contingency planning for scope risks is not too complicated. Recovery plans involve either changing the project to protect the specifications for the deliverable or dropping scope requirements. Attempting to preserve the requirements is done by adding more work to the schedule (using tactics summarized previously), using additional resources, or both. In most cases it is difficult to assess in advance the magnitude of change that this may require, as the level of difficulty in fulfilling requirements for complex projects is highly variable—from relatively trivial in some cases to impossible in others. Contingency plans for scope risks usually provide for some level of recovery effort, followed by a review to determine whether to extend the project or to modify the scope consistent with the current deadline (or, in extreme cases, to abandon the project).

For some projects, scope risks may be managed by reducing the project requirements, to provide most of the value of the project deliverable in a way that is consistent with schedule and resource objectives. The process for this, similar to that discussed in chapter 6, starts with a prioritized list of specifications. It may be possible to drop some of the requirements entirely, or to defer them to a later phase or project. There may also be potential for relaxing some of the requirements, making them easier to achieve. Although this sort of prioritization can be done effectively for some projects in advance, contingency planning for scope risks generally includes a review of project accomplishments and updating project assumptions, so your decisions on what to drop or change can be based on the most current information.

CONTINGENCY PLANNING STRATEGIES FOR
SCHEDULE RISKS

Whenever a risk results in a significant delay, the contingency plan must seek an alternate version of the workflow that provides either a way to expedite upcoming work so you can resume the project plan at some later point or a way to complete the project on some alternate basis that minimizes impact to the project deadline.

Recovery involves the same concepts and ideas used for schedule compression, discussed in chapter 6. The baseline plan will require changes, so contingency plans must provide for the effort needed for recovery by shifting, changing, or eliminating scheduled work. You may be able to delay the start of less crucial planned activities, postponing them to later in the project. Any noncritical activity work that is simultaneous with or scheduled to follow the risk event could be interrupted or postponed to allow more focus on recovery. Some activity dependencies might be revised to allow project activities to progress out of the planned sequence, freeing contributors to work on recovery. In each of these cases you will be starting work later in the schedule than initially planned. This will potentially increase the impact of future risks and may create new failure modes as additional project work becomes schedule critical.

It may even be possible to eliminate planned work if it is nonessential, or to devise quicker approaches for project activities that could obtain similar, but possibly less satisfactory, results. In some cases, it may be possible to defer these decisions to eliminate work or adopt shortcuts until later in the project, using them on an as-needed basis.

Crashing project activities scheduled for later in the project to compress their duration can also help if the project has sufficient budget reserve or access to additional staffing. Reduced durations can permit later start dates for scheduled work and potentially free up project effort for recovery. Simply adding staff to the project to work on recovery may also be an option, if you can get commitment from additional contributors. If you do plan to add people, include all training and project familiarization required as part of your baseline plan to minimize the disruption caused when you add new staff during a project. Without adequate preparation, absorbing new contributors can result in even greater impact and delay.

It may not be possible to replan the project to protect the deadline, especially if the risk relates to work near the end of the project. In such cases, the goal of contingency planning will be to minimize overall slippage and to provide the information necessary to quickly document a new, delayed completion date.

A generic schedule contingency strategy involves establishing schedule reserve for the project. Establishing schedule reserve is explored in more detail in chapter 10.

CONTINGENCY PLANNING STRATEGIES FOR RESOURCE RISKS

For risks that require significant additional resources, contingency planning involves revising the resource plans to protect the project budget, or at least to limit the damage. Again, the process for this mirrors the discussion for dealing with resource constraints in chapter 6.

The most common strategy is also one of the least attractive—working overtime and on weekends and holidays. This tried-and-true recovery method works adequately on most projects, providing the resource impact is minimal and project staffing is not already working significantly beyond the normal workday and workweek. If the amount of additional effort required is high, or the project team is stretched too thin when the risk occurs, this contingency strategy can backfire and actually make things worse by lowering motivation and causing staff turnover.

For some projects, there may be contributors who are assigned to the project but are underused during part of it. If this is the case, shifting work around in the schedule may allow them to assist with risk recovery and still effectively meet other commitments. This tactic, like dealing with schedule risks using float, tends to decrease your management flexibility and increase overall project risk.

Eliminating later work or substituting approaches other than those planned may also reduce the resources needed for the project, but whenever this is actually feasible it is generally more appropriate to do it as part of your baseline plan. If the work is not essential, or there is a quicker way to obtain an acceptable result, those decisions ought to be part of your basic plans, not held in reserve as recovery tactics.

Particularly for resource risks, it may be impossible to avoid damage to the overall resource plan and budget. All adverse variances increase the total project cost, so there may be few (or no) easy ways left to cut back other expenses to compensate.

Minimizing the impact of risk recovery involves contingency planning that revises resource use in ways that protect the budget as much as possible. Tactics such as assigning additional staff to later critical path activities or "borrowing" people from other, lower-priority projects may have little budget impact. Expediting external activities using incentive payments and outsourcing work planned for the project team may also be possible, but seek approval in advance for the additional cost as part of your contingency planning. If a contingency plan requires any training or other preliminary work to be effective, prepare for this by scheduling the needed activities early in your baseline project plan.

A generic resource contingency strategy involves establishing a budget reserve for the project, similar to the schedule reserve discussed earlier. Budget reserve is discussed further in chapter 10.

Risk Acceptance

For most significant risks, a prudent project leader will either develop preventative responses, contingency plans, or both. However, you cannot, nor should you, develop responses for all identified risks. Some will be accepted as part of your project environment. Acceptance does not mean ignoring these risks, but it does mean that you plan to take no action on them in advance.

Lower priority risks, those having more trivial consequences toward the bottom of your rank-ordered risk register, rarely warrant much proactive attention. For some major risks you may lack any effective response, and for still others it may not seem worthwhile to invest time planning for recovery. Risks such as these (assuming that the project facing them still makes business sense) are generally accepted.

Acceptance as a general risk management technique also includes both transfer and contingency planning. You also will accept the residual risk that remains after adopting mitigation strategies and escalating the ownership of risks to other stakeholders. In all of these situations, the risk causes remain, and you will need to deal with the effects of the risk should it happen.

For risks where you develop contingency plans and most risks where you are able to transfer some of the consequences to others, you will develop plans in advance to assist in recovery. For much residual risk, though, specific consequences may not be clear in advance. It may be impossible to do much preparatory planning for recovery. For example, unsuccessful adoption of new technologies or hardware on a project could result in many types of problems, ranging from the trivial to the insurmountable.

As you work to finalize the status of all accepted risks, thoroughly review each item in your risk register that represents significant residual risk. Discuss risks you are planning to accept having significant (or unknown) impact with your sponsor and stakeholders, and secure project-level schedule and budget reserves to assist managing them. In addition to "hoping for the best," identify triggers and owners for all significant accepted risks in your risk register and prepare to actively monitor work related to them as your project proceeds.

DOCUMENTING YOUR RISK PLANS AND RISK OWNERS

For risks with multiple potential consequences or particularly severe effects, you may want to generate more than one contingency plan. Before finalizing a contingency plan (or plans), review them for overall cost and expected effectiveness. If you do develop more than one response for a risk, prioritize the plans, putting first the plan you think will be most effective.

Document all contingency plans, including the same level of detail as in your project plans: WBS, estimates, dependencies, schedule, resources required, the expected project impact, and any relevant assumptions. For each risk response plan, clearly specify the trigger event that will reveal the risk has happened. Also, include the name of the owner who will monitor the risk trigger, maintain the contingency plan, and be responsible for its execution if the risk occurs.

As part of the overall project documentation, document your risk response plans and work to make the risks visible. One method for increasing risk awareness is to post a "Top Ten" risk list (revised periodically) either on the project website or with posters on the walls of project work areas. Ensure adequate distribution and storage of all risk plans, and plan to review risk management information during project meetings and overall reviews at least quarterly.

Maintain your risk register as part of your overall risk management plan, and use it to monitor risks. For each risk listed, include information such as:

- A detailed description of the risk
- The risk owner, plus any others with assigned roles and responsibilities
- Activities and efforts affected by the risk (including WBS codes or other references)
- Any qualitative or quantitative risk analysis results (probability, impact, and overall assessment)
- A summary of risk response actions in the project plan
- The risk trigger event
- Expected residual risk exposure
- A summary of contingency and fallback plans

Add risk plans to the other project documentation, and choose an appropriate location for storage and archiving that is available to all project contributors and stakeholders.

MANAGING A SPECIFIC RISK

Some years ago, a large multinational company initiated a year-long effort to establish a new European headquarters. Growth of the organization's presence over many decades had spread people, computers, and other equipment all over Geneva, Switzerland, and the inconvenience and expense for all of this had become unacceptable. The goal was to consolidate all the people and infrastructure into a modern, new headquarters building. This effort involved a number of high-profile, risky projects, and I was asked to manage one of them.

One particularly risky aspect of the project involved moving two large, water-cooled mainframe computers out of the older data center where the systems had operated for many years into a modern computer room in the new headquarters building. In the new location, the systems would be collocated with all the other headquarters computers and the telecommunications equipment that tied them to other sites in Europe and around the world. Both mainframe systems were critical to the business, so each was scheduled to be moved over a three-day holiday weekend. It was essential that each system be fully functional in the old data center at the end of the week before the move, and fully functional in the new data center before the start of business following the holiday, three days later.

Most of the risks were fairly mundane, and they were managed through thorough planning, adequate staffing, and extensive training—all committed months in advance. Other precautions, such as additional data backups, were also taken. The move itself was far from mundane, though, because the old data center, for some reason, had been established on the fifth floor of a very old building. The elevator in the building was small, about one meter square, and could carry no more than the weight of three or four people (who had to be on very friendly terms). When the systems were originally moved into the building, a system-sized door had been cut into the marble facade of the building, and a crane with a suspended box was used to move the systems into the data center. Over the years, upgrades and replacements had been moved in and out using the same method.

Up to the time of this project, only older hardware being replaced had ever been moved out of the data center this way. In these cases, if there had been a mishap it would not have affected operations, because the older systems were only moved out once the replacement systems were successfully moved in and operational. For the relocation project, this was not the case. Both systems had to be moved out, transported, and reinstalled successfully. Any problem that arose twenty meters in the air would result in a significant and expensive service interruption that would last far longer than the allocated three days.

The new data center was, sensibly, at ground level: Eliminating the need to suspend multimillion-dollar mainframes high in the air was one of the main objectives of the relocation project. Successful completion of the project would establish ground-level systems in the new data center, and result in far easier maintenance for the future.

In addition to the obvious risk of a CPU plummeting to the ground, the short timing of the project also involved risks such as weather, wind, traffic, injuries to workers, problems with the crane, and many other potential difficulties. The assessment for most of these other risks resulted in adjustments in staffing, updates to the plan, or acceptance (depending on staff experience and confidence that most of the anticipated problems could be dealt with during the move).

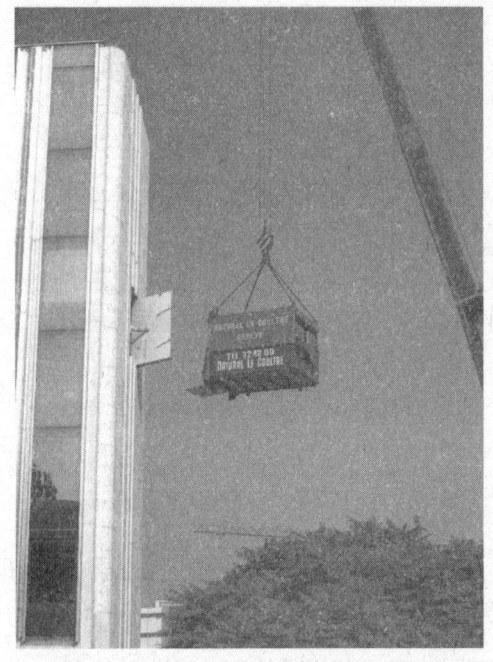

The one remaining risk that concerned all of us was that one of the mainframe computers might fall and smash into the sidewalk. The consequences of this could not be managed during the three-day weekend, so a lot of analysis went into exploring ways to manage this risk.

Risk assessment was the subject of significant debate, particularly with regard to probability. Some thought it "low," citing, "This is Switzerland; we move skiers up the mountains this way all the time." Others, particularly people from the United States, were less optimistic. In the end, the consensus was "moderate." There was less debate on risk impact, which in this case was quite literal. A large crater in the pavement would be evidence of huge physical impact, with computer parts bouncing for blocks around. (To say nothing about the major issues and concerns over cost, delay, safety, and noise.)

The primary measurable risk impacts were in time and expense, and deemed "high," so considerable planning went into mitigating the risk. A number of ideas were explored, including disassembly of the system for movement in pieces using the elevator, using an external lift mechanism secured to the outside of the building (the two systems were to be moved a month apart, so the investment would have covered both), using padding or some sort of cushion on the ground, and a number of other even less practical ideas. The disassembly idea was considered seriously, but deemed inappropriate because of timing and the discouraging report from the vendor that "those systems do not always work right initially when we assemble them in the factory." The external lift idea was a good one, but hardware that could reach to the fifth floor was unavailable. A large net or cushion would have minimized the spread of debris, but seemed unlikely to ensure system operation. It was not until the problem was reframed that the best idea emerged. The risk was not really the loss of that particular system; it was the loss of a *usable* system.

A plan to purchase a new system and install it, in advance, in the new data center would make the swift and successful move of the existing hardware unnecessary. Once operations were transferred to the new hardware, the old system could be lowered to the street, and if successful, sold as used equipment. This was an effective plan for avoiding the risk, but it had a big problem—cost. The difference between the salvage value of the current machine and the purchase price of a new one was roughly $2 million. This investment was far higher than the expected consequences of the risk, so it was rejected as part of the plan. We decided to take as many precautions as possible, and accept the risk.

All this investigation made the contingency planning easy, as the research we had done into acquiring a new system was really all that was necessary. We ordered a new system and got a commitment from the vendor to fill the order with the next machine built if there were any problems moving the existing system. (The vendor representatives were happy to agree to this, as they were heavily involved in many aspects of the relocation.) Once the move had been completed successfully, the order could be canceled with no penalty.

The consequences documented for the contingency plan were that the system would be unavailable for about three weeks, and the incremental cost of the replacement system would be roughly $3 million.

As it happened, the same staff and basic plan was employed for both mainframe moves, and both went without any incident. Although the contingency plan was not used, everyone felt that the risk planning had been a good investment. The process revealed clearly what we were facing and it heightened our awareness of the overall risk. It also uncovered many related smaller problems that we were able to eliminate, which saved time and made the time-critical holiday weekend work much easier. It also made all of us confident that the projects had been carefully and thoroughly planned, and that we would be successful. Even when risk management cannot eliminate all the risks, it is worthwhile to the project.

BOW-TIE ANALYSIS FOR DOCUMENTING RISK RESPONSES

As discussed in chapter 6, bow-tie analysis provides a graphic technique for documenting the root causes of risks. In addition to this, it is also a powerful way to show the consequences of a risk, along with the actions planned to manage it both before and (if needed) after. "Bow tie" derives from the overall appearance of the graphical format. The causes and preventions fan in from the left into the risk event in the center. Responses and consequences fan out to the right. The narrowing of the graph in the center (similar in appearance to a bow tie) focuses on the point where control could be lost. Figure 8-7 is the generic bow-tie diagram from chapter 6.

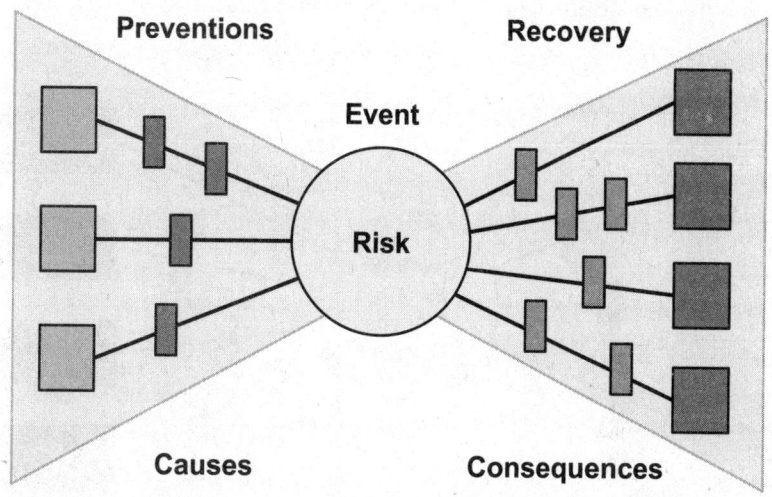

Figure 8-7: A Generic Bow-Tie Diagram

Bow-tie analysis and diagrams are often used for risks involving public health and safety exposures, such as for airline safety, tunnels, bridges, dams, power plants, and many other significant sources of public concern. They can be very effective in conveying a thorough summary of the risk situation and the effectiveness of the strategies in place for dealing with it. Bow-tie diagrams provide a simple format for displaying the information in your project risk register.

Bow-tie fault tree and recovery analysis can also be a useful tool for failure diagnosis, and was employed following the massive oil spill in 2010 following the failure of the BP Deepwater Horizon oil drilling mechanism. A fault tree showing the sources of the problems in the Gulf of Mexico coupled with analysis of the recovery effort helped in establishing needed preventive and recovery requirements for future subsurface marine oil wells.

Figure 8-8 shows a partial bow-tie analysis for the computer system relocation outlined in the previous section.

■ **Figure 8-8:** Bow-Tie Analysis Example

Key Ideas for Managing Activity Risks

- Determine root causes.
- Avoid, mitigate, or transfer risks with adverse consequences whenever feasible.
- Develop contingency plans for remaining significant risks.
- Document risk plans and keep risk data visible.
- Monitor all risks in your risk register.
- Thirty grams of prevention is worth half a kilogram of cure (approximately).

PANAMA CANAL: RISK PLANS (1906-1914)

Risk management represented one of the largest investments for the Panama Canal project. Of the risks mentioned in chapter 7, most were dealt with using effective, and in several cases innovative, means.

The risk of disease, so devastating on the earlier project, was managed through diligence, science, and sanitation. The scale and cost of this effort were significant, but so were the results. Widespread use of methods for mosquito control under the guidance of Dr. William Gorgas was effective on a scale never seen before. Specific tactics used, such as frequently applying thin films of oil on bodies of water and the disciplined dumping of standing water wherever it gathered (which in a rainforest was nearly everywhere), were so effective that their use worldwide in the tropics continues to this day. Once the program for insect control was in full effect, Panama was by far the healthiest place anywhere in the tropics. Yellow fever was eliminated. Malaria was rare, as were tuberculosis, dysentery, pneumonia, and a wide range of other diseases common at the time. Not only were the diseases spread by mosquitoes virtually eliminated, work also went much faster without the annoyance of the omnipresent insects. Although some estimates put the cost at US$10 for every mosquito killed, the success of the canal project depended heavily on Dr. Gorgas to ensure that the workers stayed healthy. This risk was managed thoroughly and well.

For the risk of frequent and sudden mudslides, there were no elegant solutions. As the work commenced, it seemed to many that "the more we dug, the more remained to be dug." Unfortunately, this was true; it proved impossible to use the original French plan for the trench in the Culebra Cut to have sides at

45 degrees (a 1:1 slope). This angle created several problems, the largest of which was the frequent mudslides. In addition, the sides of the cut pressed down on the semisolid clay the excavators were attempting to remove, which squeezed it up in the center of the trench. The deeper the digging, the more the sides would sink and the center would rise; like a fluid, it would ooze in to seek its level. The contingency plan was inelegant but ultimately effective— more digging. The completed cut in the central portion of the canal had an average 4:1 slope, which minimized the mudslides and at least partially stabilized the flowing clay. This brute-force contingency plan not only resulted in much more soil to dispose of, it represented about triple the work. Erosion, flowing clay, and occasional mudslides continue to this day, and the canal requires constant dredging to remain operational.

Dealing with the risks involved with building the enormous locks required a number of tactics. As with the mudslides, the massive concrete sides for the locks were handled by brute force and overengineering. Cement was poured at Panama on a scale never done before. The sides of the locks are so thick and so heavily reinforced that even after over a century of continuous operation, with thousands of ship passages and countless earthquakes, the locks still look much as they did when they were new.

The mechanical and electrical challenges were quite another matter. The locks were colossal machines with thousands of moving parts, many huge. Years of advance planning and experimentation led to ultimate success. The canal was a triumph of precision engineering and use of new steels. Vanadium alloy steels used were developed initially for automotive use, and they proved light and strong enough to serve in the construction of doors for the locks. Holding the doors tightly closed against the weight of the water in a filled lock required a lot of mass, mass that the engineers wanted to avoid moving each time the doors were opened or closed. To achieve this, the doors are hollow. Whenever they are closed, they are filled with water before the lock is filled, providing the necessary mass. The doors are then drained before they are opened to allow the ships raised (or lowered) in the locks to pass through.

Even with this strategy, moving doors of this size and weight required the power of modern engines. The choice of electrical operation was complicated and required much innovation (the first all-electric factory in the United States was barely a year old at the time of this decision), but electricity did provide a number of advantages. With electric controls, the entire canal system could be controlled centrally. Scale models were built to show the positions of each lock in detail. The lock systems were all controlled using dials and switches on the model with mechanical interlocks beneath the model prevent errors in operation, such as opening the doors on the wrong end of a lock, or opening them before the filling or draining of water is complete. In one place, operators could monitor overall status for all twelve locks.

When George Goethals began to set all of this up, he realized that neither he nor anyone else had ever done anything like it. For most of the controls and the more than 1,000 electric motors the canal required, Goethals managed risk by bringing in outside help. He awarded a sizable contract to a rapidly growing US company known for its expertise in electrical systems. Although it was still fairly small and not known internationally, the General Electric (GE) Company had started to build a worldwide reputation by the time the Panama Canal opened. This was a huge contract for GE, and it was the company's first large government contract. Such a large-scale collaboration of private and public organizations was unknown prior to this project. The relationship used by Goethals and GE served as the model for the Manhattan Project during World War II and for countless other modern projects in the United States and elsewhere. For good or ill, the rise of the modern military-industrial complex began in Panama.

Despite the project's success in dealing with most risks, explosives remained a significant problem throughout construction. As in many contemporary projects, loss of life and limbs while handling explosives was common. Although stringent safety precautions helped, the single largest cause of death on the second Panama Canal project was TNT, not disease. For this risk, the builders found no solutions or viable alternatives, so throughout the project they were quite literally "playing with dynamite."

CHAPTER 9

QUANTIFYING AND ANALYZING PROJECT RISK

"Knowledge is power."

—FRANCIS BACON

Information is central to managing projects successfully. Knowledge of the work and potential risk serves as the first and best defense against problems and project delay. The overall assessment of project risk provides concrete justification for necessary changes in the project objective, so it is one of the most powerful tools you have for transforming an impossible project into one that can be successful. Project-level risk rises steeply for projects with insufficient resources or excessively aggressive schedules, and overall project risk assessments offer compelling evidence of this exposure. Broadly recognizing project risk also helps in setting expectations for the project appropriately, both for the deliverables and for the work that lies ahead. The focus of this chapter is analyzing risk at the project level, building on the foundation of analysis and response planning for identified activity risks discussed in chapters 7 and 8.

PROJECT-LEVEL RISK AND VUCA

Considered one by one, the known risks on a project may seem relatively easy to deal with, overwhelming, or anywhere in between. Assessing risk at the activity level is necessary, but it is not sufficient. You also need to develop a sense of overall project risk. Overall project risk arises, in part, from all the aggregated activity-level risk data, but it also includes other factors affecting the project as a whole. Chapter 3 introduced several high-level project risk assessment ideas that considered overall factors, such as familiarity with the work and project scale, that may be available during initial project definition. It is also useful to revisit those high-level techniques—the risk framework, the risk complexity index, and the risk assessment grid—as your plans come together and update them based on your deeper understanding.

Detailed project analysis and planning provide much more information, data that you can use to assess project risk more precisely and thoroughly. In this chapter we will explore a number of useful techniques that take advantage of your increasing project understanding to gauge project risk. Overall project risk assessments based on planning data will help you make better decisions, build support for changes to project goals, and better control your project.

Another useful perspective on overall project risk considers the factors of VUCA (volatility, uncertainty, complexity, and ambiguity) on a project as a whole. In earlier chapters we noted that *uncertainty*—lack of predictability—is related to nearly half of the slippage in the PERIL database. *Complexity* is next, with over 20 percent causing scoping and schedule problems due to inadequate understanding of project problems and challenges. *Ambiguity* and *volatility* are about equally at the root of the rest of the PERIL damage, primarily producing scoping problems through insufficient clarity or excessive change. VUCA factors create specific activity risks for which you can develop responses like those explored in chapter 8, but VUCA factors can also affect your entire project.

Other common sources of overall project risk include:

- **Unrealistic deadlines:** High-tech projects often have inappropriately aggressive schedules.
- **No or few metrics:** Measures used for estimates and risk assessment are inaccurate guesswork.
- **"Accidental" project leaders:** Projects are led by team members skilled in technical work but with no project management training.
- **Inadequate requirements and scope creep:** Poor initial definition and insufficient specification change control are far too common (and relate to both ambiguity and volatility).
- **Project size:** Project risk increases with scale; the larger the project, the more likely it is to fall short of its objectives or fail.

Some of these project-level risks are well represented in the PERIL database, especially scope creep. Methods for determining overall project risk can be effective in both lowering their impact and determining a project's potential for trouble. In addition, overall risk assessment scores can:

- Build support for less risky projects and terminate (or modify) excessively risky ones
- Compare projects and help set relative priorities

- Provide data for renegotiating overconstrained project objectives
- Assist in justifying adequate management reserves
- Facilitate effective communication and build awareness of project risk

The techniques, tools, ideas, and metrics described in this chapter address these issues.

AGGREGATING RISK RESPONSES

One way to start assessing overall project risk is to "add things up." Quantitative data in your risk register provide several candidates for this:

- Cumulative expected consequences of risks
- Collective contingency plan requirements
- Aggregate "worst-case" risk-adjusted project impacts

For the first idea, you can sum the "loss times likelihood" consequences for all the risks representing significant impact. To generate this, you need to add up the estimated costs (or delays) involved multiplied by the corresponding risk probabilities for the risks listed in your risk register.

Another perspective on project-level risk accumulates the consequences of using contingency plans. To develop a sense of overall project risk, you sum the "expected" costs for all the plans—their estimated costs weighted by estimated risk probabilities. Similarly, you can calculate the total expected project duration increase required by the contingency plans using the same probabilities. For example, if a contingency plan associated with a risk having a

10 percent probability will cost $10,000 and slip the project by ten days, the contribution to the project totals will be $1,000 and one day (assuming the activity is critical), respectively.

You may also evaluate overall risk using the differences between risk-adjusted project estimates (using the PERT weighted formula or other range estimate assessments) and your "most likely" single-point activity estimates.

Each of these ideas will provide insight into the overall exposure your project is facing. These ideas will tend to underestimate total risk, however. There are several reasons for this, starting with the fact that each of these methods assumes that all project risks are independent. In reality, most project risks tend to be highly correlated. The assumption of negligible dependence is generally inappropriate because most project risks become much more likely following earlier risks events. Project activities are linked through common methodologies, staffing, and other factors. Also, projects have a limited staff, so whenever there is a problem, much of the project leader's attention (as well as that of the project team) will focus on recovery. Distracted by problem-solving, everyone will pay less attention to all the other project activities, making additional trouble elsewhere that much more likely.

Another reason that using these methods underestimates overall project risk is that the weighted sums fail to account for project-level risk factors. Overall project-level risk factors include:

- Inexperience of project manager
- Weak sponsorship
- Reorganization or business changes
- Regulatory issues
- Lack of common practices (life cycle, planning, and so forth)

- Market window or other timing assumptions
- Insufficient risk management
- Inadequate project decomposition resulting in inefficient workflow
- Unfamiliar levels of project effort
- Low project priority
- Poor motivation and team morale
- Weak change management control
- Lack of customer interaction
- Communications issues
- Poorly defined infrastructure
- Inaccurate (or no) metrics
- And of course, VUCA

The first two factors on the list deserve particular attention. If you personally have little experience running similar projects successfully, plan to increase the summed risk impacts by at least 10 percent. Similarly, if your project appears to have minimal management support, increment the overall project risk assessment by another 10 percent. Review the remaining listed factors and adjust for any of the other considerations relevant to your project. Even after these adjustments, the risk assessment will still be somewhat conservative, because the aggregated sums consider only known, identified risks; impact from "unknown" project risk is missing.

Despite all of this, accumulating what your risk register tells you about specific risks does provide a sense of how much trouble you are facing. If aggregated risk impact for either time or cost exceeds 20 percent of your current plan, your project is very risky. For particularly risky projects, prepare to use this project risk data

concerning possible cost and schedule consequences to negotiate project adjustments, justify project-level reserves, or both.

PROJECT MODELING AND SIMULATIONS

The purpose of considering overall project uncertainty is to determine realistic bounds for potential project outcomes. Single-value estimates lead to deterministic-looking project analyses with crisp, exact schedules and budgets. In reality every project estimate can be incorrect, some by a wide margin. Three-point estimating and related techniques challenge the illusion of precision and are useful for exploring the spectrum of possible project outcomes. Using "optimistic/pessimistic" or worst-case estimates (discussed in chapters 4 and 5 with regard to estimate uncertainty and in chapter 7 for analysis of activity risks) provides a straightforward approach for capturing the range of possibilities. Models such as PERT use three-point estimate data to gauge project uncertainty. Computer simulation techniques support the use of more complicated (though not necessarily more meaningful or accurate) statistical distributions and range data. Even "eyeball" project analysis based on worst-case estimates and drawing freehand, bell-shaped distributions can provide valuable insight into project risk and uncertainty.

PERT and Similar Techniques for Project Risk Analysis

As discussed in earlier chapters, PERT was the first method that attempted to use systematic risk analysis to quantify overall project risk. The principal objective of PERT was to use detailed risk data at the activity level to better predict project outcomes. For schedule analysis, project teams were requested to provide three estimates: a "most likely" estimate that they believed would be the most common duration for work similar to the activity in question, and two additional estimates that defined a range around the "most likely" estimate. The goal was to include all realistic possibilities for work duration.

Figure 9-1 shows a typical time distribution for PERT, defined by the three estimates: an "optimistic" estimate, t_o; at the low end, a "most likely" estimate, t_m at the peak somewhere in the middle; and a "pessimistic" estimate, t_p, at the high end.

Figure 9-1: PERT Estimates

Originally, PERT analysis assumed a continuous "Beta-type" distribution of outcomes defined by these three parameters, shaped as in the graph in figure 9-1. The Beta distribution was chosen because it was relatively easy to work with and it could skew to the left (as in figure 9-1) or to the right based on the three estimating parameters. (When the estimates are symmetric, the Beta distribution is equivalent to the normal distribution: a Gaussian, bell-shaped curve.) Using the three-point estimate data, you can calculate an expected estimate t_e representing the 50 percent point for the distribution using a simple weighted average. For duration estimates using the Beta distribution, the mean and standard deviation are estimated with the formulas introduced in chapter 4:

$t_e = (t_o + 4t_m + t_p)/6$, where:

t_e is the "expected" duration (the statistical mean).

t_o is the "optimistic" duration.

t_m is the "most likely" duration.

t_p is the "pessimistic" duration.

and for the standard deviation (σ):

$\sigma = (t_p - t_o)/6$

For a project with a single, dominant critical path, the expected duration for the project is the sum of all the expected (mean) durations along the critical path. The standard deviation for such a project, one measure of overall project risk, can be calculated from the estimated standard deviations for the same activities. PERT used the following formulas:

$$t_{proj} = \sum_{i\,=\,CP_{first}}^{CP_{last}} t_{e_i} \qquad \sigma_{proj} = \sqrt{\sum_{i\,=\,CP_{first}}^{CP_{last}} \sigma_i^2}$$

where:

t_{proj} = Expected project duration

CP_i = Critical path activity i

t_{e_i} = "Expected" CP estimate for activity i

σ_{proj} = Project standard deviation

σ_i^2 = Variance for CP activity i

These formulas are actually only valid for projects having a single dominant critical path. When there are additional paths that are roughly equivalent in length to the longest one, the PERT formulas will systematically underestimate the expected project duration and they will overestimate the standard deviation whenever the critical path method (CPM) analysis reveals more than one sequence of activities that could blow past the deadline. Basic PERT calculations using expected durations will calculate a resulting project with a somewhat longer predicted critical path, but the reality is worse than that.

The main reason for this inaccuracy was introduced in chapter 4, in the discussion on multiple critical paths. The simple project considered in chapter 4 had the network diagram in figure 9-2, with one critical path across the top ("A-D-J") and a second critical path along the bottom ("C-H-L").

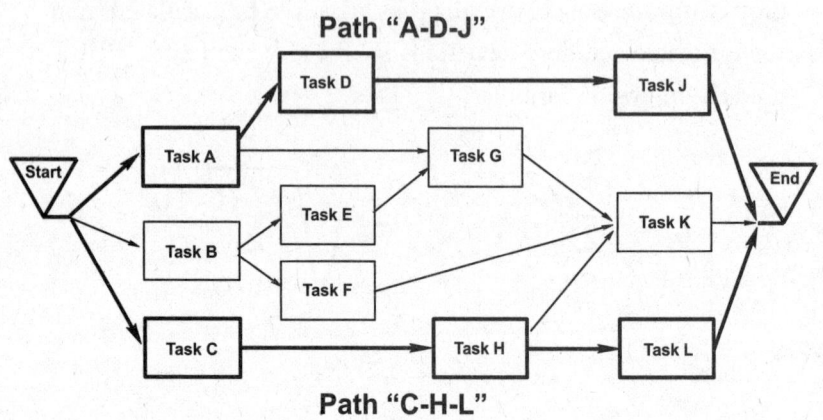

■ **Figure 9-2:** Project with Two Critical Paths

PERT-based calculation for this scenario will generate a slightly longer duration for each of the critical paths, and then attribute the greater of the two slips to the project as a whole. As the discussion in chapter 4 showed, each of the paths is a failure mode, so both should contribute to project risk and if all estimates are at the "50 percent" point there is about one chance in four that the project would complete on time or earlier than the expected project duration.

Because either of the parallel critical paths may end up being the longest, each contributes to potential project slippage. To see this more explicitly, figure 9-3 shows a range of "bell-shaped" outcomes for the two critical paths. The distribution for the project as a whole has about one-quarter of the left tail below the expected dates (similar to the table in chapter 4), with the distribution peak and right tail above it. The resulting project distribution is still basically bell-shaped, but compared with the distributions expected for each critical path, it has a larger mean and is narrower (having a smaller standard deviation).

Figure 9-3: PERT Results

To consider this quantitatively, imagine a project plan using "50 percent" expected estimates that has a single dominant critical path of 100 workdays (about five months) and a standard deviation of 5 workdays. (If the distribution of expected outcomes is assumed symmetric, the PERT optimistic and pessimistic durations—plus or minus three standard deviations—would be roughly 85 workdays and 115 workdays, respectively.) PERT analysis for the project says you should expect the project to complete in five months (or sooner) five times out of ten and in five months plus one week over eight times out of ten (mean plus one standard deviation, about 5/6 of the time)—pretty good odds.

If a second critical path of 100 workdays is added to the project with similar estimated risk (a standard deviation of five workdays), the project expectation shifts to one chance in four of finishing in five months or sooner. (Actually, the results of simulating this using 1,000 runs shows 25.5 percent. The results of a simulation almost never exactly match the theoretical answer. We will explore using simulations for project risk analysis next.) In this two-path case, the average expected project duration is a little less than 103 workdays, and the similar "5/6" point is roughly 107 workdays. This is a relatively small shift (about one-half week) for the expected project, but it results in the very large shift in the probability of meeting the deadline objective of 100 days—from one chance in two to one chance in four.

Similar analysis for three and four parallel critical paths produces the results you would expect. For three paths of 100 workdays, the project expectation falls to one chance in eight of completing on or before 100 workdays (a simulation of this showed 13 percent) and an expected duration of roughly 104 workdays. The project with four failure modes has one chance in sixteen (6.3 percent in the model), and the mean for the project is a little bit more than 105 workdays. The resulting histogram for this case is in figure 9-4, based on 1,000 samples from each of four independent, normally distributed parallel paths with mean of 100 workdays and a standard deviation of 5 workdays. (The jagged distribution is typical of simulation output.)

■ Figure 9-4: Histogram Generated by Simulation

For cases with multiple critical paths, the mean of the distribution for project duration increases and the range compresses somewhat, reducing the expected standard deviation. This is because the upper data boundary for the analysis is unchanged, while each additional critical path further limits the effective lower boundary. For the case in figure 9-4, the project duration always equals the longest of the four, and it becomes less and less likely that this maximum will be near the optimistic possibilities with each added path. Starting with a standard deviation for each path of five workdays, the resulting distribution for a project with two similar critical paths has a standard deviation of about 4.3 workdays. For three paths it is just under four workdays, and with four it falls to roughly 3.5 workdays, as seen in figure 9-4. The resulting distributions also skew slightly to the left, for the same reasons; the data populating the histograms is being compressed, but only from the *lower* side.

PERT-type analysis is most commonly performed using duration estimates, but it also applies to effort and cost estimates. As with schedule analysis, three-point cost estimates can be used to generate expected activity costs, and sum them for the entire project. Because all costs are cumulative, the PERT cost analysis formulas analogous to those for time analysis deliver results roughly equivalent to simulation.

One additional factor that reduces the accuracy of PERT models is that by default all risks are assumed to be independent. All the formulas treat each activity and event on its own, but project risk situations are rarely independent. Risks are generally highly correlated, because of shared staff and resources, root causes that recur, similar analysis defects, or just because of the increased stress that accompanies a setback. Problems in one part of a project's plan often cascade into other parts so PERT-type assessments will tend to underestimate the overall potential for adverse project impact.

Software for Project Modeling and Decision Support

Computer analysis was impractical before the 1960s (which is why PERT initially depended on simplified approximations). Once computers were widely available, analysis using Monte Carlo simulation and other techniques began to be used to analyze many kinds of complex systems, including projects. Initially, this sort of analysis was very expensive (and slow), so it was undertaken only for the largest, most costly projects. This is no longer an issue with today's modeling tools and inexpensive desktop systems.

Computer simulation analysis of project activity networks can provide a better view of the spectrum of possible outcomes, including for projects having lots of failure modes. Instead of using the calculated weighted averages of PERT to assess project schedule risk, computer simulations can generate new duration estimates consistent with defined activity ranges over and over. The simulation process uses these estimates to repeatedly calculate the project's overall duration using CPM over many cycles. The resulting histograms can display possible project outcomes based on "running a project" hundreds, or even thousands, of times.

Today's computer simulation and modeling tools for project management offer many alternatives to PERT's Beta distribution. As discussed in chapter 7, you may select triangular, normal, Poisson, and many other distribution types, or even create a list of discrete estimates associated with various outcomes. (For example, you may expect a 50 percent probability that the activity will complete in fifteen days, a 40 percent chance that it will complete in twenty days, and a 10 percent chance that it will complete in thirty days. Such scenarios are generally based on probabilities associated with known risks for which "worst-case" incremental estimates are made—the five-day slip associated with a contributor who may need to take a week of leave to deal with a family situation, or the fifteen-day slip associated with a problem that requires completely redoing all the work.)

As discussed in chapter 7, the precise choice of a distribution shape does not matter much, even for activity-level risk analysis. At the project level it becomes even less relevant. The reason for this is the "central limit theorem," well established by statisticians. When summing randomly generated samples from most types of statistical distributions (including all the realistic ones), the probability density function of the result always resembles a normal, Gaussian distribution. The more items in the sum, the closer the overall distribution will approximate a bell shape. This is why analysis for a project with a single, dominant critical path always shows a symmetric, bell-shaped curve.

The issue of data quality for schedule risk analysis was also significant for early computer-based project analysis, and this drawback persists. Generating range estimates remains difficult, especially when defined in terms of "percent tails," as is often done when describing three-point estimates in project management literature. Considering that the initial single-point "most likely" estimates are usually not all that dependable to start with, the additional upper and lower boundary estimates are likely to be even worse. Because at least some of the input data is inexact, "garbage in/garbage out" skepticism is always a valid concern for Monte Carlo schedule analysis.

This, added to the temptation for misuse of the "optimistic" estimates by overeager managers and project sponsors, has inhibited widespread use of computer simulation in many project environments. This is unfortunate, because even if range estimate analysis is only applied to specific critical activities using manual approximations, it can still provide valuable insight into project-level risk. Some effective methods require only modest additional effort, and there are a range of possible techniques, from manual approximations to full computer simulation. A summary of choices follows.

MANUAL APPROXIMATIONS

One way to apply these concepts was discussed in chapter 4. If you have entered your project workflow information into the database of a project scheduling tool and done a thorough job of identifying logical sequencing information, much of the necessary work for first-cut project-level timing assessment is already done. The duration estimates in the database are a reasonable first approximation for the optimistic estimates, or the most likely estimates (or both). To get a sense of project risk, make a copy of the database and enter new estimates for every activity where you have a worst-case estimate based on the impact information in your risk register. A Gantt chart based on these larger estimates will show overall project slippage. By associating a normal distribution with these points, you may infer a rough approximation of a PERT-type analysis.

The method used for scaling and positioning the bell-shaped curve can vary, but at least half of the distribution ought to fall somewhere between the original schedule end point and the resulting "pessimistic" version. Because it is very unlikely that everything that could go wrong in the project will do so, the upper boundary should line up with a point several standard deviations above the mean, far out on the distribution tail. (Keep in mind, however, that even your "worst" worst-case schedule accounts for none of the *unknown* project risk.) The initial schedule end point is probably somewhere below the mean of the distribution; the exact placement should be based on whether you believe your estimates are conservative or aggressive. A histogram similar to figure 9-5, using the initial plan as about the 20 percent point (roughly one standard deviation below the mean) and the worst-case plan

Figure 9-5: "PERT" Approximation

to define the 99 percent point (roughly three standard deviations above the mean), could serve as a first approximation.

The cumulative graph of project completion probabilities equivalent to figure 9-5 looks like figure 9-6.

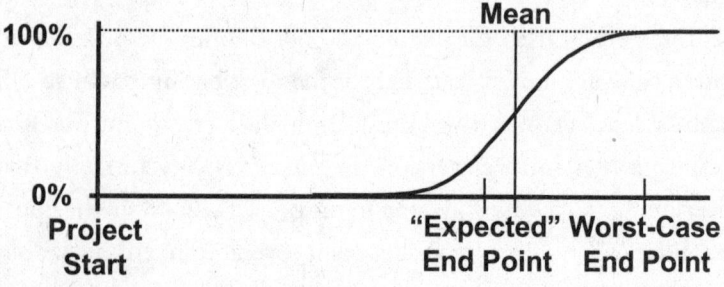

Figure 9-6: Cumulative "PERT" Estimates

Although this sort of analysis remains subjective, the additional effort it requires is small once you have a preliminary schedule for the project, and it can provide valuable insight into project risk.

One of the most beneficial things about techniques that make schedule risk visible is that they provide concrete results. When you review a specific analysis, it will either look reasonable or it will seem "wrong." If the results seem realistic, they are probably useful. If they do not look credible, it usually indicates that additional planning is warranted. Improbable-looking results are a good indication that your activity list is incomplete, your estimates are inaccurate, you missed some dependencies, you have underestimated some risks, or your preliminary plan has some other defect.

Even this "quick and dirty" type of schedule risk approximation provides insight into the thoroughness of your project plan.

COMPUTER SPREADSHEETS

The next step up in sophistication and effort involves computer spreadsheets. This is particularly useful for resource analysis, because cost and effort for the work at the project level are cumulative. Spreadsheets are a very easy way to quickly assess three cost (or effort) estimates to derive an overall project-level budget analysis. A list of all the activities in one column with the "most likely" and range estimates in adjacent columns can be readily used to calculate expected estimates and variances for both the activities and for the project as a whole. Using the PERT formulas for cost, it is simple to accumulate and evaluate data from all the project activities (not just from the critical path). The sum of all the expected costs and the calculated variance can be used to approximate project budget risk. Assuming a normal distribution centered on the sum of the expected cost estimates with a spread defined by the calculated standard deviation approximates the range that may be expected for project cost.

Spreadsheet analysis can also provide insight for overall schedule risk, but because duration estimate inaccuracies matter only for critical (and near-critical) work, the scheduling tool methods mentioned previously will be more useful.

COMPUTER SCHEDULING TOOLS

True Monte Carlo simulation analysis capability is not common in most low-end and midrange computer-based scheduling tools, and what is built in to support three-point activity duration estimates tends to be implemented in quirky and mysterious ways. It is impractical to list all the available scheduling tools here, so the following discussion characterizes them generically.

There are dozens of such tools available for project scheduling, ranging from minimalist products that implement rudimentary activity "to do" lists to high-end, web-enabled enterprise applications. Often, families of software offering a range of capabilities are sold by the same companies. Most project management scheduling tools provide a method for determining the project critical path. Robust schedule risk analysis using most of these tools, even some fairly expensive ones, often requires the manual analysis techniques discussed previously or purchase of additional, specialized software (more on this specialized software follows). In general, scheduling tools are set up for schedule analysis using single-point estimates to determine critical path, so three-point estimate analysis requires several copies of the project data (or parallel schedule copies for "what if?" analysis) to analyze potential schedule variance. Some products (including Microsoft Project) do provide for entry of three-point estimates and some rudimentary analysis, but this is typically based on calculations (as with PERT), not simulation.

Some high-end project management tools, which are both more capable and more costly than the more ubiquitous midrange tools, do provide integrated Monte Carlo simulation analysis, either built-in or as optional capabilities. Even with the high-end tools, though, schedule simulation analysis requires an experienced project planner with a solid understanding of the process.

COMPUTER SIMULATION TOOLS

Tools that provide true Monte Carlo simulation functionality are of two types, designed either to be integrated with a computer scheduling tool or for stand-alone analysis. Again, there are many options available in both of these categories.

There are quite a few applications designed to provide simulation-based risk analysis that either integrate into high-end tools or "bolt on" to midrange scheduling packages. If such an add-on capability is available for the software you are using, simulation analysis can be done without having to reenter or convert any of your project data. With the stand-alone software, project information must be input a second time or exported. Unless you also need to perform nonproject simulation analysis, Monte Carlo simulation tools designed to interface directly with scheduling applications are generally a less expensive option.

In addition to products specifically designed for Monte Carlo schedule analysis, there are also general-purpose simulation applications available, including decision support software and general-purpose statistical analysis software. For the truly masochistic, it is even possible to do Monte Carlo simulations using only a spreadsheet. (Microsoft Excel, for example, includes functions for generating random samples from various distribution types as well as statistical analysis functions for interpreting the data.)

Whatever option you choose, there are trade-offs. Some techniques are quick and relatively easy to implement, providing subjective but still useful insight into project risk. Other full-function Monte Carlo methods offer very real risk management benefits, but they also carry costs, including investment in software, generation of more data, application expertise, and increased effort. Before deciding to embark on an elaborate project using Monte Carlo simulation analysis, especially the first time, carefully consider the costs and added complexity.

A primary benefit of any of this risk analysis is the graphic and visible contrast between the deterministic-looking schedule generated by point-estimate critical path methods, and the more realistic range of possible end points (with associated probabilities) that emerges from simulation methods. The illusion of certainty fostered by single-estimate Gantt charts is inconsistent with the actual risk present in modern projects. The visible variation possible in a project is a good antidote for excessive project optimism.

And even the output of simulation methods may foster an illusion of precision. The accuracy of the output and graphical displays generated by Monte Carlo models can never be any better than that of the least precise inputs. Rounding duration estimates to whole days for input is general practice, yet simulation software typically produces results displaying many decimal places. This is particularly ironic considering the quality of typical project estimates.

In project environments that currently lack systematic project-level risk analysis, it may be prudent to begin with a modest manual approximation effort on a few projects, and expand efforts over time for future projects.

INTEGRATED SCHEDULE/COST ASSESSMENT

In the discussions of schedule and resource risk earlier in the book, there is a good deal of emphasis on the interrelationship between time and cost, particularly in relation to duration and cost/effort estimating. It is always risky to advance a project where the timing estimates are inconsistent with the staffing or financial assumptions.

The linkage between schedule and cost is also significant at the overall project level. Aggregated schedule risk (whether assessed by summing risk consequences or by using modeling or simulation techniques such as those discussed previously) will invariably affect costs. There are a number of reasons for this, including:

- Work that takes longer than expected nearly always requires additional effort, and therefore increases cost.

- Slippage of activities and milestones often results in expediting, crashing, or other resource-intensive tactics for later work, in an attempt to recover the schedule.
- Doing work later than it was originally scheduled may entail additional expense, including contract fee adjustments, replacement of perishable or other time-sensitive resources, extended use of facilities or specialized expertise, last-minute rescheduled travel, and other unexpected costs.
- Penalties and other direct financial consequences may be triggered by any deadline delays (often accompanied by a reduction in the value of late deliverables).

Carefully consider the cost consequences of your overall project schedule uncertainty, both within your project and on other work and parallel projects that could be affected by extended resource usage, slippage of critical dependencies, "borrowed" staff, and other factors.

SYSTEM ANALYSIS

It is always wise to revisit your scope risks as part of your overall project risk assessment, particularly for projects delivering complex systems. Review your plans and initial design work, examining your scope holistically. Inspect your flowcharts, functional block diagrams, defined cases, subsystem decomposition, function or feature point assessment, or other complexity analysis. Look for potential failure modes, excessive interdependencies or other linkages, and other system-level indications of structural risk.

Contrast your analysis with that done for similar, past projects, and use their experiences encountering unanticipated system difficulties as a guide when assessing system-related project risk. If you lack past assessments of complexity, consider reviewing the initial documents for previously completed work to create some, and resolve to start collecting data going forward.

CRITICAL CHAIN CONSIDERATIONS

Critical chain project management (CCPM) continues to enjoy some popularity in project management circles. Discussion of CCPM started with the "business novel" *Critical Chain* published in 1997 by Eliyahu Goldratt. The book describes applying concepts of the "Theory of Constraints" to project plan analysis. The essential notion of the Theory of Constraints is based on identifying resource constraints (or bottlenecks, or pinch points) and then eliminating or neutralizing them. The Theory of Constraints can be extraordinarily effective when fine-tuning the workflow for manufacturing processes. Because projects are also about workflow, Goldratt asks, "Why not use the Theory of Constraints to optimize them, too?" The basic steps for constraint management are:

- **Identify** the most significant constraint.
- **Exploit** it by rescheduling preceding work to ensure the constraint (or bottleneck process) is running without interruption.
- **Subordinate** other processes to the constraint, providing buffer capacity where needed to maximize throughput.
- **Elevate** the constraint, by increasing its capacity. Add resources where needed to alleviate bottlenecks and improve related processes.

- **Repeat**. Once you are successful in removing the worst constraint, a new pinch point will appear. Continuously improve to optimize the system.

Applying these ideas to a project may result in more robust, appropriate project plans. However, this may also result in riskier projects with more numerous failure modes. CCPM is often characterized as a way to compress project schedules, based on the assumption that almost all duration estimates are "padded" and can be reduced. Once all project estimates have been trimmed and a new critical path calculated, portions of the time "saved" can be allocated back to small *feeding buffers* along the new critical path(s), and as a *project buffer* at the end of the project. Buffers are owned at the project level, and the resulting project, including all the buffers, is assumed to be both realistic and significantly shorter than the original plan. There are a few reasons to be skeptical of this for real projects.

First, CCPM project analysis starts with the assumption that duration estimates are uniformly too conservative and can be trimmed (using arbitrary percent reductions, analysis based on "procrastinating student" syndrome, assumptions derived from "Parkinson's Law," or other concepts). Data in the PERIL database (not to mention common sense) should at a minimum lead to healthy skepticism about this; estimates are frequently too optimistic to start with, not systematically too long.

In addition, projects are unique and inherently uncertain. It is perfectly reasonable to optimize a manufacturing or other process that will be used over and over, and for these processes you can collect precise, reliable measurements to support your optimization efforts. Most projects are poor candidates for a significant optimization effort because most will only be executed once. Unless you have a succession of repetitive projects such as building rowhouses in a planned development, there may be little to gain from the sort of analysis CCPM requires. The lack of reliable data (remember, most project estimates are at least partially based on guesses) provides another reason to be reluctant to engage in excessive analysis.

CCPM also explicitly assumes that there will never be any multitasking or sharing of resources between projects. While this may be desirable, it is not realistic for actual modern projects.

Nonetheless, the main concepts of CCPM address project realities that are familiar to most project leaders. The uniqueness of CCPM lies more in its vocabulary than in its substance. Setting arbitrary project deadlines unrelated to schedule analysis is not at all uncommon. Aggressive deadlines are often a result of pursuing a top-down goal, an "opportunity choice" made at project initiation that results in high project schedule uncertainty (with very little chance of on-time completion). The buffers of CCPM, particularly the "project buffer" at the end, are equivalent to schedule reserves, which are a widely understood and common technique for managing overall project risk.

Even though CCPM is based on shaky assumptions and uses confusing terminology, some of its conclusions are consistent with well-established techniques for understanding and managing overall project risk. That said, project leaders who adopt CCPM concepts will be wise to remain wary of unrealistic, arbitrary assumptions. They will work to size the buffers consistently with overall project risk and retain ownership and control of all buffers and reserves at the project level. In project environments that discourage establishing and managing reserves, adopting some CCPM concepts could prove helpful.

QUESTIONNAIRES AND SURVEYS

Questionnaires and surveys are a time-honored technique for assessing project risk. These can range from simple, multiple-response survey forms, to assessments using computer spreadsheets, Web surveys, or other computer tools. However you choose to implement a risk assessment survey, it will be most effective if you tailor it to your project.

Many organizations have and use risk surveys. If there is a survey or questionnaire commonly used for projects similar to yours, there may be very little customizing required. Even if you have a format available, it is always a good idea to review the questions and fine-tune the survey before using it. If you do not have a standard survey format, the following example is a generic three-option risk survey that can be adapted for use on a wide range of technical projects.

This survey approach to risk assessment also works best when the number of total questions is kept to a minimum, so review the format you intend to use and select only the questions that are most relevant to your project risks. An effective survey may not need to probe more than about a dozen key areas—never more than about twenty. If you plan to model yours on the following survey, review each of the questions and include only the subset that is most relevant to your project. If you develop your own survey, limit the number of responses for each question to no more than five clearly worded responses. Ensure that the listed responses address all relevant possibilities, with no gaps or overlaps (for example: "1 or less," "Between 1 and 5," "5 or more").

Recently, I had the opportunity to help revise a risk assessment survey implemented using a Microsoft Excel spreadsheet. There were a dozen items included, and each was given a score from 1 (low risk) to 5 (high risk). The 12 areas probed were:

1. Completeness of business requirements
2. Estimated labor effort
3. Likelihood of scope change
4. Use of remote staff
5. Credibility of project objective
6. Accuracy of cost estimates
7. Experience with required technology
8. Expected staff stability
9. Use of new skills or contract staff
10. External dependencies
11. Accuracy of duration estimates
12. Other potential risk factors

For each item, the spreadsheet provided a detailed description and guidance for the five possible responses. As an example, for item two, this additional information was included: "This item addresses scale. Assess project risk based on staff effort. 1. Project is less than 3,000 person-hours; 2. Project is under 6,000 person-hours; 3. Project is under 10,000 person-hours; 4. Project is under 25,000 person-hours; 5. Project exceeds 25,000 person-hours."

The items were not equally weighted. Of the first eleven items listed, the initial four had a slightly higher weight and the last three had slightly lower. The weighted calculation generated a risk assessment rating between 1 and 5 for each project. Item twelve was not used unless its value exceeded the overall calculated risk score for the first eleven. If it was greater, that score replaced the calculated risk score.

Every project, regardless of size, was required to submit the risk survey. The survey was put to several uses. Any project with a low-risk score (1 or 2) was eligible to use a minimized version of the standard project methodology and required to submit fewer documents and reports. Projects having a high-risk score (4 or 5) were required to include a budget reserve of at least 10 percent to be used in managing risk. These surveys also provided data for analyzing risk across the portfolio of many hundreds of projects executed in the organization each year.

Once you have finalized the risk assessment questionnaire, the next step is to get input from each member of the core project team. Ask contributors who participated in project planning to respond to each question, and then collect their data.

Risk survey information is useful in two ways. Its main purpose is to produce an assessment of overall project risk. This can be used to compare projects, to set expectations, and to establish risk reserves. Another value is identifying weaknesses and widespread sources of project-level risk—through questions where responses consistently fall into the high-risk categories. Risk surveys can be very compelling evidence for needed changes in project infrastructure, organizational practices, or other aspects that increase risk. For high-risk factors, ask, "Do we need to settle for this? Are there changes we should consider that could reduce project risk?"

As you assess survey responses, also investigate any questions to which your contributors give widely divergent responses. Differences can reveal incomplete comprehension, ambiguity, or other problems. Conduct additional discussions to establish consensus, increase clarity, and build common understanding within your project team.

Instructions for a Sample Project Risk Questionnaire

Before using the following qualitative survey, read each one of the questions and make changes as needed to reflect your project environment. Eliminate irrelevant questions and add new ones if necessary to reflect risky aspects of your project. Effective surveys are short, so limit the survey to ten to twenty total questions. Section 2, "Technical Risks," normally requires the most intensive editing. The three sections focus on:

- Project external factors (such as users, budgets, and schedule constraints)
- Development issues (such as tools, software, and hardware)
- Project internal factors (such as infrastructure, team cohesion, and communications)

Distribute copies to key project contributors and stakeholders, and ask each person to select one of the three choices offered for each question. To interpret the information, assign values of 1 to selections in the first column, 3 to selections in the middle column, and 9 to selections in the third column. Within each section, sum up the responses, then divide each sum by the number of responses tallied. Within each section, use evaluation criteria such as:

- Low risk: 1.00 to 2.00
- Medium risk: 2.01 to 4.00
- High risk: 4.01 to 9.00

Average all questions to determine overall project risk, using the same criteria. Although the results of this kind of survey are qualitative, they can help you to identify sources of high risk in your project. For any section with medium or high risk, consider changes to the project that might lower the risk. Within each section, review all responses in the third column. Brainstorm ideas, tactics, or project changes that could shift the response, reducing overall project risk.

Example Questions for a Risk Questionnaire

For each question that follows, choose the response that best describes your project. If the best response seems to lie between two choices, check the one of the pair farther to the right.

SECTION 1.

PROJECT PARAMETER AND TARGET USER RISKS

1-1. SCOPE (PROJECT DELIVERABLE SPECIFICATION) STABILITY.		
❑ Change is unlikely	❑ Small change is possible	❑ Changes are likely or definition is incomplete
1-2. PROJECT BUDGET/RESOURCES.		
❑ Committed and realistic	❑ Probably sufficient, with margin/ reserve defined	❑ Insufficient or unknown
1-3. PROJECT DEADLINE.		
❑ Realistic	❑ Possible; margin/ reserve defined	❑ Overly aggressive or unrealistic
1-4. TOTAL PROJECT LENGTH.		
❑ Less than 3 months	❑ 3–12 months	❑ More than 12 months
1-5. TOTAL EFFORT-MONTHS ESTIMATED FOR THE PROJECT.		
❑ Less than 30	❑ 30–150	❑ More than 150

1-6. PEAK SIZE OF CORE PROJECT TEAM (KEY CONTRIBUTORS CRITICAL TO THE PROJECT).

❑ 5 or fewer	❑ 6–12	❑ More than 12

1-7. PROJECT MANAGER EXPERIENCE.

❑ Finished more than one comparable project successfully	❑ Finished a project about the same size successfully	❑ None, or only has done smaller or shorter projects

1-8. USER SUPPORT FOR THE PROJECT OBJECTIVE (SCOPE, SCHEDULE, AND RESOURCES).

❑ Enthusiastic	❑ General agreement	❑ Small or unknown

1-9. PRIORITIZATION OF SCOPE, SCHEDULE, AND RESOURCES (CONSTRAINED, OPTIMIZED, ACCEPTED).

❑ Known and agreed upon; only one parameter constrained	❑ Two parameters are constrained, but one is flexible	❑ No priorities set or all parameters are constrained

1-10. NUMBER OF DIFFERENT TYPES OF USERS (MARKET SEGMENTS).

❑ 1	❑ 2	❑ 3 or more

1-11. PROJECT TEAM INTERACTION WITH USERS DURING PROJECT.

❑ Frequent and easy	❑ At project start and end only	❑ Little or none

1-12. USER NEED FOR THE PROJECT DELIVERABLE.

❑ Verified as critical to user's business	❑ Solves a problem; increases user efficiency	❑ Not validated or unknown

1-13. USER ENTHUSIASM GENERATED BY THE PROJECT DELIVERABLE AT PROJECT START.

❑ High	❑ Some	❑ Little or none

1-14. USER ACCEPTANCE CRITERIA FOR THE PROJECT DELIVERABLE.

❑ Well defined	❑ Nearly complete	❑ Definition incomplete

1-15. USER ENVIRONMENT AND PROCESS CHANGES REQUIRED TO USE THE PROJECT DELIVERABLE.		
❏ None	❏ Minor	❏ Significant
1-16. USER INTERFACE TO OPERATE OR USE THE PROJECT DELIVERABLE.		
❏ Identical to one now in use	❏ Similar to one now in use	❏ New or represents major changes
1-17. TESTING PLANNED WITH ACTUAL USERS OF THE PROJECT DELIVERABLE.		
❏ Early, using models or prototypes	❏ Mid-project, at least for key subdeliverables	❏ Late in project; Beta test

SECTION 2.

TECHNICAL RISKS—GENERAL

2-1. COMPLEXITY OF DEVELOPMENT.		
❏ Less than recent successful projects	❏ Similar to recent successful projects	❏ Unknown or beyond recent similar projects
2-2. DEVELOPMENT METHODOLOGY.		
❏ Standardized	❏ Similar to other recent projects	❏ Ad hoc, little, or none
2-3. MINIMUM TEAM EXPERIENCE WITH CRITICAL DEVELOPMENT TECHNOLOGIES.		
❏ More than 1 year	❏ 6 months to 1 year	❏ Little or none
2-4. TOOLS, WORKSTATIONS, AND OTHER TECHNICAL RESOURCES.		
❏ Established, stable, and well understood	❏ All have been used before	❏ Some new facilities or tools required
2-5. PLANNED REUSE FROM EARLIER PROJECTS.		
❏ More than 75 percent	❏ 40 percent to 75 percent	❏ Little or none

2-6. EARLY SIMULATION OR MODELING OF DELIVERABLE.		
❏ Will be done with existing processes	❏ Planned, but will need new processes	❏ Not planned or not possible

2-7. TECHNICAL INTERFACES REQUIRED (CONNECTIONS OF THIS PROJECT'S DELIVERABLE INTO A LARGER SYSTEM OR TO DELIVERABLES FROM INDEPENDENT PROJECTS).		
❏ None (stand-alone) and well understood	❏ Less than 5 and all are to existing systems	❏ More than 5 or more than 1 that is new (parallel development)

HARDWARE

2-8. HARDWARE TECHNOLOGY INCORPORATED INTO DELIVERABLE.		
❏ All established, existing technology	❏ Existing technology in a new application	❏ New, nonexistent, or unknown technology

2-9. TESTING.		
❏ Will use only existing facilities and processes	❏ Will use existing facilities with new processes	❏ Unknown, or new facilities needed

2-10. COMPONENT COUNT.		
❏ Number and type similar to recent successful projects	❏ Similar number but some new parts required	❏ Unknown, larger number, or mostly unfamiliar components

2-11. COMPONENT SOURCES.		
❏ Multiple reliable, managed sources for all key components	❏ More than one identified source for all key components	❏ A single (or unknown) source for at least one key component

2-12. COMPONENT AVAILABILITY (LEAD TIMES, RELATIVE TO PROJECT DURATION).

❏ Short lead time for all key components	❏ One or more key components with long, but known, lead times	❏ One or more key components with unknown lead time

2-13. MECHANICAL REQUIREMENTS.

❏ All significant processes used before	❏ Some modification to existing processes required	❏ New, special, or long lead processes needed

SOFTWARE

2-14. SOFTWARE REQUIRED FOR DELIVERABLE.

❏ None or off-the-shelf	❏ Mostly leveraged or reused	❏ Mostly new development

2-15. SOFTWARE TECHNOLOGY.

❏ Very high-level language (4 or 5GL) or app development tool	❏ Standard language (C++, Java, Python, Visual Basic)	❏ New, low-level, or obsolete language (assembler, COBOL)

2-16. DATA STRUCTURES REQUIRED.

❏ Not applicable or relational database	❏ Other database or well-defined files	❏ New data files

2-17. DATA CONVERSION REQUIRED.

❏ None required	❏ Minor	❏ Major or unknown

2-18. SYSTEM COMPLEXITY.

❏ No new control or algorithm development	❏ Little new control or algorithm development	❏ Significant new or unknown development

2-19. PROCESSING ENVIRONMENT OF DELIVERABLE.

❏ Single system	❏ Multisystem but single site	❏ Distributed, multisite system

SECTION 3. STRUCTURE RISKS

3-1. PROJECT SPONSORSHIP AND MANAGEMENT COMMITMENT TO PROJECT OBJECTIVE (SCOPE, SCHEDULE, AND RESOURCES).

❑ Enthusiastic	❑ Supportive	❑ Neutral or none

3-2. PROJECT PRIORITY.

❑ High	❑ Moderate	❑ Low

3-3. PROJECT MANAGER EXPERIENCE.

❑ Success on recent similar project	❑ Managed part of a recent similar project	❑ Low or none on this sort of project

3-4. PROJECT MANAGER AUTHORITY.

❑ Most project decisions made by PM	❑ Limited decision-making and budget control	❑ None; all key decisions escalated to others

3-5. PROJECT MANAGER FOCUS.

❑ Full time on this project	❑ More than half time spent managing this project	❑ Less than half time spent managing this project

3-6. PROJECT PLAN.

❑ Plan is realistic and bottom-up	❑ Plan seems possible and has defined reserve for schedule/budget	❑ Plan is unrealistic or no plan exists

3-7. PROJECT VERSION CONTROL AND CHANGE MANAGEMENT.

❑ Well-defined and rigorously used processes	❑ Informal but effective processes	❑ Little or no change control

3-8. PROJECT LIFE CYCLE.

❑ Well-defined with clear milestones and phase deliverables	❑ Defined but not rigorously used	❑ No formal life cycle

3-9. PROJECT STAFFING.

❏ Available and committed	❏ All key people identified	❏ Significant staffing unknowns remain

3-10. SUBPROJECTS.

❏ This project is independent of other work	❏ All related subprojects are well defined and coordinated	❏ Related subprojects are loosely coupled or not clearly defined

3-11. PROJECT WORK ENVIRONMENT.

❏ Your site; workplace known and conducive to project progress	❏ Some work must be done in an unknown or poor work environment	❏ Mostly offsite or in a poor work environment

3-12. STAFFING COMMITMENT.

❏ All key people are full-time	❏ Mix of full-time and part-time staffing	❏ All part-time or external staffing

3-13. TEAM SEPARATION.

❏ Collocated	❏ Single site	❏ Multisite

3-14. TEAM ENTHUSIASM FOR THE PROJECT.

❏ High	❏ Adequate	❏ Reluctant or unknown

3-15. TEAM COMPATIBILITY.

❏ Most of team has worked together successfully	❏ Some of team has worked together before	❏ New team

3-16. LOWEST COMMON MANAGER FOR MEMBERS OF THE CORE PROJECT TEAM.

❏ Project leader	❏ Up to two levels in same organization	❏ More than two levels up, or none

3-17. NUMBER OF OUTSIDE ORGANIZATIONS OR INDEPENDENT PROJECTS THAT THIS PROJECT DEPENDS ON FOR INPUTS, DECISIONS, OR APPROVALS.

❑ None	❑ One other	❑ More than one

3-18. PROJECT DEPENDENCE ON EXTERNAL SUBCONTRACTORS OR SUPPLIERS.

❑ Little or none (<10 percent)	❑ Minor (10–25 percent)	❑ Significant (>25 percent)

3-19. QUALITY OF SUBCONTRACTORS.

❑ High—with relevant experience (or no subcontractors used)	❑ Good—solid references from trusted sources	❑ Doubtful or unknown

3-20. PROJECT COMMUNICATION.

❑ Frequent (weekly) face-to-face status gathering and written reporting	❑ Sporadic, informal, or long-distance status and reporting	❑ Ad hoc or none

3-21. PROJECT TRACKING.

❑ Frequent (weekly) reporting of actual progress vs. plan	❑ Project leader tracks and deals with plan exceptions reactively	❑ Informal or none

3-22. PROJECT DOCUMENTATION.

❑ Accurate, current documents are online for project team	❑ Current status and schedule are available to project team	❑ Documents known only to project leader, or none

3-23. PROJECT ISSUE RESOLUTION.

❑ Well-defined process; issues tracked and closed promptly	❑ Informal but effective process	❑ Issues are not easily resolved in a timely fashion

ANALYSIS OF SCALE

Quantitative project analysis using all the preceding techniques, with either computer tools or manual methods, is based on details of the project work—activities, worst cases, resource issues, and other planning data. It is also possible to assess risk based on the overall size of the project, because the overall scale is another important risk factor. Projects as little as 20 percent larger than previous work represent significant incremental risk.

Analysis of project scale is generally based on the overall effort required by the project plan. Projects fall into three categories— low risk, normal risk, and high risk—based on the anticipated effort compared with earlier, successful projects. Scale assessment begins by accumulating the data from the bottom-up project plan to determine total project effort, measured in a suitable unit such as "effort-months." The calculated project scale can then be compared with the effort actually needed to complete several recent, similar projects. In selecting comparison projects, look for work having similar deliverables, timing, and staffing to make the comparison as relevant as possible. If you lack effort-month data for the other projects, you can do a rough estimate using staffing levels and project duration. If there were periods in the comparison projects where significant overtime was used, especially toward the end, also include that effort. The numbers generated do not need to be precise, but they ought to fairly represent the amount of overall effort actually required to complete the comparison projects.

Using the total of planned effort-months for your project and an average from the comparison projects, determine the risk:

- **Low risk:** Less than 60 percent of the average
- **Normal risk:** Between 60 percent and 120 percent of the average
- **High risk:** Greater than 120 percent of the average

These ranges center on 90 percent rather than 100 percent because the comparison is between actual past project data, which includes all changes and risks that occurred, and the current project plans, which do not. Risk arises from other factors in addition to size, so consider raising the risk assessment one category if:

- Your schedule is significantly compressed
- Your project involves new methods or technology
- 40 percent of your project resources are either external or unknown

PROJECT APPRAISAL

Analysis of project scale can be taken a further step, both to validate the project plan and to get a more precise estimate of risk. The technique requires an "appraisal," similar to the process used whenever you need to know the value of something, such as a piece of property or jewelry, but you do not want to sell it to find out. Value appraisals are based on the recent sale of several similar items, with appropriate additions and deductions to account for small differences. If you want to know the value of your home, an appraiser examines it and finds descriptions of several comparable homes nearby that have been sold recently. If a comparison home has an extra bathroom, a small deduction is made to its purchase price; if your house has a larger, more modern kitchen, the appraiser makes a small positive adjustment. The process continues, using at least two other homes, until all factors normally included have been assessed. The average adjusted price that results is taken to be the value of your home—the current price for which you could probably sell it.

The same process can be applied to projects, because you face a similar situation. You would like to know how much effort a project will require, but you cannot wait until all the work is done to find out. The project appraisal process begins by selecting two or three recently completed similar projects for which you can determine the number of effort-months that were required. (Appraisals begin with the same data as the analysis of scale technique.)

From your bottom-up plan, calculate the number of effort-months your project is expected to take. The current project can be compared to the comparison projects, using a list of factors germane to your work. Compared factors relevant to the scope, schedule, and resources for the projects, as in figure 9-7 (which was quickly assembled using a computer spreadsheet).

This technique is most useful when the comparison projects are as similar as possible to your current project, using small adjustments to arrive at a plausible result. If a factor seems "similar," no adjustment is made. When there are differences, adjust conservatively, such as:

- **Small differences:** Plus or minus 2 to 5 percent
- **Larger differences:** Plus or minus 7 to 10 percent

The adjustments are positive if the current project is "bigger," and negative if the comparison project seems more challenging.

The first thing you can use a project appraisal for is to test whether your preliminary plan is realistic. Whenever the adjusted comparison projects average to a higher number of effort-months

Project: ___Zinfandel___   Effort-Months (Planned) | 100 |

		Project A		Project B		Project C	
		Comparison	Change in Effort	Comparison	Change in Effort	Comparison	Change in Effort
Effort-Months (Actual)		110		80		107	
Scope:	Functionality	Similar	0	3%	2.4	Similar	0.0
	Usability	−3%	−3.3	Similar	0	Similar	0.0
	Reliability	Similar	0	3%	2.4	Similar	0.0
	Performance	5%	5.5	Similar	0	−3%	−3.2
	Supportability	Similar	0	Similar	0	Similar	0.0
	Technology	−5%	−5.5	5%	4	−3%	−3.2
Resources:	Maximum staff	−3%	−3.3	3%	2.4	−5%	−5.4
	Control	Similar	0	Similar	0	Similar	0.0
	Staff experience	3%	3.3	Similar	0	Similar	0.0
	Geographical separation	Similar	0	5%	4	Similar	0.0
Schedule:	Total length	−5%	−5.5	Similar	0	3%	3.2
	Net adjustments	−8%	−8.8	19%	15.2	−8%	−8.6
	Indicated effort-months		101.2		95.2		98.4

Mean effort-months | 98.3 |

■ **Figure 9-7:** Project Appraisal

than your current planning shows, your plan is probably missing
something. Whenever the appraisal indicates a difference greater
than about 10 percent compared with the bottom-up planning,
work to understand why. What have you overlooked? Where are
your estimates too optimistic? What activities have you not captured? Also, compare the project appraisal effort-month estimate
with the resource goal in the original project objective. A project
appraisal can provide early warning of potential budget
problems.

One reason project appraisals will generally be larger than the
corresponding plan is due to risk. The finished projects include the
consequences of all risks, including any that were "unknown" and
invisible early in the work. The current project planning includes
data on only the known risks for which you have incorporated risk

prevention strategies. At least part of the difference between your plan and an appraisal is due to the comparison projects' additional risks, contingency plans, and other risk recovery efforts.

In addition to plan validation, project appraisals are useful in project-level risk management. Whenever there is a major difference between the parameters of the planned project and the goals stated in the project objective, the appraisal shows why convincingly and in a very concise format. An appraisal may also be useful for assessing risk due to scale, and may provide data needed to justify project-level resource reserves.

A project appraisal can provide a compelling way to initiate discussion of options, trade-offs, and changes required for over-constrained projects with your project sponsor. Chapter 10 will address gaining approval for adjustments to project goals and commitments.

SCENARIO ANALYSIS

Computer simulation using range estimates for cost and duration represents one type of scenario analysis. You can also deepen your insight into overall project risk through the use of narratives. Review your plans, playing a "movie in your head" as you consider the scheduled work, week by week. Look for instances where parallel projects or other work may be in conflict. Consider staffing profiles, and verify that shared or scarce resources will be sufficient. Overall, imagine the work as you expect it to proceed, and think about what will be keeping you up at night.

Another powerful technique for probing overall project risk is related to root-cause analysis. Chapter 6 discussed using specific descriptions of project problems to stimulate brainstorming about their sources and causes. The same idea can be applied to the project as a whole, through a project "premortem." Similar to a project retrospective or lessons learned exercise, this analysis probes for the reasons and causes behind significant problems and modes of project failure. Begin tapping into "prospective hindsight" by making a list of possible ways the project could fail. Challenge your team members and stakeholders to supply reasons for the failure. Such discussions cannot only reveal significant shortcomings in your planning processes, they can also help people see the project more realistically.

Note the portions of your schedule or plans that represent the greatest potential exposure, initiate further analysis, and consider possible plan adjustments to better manage the risks.

PROJECT METRICS

Project measurement is essential to risk management. It also provides the historical basis for other project processes such as estimation, scheduling, and resource planning. Metrics drive behavior, so selecting appropriate factors to measure can have a significant effect on motivation and project progress. HP founder Bill Hewlett is quoted as saying, "What gets measured gets done." Metrics provide the information needed to improve processes and to detect when you should modify or replace an existing process. Established metrics also are the foundation of project tracking and control, establishing the baseline for measuring progress. Defining, implementing, and interpreting a system of ongoing measures is not difficult, so it is unfortunate that on many projects it is done either poorly or not at all.

Establishing Metrics

Before deciding what to measure, carefully define the behavior you want and determine what measurements will be most likely to encourage that behavior. Next, establish a baseline by collecting enough data to determine current performance for what you plan to measure. Going forward, you can use metrics to detect changes, trigger process improvements, evaluate process modifications, and make performance and progress visible.

The process begins with defining the results or behavior you desire. For metrics in support of better project risk management, a typical goal might be "Reduce unanticipated project effort" or "Improve the accuracy of project duration estimates." Consider what you might be able to measure that relates to the desired outcome. For unanticipated project effort, you might measure "Total effort actually consumed by the project versus effort planned." For estimation accuracy, a possible metric might be "Cumulative difference between project estimates and actual durations, measured at the project conclusion."

Metrics are of three basic types: predictive, diagnostic, and retrospective. An effective system of metrics will generally include measures of more than one type, providing for good balance.

Predictive metrics use current information to provide insight into future conditions. Of the three types of metrics, predictive measures are the least precise, because they are based on speculative plan-based information. Predictive metrics include all the various project estimates, anticipated project "return on investment," the output from the quantitative risk management tools, and most other measurement forecasts based on planning data.

Diagnostic metrics are designed to provide current information about a system. Based on the latest data, project diagnostic metrics assess the state of a project as it progresses and may detect anomalies or reveal future problems. The "unanticipated effort" metric suggested previously is based on earned value, a project metric discussed next.

Retrospective metrics report after the fact on how the process worked. Backward-looking project metrics report on the overall effectiveness of processes and are useful in tracking project trends. Retrospective metrics can be used to calibrate and improve the accuracy of corresponding predictive metrics for subsequent projects.

Measuring Projects

The following section includes a number of useful project metrics. No project will need to collect all of them, but one or more measurements of each type of metric, collected and evaluated for all projects in an organization, can significantly improve the planning and risk management for future projects. These metrics relate directly to projects and project management. Further discussion of metrics related to financial measures follows this section.

When implementing any set of metrics, you need to spend some time collecting data to validate a baseline for the measurements before you make any decisions or changes. Until you have a validated baseline, measurements will be hard to interpret, and you will not be able to determine the effects of process modifications that you make. You will find more discussion on selecting and using metrics in chapter 10.

PREDICTIVE PROJECT METRICS

Most predictive project metrics relate to factors that can be calculated using data from your project plan. These metrics are fairly easy to define and calculate, and they can be validated against corresponding actual data at the project close. Over time, you want to drive the predictive measures and corresponding retrospective results into closer and closer alignment—making your forecasts and estimates more and more accurate. Measurement baselines are set using project goals and planning data.

Predictive project metrics can also serve as a distant early warning system for project risks. These metrics use forecast information during the early stages of work to highlight unrealistic assumptions, significant potential problems, and other sources of project risk. Because they are primarily based on plans and expectations rather than measured data, predictive metrics are generally the least accurate of the three types and often are reported using ranges or error bars. Predictive project measures support risk management in a number of ways:

- Determining project scale
- Identifying the need for risk mitigation and other project plan revisions
- Determining situations that require contingency planning
- Justifying schedule and budget reserves
- Supporting project portfolio decisions and validating relative project priorities

Predictive metrics are useful in helping you anticipate potential project problems. One method of doing this is to identify any of these predictive metrics that is significantly larger than typical for past, successful projects—a variance of 15 to 20 percent represents significant project risk. A second use for these metrics is to correlate them with other project properties. After measuring factors such as unanticipated effort, unforeseen risks, and project delays for ten or more projects, some of these factors may reveal sufficient correlation to predict future risks with fair accuracy. Predictive project metrics include:

SCOPE AND SCALE RISK

- Size-based deliverable analysis (part counts, number of major deliverables, lines of noncommented code, flowchart components, modules on system diagrams)
- Project complexity (interfaces, algorithmic assessments, technical or architecture analysis)
- Volume of expected changes
- Number of planned activities

SCHEDULE RISK

- Project duration (elapsed calendar time)
- Total length (sum of all activity durations if executed sequentially)
- Logical length (maximum number of activities on a single network path)
- Logical width (maximum number of parallel activities)
- Activity duration estimates compared with worst-case duration estimates
- Number of critical (or near-critical) paths in project network
- Logical project complexity (the ratio of activity dependencies to activities)
- Maximum number of predecessors for any milestone ("fan-in")
- Total number of external predecessor dependencies
- Project independence (ratio of internal dependencies to all dependencies)

- Total float (sum of total project activity float)
- Project density (ratio of total length to total length plus total float)

RESOURCE RISK

- Total effort (sum of all activity effort estimates)
- Total cost (budget at completion)
- Staff size (full-time equivalent and/or total individuals)
- Activity cost (or effort) estimates compared with worst-case resource estimates
- Number of unidentified activity owners
- Number of staff not yet assigned or hired
- Number of activity owners with no identified backup
- Expected staff turnover
- Number of geographically separate sites

FINANCIAL RISK—EXPECTED RETURN ON INVESTMENT (ROI)

- Payback analysis
- Net present value
- Internal rate of return

OVERALL RISK

- Number of identified risks in the project risk register
- Quantitative (and qualitative) risk assessments
- Adjusted total effort (project appraisal: comparing baseline plan with completed similar projects, adjusting for significant differences)
- Survey-based risk assessment (summarized risk data collected from project staff, using selected assessment questions)

- Aggregated overall schedule risk (or aggregated worst-case duration estimates)
- Aggregated resource risk (or aggregated worst-case cost estimates)

DIAGNOSTIC PROJECT METRICS

Diagnostic metrics are based on measurements taken throughout the project, and they are used to detect adverse project variances and project problems either in advance or as soon as is practical. Measurement baselines are generally set using a combination of stated goals and historical data from earlier projects. Diagnostic metrics are comparative measures, either trend-oriented (comparing the current measure with earlier measures) or prediction-oriented (comparing measurements with corresponding predictions, generally based on planning).

Based on project status information, diagnostic project metrics assess the current state of an ongoing project. Risk-related uses include:

- Triggering risk responses and other adaptive actions
- Assessing the impact of project changes
- Providing early warning for potential future problems
- Determining the need to update contingency plans or develop new ones
- Deciding when to modify (or cancel) projects

A number of diagnostic project metrics relate to the concept of earned value management (EVM). These metrics are listed with resource metrics below and described following this list of typical diagnostic project metrics:

SCOPE RISK

- Results of tests, inspections, reviews, and walk-throughs
- Number and magnitude of approved scope changes

SCHEDULE RISK

- Key milestones missed
- Critical path activity slippage
- Cumulative project slippage
- Number of added activities
- Early activity completions
- Activity closure index: the ratio of activities closed in the project so far to the number expected

RESOURCE RISK

- Excess consumption of effort or funds
- Amount of unplanned overtime
- Earned value (EV): a running accumulation of the costs that were planned for every project activity that is currently complete
- Actual cost (AC): a running accumulation of the actual costs for every project activity that is currently complete
- Planned value (PV): a running accumulation of the planned costs for every project activity that was expected to be complete up to the current time
- Cost performance index (CPI): the ratio of earned value to actual cost
- Schedule performance index (SPI): the ratio of earned value to planned value

- Cost variance (CV): the difference between earned value and actual cost, a measurement of how much the project is over or under budget
- Schedule variance (SV): the difference between earned value and planned value

OVERALL RISK

- Risks added after project baseline setting
- Issues opened and issues closed
- Communication metrics, such as volumes of email and voicemail
- The number of unanticipated project meetings
- Measured impact on other projects
- Risk closure index (ratio of risks closed in a project divided by an expected number based on history)

Many of the metrics listed here are self-explanatory, and many are routinely included in status reporting. Exceptions include the EVM metrics—EV, AC, PV, CV, SV, CPI, SPI, and the rest of the EVM alphabet soup. The definitions make them seem complex, but they really are not that complicated. EVM is about determining whether the project is progressing as planned, and it begins with allocating a portion of the project budget to each planned project activity. The sum of all these allocated bits of funding must exactly equal 100 percent of the project staffing budget. As the project proceeds, EVM collects data on actual costs and actual timing for all completed activities so that the various metrics, ratios, and differences may be calculated. The definitions for these diagnostic metrics are all stated in financial terms here, but the mathematics of EVM is identical for equivalent metrics that are based on effort data, and a parallel set of metrics defined this way may be substituted. The terminology for EVM has changed periodically, but its basic concepts have not.

The basic principle of EVM is that every project has two budgets and two schedules. It starts with one of each, making up the baseline plan. As the project executes, another schedule and another budget emerge based on actual project progress data.

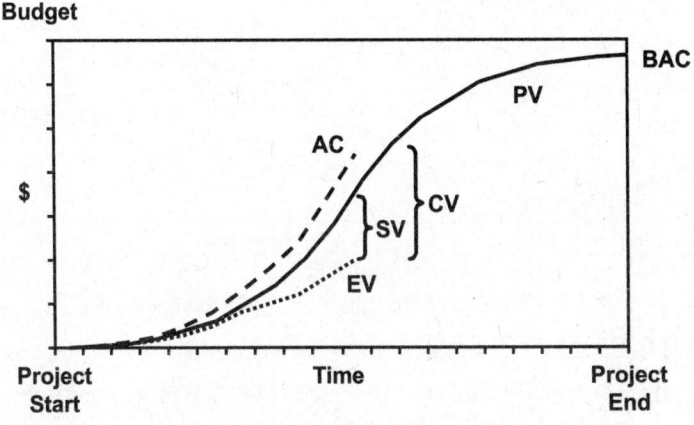

Figure 9-8: Selected Earned Value Measurement Metrics

The combination of planned funding and timing may be graphed as the curve labeled PV in figure 9-8, starting at zero and meandering up and to the right until it reaches the data point that represents the scheduled end of the project and the cumulative funding for the project. (The metric for the total budget is Budget at Completion, marked as BAC in figure 9-8.) The expected funding consumption curve describes the Planned Value (PV) metric. The combination of actual spending and actual activity completion may be plotted as the Actual Cost (AC) metric. These two metrics may be calculated at any point in the project, and if the project is exactly on schedule they may be expected to match. If they do not, something is off track. Because PV and AC are based on different schedules and budgets, you cannot really tell whether there is a timing problem, a spending problem, or some combination. To unravel this, you can use the Earned Value (EV) metric. As project work progresses, EV accumulates the cost estimates associated with the work, and it may also be plotted on the graph. These three basic EVM metrics are presented in the following table.

		BUDGETS	
		Planned Expenses	Actual Expenses
SCHEDULES	Planned Schedule	Planned Value (PV)	
	Actual Schedule	Earned Value (EV)	Actual Cost (AC)

As a project progresses, both PV and AC may be compared with EV. Any difference between AC and EV—in figure 9-8 shown as Cost Variance (CV)—must be due to a spending issue, because the metrics are based on the same schedule. Similarly, any difference between PV and EV—Schedule Variance (SV) on the graph—must be due to a timing problem. There are indices and other more complex derived metrics for EVM, but all are based on the fundamental three: EV, PV, and AC.

There is much discussion concerning the value of EVM. It typically can accurately predict project overrun at the point where 15 percent of the project budget is consumed, so it can be very useful. It also requires quite a bit of overhead. For many types of projects, tracking data at the level required by EVM may be considered overkill.

If the metrics for EVM seem impractical for your projects, the related alternative of activity closure index (listed with the schedule metrics) provides similar diagnostic information based on the higher granularity of whole activities. This metric provides similar information with a lot less effort. Activity closure rate is less precise, but even it will accurately spot an overrun trend well before the project halfway point.

RETROSPECTIVE PROJECT METRICS

Retrospective metrics determine how well a process worked after it completes. They are the project environment's rearview mirror. Measurement baselines are based on history, and these metrics are most useful for longer-term process improvement. Use retrospective project metrics to:

- Track trends
- Validate methods used for predictive metrics
- Identify recurring sources of risk
- Set standards for reserves (schedule and/or budget)
- Determine empirical expectations for "unknown" project risk
- Decide when to improve or replace current project processes

Retrospective project metrics include:

SCOPE RISK

- Number of accepted changes
- Number of defects (number, severity)
- Actual "size" of project deliverable (parts, major deliverables, lines of code, components, modules)
- Performance of deliverables compared to project objectives

SCHEDULE RISK
- Actual project duration compared to planned schedule
- Number of new unplanned activities
- Number of missed major milestones
- Assessment of duration estimation accuracy

RESOURCE RISK
- Actual project budget compared to planned budget
- Total project effort
- Cumulative overtime
- Assessment of effort estimation accuracy
- Life cycle effort percentages by project phase
- Added staff
- Staff turnover
- Performance to standard estimates for standardized project activities
- Variances in travel, communications, equipment, outsourcing, or other expense subcategories

OVERALL RISK
- Late project defect correction effort as a percentage of total effort
- Number of project risks encountered
- Project issues tracked and closed
- Actual measured ROI

FINANCIAL METRICS

Project risk extends beyond the normal limits of project management, and project teams must consider and do what they can to manage risks that are not strictly "project management." There are a number of methods and principles used to develop predictive metrics that relate to the broad concept of "return on investment" (ROI), and an understanding of these is essential to many types of technical projects. As discussed in chapter 3 with market risks, ROI analysis falls only partially within the traditional boundaries of project management. Each of the several ways of measuring ROI comes with benefits, drawbacks, and challenges.

The Time Value of Money

The foundation of most ROI metrics is the concept of the time value of money. This is the idea that a quantity of money today is worth more than the same quantity of money at some time in the future. How much more depends on a rate of interest (or discount rate) and the amount of time. The formula for this is:

$PV = FV/(1 + i)^n$, where:
PV is present value
FV is future value
i is the periodic interest rate
n is the number of periods

If the interest rate is 5 percent per year (0.05) and the time is one year, $1 today is equivalent to $1.05 in the future.

Payback Analysis

Even armed with the time value of money formula, it is rarely easy to determine the worth of any complex investment with precision, and this is especially true for project investments. Project analysis involves many (perhaps hundreds) of parameters and values, multiple periods, and possibly several interest rates. Estimating all of this data, particularly the value of the project deliverable after the completion of the project, can be very difficult.

The most basic ROI model for projects is simple payback analysis, which assumes no time value for money (equivalent to an interest rate of zero). This type of ROI metric has many names, including break-even time, payback period, or the "return map." Payback analysis adds up all expected project expenses and then proceeds to add expected revenues, profits, or accrued benefits, period by period, until the value of the benefits balances the costs. As projects rarely generate benefits before completion, the cumulative financials swing heavily negative, and it takes many periods following the first revenues and benefits to reach "breakeven."

■ **Figure 9-9:** Simple Payback Analysis

The project in the graph in figure 9-9 runs for about five months, with a budget of almost $500,000. It takes roughly another six months to generate returns equal to the project's expenses. Simple payback analysis works fairly well for comparing similar-length projects to select the options that recovers costs most rapidly. Payback analysis has the advantage of simplicity, using predictive project cost metrics for the expense data and sales or other revenue forecasts for the rest.

Refining simple payback analysis to incorporate interest (or discount) rates is not difficult. The first step is to determine an appropriate interest rate. Some analyses use the prevailing cost of borrowing money, others use a rate of interest available from alternative investments (such as bonds), and still others use rates based on business targets. The rate of interest selected can make a significant difference when evaluating ROI metrics.

Once you have determined the interest rate, each of the expense and revenue estimates can be discounted back to an equivalent present value before it is summed. The discounted payback or break-even point again occurs when the sum, in this case the cumulative present value, reaches zero. For a nonzero interest rate, the amount of time required for payback will be significantly longer than with the simple analysis, since the farther in the future the revenues are generated, the less they contribute due to the time value of money. Discounted payback analysis is still relatively easy to evaluate, and it is more suitable for comparing projects that have different durations.

Payback analysis, with and without consideration of the time value of money, is often criticized for being too short-term. These metrics determine only the time required to recover the initial investment. They do not consider any benefits that might occur following the break-even point, so a project that breaks even quickly and then generates no further benefits would rank higher than a project that takes longer to return the investment but represents a much longer, larger stream of subsequent revenues or benefits.

Net Present Value

Net present value (NPV) is another method to measure project ROI. NPV follows the same process as the discounted payback analysis, but it does not stop at the break-even point. NPV includes all the costs and all the anticipated benefits throughout the expected life of the project deliverable. Once all the project costs and returns have been estimated and discounted to the present, the sum represents the total present value for the project. This total NPV can be used to compare possible projects, even projects with very different financial profiles and time scales, based on all future project benefits.

NPV effectively determines the overall expected return for a project, but it tends to favor large projects over smaller ones, without regard to other factors. A related idea for comparing projects normalizes their financial magnitudes by calculating a profitability index (PI). The PI is a ratio, the sum of all the discounted revenues divided by the sum of all the discounted costs. PI is always greater than one for projects that have a positive NPV, and the higher the PI is above one, the more profitable the project is expected to be.

Even though these metrics require additional data—estimates of the revenues or benefits throughout the useful life of the deliverable—they are still relatively easy to evaluate.

Internal Rate of Return

Another way to contrast projects of different sizes is to calculate an internal rate of return (IRR). IRR uses the same estimates for costs and returns required to calculate total net present value, but instead of assuming an interest rate and calculating the present value for the project, IRR sets the present value equal to zero and then solves for the required interest rate. Mathematically, IRR is the most complex ROI metric, as it must be determined using iteration and "trial and error." For sufficiently complicated cash flows, there may even be several values possible for IRR. (This occurs only if there are several reversals of sign in the cash flows, so it rarely happens in project analysis.) These days, using a computer spreadsheet makes determining IRR fairly straightforward, if good estimates for costs and revenues are available. For each project, the interest rate you calculate forecasts how profitable the project would be as an investment.

Using ROI Estimates

All of these ROI methods are attempts to determine the "goodness" of financial investments, in this case, projects. Theoretically, any of these methods provides an effective way to select a few promising projects out of many possibilities, or to compare projects with alternative investment opportunities.

Because of their differing assumptions, these methods may generate inconsistent ranking results for a list of potential projects, but this is rarely the biggest issue with ROI metrics. In most cases the more fundamental problem is with input data. Each of these methods generates a precise numeric result for a given project, based on some analysis of "What's it cost?" and "What's it worth?" For many projects, this input data comes from two sources that are historically not very reliable: project planning data and sales forecasts. Project planning data can be made much more accurate as planning progresses using metrics and adjustments for risk. Unfortunately, project ROI calculations are generally made before much, if any, planning is done. When projects are initiated, project cost data is mostly based on vague information or guesswork. In many cases the "What's it cost?" estimate comes from top-down wishful thinking completely unrelated to planning.

Estimates of "What's it worth?" can be even more problematic. These assumptions are very uncertain (based on sales projections or other speculative forecasts). Not only that, they are almost always much larger numbers, so they are more significant in the calculations. In many cases for product development projects, revenue estimates are higher than costs by an order of magnitude or more. Even small estimating errors can result in large ROI variances.

The predictive value of ROI measures calculated in advance of projects can never be any more trustworthy than the input data, so skepticism is warranted. Retrospective ROI metrics can be very accurate when calculated after projects are completed, but this is rarely done (at least in part because it would embarrassingly reveal how inaccurate the initial projections were).

Key Ideas for Project Risk Analysis

- Survey contributors and stakeholders for risk assessments.
- Use worst-case estimates, contingency plan data, or Monte Carlo simulation analysis to assess project uncertainty.
- Estimate project scale in effort-months.
- Establish and use project metrics.

PANAMA CANAL: OVERALL RISKS (1907)

When John Stevens first arrived in Panama, he found a lack of progress and an even greater lack of enthusiasm. He commented, "There are three diseases in Panama. They are yellow fever, malaria, and cold feet; and the greatest of these is cold feet." For the first two, he set Dr. William Gorgas to work, and these risks were soon all but eliminated from the project.

For the "cold feet," Stevens himself provided the cure. His intense planning effort and thorough analysis converted the seemingly impossible into small, realistic steps that showed that the work was feasible. Over time the ways and means for getting the work done became well documented and credible. Even though there were still many specific problems and risks on the project, Stevens had demonstrated that the overall project was truly possible. This was quite a turnaround from John Wallace's belief that the canal venture was a huge mistake.

With Stevens's plan, nearly every part of the job relied on established techniques, and almost all the work required had successfully been done elsewhere. Project funding was guaranteed by the US government. There were thousands of people able, and very willing, to work on the project, so labor was never an issue. The rights and other legal needs were not a problem, especially after Theodore Roosevelt's manipulations both in the United States and in Panama. What continued to make the canal project exceptional was its enormous scale. As Stevens said, "There is no element of mystery involved, the problem is one of magnitude and not miracles."

Planning and a credible understanding of overall project risk are what convert the need for magic and miracles (which no one can confidently promise to deliver) into the merely very difficult. Projects that are seen as challenging but possible are the ones that succeed; a belief that a project can be completed is an important factor in how hard and how well people work. When it looks as though miracles will be necessary, people tend to give up, and their skepticism may very well make the project impossible.

CHAPTER 10

MANAGING PROJECT RISK

"Let us never negotiate out of fear, but let us never fear to negotiate."

—JOHN F. KENNEDY

I t is rare to encounter a project where everyone involved feels things are adequately under control. There never seems to be enough time, funding and staffing are below what you would like, and there are generally a few technical challenges yet to figure out. Managing project-level risk involves understanding all of this well enough early in your work to set realistic project expectations and, if necessary, to negotiate at least minor changes to project goals. Although completely dealing with project risks and issues is never possible, shifting things to minimize the worst problems may be enough. Once a project is seen to be feasible, hard work, with a bit of inspiration, cleverness, and luck, will often be sufficient to let you close the rest of the gap.

Managing project risk begins with the risk assessments and plans of the preceding chapters. This chapter builds on that foundation, discussing how to effectively use risk and project data to influence necessary changes, to clearly communicate project risks, and to adopt ongoing risk management practices that detect new risks promptly and minimize problems throughout the project.

PROJECT DOCUMENTATION REQUIREMENTS

One of the only things less interesting than assembling project documentation is reading a lengthy description of what it "must" include. Because today's projects come in all sizes, shapes, durations, and complexities, the requirements for project documentation—the written descriptions for project deliverables, plans, and other relevant information—vary a great deal. Whether the documentation is lengthy and elaborate or mostly informal, it serves as your foundation for project execution and control. Project teams that fail to put adequate documentation in place know too little about their projects and they carry more risk. In addition, when you lack data, you have a much lower chance of influencing necessary changes to your project because your proposals and negotiations will lack the compelling data facts needed to support them. Although it is certainly possible to overinvest in project documentation, it is far more common to create too little. Prudent project risk management tends to err on the side of capturing more, rather than less, data.

Project documentation is most effective when it is available in "layers." At the most detailed level, there is the thorough, everything-including-the-kitchen-sink version of the project plan needed by the project team. For others, such lengthy detail is neither necessary nor appropriate. You also need clear, summary-level documentation to use in discussions with sponsors, key stakeholders, and others who are less involved with the project but will be involved with project discussions, negotiations, decisions, escalations, problem-solving, and other project interactions.

Thorough project documentation created during your planning and risk assessment provides the foundation needed to validate your project plans. It also provides the leverage you need to negotiate project modifications when it is necessary to transform an overconstrained project that is sure to fail into one that is realistic. You will be overwhelmed by risk whenever your project baseline plans are inconsistent with stated project objectives. Thorough, realistic documentation also supports ongoing risk management through periodic plan reviews and an effective data-driven change management process.

Project documents fall into three categories: definition documents, planning documents, and periodic project communications.

Definition documents are generally assembled first. They include items such as:

- A high-level project overview
- A scope statement and a summary of the project objective
- The project charter (or "data sheet," project proposal, or whatever the overall description of the project may be called)
- Deliverable evaluation and acceptance criteria
- Project stakeholder and sponsor analysis
- Project staffing and organization information
- Significant assumptions and project constraints
- Methodologies or life cycles to be used
- Risk management plans
- Process documentation for managing specification changes

Additional necessary documentation may include detailed specification documents, a high-level project financial analysis, the project budget, detailed release requirements, any market research reports or user investigations, and any other specific project data required by your organization.

Planning documents are also assembled in the earliest project stages, but they may be expected to evolve and be augmented throughout the project as a result of new information or approved changes. Typical project planning documents are:

- The project work breakdown structure (WBS) and activity list
- The project schedule
- The project resource plan
- Functional plans (for quality, support, test, contracting, and other aspects)
- The risk register and risk management plans
- Documented baseline project commitments

Periodic project communications accumulate throughout the project. They will include items such as:

- Status reports
- Meeting minutes
- Issue logs
- Specification change notifications and reports
- Project reviews
- Phase transition, development iteration, or stage-gate documentation
- Interim and final project retrospective reports and "lessons learned"

Project documents are most useful when they use a consistent, easy-to-read format, so adopt an existing format (or define one) that seems appropriate for each piece of documentation and stick with it. Especially for lengthy documents, use a format that begins with a high-level summary or abstract that is no longer than half a page of text. It is always risky to bury important information on page 43 of a project report. For each project document, identify an owner (often the project leader) who will be responsible for creation, maintenance, and distribution. Define how to manage changes to documents such as requirements, specifications, and plans. When there are approved changes, determine how you will provide up-to-date documents and mark old versions obsolete.

Documents have value only if the people who need them have ready access to them. Storing documents online (with appropriate access security) is an effective way to ensure that all team members will have access to, and will be working from, the same information. Establish a centralized location for any paper documents (or several, for geographically separated teams) that is well known and easily accessed. Whether your project documents are in a notebook, in a file cabinet, or on a server, keep them available and up-to-date.

PROJECT STARTUP

One significant source of risk for modern projects is a lack of team cohesion, particularly for projects that have geographically separated teams. Completing a difficult project requires teamwork, trust, and a willingness to look out for and help other team members on the project. Under tension, chains tend to break at the weakest link; projects staffed by "virtual" teams have nothing but weak links.

One method for minimizing the risks that result when projects must be staffed by people who do not know each other is conducting a project startup workshop. A startup workshop (sometimes referred to as a project launch, a kickoff meeting, a planning workshop, or a project initiation meeting) is an event intended to initiate project processes and begin to build teamwork. A well-run startup will achieve a common understanding of the project goals and priorities and help you avoid wasted time and redundant effort. Establishing a cohesive team will ensure a fast, efficient start for the project.

You may even benefit from holding this sort of workshop several times during a project: early in the planning process, at the start of project execution, and before each major new phase of the project. The precise objectives will vary somewhat for workshops held at these different times, but all startups focus on team-building and on common project understanding. Achieving these objectives will substantially reduce many types of project risk.

Justifying and Preparing for the Workshop

One reason given for not holding startup workshops is cost. Particularly for global teams who must travel to take part in a face-to-face workshop, costs and travel time can be significant. But the cost of not doing a project startup is also high; serious problems and loss of productivity arise whenever people are uncooperative or misunderstand information in complex projects. For most projects it is not a choice between the expense of a project startup workshop and saving money; the choice is between investing a relatively small amount of time and money early or spending a lot more time and money on inevitable problems later in the project. Establishing common objectives and language for the project and building relationships among the project team members minimizes risk and creates the environment needed for a successful project.

Work to justify a face-to-face startup workshop early in the project. If the timing or cost aspects of a project startup genuinely make an in-person meeting impossible, at least plan and hold a meeting, or a series of meetings, using videoconferencing or other teleconferencing technology. Such a meeting is less effective for building relationships and trust, but it will be much better than doing nothing.

Productive project startup workshops require a well-planned agenda and sufficient time to carry it out. Determine the people who should participate in the workshop and get their commitment to attend. Prepare and distribute all the information that participants will need to review in advance, and plan to have all needed project information available throughout the workshop.

Holding the Workshop and Following Up

Begin the project startup workshop with personal introductions, focusing especially on contributors who don't know each other. Open the meeting with a review of the agenda, project objectives, ground rules, prevailing assumptions and constraints, and other necessary background information.

Throughout the workshop, have someone capture issues, questions, action items, and other data produced by the team. As the workshop progresses, work together with the attendees to review, develop, and improve the project definition and planning documents.

Toward the end of the workshop, review the issues captured and assess them for project risks. Risk identification is a significant byproduct of startup workshops, so explicitly add any newly uncovered risks and significant issues to your project risk register for further analysis and follow-up. Wrap up the workshop by identifying assignments, due dates, and owners for all action items and other required additional work. Close the meeting by thanking the participants for their contributions.

After the workshop, integrate the work done during the workshop into the appropriate project documents, and put the updated documentation where it can be referenced and used. Analyze new risks and plan responses for any that are significant. Follow up on all action items and other assignments made during the workshop, by either promptly bringing them to closure or by incorporating the needed work into your project plans.

SELECTING AND IMPLEMENTING PROJECT METRICS

Project metrics are fundamental to project risk management. Some metrics relate to risk triggers, and others may provide trend data that foreshadows future project problems. A project is a complex system, so you will need a number of metrics to adequately monitor progress. Defining too many metrics also causes problems, starting with the excessive cost and effort required to collect them. Strive to define a minimum set of project metrics that you need to give a balanced view. Chapter 9 lists a wide range of typical project metrics.

Selecting Metrics

Useful metrics are objective; if they are evaluated by several people, each person will get the same result. Good metrics are also easy to understand and to collect. Clarify how and what you need to measure, and verify through discussion that everyone involved has a consistent understanding of the process. Define the units and precision to be used for the measurements, and use the same units for all collection, evaluation, and reporting. For example, you might decide that all measurements for duration estimates be rounded to the nearest full workday. Also, determine how often to measure. You need to collect data frequently enough to support the results you desire, but not so often that it creates unnecessary overhead. Capturing data too often may also generate "noise," variations in the data that have little or no meaning.

Prioritize any metrics you are considering, using criteria such as linkage to desired behaviors, relationship to risks, contribution to potential process improvement, or availability of data. Collect only metrics that will make a meaningful difference; never collect data just because you can. An effective set of metrics also provides tension—improvement of one measure may diminish another one. Opposing a metric measuring speed of execution with another measuring defects or quality will result in more appropriate behavior than either measurement by itself. Work to minimize "gaming" of the metrics by eliminating factors that might improve the measurement without achieving any desired results. It is possible to subvert almost any metric, so define them in terms that minimize differing interpretations and "loopholes."

Finally, work to ensure that any metrics collected are used primarily for process monitoring and improvement, not as a basis for punishment. Metrics are powerful tools for identifying opportunities for beneficial change and determining trends, but the quality of the data that people provide will be less useful if they know that it will also be used in evaluating their performance. Once metrics are identified with processes used to rank and cancel projects, the reliability of future data deteriorates substantially. Use metrics for process control and improvement, not to generate criticism of the project team. If any personal information is involved, ensure that the measurements are kept confidential.

Implementing Metrics and Collecting Data

Before you start to use a project metric, work to get consensus from all members of the project team on the definition, the planned collection and use of the data, and the meaning of the results. Get commitment from everyone who will collect or supply data in advance, and seek agreement not to "game" the metrics.

After defining a set of metrics, the next step is to define an acceptable or desirable normal range. For well-established metrics, baselines may already be documented. For new measures, or for metrics used in a new application, you need to establish a "normal" data range. Although you can begin with an educated guess as a provisional baseline, you should use the first several cycles of data collected to confirm it. Until you have established the baseline using measurements, resist the temptation to make decisions and process changes.

Document each metric and its parameters, and provide this data to everyone involved. Include information such as the name of the metric, the intended objective, data required, measurement units, measurement frequency, the method for data collection, any formulas used, the target acceptable range, and who is responsible for making the measurement.

After setting a measurement baseline, collect project data as planned, and use the information to guide your project decisions. Set baselines for diagnostic metrics early in projects, using current data or data from similar earlier projects. For retrospective metrics, set baselines using existing data from earlier projects, or wait until several completed projects have collected the data required. For predictive metrics, establish corresponding retrospective metrics (for example, validate financial return on investment predictions against actual performance), and establish norms that plausibly connect to the desired results. Retain some skepticism when collecting project metrics, review the data you receive, and confront any suspected gaming of the measurements. Periodically reevaluate all metrics, especially after significant organizational or process changes. Following changes, revalidate the baselines and acceptable ranges for each of your metrics.

Throughout the process, make the measurements visible. Report the status of project progress and measures as planned to all project stakeholders who use the information or will be affected by it. Be prompt in evaluating and reporting the data to ensure timely feedback and early detection of significant variances.

ESTABLISHING PROJECT RESERVES

Imagine a large target with a big, red, circular bullseye in the center. If you stand two meters away from the target and aim a target rifle right at the center, you should have no difficulty hitting the middle of the bullseye. If you were to repeat the shot, but this time from two hundred meters away, the situation changes. For the second shot, simply aiming at the bullseye will no longer be effective, because you can no longer rely on the projectile to fly in a straight line. If you aim at the center of the target, you will hit below its center. The parabolic arc that controls the flight of the bullet was described with precision hundreds of years ago by Sir Isaac Newton, and the principle is so well understood that even a typical middle manager would not be tempted to hike out and give the bullet a lecture on "flying smarter, not harder." Everyone knows that you need to aim higher than the point you wish to hit, to compensate for the effects of gravity.

Simple, short projects are analogous to the first shot. Setting a date and planning to hit it will work more often than not, because the time window is brief, the work is fairly obvious, and the risks are small. For complex projects, though, the analogy of the second shot is better. The longer duration, with substantial unknowns and risks, is a different situation. As with gravity for the flying bullet, risk has an effect on the trajectory of a project. Project plans that set deadlines to line up exactly with the final planned activities have little chance of completing on time, even when the plans are based on reasonable, realistic estimates. The "force" of risk makes such a schedule unreliable.

Management reserve is a general tactic for dealing with project risk that helps to compensate for uncertainty. Reserve—in time, in budget, or in both—based on expected risk may be used to develop credible schedules and set reasonable expectations. Establishing reserves is not about padding estimates or making scheduling choices to accommodate sloppiness or team sloth; it is about using risk assessment information to set appropriate buffers at the project level to allow the project to deliver on commitments. In effect, management reserve is about setting project objectives with ranges, with the size of the range, or reserve, defined using project-level risk assessments.

Management reserve is based on two factors: expected impact from known risks (based on contingency plans, worst-case scenarios, and consequences of known risks you have elected to accept), and unknown risk. Data for the first factor, discussed in detail in earlier chapters, comes from planning processes. Unknown risk, by definition, is risk you are unable to anticipate or describe. Explicit planning for unknown risks is not possible, but metrics from earlier projects can provide guidance on the magnitude of exposure. Using project risk assessment data and metrics, you can estimate appropriate schedule and budget reserves. In effect, management reserve provides a generic contingency plan for your overall project. Reserve is never allocated to the activity level, and it is managed exclusively by the project leader, not by activity owners.

Schedule Reserve

Management reserve for schedules may be implemented in several ways. The simplest method is to estimate the amount of expected schedule exposure, and then develop a plan that supports completion of the project earlier than the required completion date by that amount. In dealing with problems, project slip that stays within the reserve will still permit you to meet the project commitment. The published project schedule either could show only the more aggressive, target completion date, or it could show the target date as a milestone followed by a dummy activity, and then the committed deadline. The dummy activity can have a name such as "allowance for risk," and it has a duration estimate equal to the schedule reserve.

For known risks, the amount of reserve needed for a given project can be anticipated using methods that have been described in earlier chapters of this book. From chapter 4, the idea of worst-case estimates provides one source. Using the "most likely" duration estimates establishes one possible project end date. Schedule analysis based on the worst-case estimates calculates a second end date for the project further out. Some fraction of the difference between these two dates can be used to determine the required reserve. How you do this depends on your confidence in the data, but it is common to use about half of the difference as a reserve—managing the work using the "most likely" schedule, but setting the project deadline to be a date midway between that schedule and the worst-case end date.

A second method for determining schedule reserve is based on data from contingency plans plus an allowance based on known, accepted risks. This process uses the method discussed in chapter 9 to aggregate activity risk data. In this case, you would track and manage your project using the project plan as a target, but your committed deadline would be later by a duration defined by the cumulative expected consequences of your known risks.

A third way to assess schedule reserve using data from known risks, also discussed in chapter 9, relies on PERT analysis or Monte Carlo simulations. Histograms or expected distributions can also be used to estimate required reserve, by determining the duration between the "most likely" (30 to 50 percent likelihood) date and some higher probability point farther out that is consistent with your project's risk tolerance. Again, your plan supporting the "most likely" dates can be used to manage the work and define the early point of a range window of acceptable dates. The upper boundary of the window will be the project commitment.

Estimating schedule reserve using any of these ideas will still necessarily be incomplete. These calculated allowances for reserve are based only on known risks. Without consideration of your unknown risk, you will underestimate the reserve allowance you need, perhaps significantly. If you have historical measures from past projects that track typical schedule impact from unanticipated problems, use them to include an appropriate margin for this in your required reserve.

One common example of reserve for unknown risk is explicit in many kinds of project plans. At the end of many construction and relocation projects there is an activity scheduled called a "punch list," or something similar. The purpose of this activity is to fix and close out all the defects, problems, omissions, or other issues that will accumulate on a list during the project. At the start of the project, a duration estimate based only on the list would logically be zero—there are no defects yet identified. Because a duration estimate cannot be based on explicit knowledge of the work, it is based on the history of dozens, or hundreds, of similar projects. Experience from earlier work tells you how much time and effort, on average, you can expect between completion of the final scheduled activities and customer sign-off. Metrics that measure unscheduled effort, the number of activities added during projects, underestimated activities, and other indicators of plan incompleteness are all useful for estimating typical "unknown" risk.

An alternative method for estimating the schedule consequences of unknown risk is the project appraisal idea discussed in chapter 9. The comparison projects include the effects of unknown risk, where your planned current project does not. Part of any difference shown in such an assessment is due to unknown risk.

The amount of required schedule reserve varies greatly depending on the type of project. A reserve of only a few days may be appropriate for short, routine projects. For complicated, aggressive projects, target dates may need to be established weeks, or even months, before the committed deadline to deal with the many possible problems and potential sources of slippage. Whether the reserve is short or long, remember that it, like schedule float, belongs to the project as a whole. It is available only for problem-solving, not for personal convenience. Using reserve established to manage project risk for other purposes (especially for scope creep) increases project risk.

The best way to handle schedule reserve will vary. On some projects, reserve is discussed and managed in the open. Schedules posted and distributed reflect its existence, and the status of remaining schedule reserve is discussed in status meetings with other topics. On other projects, the management of reserve is more covert. As far as the teams on these projects know, the deadline for the project is the date that follows the final activity in the plan.

Although this has the desired effect of focusing attention on getting the work done as promptly as possible, it is inconsistent with open and honest project communications. The alternative of managing the reserve openly is usually the better method, but it may be undermined unless you effectively guard against two potential issues: scope creep and Parkinson's Law.

Scope creep, as evidenced in the PERIL database, is a common issue. The more time a project team spends thinking about and doing the work, the more ways they come up with to make it "better." In projects that possess a time buffer for risk management, the temptation may become overwhelming to add and modify the project scope, because "we have the time available." On all projects, risk management depends on disciplined and thorough control of changes, and this is particularly true of projects that have visible schedule reserve. Schedule reserve should be used only to accommodate project changes that are a direct result of project problem-solving and issue resolution. Schedule reserve is not a tool for project "improvement."

The second issue, Parkinson's Law—work expands to fill the time available—also presents a significant challenge. Misuse of schedule reserve, particularly unused reserve still available late in the project, is a constant temptation. One method for guarding against this is to establish the available window of time for project completion, and to set up rewards for the team proportionate to any unused reserve at the end of the project. Incentives for avoiding misuse of the reserve can be effective, but they must be developed carefully so that they are effective in discouraging misuse and scope creep.

The best methods for reserve management ensure that all decisions are ultimately in the hands of a project leader who will apply the available reserve as intended, to deal with real-time problems, issues, and conflicts. This way, the established reserve operates to counteract the effect of risk and helps aggressively scheduled projects to meet goals and complete on or before their committed deadlines.

Budget Reserve

Resource analysis and risk data often reveals significant potential expense exposure. If so, establishing a reserve for resources at the project level will enable you to expedite work, add additional staff, or take other necessary actions that may be needed to stay on schedule.

The amount of reserve needed is estimated similarly to the schedule reserve discussed earlier, using worst cases, contingency plans, and budget analysis. For unknown risk, estimate reserve using financial metrics from earlier projects. Base your determination of required budget reserve on the best data you have available.

Again, the challenge is to be aware of the budget reserve while resisting the temptation to use it for project modifications that have nothing to do with risk. It is usually somewhat easier to manage budget reserve than schedule reserve, because decisions concerning money and resources are generally made by the project leader, and sometimes even higher in the organization.

Using Management Reserve

Although determining a prudent allowance for schedule and/or budget reserve is the first step, setting it up requires discussion, negotiation, and approval from project sponsors and stakeholders. You will need all the planning and other data you used to calculate required reserves, but this is not sufficient. You also need to identify and factor in your project constraints. Requesting schedule reserve that is not consistent with a required completion date for the project probably makes no sense, nor would a proposed budget reserve that exceeds the expected benefit for the project. Work to keep your analysis consistent with the goals and objectives for the project, and understand that when your estimate for reserve exceeds what is logical for the project, project risk is high. For cases where needed reserves seem excessive, abandoning the project in favor of better alternatives could be the best decision.

MANAGING FOR VUCA

Throughout this book we have explored the effects of volatility, uncertainty, complexity, and ambiguity (VUCA) on projects. Although the acronym originated within the defense community as they were responding to the 9/11 terrorist attacks in 2001, VUCA has evolved into a focus for business writers and project leaders. And as evidenced by damage documented in the PERIL database, dealing more effectively with these factors will certainly reduce overall project risk. In the PERIL database, uncertainty was responsible for almost half of the impact, followed by complexity, ambiguity, and volatility.

Bob Johansen (a business thought leader with the Institute for the Future in Silicon Valley) provides some perspective on countering VUCA in his book *Leaders Make the Future*. He suggests a set of positive VUCA strategies for better dealing with these challenges:

- **Vision** to minimize volatility
- **Understanding** to reduce uncertainty
- **Clarity** to decrease complexity
- **Agility** to manage ambiguity

We will explore these ideas and others for managing project risk related to each of the VUCA factors, starting with uncertainty.

Reducing Project Uncertainty

Uncertainty is often used as a synonym for risk, so it is unsurprising that "lack of predictability" is the most problematic of the VUCA factors in the PERIL database, representing nearly half of the total impact. Because projects are unique undertakings, some level of uncertainty is inevitable. At the project level, however, there are many things you can do to minimize what you don't know, starting with the sort of in-depth analysis and planning outlined in earlier chapters.

Thorough understanding is key to decreasing the level of overall project uncertainty. Do this through investigations, analysis, planning, collaborative discussions, and other project management techniques. Uncertainty increases along with scale and duration, so whenever possible set shorter-term, more easily understandable project goals aligned with phases, stages, or iterations.

Strive to establish consistent understanding of the overall project by all contributors, through education, training, development, and collective activities such as workshops, meetings, and reviews. As you interact with team members and stakeholders, ask lots of questions and use active listening to uncover pockets of inadequate understanding.

In all project estimating and forecasting, use ranges to make uncertainties visible, and probe for the sources and consequences of possible worst cases. Establish a central project management information system to archive project documents and plans where all involved can have easy access.

Decreasing Project and System Complexity

Difficulty understanding interactions within projects, especially larger ones, also causes a lot of project pain. Project complexity has many sources, including scoping and system aspects, complicated workflow, and organizational staffing. Developing greater clarity through decomposition can help in each of these areas. For complex deliverables having many components and a hierarchy of requirements, system analysis will assist you in understanding interrelationships and interfaces. When project workflow involves handoffs and interactions between teams working independently, program-level planning techniques will help you identify potential roadblocks and other problems. If overall staffing involves a team large enough to require a multilevel staffing chart, organizational planning techniques can be useful. Dealing with significant project complexity requires program management techniques (to be explored in more detail in chapter 13).

Complexity also arises from adopting novel approaches, equipment, and technologies. Wherever possible, consider simplifying methods, solutions, and hardware. Even though doing things "the same old way" might motivate team members less, using existing methods and exploiting established results that have worked previously can significantly decrease the complexity you face.

Working through complex challenges requires time. Provide as much as possible by scheduling risky, complicated activities as early in the project as possible. Plan for diligent monitoring of project tasks and prepare to respond promptly to any variances or issues. Establish reliable processes for escalating quickly when necessary, and implement course corrections based on "Plan-Do-Check-Act."

Managing complexity is also easier if you can obtain subject matter expertise to assist in areas where your team has deficiencies. In addition to schedule and budget reserve, establish a "talent reserve" by identifying any skills, knowledge, or experience required for your project that are missing or inadequate. Encourage team members to get training, find mentors, or otherwise build their talents. Having more people with broader expertise will not only help you deal with complexity, it will also provide for quicker and more effective response to project risks, issues, and problems as they arise.

Managing Project Ambiguity

High-level objectives used to start most projects are generally quite open to interpretation. The longer this ambiguity persists, the more harm it causes; scoping gaps—legitimate scope requirements discovered late in the project—caused over 40 percent of the scope-related impact in the PERIL database. Insufficient clarity is a major source of overall project risk.

When project objectives are poorly defined, agile methods or phased efforts can help. Setting relatively short-term project goals for the next phase, stage, or iteration and using feedback to solidify ongoing work can reduce ambiguity. Agile methods significantly improve the precision of scoping detail by validating detailed requirements one step at a time based on evolving benefits and results.

Look for ways early in the project to test, model, inspect, experiment, and gather feedback on any deliverable details that appear incomplete or "fuzzy." Focus initial project work on determining what is feasible, and use this to provide a foundation for documenting the project baseline.

Dealing with ambiguity also requires effective communications and documentation. Logically organize and thoroughly document project plans, objectives, data, and reporting. Work to clearly define all terminology, and avoid jargon, acronyms, and "technobabble."

Minimizing Project Volatility

Unpredictable change threatens projects of all types. Scope creep—nonmandatory scoping changes—and scoping gaps represented over 70 percent of the pain related to scope issues in the PERIL database. As with ambiguity, much of this originates with insufficient initial precision regarding project deliverables.

A vivid project vision can help avoid unanticipated changes by providing a clear and motivating statement describing why the project matters. An effective vision uses compelling language to summarize how successful project completion will result in a better future. A useful, compelling project vision is durable and is not likely to change over time. Good vision statements are also motivating. When project contributors care about the vision, they commit to the goals and strive to deliver expected results even when the going gets hard.

As you interact with key stakeholders, ask questions and use active listening to uncover inadequate understanding or differing expectations. Probe to uncover any lack of agreement on goals or requirements. When project plans are coming into focus, quantify the value of the expected benefits and results. Use the information to obtain buy-in from key stakeholders early, before committing to a formal baseline. Work to secure and maintain strong project sponsorship based on clearly stated and documented objectives.

Establish effective processes for prioritizing and managing scoping changes as the project progresses, with firm commitment that all change decisions will consider consequences to the project vision and benefits. Ensure that any approval of changes will rely on realistic assessment showing that the value of the change significantly exceeds its cost. We will explore establishing effective specification change management processes later in this chapter.

PROJECT BASELINE NEGOTIATION

Managing project risk nearly always involves some shift in the project objective. In the unlikely event that your bottom-up plans and risk assessment are wholly consistent with the initial project goals, no negotiation is necessary; validating the plan and documenting the baseline is all that you need to do. For most projects, however, there will be issues to confront, often significant ones.

Project negotiation serves a number of purposes. The most obvious one is to shift an overconstrained project enough to bring it in line with a realistic plan. Other reasons for negotiation include securing sponsor support, setting limits on project scope, and managing expectations.

Strong Sponsorship

Risky projects need all the help they can muster, so work to get and retain high-priority and visible support for your project. Projects that have substantial risk are generally undertaken because there are large potential benefits expected, so ensure that all discussions of the project emphasize the positive results that will come from the project, not just the risks, problems, and challenges. Build awareness of your project, early and often, so that your management will continue to support the project in its words and actions. Particularly on risky projects, you need commitment for quick resolution of escalated issues, protection of the project team from conflicts and nonproject commitments, and adequate management reserve. You may also want sponsor approval for training to acquire new skills and to streamline or change processes.

The sponsor can also lower risk for the project by aggressively removing organizational barriers and administrative overhead, and by dealing with factors that may inhibit fast execution of the project. Conversely, management can exacerbate risk by contributing to these factors and initiating new work that requires people currently assigned to your project. Strong, continuing sponsorship is one of the key factors that separates risky projects that succeed from those that crash and burn.

Setting Limits on Project Scope

Another goal of project negotiation is to set boundaries for the project. A great deal of risk for complex projects, discussed in chapter 3, arises from the fact that there may be lingering ambiguity and any number of different expectations concerning what, exactly, your project is supposed to produce. Even though you and your project team probably have a relatively clear definition as the planning and risk analysis come to closure, there still may be residual "fuzziness" in other quarters. The project scope must be just as clear as the deadline, to everyone involved.

Work to focus discussions with sponsors and key stakeholders around unambiguous scoping documentation that clearly states both what the project will include and what it *will not* include. Even projects employing agile methods benefit from establishing limits and expectations for deliverables early in the work; understanding the overall objectives and credible foundations for creating value will establish boundaries for delivery of useful, cost-effective results. Setting limits on scope early, using "is/is not" scope descriptions that are clear to all, will either validate the project team's conceptions or trigger discussions and necessary adjustments. Making needed scope corrections at the project's inception lowers overall risk and establishes consistent expectations for all parties.

Fact-Based Negotiation

Project baseline negotiation requires your definition and planning documents. Initial discussions will focus on summaries, so writing clear, informative summaries is essential. In preparing project information for discussion, include a high-level summary of objectives, a milestone project schedule, a high-level work breakdown structure, a project appraisal, and a summary of major assumptions and risks. If your planning shows a major mismatch between the current project plan and the requested project goals, prepare and bring several high-level proposals describing project alternatives.

With this data in hand, your next step is to set up a meeting with the project sponsor to discuss the project, the results of your planning, and, if necessary, the alternatives. Begin the discussion with a presentation of your planning results. Whenever your project plan is inconsistent with the project as initially conceived, you need to negotiate changes. Changes to consider include requesting additional resources, extending the deadline, getting contributors with more experience, building skills using the people you have, reducing project scope, or any number of other options.

Having data is critical for your success, because the balance of power in such negotiations is not in your favor. Although it is relatively easy for sponsors and managers to brush aside concerns and opinions, it is much more difficult for them to dismiss hard facts. When there is a significant difference between project expectations for timing and resources as seen by the project team and their management, a half-page project appraisal (described in chapter 9) can be a good starting place for the discussion, showing why the requested project is not likely to be done as quickly or inexpensively as desired. ("Remember this project? That's the one we tried to complete in two months, and it ended up taking six.")

When requested to do a project much faster than is possible, your project Gantt chart, showing all the activities and durations, is an effective tool. When the proposed deadline is far too short to accommodate the work, hold up the chart and say that you can only do it on schedule if the sponsor will select some activities to delete. Most sponsors will quickly back down and begin a productive discussion of alternatives, rather than randomly removing work they probably do not understand. Any project information backed up by historical, documented data can be a good starting point for a fact-based, not emotion-based, negotiation.

Reducing project risk through negotiation is best done with the ideas outlined by Roger Fisher, William Ury, and Bruce Patton of the Harvard Negotiation Project in their book *Getting to Yes*. Their process of principled negotiation is effective for "win-win" negotiations, where all parties get at least some of what they seek. In project negotiations where only the sponsor "wins," everyone loses. It does no one any good to force a commitment to an impossible project. The team and project leader lose because they are stuck with a doomed project. The sponsors, managers, and customers lose too, because they do not get what they expect and need. Principled negotiation, done early, is essential for dealing with unrealistic projects.

Some useful ideas for project negotiations include separating the people from the issues and focusing on interests, not positions. By sticking to facts and mutually understood needs, you raise the discussion beyond "This project is hard" on the project side and "You are the best project leader we have" on the other. Although both of the statements may be true, neither one actually addresses the real issue—that the project objective, as stated, is not possible. As you prepare for negotiation, develop project alternatives that provide for mutual gain, such as exploring opportunities that could increase the original project's benefits, or segmenting the project into a sequence of shorter projects capable of delivering value earlier. In your negotiations, base decisions and analyses on objective criteria. Brainstorm, problem-solve, and get everyone involved in seeking better options. Ask lots of questions, and focus on resolving the issues, not just arguing about the project.

Your biggest asset in all of this is your knowledge. As a result of your project planning, no one alive knows more about the project than you do. You also have a track record and credibility, built up over a body of prior work. The managers and project sponsors are aware of this; that is why they requested that you lead the project. Proceed with negotiations using your technical and planning expertise, and the experience of your project team.

Lay out the consequences of accepting a commitment to a project with excessive residual risk in clear, fact-based terms. By using conservative assumptions to support the analysis of the potential project problems, you will end up with one of three possible results. The most desirable outcome is shifting the project objective in line with, or at least reasonably close to, your plan. For other projects, realistic analysis of the work and risks may lead to the conclusion that the project is not a good idea, and it is taken no further. Either of these outcomes will avoid a failed project.

The third possibility is that your data may not be sufficiently compelling or that your sponsors will ignore it. In this case, you may end up forced to commit to an infeasible project, with no realistic plan to support it. Should this happen, document the situation for future reference, to make it less likely to recur. Then you can try your best and hope for miracles (or update your résumé).

PROJECT PLAN VALIDATION

Following discussion and negotiation, validate that you have consensus on the project. Verify that you have a plan supporting the project objective that is acceptable to the project sponsor and key stakeholders as well as to you and your project team.

Use the project documents from the planning processes, with any negotiated modifications, to establish the project baseline plan of record. Before finalizing the plan, review it to ensure that it includes periodic risk reassessment activities throughout (at least at major phase milestones). During these reviews, additional risks not apparent at project start will be identified, and your contingency plans can be updated.

Publish the final versions of the project documents and distribute them so that the project team can access and use them to manage progress throughout the project. Put your project documents online or in another location where everyone has access to current versions at any time. If you use a computer scheduling tool for project tracking, save the project schedule as a baseline and begin tracking activity status in the database.

When you set the project baseline, freeze specifications for at least the initial development effort and delivery of results. Set both the project scope definition and your baseline plan at the same time, and change neither one without using an established process like that described in the next section to manage specification changes. Freezing the overall schedule and resources on a project while allowing the scope to continue to meander is a massive source of project risk.

For risk visibility, create a "Top Ten" list of the most significant known risks for the current phase of your project, and post it where the project team will be aware of it—in the team workplace, on the project website, or in some other prominent location. Commit to periodically reviewing and updating the list throughout the project.

SPECIFICATION CHANGE CONTROL

Once the project plan has been accepted by all stakeholders and you have locked in your requirements, initiate an effective process to carefully manage all proposed scoping changes. After the project documents are agreed to by all appropriate decision-makers—the project sponsor, customers, stakeholders, and others—it is risky to allow unexamined changes into the project. Although new information flows around modern projects continuously, maintaining specification control is crucial for project success. Unmanaged change leads to slipped schedules, budget problems, and other consequences, as the PERIL database shows. Even on projects employing agile methods where evolution of scope for future development iterations is inevitable, you need to manage risk through scrupulous control of changes during each development cycle (and often for one or more subsequent iterations as well).

Having a process for submission, analysis, and disposition for each proposed change lowers the risks, especially if "reject" is the default decision for submitted change requests. An effective change management process puts the burden of proof on each change request; all changes are considered unnecessary until proven otherwise.

Another requirement for effective change control is giving the people responsible for the change process the authority to enforce their decisions. Change approvers need the power to say "no" (or at least "not yet") and make it stick. For reasons of efficiency, some change processes establish change screeners, who initially examine any proposed change and determine when (or even if) a change will receive further consideration.

Even the most rudimentary project change control processes should be documented, in writing. The formality of the actual process adopted varies a great deal with project type, but at a minimum, it should include:

- Logging and tracking of all change requests
- A defined process for analyzing all proposed changes
- Documented criteria for accepting, rejecting, or deferring changes
- Communication of decisions and status

Change Submissions

Ideas for change generally begin with problem-solving or from recognition of an opportunity. Submissions should include information such as:

- Why the change is needed
- An estimate of expected benefits from the change
- The estimated impact of the change on schedule, cost, and other factors
- Specific resources needed for the change

Document all changes submitted, and maintain an up-to-date log (or "burn-down" list, or backlog) of submitted change proposals throughout the project. Following submission, examine each submitted change, and if the information is unclear or key data is missing, return the request to the submitter for correction.

Change Analysis

Analyze all changes for both impact and cost/benefits. Impact assessment parallels the processes used for impact analysis of risks. It begins with high-level categorization of change impact:

- **Small:** minor effect on the deliverable or project plan
- **Medium:** functional change to the deliverable but little project impact
- **Large:** major change to project object and the deliverable

Evaluate the costs and benefits of the change. Each change presumably has some benefits, or it would not have been submitted. The expected benefits need to be estimated and verified so they can be compared with the expected costs and other consequences.

Changes generally fall into one of several categories. Many proposed changes resolve problems encountered on the project or fix something that is not functioning as required. The benefits of these changes relate to the avoided expense or time slippage that will persist on the project until the problem is solved. Other changes arise from external factors such as new regulatory or safety requirements, the need to comply with evolving standards, or actions by competitors. These types of change, which are solving real problems, addressing firm requirements, and reacting to adverse shifts in the environment, are often unavoidable. Your project deliverable will lose much, if not all, of its value unless the changes are made. The benefits of both kinds of "mandatory" changes are usually sufficient to justify their serious consideration.

Other project changes are intended to make the project "better" and are on less solid ground—changes that add something to the deliverable, alter something about the deliverable to improve it, or introduce new processes or methods to be used for project work. The benefits of these changes are more speculative, and thus harder to assess. Credible estimates for increased sales, revenue, or usefulness as a result of the change are difficult, and they tend to be optimistic. Although some opportunities for change may result in significant benefits, many changes intended to make projects "better" generate unintended consequences and result in benefits that are far smaller than expected (or even nonexistent). Overall impact to a project may also be difficult to estimate, particularly if the change involves adopting a new approach to the work. Effective change management systems are highly skeptical of these discretionary modifications and tend to reject them. When outright rejection is not possible, the process should at least be adept at saying "not yet." This allows the project to proceed as planned and later embark on a follow-on effort to pursue the ideas or reconsider them to be part of a future development iteration.

In all cases, a rational consideration of the net benefit of the change—the reasonably expected benefits less the estimated costs and other consequences—must be the basis for any good decision. This analysis should apply to all submitted changes, regardless of their origin. If customers submit changes, the specific consequences in terms of timing and cost must be visible to them, and generally borne by them as well. If a project contributor submits a change, he or she should provide ample documentation for it and expect to fight hard to get it approved. Politically, the most difficult situations arise from the changes requested by sponsors and management. Although it is never easy to say "no" to the people you work for, the existence of a documented process that has been approved to manage project change is a vital initial step, and clear, data-supported descriptions of the consequences of requested changes are also necessary. As with risk management generally, effectively managing risk associated with scope changes relies on thorough, credible project planning data.

Disposition Options

For each potential change, you have four options: approval, approval with modification, rejection, and deferral. The process for making a decision on each proposed change uses the results from the analysis and documented information on project objectives and priorities to make a business decision. The primary criterion for the decision will generally be the assessment of benefits versus costs, weighing the relative advantages and disadvantages of each change. The level of formality tends to scale with project size and complexity, but two aspects of the decision process are universal. The first requirement is to make decisions promptly. Change requests, particularly those that address problems, need quick attention. The value of urgent changes can diminish significantly as they sit, so ensure that such changes are considered and closed without undue delay. Even scope management processes that defer significant changes to the end of a phase or development iteration need an exception process for occasional prompt action. The second need is for consistent adherence to agreed-upon requirements for decisions. Some change systems are based on approval by a majority of those involved; some require unanimity; and still others grant veto powers to some approvers who have greater organizational authority. Effective change systems avoid having too many decision-makers required for approval to minimize scheduling problems and shorten debates, and they provide named backup approvers who can act whenever a designated approver is not available.

An effective change management process always starts with the presumption that proposed changes are unnecessary, and rejects all changes that lack a compelling, credible business case. Carefully examine even changes that have demonstrable benefits to determine whether some parts of the change may not be needed, or whether the change could be deferred to a later project, phase, or development iteration—especially if the impact significantly interferes with committed project objectives. Approval and acceptance of changes should be relatively rare, and reserved for the most compelling requirements for problem-solving or delivering significant business value. The more change a project is subject to, the higher the risk. Whatever the decision, close out all requests quickly, within the documented time goals established for the process. Also, promptly escalate any issues or conflicts that cannot be resolved at the project level.

Communicating the Decision

As each decision is made, document it in writing. Include the rationale for the decision and a brief description of any project impact. Prepare and distribute a summary of the pending, accepted, and rejected change proposals to project stakeholders and to your project team members.

Whenever a change is not approved, respond to the submitter with an explanation, including the rationale for the decision. If there is a specific process for appeal and reconsideration, provide this information to the submitter as well.

For any accepted changes, update all relevant project documents—the work breakdown structure, estimates, schedules, specifications and other scope documents, the project plan, charts, or any other project documents that an approved change affects.

Even for rejected changes, retain the proposals in the project archives. The "good ideas" may be worthy of consideration in follow-on projects, in parallel projects, or in a later phase of work. When your project is over, you can use the change history to reduce risk on future projects by carefully reviewing the process, the decisions made, and the consequences (both intended and unintended).

Key Ideas for Managing Project Risk

- Hold a project startup workshop.
- Select and use appropriate project metrics.
- Determine and establish the required project reserve.
- Consider your VUCA factors.
- Negotiate and commit to credible project objectives.
- Manage scope and control specification changes.

PANAMA CANAL: ADJUSTING THE OBJECTIVE (1907)

Setting a concrete objective for a project is not necessarily a quick, easy process. In the case of the Panama Canal, although Theodore Roosevelt made the decision to build the canal and the Senate approved the commitment in early 1904, the specifics for exactly what sort of canal would be built were still not settled nearly two years later. All the data accumulated by John Stevens led him to the same conclusion ultimately determined by the French engineers—building a sea-level canal at Panama was not feasible. He estimated that a lock-and-dam canal could be completed in nine years, possibly eight. A sea-level canal could not be built in less than eighteen years, if at all. He convinced Theodore Roosevelt of this, and he thought the matter was settled.

But it was not settled. In spite of the French experience, the lock-and-dam versus sea-level debate was still going strong in the US Senate in 1906. Showing much of the same diligence and intelligence one might expect of today's Senate, they took a vote on how to build the canal. They approved construction of a sea-level canal by one vote. One unavoidable observation from study of past projects is that things change little over time, and politics is rarely driven by logic.

John Stevens had just returned to Panama from Washington in 1906, and although he was quite busy with the project, he turned around and sailed back to the United States. He met extensively with members of both the US House of Representatives and the Senate. He patiently explained the challenges of a sea-level canal in a rainforest with flooding rivers. He developed data, drew maps, and generally described to anyone who would listen all the reasons why the canal could not be built at sea level. As was true earlier for the French, the main obstacle was the flooding of the Chagres River, which flows north into the Gulf of Mexico parallel to the proposed canal for roughly half of its route.

Stevens spent a lot of time with one ally, Senator Philander Knox. Senator Knox was from Pennsylvania—specifically, he was from Pittsburgh, Pennsylvania. Stevens worked with Knox on a speech in which the senator described in detail why the canal must be constructed with dams and locks. By all reports, it was an excellent speech, delivered with great eloquence and vigor. (It was probably not entirely a coincidence that a sea-level canal required none of the locks, steel doors, and other hardware that would come from Senator Knox's friends in the foremost steel-producing city in the Americas.)

Despite all of this, thirty-one senators still voted for a sea-level canal. Fortunately for the project and for Stevens, thirty-seven senators were paying attention, and the design Stevens recommended was approved.

It had taken him more than a year, but finally John Stevens had his plan completed and approved. Defending the feasible plan required all of his data, principled negotiation, and a great deal of perseverance, but he ultimately avoided the costly disaster of a second impossible canal project at Panama.

CHAPTER 11

MONITORING AND CONTROLLING RISKY PROJECTS

"Adding manpower to a late software project makes it later."

—FRED BROOKS, author of *The Mythical Man-Month*

Apart from phrasing (replacing the very 1970s *manpower* with *people* or *staff*), it's hard to quibble with Fred Brooks's statement. In fact, the effect described by Brooks applies to projects of almost any type, not just software projects. Adding contributors to a late project never seems to help very much, because the first thing that new people on a project need is information, so they ask blizzards of questions. Responding to these questions distracts the overworked people already on the project, which further slows progress. There are other reasons adding staff late in a project can be counterproductive, such as the need to build trust and to move through the team-building stages of "forming, storming, and norming." Adding staff is not the real problem, though. It is adding staff too late. One goal of disciplined project tracking is to detect staffing shortfall issues early enough to avoid the need for chaotic, and seldom successful, heroic measures.

Effective monitoring will help you find and fix problems while they are still small and stay out of trouble in the first place.

Risk management cannot end with the initial planning. Your project starts with its plan, just as a lengthy automobile trip begins with an itinerary based on maps and other information. But what trip ever goes exactly as planned? As the driver continues on the trip, small adjustments based on events and conditions are necessary. More serious issues such as vehicle problems or automobile accidents may result in major modifications to the itinerary. Throughout the trip, the driver must remain alert and reasonably flexible. Managing risk in projects is about detecting things that are not proceeding as planned in your project. Like the driver who must remain alert and responsive to things that happen on the road, the project leader uses tracking, reviews, and reapplication of the planning concepts discussed in the preceding chapters to adjust to the prevailing project conditions, seeking to bring it to successful closure.

Effective project risk management relies on frequent reassessment of new information and status as the work proceeds. You cannot know everything about the work at the beginning, particularly for longer, complex projects. Periodic project reviews are necessary to keep the project moving and productive.

DON'T PANIC

The main focus of this chapter is ongoing execution of a project with as few detours and as little aggravation as possible. Risk planning helps to reveal what might go wrong, so you can have responses ready to deal with much of it. Project work is unpredictable, though, so unexpected things will happen. Effective project leaders strive to remain calm when problems arise. Risk management depends on level-headed analysis and prompt action, so work to remain composed. Recovery from problems not only depends on a prompt and appropriate response, it also depends on competent execution. You will stay on track more successfully by heeding Rudyard Kipling: "If you can keep your head when all about you/Are losing theirs and blaming it on you. . . ."

This is much easier to say than to do, but minimizing emotions and chaos in a crisis is the fastest route to problem recovery. Stress causes inefficiency and mistakes and raises the likelihood of future risks, so do your best to keep things running smoothly throughout your project—even when things seem to be falling apart. Panic will only make things worse.

APPLYING THE PLAN

Predictable project progress depends on your baseline project plan. The plan is now the roadmap for your work, and you can begin tracking status and updating your project database with actual results. Status information is primarily useful in assessing progress, but it also provides early warnings for risks. In addition, status data supports longer-term risk management by revealing opportunities and overall process improvements you can act on during project reviews and postproject analysis.

Risk management relies on systematic project tracking to provide the information necessary for proactive detection of project problems while they are still small and easily solved. Project tracking helps you anticipate potential problems, allowing the project to avoid at least some of them. Disciplined tracking makes it difficult to ignore early warning signals, and it provides the data you will need for an effective response. Without accurate, timely information, project problems remain out of sight.

Hidden problems will occur without warning, inflicting serious damage to your plans.

Credible status data also can reduce the project worries and team stress that arises from a lack of good information. Even when the project status reveals bad news, the true situation viewed with credible information is nearly always less dire than the alternatives that people dream up when they lack data. In addition, detailed status often reveals root-cause and other information you need for recovery. Factual information helps dampen both excessive optimism and pessimism, neither of which is helpful to a project.

Dogmatic collection of project status and frequent comparison to the plan guards against a common project risk—"safe so far" project reporting. As long as project deadlines are still way out in the future, no project is officially late. If there is little or no credible data, project reporting can continue to say that the project is doing fine. Only at the deadline, or perhaps a little before it, does the project leader publicly admit that the project will not meet its schedule commitment. This is analogous to a man who falls off a ten-story building and reports as he passes by each row of windows, "Safe so far!"

Projects become late one day at a time. Failure to detect this as soon as possible allows schedule and other risks to remain undetected, and possibly grow until they overwhelm the project.

PROJECT MONITORING

Project monitoring can begin as soon as there is a clear, validated baseline plan that has been approved by the project sponsor and accepted by the project leader and team. Other prerequisites for effective project tracking are a functioning communications infrastructure, disciplined tracking methods, and thorough project planning data available to all team members and stakeholders.

Decisions Related to Monitoring

Specifics concerning project status collection and storage are basic decisions that you need to make as part of the initial project infrastructure for your project.

You need to commit to an appropriate frequency and method for status collection. Tracking on most projects is done weekly, but for very short (such as the development iterations in agile projects) or very urgent projects, daily data collection may be warranted. For long projects, less frequent data collection may be acceptable, but a cycle longer than two weeks is inconsistent with good risk management. Online or email status collection is most common, but any method that is effective and provides hard data can work.

On large, complex, multiteam programs, consistent data collection is essential, and the volume of status information can become quite a burden. One way to manage this is through a centralized project office, responsible for assembling, summarizing, and analyzing the data consistently for all the project teams. This ensures current, consistent data, and also permits use of more complex scheduling tools without the cost of so many copies and the considerable effort that would be required for all the project leaders to master the tool.

Project status meetings are also usually weekly. When face-to-face meetings are not possible, use the best available telecommunications methods. The frequency and methods used vary from project to project, but risks rise steeply when reports, meetings, and other communication are less frequent than weekly.

Decisions on how and where to store the project status information are also important. Online storage of project data is best, because it provides the project team access at any time. Determine the tools and systems to be used for collecting and storing the data, and set up appropriate security so that only team members who should be updating project information will be able to modify it.

The precise details for these decisions related to project monitoring will affect your ability to manage risk, so commit to methods and frequencies that will best serve your project.

Project Information

Project status information is of two types: hard data (facts and figures) and soft data (anecdotal information, rumors, and less specific information). Both types of data are useful for risk management. Hard data includes the "real-time" diagnostic project metrics discussed in chapter 9—showing how project work is proceeding. Some of the hard data collected will relate to, or may even be, risk event triggers, and other data may reveal dangerous trends. Soft data can help you understand the causes for your project status; it may also provide early warnings of future problems and risks.

Hard data: Hard project data includes metrics that assess progress, including revised start and completion estimates for future work. Hard data collection should be routine, easy, and efficient. Project contributors are so busy that if collecting hard status information is not simple, it will not get done. At a minimum, collect:

- Schedule data, such as activities completed and activities scheduled but not completed, milestones completed or missed, actual activity start and finish dates, and duration remaining for incomplete activities

- Resource data, including actual effort consumed, cost data, remaining effort for incomplete work, and missing resources
- Data regarding issues, problems, and specification changes

Soft data: Additional information of a less tangible nature also permeates your project. Information about the project contributors may alert you to potential threats to needed resources, individual productivity, and other potential sources of project risk. Changes in the work environment, a rumored reorganization or layoff, or individual team members having personal problems may also adversely affect upcoming project work. Soft data may also provide information on opportunities to help the project. Soft project data includes issues such as:

- Conflicts arising from expected new projects or other work
- Falling productivity of individual team members
- Imminent infrastructure changes that could affect your project
- Delayed changes required by your project
- Potential problem situations with a common, persistent root cause
- Upcoming situations requiring more authority than you have
- Long delays getting resolution of escalated issues and decisions

THE STATUS CYCLE

Project monitoring depends on a four-stage cycle that repeats periodically (generally weekly) throughout the project. The first stage is inbound communication, *collecting project status information*. The second stage of the cycle detects differences by comparing the status to the plan, evaluates the metrics, and *analyzes variances*. The third stage *develops issues responses* or problems detected. The fourth and final stage is outbound communication and *project reporting*, keeping people aware of what has happened in the project.

The monitoring cycle provides for analysis and planning after collecting project status information, but before project reporting. This lets you include your responses to any issues or problems in your project status report. Any bad news you report will be received better if it is accompanied by credible plans for recovery.

Collecting Project Status

Collecting project status is primarily your responsibility as the project leader. Status data is your "dashboard" for the overall health of your project. Whatever data you decide to collect, be dogmatic in collecting it. Projects using agile methods often employ daily "stand-up" meetings where status is quickly reported by all on three items: What was done yesterday, what will be done today, and any expected issues. Project risk management requires data, so do what you must to keep it flowing.

There are a number of factors that can impede status collection. One pitfall is to collect project status only "when there is time." As busy projects proceed, the work intensifies and problems, distractions, and chaos build. It may be tempting in times of stress to skip a status collection cycle. Especially during significant problems, it is very risky to lose information. You may even find it necessary to intensify data collection during problems or near project completion.

Other things to guard against are collecting data and then misusing it or not using the information at all. After you collect status information from your team, at least incorporate a summary of it into your overall project status report. When you fail to use what you collect, your team members will either stop sending it or will put no effort into supplying meaningful data. Misuse of status information can also be a major problem. When the status you receive is bad news, your first temptation may be to grab a chair and break it over the head of the person who sent it, or at least yell a lot. One of the hardest things a project leader has to learn is not to shoot the messenger. You need to respond positively, even to bad news. Thanking people for bad news is never easy, but if you routinely punish team members for providing honest data, you will quickly stop hearing what you need to know and project risks will escalate. It is much better to mentally count to ten, and then offer a response such as, "Well, I wish you had better news, but I appreciate you raising this issue promptly. What will help get you back on schedule?" The sooner everyone begins to focus on soft data such as this, the earlier things can get back on track.

Variance Analysis

After collecting status, look for project problems by analyzing variances. Variance analysis involves comparing the status information with the project baseline plan to identify any differences. Determine the impact of any variances, both positive and negative; positive variances may provide opportunities for improved execution of future work, and negative variances need attention so that they do not send the project spiraling out of control.

For any variances you detect, particularly large ones, spend a moment validating the differences. Before spending time on impact analysis, check with the people who provided the data to make certain that the problems (or for positive variances, any apparent opportunities) are real. For each difference, determine the root cause of the variance, not just the symptoms. (Chapter 8 explores root-cause analysis.) Work with both hard and soft project data to understand why each variance occurred. Metrics seldom slip out of expected ranges in isolation; the project schedule, resources, and scope are all interrelated, so problems with one of these parameters will probably affect the others.

Armed with the underlying cause of each variance, you can best decide how to respond. Dealing with the root cause of problems and issues also prepares you to better anticipate similar problems later in the project. In variance analysis, focus on understanding the data; never just look for someone to blame.

Schedule metrics: Variance analysis generally starts with schedule data, whether positive or negative. If there are positive variances—work completed early—there may be an opportunity to pull in the start date of other work. It is also worthwhile to discuss the early finish with the activity owner to see whether it is the result of an approach or method that could be applied to similar work scheduled later in the project, or whether you could plausibly reduce any duration estimates for later.

The more common situation is an adverse variance, which for critical activities will impact the start of at least one following project activity. Unless work affected by the slip can be compressed, critical slippage may cascade to all of the activities and milestones later in the project, including the final deadline. Even for noncritical activities, adverse variances are worth investigating; the slip may exceed the flexibility in the schedule, or it might reveal an analysis error that could invalidate duration estimates for additional project activities—some of which may be critical.

Finally, schedule variances may be due to root causes that were not detected during risk analysis. If the root cause of a slip suggests new risks and project failure modes, add them to your risk register plan for additional risk analysis and response planning.

Resource metrics: Resource variances are also significant. Metrics related to earned value management (EVM) can be particularly useful in examining resources throughout the project. EVM metrics, such as the cost performance index (CPI), measure the effort or money consumed by the project in relation to the plan. If the consumption is low (CPI less than one) but the schedule progress is adequate, there may be an opportunity to complete the project under budget. If it is too low and the schedule is also slipping, the root cause is likely to be inadequate staffing or constraints on some other resource. Whenever project progress is too slow because of insufficient resources, escalate the situation to higher management promptly, especially if your project is not getting resources that have been previously committed.

Whenever resources are being used in excess of what is expected—that is, when CPI is higher than one or some related metric shows your "burn rate" is too high—the variance is almost certainly a serious problem. The likelihood is strong that the project will ultimately require more resources to complete than the plan indicates, because it is very difficult to reverse resource overconsumption problems. Even as early as 20 percent of the way through the project schedule, a project with an adverse CPI variance has essentially no chance of finishing within budget. Using more resources than planned may cause your project to hit a limit on staff, money, or some other hard constraint, and halt the project well before it is completed. Publicly admitting to this sort of problem is never easy, but if you wait it will be worse. Resource overconsumption issues increase with time, and the options for recovery diminish later in the project. Sympathy from your project sponsors and stakeholders will drop from little to none at all if you wait too late to deliver bad news.

Some resource issues are acute, having impact on only a short portion of the project; others are chronic and will recur throughout the work. Chronic situations not only create project budget problems, they also may lead to frequent overtime and constant stress on project staff. Risk probabilities rise with increased stress and lowered motivation. Chronic resource problems may also have an impact on your ability to execute existing contingency plans.

Scope metrics: Although schedule and resource data provide the most common status variances, at least some of the data relates to the project deliverables. The results of tests, integration attempts, feasibility studies, and other work will either support expectations set out in the project requirements, or they will not. Significant variances related to scope may indicate a need to propose project changes. Major variances may even foreshadow ultimate project failure.

If a scope-related metric shows a better result than what was expected, explore whether there may be an opportunity for the project to deliver a superior result within the same time frame and budget. It may even be possible to deliver the stated result sooner or less expensively. Although this situation is relatively rare, it does happen, and how best to exploit such opportunities may not be obvious. Discuss them with your project sponsors, customers, and key stakeholders before adding something to the project scope "just because you can." Use your change management process to assess the value and utility of any additional deliverable scope before incorporating it into the project.

When scope-related data indicates a problem that can be resolved with additional work, it will likely affect the project schedule, resources, or both. Develop plans for various combinations of additional time and/or funding you would need to deliver the expected results. Considering your project's priorities, assess the alternatives, and prepare a summary of the most palatable option (or options) and the required changes to the project objective.

If you cannot resolve a scope problem with extra work, your remaining options are to modify the deliverable or to abandon the project. Like resource overconsumption problems, scope under-delivery issues are always difficult to deal with. Some projects choose to hide the problems, hoping that someone comes up with a brilliant idea to close the gap between what is desired and what can credibly be delivered. This is a very high-risk strategy that seldom works. The best course is to raise the issues as soon as you have validated the data. If you do this early, project options are more numerous, the total investment in the project is still relatively small, and expectations are less "locked in." For some projects, delivering a diminished result may be acceptable, but for others under-delivery will not be an option. Aborting a project is always painful and unpleasant, but it's a terrible idea to delay the inevitable. When a project deliverable proves to be demonstrably impossible, the best time to change (or kill) it is early, not late.

In addition to the impact on the current project, scope problems may affect other projects. Inform the leaders of projects depending on your deliverable (or who may be using similar flawed assumptions), so that they can develop alternate strategies or work-arounds.

Overall impact: Once you have completed your variance analysis, document the impact. List the consequences of each variance in terms of:

- Predicted schedule slip
- Budget or other resource requirements
- The effect on the project deliverable
- Impact on other projects

Trend analysis: Project data trend analysis may reveal potential future risks and disruptions. Trend analysis need not necessarily be part of each monitoring cycle, but periodically it is prudent to review the bigger picture. When the resource consumption rates or cumulative slip for the project head in dangerous directions, trend data will help you see it. The earlier you can detect an adverse trend, the more options you will have for correcting it. Trend data may reveal a need to adjust the project end date, increase the budget, request more staff, renegotiate contracts, or modify the project deliverables. If so, the earlier you start, the better your chances for success.

Unfavorable trends detected early in the project can show the need for change when there is much more tolerance for it. Near the start of a project the objectives remain somewhat flexible in the minds of the project sponsors, stakeholders, and contributors. Ignoring or failing to detect adverse trends in the status data is very risky. If trend information, for example from Earned Value metrics, indicates a problem and you do nothing, the trend is likely to continue and grow. Ultimately, something will have to be done. As it gets later in the project, the options diminish and the changes required to reverse the trend become more expensive and less likely to help. Also, late project interventions often create additional problems and may even result in project failure.

Detecting and dealing with adverse project trends early enough avoids the late project changes and cancellations that are so demotivating for project teams. After having worked for months, or even years, on a project, even small changes to the deliverable can be devastating to contributors. Allowing everyone to identify with an aggressive, high-tech, bleeding-edge objective for the bulk of the project and then having to chop the heart out of it at the last minute in order to ship something on time is demoralizing and embarrassing. People identify with the work they do, so late project changes are taken very personally. If this happens often, motivation on subsequent projects will drop. Project staff will stop caring about their work and will not trust the people who lead and sponsor them. Today's complicated projects are successful not because they are easy; they succeed because people care about them. Anything that interferes with this raises project risk to insurmountable levels.

Issue Response

Once you have determined the source and magnitude of any status problems, you have a basis for response. Treat significant differences between the plans and reported project performance as issues. Work to address each situation soon after detection, while problems are smaller and responses will cause minimum disruption.

Responding to project issues resembles risk response planning, discussed in chapter 8. In fact, for issues that you anticipated as risks, the response could be as simple as implementing a contingency plan. When developing responses for project variances, consider the specifics of the problems. If the variance is small, it may be sufficient to delegate the response to the team members responsible to work to come up with a solution. Other possible responses range from very minor staffing shifts or resequencing of project activities to major changes to the project objective, or even to project cancellation. The process for issue response closely resembles the "Plan-Do-Check-Act" cycle from quality management. In planning problem responses, work quickly, but seek good solutions.

When you have captured ideas for response, analyze how each will affect project schedule, resources, and scope. Probe for possible unintended consequences, both in your project and for other related work. The best of the options developed may not present any obvious problems or require any significant project changes (sometimes the "brute force" option of working evening or weekend overtime may be the path of least resistance).

Larger problems may require major changes. If so, submit each option you are considering to your change management process for review. For significant changes, implementation may involve fundamental replanning. If so, get buy-in from the project team and key stakeholders for the revised plan. When necessary, revalidate the objective and baseline with the project sponsor, and update all affected documents.

Once a response plan is accepted, implement it. Communicate the plan and the information on required project changes to the project team and any other people involved. After taking the actions in the response plan, verify that you have solved the problem. If your actions prove ineffective, plan for additional responses, seeking better solutions.

The situation is similar to the way a fire department treats a fire. Initially a new fire is "one alarm," and one fire crew is sent out. When the fire is too large, or it spreads, the fire department escalates to two alarms, and then, if needed, to three or more. The escalation continues until the fire is brought under control. Ongoing project risk management requires the same diligence, escalation, and persistence. Significant project changes often lead to unintended consequences. During the status cycles that follow big changes, be particularly thorough in your data analysis and look for unexpected results.

Communication and Risk Reporting

The final step in the status cycle is to let people know how the project is doing. This includes project status reports and status meetings, as well as less formal communication. Successful projects depend on a solid foundation of clear, frequent communication. Without effective communication, project risks may go undetected and cannot be managed.

Communication on modern projects presents a number of growing challenges. Distance is a well-known barrier to communication. It restricts both the type and amount of communication possible, and reduces informal interaction to almost none. As project teams become increasingly global, time differences also interfere with communication. Even phoning people on global projects can be difficult. It seems that whenever you need to talk, it is the middle of the night for them. Different languages and cultures are another growing communication challenge for modern projects. Global work involves people who speak different languages and who have different ways of working and communicating. Even traditional collocated project teams are increasingly now working remotely, from home or some different location, at least part of the time. Sharing complicated technical project information among disconnected people is never easy, and omissions and misunderstandings are common. Cultural and linguistic diversity in technical work is becoming the norm, not the exception, for all types of projects. Finally, today's projects involve cross-functional project teams coming from diverse educational and work backgrounds.

It may be easier for an engineer in Ohio to communicate with an engineer in Japan than it is for either of them to communicate with a marketing manager down the hall.

As the project leader, you are the person primarily responsible for project communication. You need to rise to these challenges and minimize project communication risk. For today's projects, this requires discipline and effort.

Project status reporting: The most visible communication for many projects is a written status report. Ongoing risk management depends on clear, credible project information that is understood by everyone on the project. Status reporting that is too cursory increases risk because no one has enough information about the project to know what is happening—leading to chaos. This may occur because the project leader is busy or distracted and provides too little data. It also may be the result of "need to know" project reporting, where the project leader sends out very brief notes to each team member containing only data concerning the portion of the project that each contributor is involved with. It can even happen because the project leader dislikes writing reports. Whatever the reason, projects with too little information become very prone to risks, particularly risks related to dependencies and interfaces.

On the other hand, status reporting that rambles on and on is no better. No one has time to read it all, and although the information everyone needs is probably there, somewhere, finding it is impossible. One common reason for long reports is a project leader who solicits individual reports from the whole team and concatenates them into a compendium running to dozens of pages. Time pressure can be a factor in this; there is much truth in the old saying, "I didn't have time to write a short report, so I wrote a long one." Whatever the reason, the result of rambling reports is chaos and increased project risk, because few will have the patience or time to find the information they need.

The best reports start with a short, clear summary, including current risks. Regardless of who you are sending a status report to, begin with a brief (twenty lines or fewer—one "screen load") summary. Be aware that sometimes the summary is all that will actually be read, and that some of the stakeholders who receive your report will not need or want any more detail than this.

Follow the summary with additional needed information that is concise, honest, and clear. If you commit to weekly reporting on a specific day, do it. Understand what your stakeholders need to know and provide it in your reports, in a consistent place and format. Any important data that people notice is missing will probably result in unnecessary and time-consuming telephone calls, meetings, or other interruptions.

Following your high-level summary, your project status report may include:

- A short description of each major accomplishment since the last report. This portion of the report is an excellent place to "name names" and to recognize individual and team accomplishments.
- Activities planned during the next status period.
- A schedule summary, with planned, actual, and expected future dates.
- A resource summary, with planned, actual, and expected future resource requirements.
- Significant risks, issues, and problems with your planned responses.
- Project analysis, including an explanation of any variances, issues, and plans for resolution.

- Risk analysis, including the known risks in the near project future and the status of any ongoing risk recovery efforts.
- Additional detail, charts, and other information as needed.

Include only status information that you can substantiate in your written status reports.

Risk trigger and metric reporting: Risks in your risk register need defined triggers, specific signals that indicate that a risk has happened or is about to occur. Many triggers relate to trends or thresholds of diagnostic project metrics. Throughout your project, work with the risk owners to monitor measurements and for events that reveal the current status of your known risks.

Incorporate what you detect in your status and other reporting, in your risk register, and in any other risk-related communications. When reporting on risks, focus on metrics and other fact-based data, and for active risks include a summary of your response efforts and recovery results.

Risks as issues and risk response status: Whenever a risk occurs, it becomes an issue. (The probability is now 100 percent.) List all current risks (and their responses) in your project issue log, in addition to tracking progress in your risk register. Resist the urge to minimize the impact and consequences of risks in your status and other reporting. It is tempting to "spin" adverse events and make them appear less damaging than they are, and there are unquestionably disincentives for candor when you are having problems. Overall, though, hiding bad news will not make recovery any easier, and it will damage your credibility if (or when) you do need to escalate to get help. Visible problems are always tolerated better than those that emerge suddenly as major disasters.

Other reports and presentations: You will generally be required to do additional reporting on your project, including periodic reports in support of organizational requirements. Especially on longer projects, you will occasionally need to create higher-level reports and do presentations. Presentations are an excellent opportunity to reinforce the importance of your project, to be positive about what the team has done, and to share your plans for the future. You can also outline your current challenges, risks, and your plans for dealing with them. Presentations are a particularly effective way to renew strong project sponsorship, motivate your team, and revive project enthusiasm. All of these factors can assist in avoiding future problems and risks, especially on longer projects.

Top risks: Visibility and risk communications are powerful and effective risk mitigation strategies. Create and post a "Top Ten" list of current risks where your team members can see it, such as on a project web page, on a poster in your work area, or in your team communications. People always work to avoid risks they are aware of, particularly those where they understand the impact and consequences.

Project status meetings: Project status meetings are viewed by many as a necessary evil, and by everyone else even less positively. Project contributors, for the most part, hate meetings, especially long ones. Considering the increase in project risk that results from inadequate communication, this is unfortunate. The discussions and exchanges that occur during project status meetings are essential for avoiding risks; many potential problems never occur as a result of timely discussions and awareness developed during conversations. Holding regular status meetings, even via teleconferencing, is a potent tool for keeping difficult projects on track and risks under control.

One key to improving status meeting attendance and participation is to keep meetings short. Meetings are more interesting and energized if they focus only on important project information—what has been accomplished and what issues are pending. Problem-solving and issue resolution are unquestionably essential, but these activities rarely require the entire project staff to be involved. Delegate problem-solving and extended discussions to smaller groups, and strive to keep your meetings brief.

Effective meetings are well structured, sticking to an established agenda. They also start on time, set time limits for the agenda items, and end early whenever possible. Face-to-face communication minimizes misunderstandings and reinforces teamwork, but may not always be possible. For teleconference meetings, minimize communication risks by:

- Using the best meeting technologies available
- Ensuring that the technologies used are familiar to all participants
- Verifying that the technologies to be used are compatible and functioning, and retesting them following any changes or upgrades

However you conduct your meetings, record what was discussed and distribute meeting minutes promptly to all project contributors (and to others as appropriate). File meeting minutes in your project archives.

Informal project communications: Never limit project communications just to formal reports and scheduled meetings. Some of the most important communication on complicated projects takes place at coffee machines, in hallways, on the phone, and during casual conversations. Project risks may surface far earlier in these discussions than in more formal interactions.

Successful project leaders create opportunities for these frequent, unstructured conversations. The idea of "management by wandering around," popularized by Dave Packard and Bill Hewlett, is a particularly effective way to reinforce trust and build relationships within a project team. Even when teams are distributed and you are unable to talk frequently with people in person, there will be opportunities to do it once in a while, and you can rely on the telephone or computer networking tools in between. A great deal of "soft data" and valuable project information on project risks surfaces during casual exchanges. Effective project leaders also work to encourage interactions among project team members. Team cohesion, which correlates strongly with the amount of informal communication, is one of your best defenses against project risk.

PROJECT ARCHIVES

In addition to distributing project documents and reports to your stakeholders and contributors, you also need to retain copies as part of your project management information system (PMIS). This archive not only serves as an ongoing reference during the project, it is essential for capturing the lessons learned during postproject analysis, and it contains data that can improve risk management on future projects.

A typical project archive contains:

- Project definition documents
- All versions of project planning documents used (including proposals, charters, budgets, charts, contracts)

- Each project status report
- Other periodic project reports and communications
- Issue logs and risk registers, worksheets, and plans
- A change control history

When the project is completed, the final addition will be the postproject retrospective analysis and lessons learned.

MANAGING RISK RESERVES

Ideally, reserves for time and budget will have been established for your project in proportion to its risk. Reserves are used to enable the project to meet its commitments in the face of both anticipated and unknown challenges. Budget reserve is best used to deal with financial effects of risks and unforeseen, necessary expenses. Schedule reserve provides a buffer for recovery due to slippage caused by risk-related delays or other unplanned work. Reserves only serve to protect the project if used exclusively to support recovery. Strongly resist tapping them for scope creep, contributor convenience, or other uses unrelated to risk response.

Monitor reserves as your project progresses. If you find that you are consuming either budget or schedule reserves too fast (for example, having less than half remaining for either at the project midpoint), discuss the situation with your project sponsor and key stakeholders. Reserves are most needed as you approach project completion, so whenever your reserves drop too low, you may want to consider modifying your deadline or making other baseline adjustments.

PROJECT REVIEWS AND RISK REASSESSMENT

When you operate a complex piece of machinery such as an automobile, you frequently need to add fuel, check the oil and the air pressure in the tires, and make other minor adjustments. This is sufficient in the short run, but if you never do anything more, the car will soon break down. Periodically, you also must perform scheduled maintenance, to change the oil, replace worn-out or poorly functioning components, check the brakes and other systems, and generally bring the vehicle back into good operational condition.

A project is also a complex system. Monitoring and reporting on planned activities is necessary, not unlike adding fuel to an automobile. Unless the project is very short, however, this will not be sufficient. Longer projects also require "periodic maintenance," in the form of project reviews.

The planning horizon for some projects may be as short as a month or two, and for others it may extend to as much as a year. However, no project can plan with adequate detail beyond its planning limit, whatever it may be. Projects using agile methods conduct reviews at the close of each development iteration, generally about monthly. Project reviews allow you to take a longer view, beyond the next status report, to revalidate the project objectives, plans, and assumptions. Successful project and risk management require cycles of review and regular reassessment to keep the project on track.

Lengthy projects often involve technical complexity and a very limited planning horizon, resulting in greater project risk. Project reviews provide an effective way to better manage the unknowns and exposures. During a project review, one of three scenarios will arise. Some reviews find few issues and the project will proceed as originally expected. Other reviews will reveal changes or that additional planning is needed. These projects can move forward, but only after updating the objectives and project baseline. The third possible outcome of a project review is a recommendation to cancel future project work. Although this is not pleasant, it is ultimately better for everyone to cancel a project that will eventually fail before investing even more time and money.

Whatever other agenda items you set for your project review, plan to reconsider VUCA—any changes your project is facing related to volatility (both within and outside your project), uncertainty (remaining unknowns throughout your plans), complexity (related to your expected results and system challenges) and ambiguity (lack of clarity regarding requirements, options, or work).

As part of the review, also explicitly reassess your risks and analyze your reserves. Discuss the problems and risks you have encountered in the project so far, and brainstorm methods for avoiding similar trouble as the project proceeds. Work to identify new scope, schedule, resource, or other risks that are now visible in your project. Add the new risks to your risk register and thoroughly reassess all of them, rank-ordering the risks based on current information. Develop plans for any significant risks that lack an appropriate response.

As you review your risks, also reassess the overall risk profile for the project. As projects proceed, things change and overall risk changes with them—either increasing or decreasing. As the work proceeds and more is known, project-level risk should decrease, but every project is different and it is prudent to reassess.

A project review is also a good time to check the status of any reserves established for the project. If contingency funds are being depleted faster than expected, determine what you need to do to ensure that they will remain adequate. If you have used most (or all) of your schedule reserve, consider options for increased staffing, revising the deadline, or other alternatives. If changes to the project objective or reserves appear necessary, discuss your recommendations with your project sponsor and use your change processes to implement them.

After your review, document what you discussed and learned. Add a summary of the review to your project archive, and communicate your findings to your sponsor, related project teams, and key stakeholders.

Prepare a presentation to summarize the project's progress to date and your plans going forward. Formal presentation of project review findings can also be useful in keeping the project, with its accomplishments and challenges visible. Accentuate the positive, emphasizing the value and importance of the project. Ensuring the organization remains aware of the work, especially on lengthy projects, helps in maintaining priorities and resources and makes overall risk management less difficult.

A project review is also a good opportunity for recognition and celebration. Use your communications, reports, and presentations to highlight significant accomplishments and to publicly thank specific people and teams. Use thanks and recognition to renew enthusiasm for the project and motivate your project team. Project reviews are also a good time to celebrate your accomplishments. Long projects, especially, need more parties.

TAKING OVER A TROUBLED PROJECT

Now we look at one additional project execution risk. As the PERIL database shows, staff turnover is a significant problem. It can be an especially personal problem if the turnover results in your being asked to lead a failing project. This unfortunate situation is one of a project leader's worst nightmares. Even if you inherit a project in progress that appears to be in pretty good shape, it's best to respond to such a request with, "I'll take a look at it and let you know as quickly as possible if any changes or adjustments might be needed."

Your first order of business is to find out whatever you can about the project and get to know the team. Although it may be interesting to dig into why the prior project leader is no longer in the picture, this can probably be left for later unless the information will contribute to project recovery.

Learning about the project can begin with a review of project documents and other information in the project archive and elsewhere. If there is a well-maintained archive of project information in a PMIS, it will be invaluable. A new project leader who has access to such data still faces a daunting task but will be light-years ahead of where he or she would otherwise be. On a troubled project, though, there may be little useful information. You quickly need to do the best you can to fill in the gaps.

For current information, spend time reviewing recent status reports. Be skeptical and verify any information in them that is inconsistent with what you see. Discuss the project with each project contributor, and use these conversations to solicit suggestions for change, to build your understanding of how things are going, and to start establishing relationships and trust. Avoid making predictions or firm commitments while you investigate, but do communicate openly and let people know when you expect to have better answers.

If there is little concrete (or credible) information, you will need to initiate a very fast planning effort to develop some. Even if there is data, at least do a quick project planning review to validate it. Someone else's plan can be a good starting point, but it won't serve as a reliable foundation for project execution until it's yours. An "express" planning exercise should include, at minimum, detailed examination of all current and pending activities, verification of the project's committed scope, timing, staffing and funding, and documentation of all currently identified issues and problems.

There are many reasons that projects may be viewed as failing, so determine what the main problem (or problems) are. Some typical issues include:

- Schedule delays
- Excessive resource consumption
- Insufficient staff or other resources
- Scope not achievable using available technologies and capabilities
- Low priority
- Conflicts with other projects
- Weak sponsorship

Recovery requires prompt action, and the best strategy for this comes from the medical field: triage. Once you have determined what is not going well and listed all the project activities and issues needing attention, sort them into three categories. Some things need immediate attention and will result in permanent damage to the project if not addressed immediately. Identify and staff this work, stopping other activities with lower urgency where necessary. Other matters on your list need attention but not right now, so put them aside for the present and plan to address them soon. Other matters listed may be hopeless. Note these and move on.

This last category—hopeless issues—can be very revealing, because these legitimate project problems may provide evidence that the project as defined may be impossible. Even the issues that you can manage and resolve may require more resources or time (or both) than can be justified. Schedule time with the project sponsor to review your response actions and the overall project. Plan to discuss modifications to the project or even cancellation. Not all troubled projects can be saved, and it's better to pull the plug on a doomed project than to "throw good money after bad."

If the project is recoverable, your next steps after resolving the short-term problems will be to schedule an in-depth project review, as described previously. Your goals for this are to understand the project and engage the project team in developing current and realistic project planning information, including updated risk data. Once you have the truck back on the highway, invest the time it takes to ensure that you can keep it there and out of the ditch. Tools for this are found throughout this book.

Key Ideas for Risk Monitoring and Control

- Collect status dogmatically.
- Monitor variances and trends frequently throughout your project.
- Respond to issues and problems promptly.
- Communicate clearly and often.
- On long projects, conduct periodic risk and project reviews.
- Be skeptical whenever assuming leadership of a project. Conduct a quick, thorough review to initiate changes and "make it yours."

PANAMA CANAL: RISK-BASED REPLANNING (1908)

Project monitoring and prompt responses when needed were among the main differences between the initial nineteenth-century effort to construct the Panama Canal and the second one. No project proceeds exactly as planned, and the US canal project was no exception. It was ultimately successful because the managers and workers revised their plans to deal effectively with problems as they emerged.

As the work at Panama continued, for example, it seemed that the more they dug, the more there was to dig. Mudslides were frequent, and between 1906 and 1913 the total estimates for excavation more than doubled. The response to this problem was not terribly elegant, but it was effective. Following the report of a particularly enormous mudslide in the Culebra Cut, George Goethals remarked, "Hell, dig it out again." They had to, many times. Some risks are managed primarily through perseverance and brute force.

As time passed, a number of factors not known at the start of the project came into focus. By 1908, it became clear that new materials, including the steels to be used on the canal, were making possible the construction of much larger ships. Goethals made two significant design changes as a result of this. The first was to commit to a wider excavation of the Culebra Cut, increasing it to nearly 100 meters (from 200 feet to 300 feet) to accommodate ships wider than 30 meters sailing in each direction. Although this represented much additional digging, it also made the tasks of ongoing maintenance and dredging a little easier.

The second change was to the size of the locks. Based on Goethals's estimates of the size of future oceangoing ships, the locks were enlarged to be 110 feet wide and 1,000 feet long. This somewhat arbitrary choice of dimensions became the single most important factor in twentieth-century shipbuilding. These dimensions are the exact size of the rectangular-hulled PANAMAX ships, the largest ships that can transit the canal. Until recently, apart from oil supertankers (which are generally designed for use on single-ocean, point-to-point routes), very few ships were built any bigger than a Panama Canal lock.

In addition to making the locks larger, Goethals made another change to them. All the water used to operate the canal flows by gravity. Locks are filled from the man-made lakes above them and then emptied into the ocean. During the rainy season, this works well. In the drier parts of the year, the depth of the lakes falls, and the water level in the cut connecting them could fall too low to permit oceangoing ships to pass. To save water, Goethals redesigned each of the twelve locks with multiple sets of doors, enabling smaller ships to lock through using a much smaller volume of water.

One additional significant change was adopted midproject, primarily for security reasons. At the start of the twentieth century, the global political situation, particularly in Europe, was increasingly unstable. The geography of Panama has a long, gradual slope from the central ridge north on the Atlantic side, and a much shorter, steeper slope on the south, facing the Pacific. On the steeper Pacific slopes, the locks in the original plan were visible from the water, and Goethals, a military man, feared that the canal might be closed down by projectiles fired from an offshore warship. To avoid this, he moved the Pacific locks farther inland. The change actually made the engineering somewhat easier, as the new plan took better advantage of the more level land farther up the slope.

George Goethals minimized risk through scrupulous management of all changes, insisting throughout his tenure that "everything must be written down." Once the plan was set, the debating stopped, and all the effort went to execution.

CHAPTER 12

CLOSING PROJECTS

"History repeats itself. That's one of the things wrong with history."

—CLARENCE DARROW

Reviewing the records of many projects, it is striking how often consecutive projects fall victim to the same problems. Common issues such as inadequate staffing, top-down imposed deadlines having no relationship to the work, fixed commitments based on little or no analysis, and many other issues listed in the PERIL database plague project after project. One definition of insanity is repeating the same actions over and over, hoping for a different result. More than a little risk in most projects is a direct result of reusing the same project practices that have caused problems in the past.

Getting better results requires process improvement. Using "Plan-Do-Check-Act," you can discover ways to improve most any process. You can, as part of project closure, review the results you obtained from the processes you used. Achieving consistently better results and minimizing future risks requires you to identify what worked well and commit to repeat these processes on subsequent projects. It also requires you to identify the processes that underperformed for you and change them. Modifying a "broken" process is almost always better than trying again using methods that have failed. If the performance of your next project is still not good enough after adopting changes, you can always change it again. Postproject analysis is a powerful and effective tool for long-term project risk management.

PROJECT CLOSURE

There are a number of closure activities common to most projects, but the specifics vary a great deal with the type of project. Project closeout generally involves:

- Formal acceptance of completed project deliverables
- The final written report
- Closeout of all project contracts, documents, and agreements
- Acknowledgment of contributions
- A celebration or other event to commemorate the project
- A postproject retrospective analysis to capture the lessons learned

The most relevant of these to risk management is the retrospective analysis, which is covered in detail later in this chapter.

Formal Acceptance

One of the greatest potential risks any project leader faces is finishing the work only to be asked, on delivery, "What's this?" Scope risk management seeks to avoid this situation through validation of the initial specifications, periodic revalidation of requirements, scrupulous management of changes, and incorporating interim tests, inspections, and evaluations as the work proceeds. Defining all final acceptance testing, aligned with the initial specifications, should be one of the first activities undertaken in a complex project, as part of scope definition and planning. Even for projects using agile methods, you will be wise to develop a clear definition of the problem you are solving and what criteria an ultimate useful solution would need to meet. Scope management also requires you to modify testing and acceptance criteria throughout the project to reflect the effects of any authorized changes. If final tests and acceptance criteria are defined only late in the project, it is only through happenstance that the project deliverables will be accepted.

Managing this risk involves thorough specification of the deliverable and frequent communication throughout the project with the people who will evaluate and accept it. You can minimize the risk greatly by engaging them in discussions and evaluations of any prototypes, incremental results, models, iterative development outputs, or other interim project deliverables. Detailed, validated scope definition is the best way to minimize late project surprises.

When you have completed your project, get formal acknowledgment of this from the project sponsor, and as appropriate from the customer and key stakeholders. For projects undertaken on a fee-for-service basis, generate the final billing information and ensure that the client is properly and promptly billed. Even for projects that end in cancellation or fail to deliver on all of their objectives, you should obtain written acknowledgment whenever possible of the partial results or other accomplishments that you did successfully complete.

Final Project Report

The main purpose of a final report is to acknowledge what has been done and to communicate to everyone involved that the project is over. Most are similar to the periodic status reports issued throughout the project, but will often include additional detail. Every final project report should also thank and recognize the contributors.

Contract and Document Closeout

At project close, complete any final paperwork required for all internal agreements and external contracts that are specific to your project. Following final payments of all invoices, summarize the financial information, and close the contracts. If there are issues or problems relating to any contracts, escalate and resolve them as soon as practical. If you have had difficulties with any outside service providers, document the issues and make the information available to other project leaders to avoid similar risks in the future.

As part of project closure, add all final project documentation to your project information archive.

Acknowledging Contributions

It is a small world. When you work with people once, the chances are fairly good that you will work with them again. Managing risk in a continuing stream of projects depends on developing and maintaining trust, relationships, and teamwork. Recognizing the accomplishments and contributions that people have made is fundamental to this.

On complex projects, expertise and hard work are frequently taken for granted. When contributors finish difficult activities, often the only feedback they get is an assignment to another, even more difficult activity. Especially at the end of a project, you need to thank people, both in person and in writing. For people who work for others, also acknowledge their contributions to their management. Keep your remarks truthful, but focus on positive contributions. If it is culturally appropriate, praise people and teams publicly as well. If there are programs in place for specific rewards, such as stock options or other tangible compensation for extra effort, submit recommendations for deserving project contributors to reward them for their work.

Celebration

Whatever the atmosphere has been in the closing days of a project, bring each project to a positive conclusion. Mark the success of the project with some sort of event. Even if the project was not a success, it is good to get people together and acknowledge what was accomplished. Celebrations need not be lavish to be effective; even in businesses that may not currently be doing well financially, project teams can get together and share food and beverages that they provide for themselves. Moving on to the next project or another assignment is much easier when people have a chance to bring the last project to a friendly conclusion. If your project has a global or distributed team, arrange a similar event for each location at roughly the same time.

PROJECT RETROSPECTIVE ANALYSIS

Managing project risk on an ongoing basis requires continuing process improvement. Whether you call this effort a retrospective meeting, lessons learned, a postmortem, a postproject analysis, or something else, the objective is always the same: improving future projects and minimizing their risks. If the people who led the projects before yours had done this more effectively, your project would have had fewer risks. Help the next project leader out—it could be you.

The overall process for a project retrospective analysis is similar to the project review process discussed in chapter 11, but the focus is broader. Project reviews are primarily concerned with the remainder of the current project, using the experiences of the project so far to do "course corrections." A retrospective analysis is backward-looking and more comprehensive, mining the history of the whole project for ideas to keep and processes to change in projects generally.

Before you schedule and conduct a project retrospective, get organizational commitment to act on at least one of the resulting change recommendations. Performing postproject analyses only to discover the same process defects over and over is demotivating and wastes the time of the meeting participants. Decide how you will use the resulting information before you commit resources to the analysis.

Preparing for and Scheduling a Project Retrospective

Thorough postproject analysis requires you to have accurate, thorough project data. As you add the final project documents to the archive, determine what information you need, and ensure that it will be available for review during your project retrospective meeting. Schedule a retrospective analysis soon after your project ends, but not immediately after it. If it is too soon, final documents will be incomplete and events from the last, chaotic days of work will dominate the analysis. Don't wait more than about two to three weeks after the project, though, or important memories, particularly the less pleasant ones, will begin to fade.

Allocate sufficient time. Even shorter projects can generate enough data to justify an hour or so to look backward. Set an agenda providing time for all contributors to comment and to collect both positive results and proposals for process change.

Encourage participants to come prepared with specific examples of what went well and what changes they would recommend.

Retrospective Surveys

If your business has a standard retrospective survey form, plan to use it. A retrospective survey is an effective way to gather information about project definition, planning, defect and issue management, decision-making, teamwork, leadership, process management, managing dependencies and deliverables, testing, logistics, and other project processes. Standard formats usually have lists of statements to be rated on a scale from "strongly agree" on one extreme to "strongly disagree" on the other, and spaces for written comments.

If there is no survey form or the one you have does not include much in the way of risk information, you may find the following survey form useful.

Plan to use the survey in addition to the discussion of processes during the meeting. You can also use it to collect inputs from any project contributors who are unable to participate.

Project and Risk Management Review and Assessment

Start a retrospective meeting with a statement of objectives, and review the meeting agenda and ground rules for the meeting. At a minimum, establish a rule to maintain a focus on the processes and to avoid attacking individuals and "blamestorming."

Capture ideas generated in the meeting, focusing on "pluses" and "deltas." Start your analysis with "Positives" before moving to "Needed changes" (not "Negatives"). Collecting positives about the project first reminds people of what went well. Probe for specific opinions on project aspects that led to success. Capture what worked particularly well on your project; identify any new practices that you should repeat or extensions to existing processes that were valuable. Also reflect on significant identified risks that you managed to avoid (or opportunities you were able to take advantage of), and any actions you took to achieve this.

When most of the positives have been cataloged, turn your focus to desirable changes. Identify process areas that need improvement and practices that could be simplified or eliminated. Consider project issues and problems that you had to deal with. Review your risk registers to identify risks you encountered, along with any "unknown" risks that befell your project. Describe any changes you could implement to better insulate your project work from similar exposures. Brainstorm tactics for mitigating errors and failures, and develop process recommendations for avoiding similar problems on future projects. (As you review your experiences, you may identify aspects that could be sensitive or personal. In determining how to document and share this sort of information, always consider confidentiality and preservation of ongoing relationships.)

Throughout the meeting, work to hear from everyone, not just a vocal minority. As the allotted time winds down, summarize the recommendations, and ask each participant to nominate one recommendation that he or she believes would make the most significant difference on future projects. Work as a group to develop consensus, if possible, on the most important change, or at least generate support from the group for one or two that top the list.

Close the meeting with reflections on the process and encourage people to share what they learned from the project personally and how they plan to work differently in the future.

Documenting the Results and Recommendations

Document the meeting results in a concise format with the top recommendation (or recommendations) and key findings in a clear, short summary at the beginning. Distribute the project retrospective report to the participants for review and comment.

Project and Risk Management Process Improvement

Take the principal recommendations to your management and request support for making necessary changes. Small changes can be fairly trivial to implement, but more significant ones may require new projects and require significant data, planning, and resources to initiate. If your recommendation is rejected, discuss alternatives with the project team and investigate whether there might be other ways to at least implement portions of the recommendation that, although less effective, would be under your control.

In any case, take at least one issue emerging from every project and resolve to do something different in your next project to do something about it. Effective risk management requires your firm commitment to continuous process improvement.

Examine your overall risk management planning and effectiveness. If your project encountered any particularly surprising risks, review your overall risk assessment process, especially your estimation of probabilities. If you suspect sources of bias may be hiding risks, consider changes to your risk discovery processes. At a minimum, resolve to be more skeptical of assumptions that appear to be overly optimistic regarding negligible worst-case impact or very low likelihood.

Process improvement rests on the "Plan-Do-Check-Act" cycle, and requires persistence. Managing project risk means reusing what has worked before on your projects and fixing or replacing what has failed. Every project offers beneficial lessons learned.

Project and Risk Data Archiving

When completed, put a copy of the results in the project archive, and share the findings with others who could benefit from the information, including the leaders of similar projects. If your organization has a centralized repository for risk data, supplement it with information from your completed risk register. Although public airing of risk experience may result in some embarrassment, hiding adverse experiences will lead to repetition, further pain, needless expense, and even more embarrassment. If your organization lacks a risk data archive, start one (at least for yourself).

Key Ideas for Project Closure

- Thoroughly and accurately document the project results.
- Recognize accomplishments and thank contributors.
- Conduct a project retrospective and *use the recommendations*.
- Review your risk processes and update your data archives.

PANAMA CANAL: COMPLETION (1914)

On August 15, 1914, the first seagoing vessel crossed Panama, and the Panama Canal opened all the way through. This huge accomplishment was reported far and wide as the biggest news of the day. The attention lasted only a short time, though, as World War I broke out in Europe and quickly overshadowed the canal story.

In retrospect: The eighty-kilometer (fifty-mile) lock-and-dam canal was completed slightly more than ten years after the congressional act that initiated the work. About 5,000 additional lives were lost finishing the US project. Some died from disease, but most of the loss of life was due to handling explosives (making the total death toll as high as 30,000, including those who died in the 1800s). The canal opened six months ahead of the schedule set earlier by John Stevens, despite all the difficulties and changes. Even more remarkable, it finished at a cost US$23 million less than the budget (US$352 million had been approved). The total cost for construction was over US$600 million, including the cost of the French project. If this is not the only US government project ever to finish both early and under budget, it is certainly the largest one to do so.

Most of the credit goes to George Washington Goethals. Although he never failed to acknowledge his debt to John Stevens, nearly all the work was accomplished while Goethals was chief engineer. After the opening of the canal, Goethals remained in Panama as governor of the Canal Zone, to oversee its early operation and deal with any problems. His thoughts on completion of the work at Panama, delivered in March 1915, were:

We are gathered here tonight, not in the hope of something to be accomplished, but of actual accomplishment: the two oceans have been united. The [mud]slides hinder and prevent navigation for a few days, but in time they will be removed. The construction of the Canal means but little in comparison with its coming usefulness to the world and what it will bring about. Its completion is due to the brain and brawn of the men who are gathered here—men who have served loyally and well; and no commander in the world ever had a more faithful force than that which worked with me in building the Panama Canal.

If you were asked to name a famous engineer, Goethals would be an excellent choice. Although there are other engineers who have become famous as astronauts, politicians, and billionaires, Goethals is famous for engineering, and his name is on a major New York City bridge. His accomplishments in addition to the canal are substantial, and he remains a significant influence in civil engineering to this day. The lessons learned from this project are thoroughly documented (as with all projects undertaken by the US Army Corps of Engineers). They serve as the foundation not only for subsequent civil engineering projects but also for much of what is now recognized as modern project management.

CHAPTER 13

PROGRAM, PORTFOLIO, AND ENTERPRISE RISK MANAGEMENT

"There are risks and costs to a program of action. But they are far less than the long-range risks and costs of comfortable inaction."

—JOHN F. KENNEDY

The future, for any organization, requires action and entails risk. The subject of this book, *project* risk management, is a useful starting point for managing risk, but it may not be sufficient.

Projects are always part of something larger. Programs are made up of projects, so program risk management relies on project risk management, among other things. Project portfolios include multiple projects and may also include programs, so portfolio risk management also depends on project risk management. Enterprise risk management includes all of these types of risk management, plus additional considerations. This chapter explores the relationship of project risk management to each of these higher-level perspectives.

Earlier chapters here explored the concepts of VUCA on project risk. Volatility, uncertainty, complexity, and ambiguity are also relevant at these higher levels of aggregation, as these factors create challenges for an organization as a whole. Better managing overall VUCA should be central to risk management of programs, project portfolios, and the enterprise as a whole. This is particularly central to improving portfolio risk understanding and control.

In some organizations exploring risk through projects may be a main objective. When he retired in 2022 after six years as head of NASA, Dr. Thomas Zurbuchen noted that the key to making progress is taking smart risks, and not panicking if some risks do not work out. "The fastest way of turning off all innovation is to punish the people who do listen to you and actually are trying new things," he said. "Let's not kill them." Inevitably, not all complex projects succeed. If the overall environments are managed well, however, there is much to be gained, even from projects that may stumble.

PROJECT RISK MANAGEMENT IN CONTEXT

Project success or failure is generally measured against the triple constraint of scope, time, and cost, and the risks listed in the PERIL database reflect this perspective. The success of programs and portfolios, not to mention the health of the enterprise as a whole, depends on successful projects—those that meet the objectives that they commit to. However, at each level above the project, the connection with project risk management becomes more abstract. The focus shifts because higher-level managers are measured and evaluated based on more than the fate of any particular single project. Risk management in these other arenas extends well beyond the concerns that keep project leaders awake at night. Program risk management focuses extensively on one of the

VUCA factors, complexity. Portfolio risk management is primarily concerned with achieving financial goals. Enterprise risk management shifts attention to the longer-term health and viability of the organization as a whole.

The Focus of Program Risk Management

"Program" is a term that means different things in different contexts, but the Project Management Institute has long defined a program as a group of "related projects . . . managed in a coordinated manner." This chapter focuses on this type of program, where the main objective for program management is better overall control of interconnected projects than would be possible if they were managed individually. Programs include multiple projects that may be executed in parallel, in sequence, or both. Projects are time limited, with a specific start and finish dates. Programs may also have deadlines, but some are open ended—only the component projects have well-defined closure objectives. Programs may contain a few projects, hundreds of projects, or any number in between.

Program risk management closely resembles project risk management, and for small programs, there may be very little difference at all. Risk management for the program can be little more than aggregation of the risk plans and strategies for the included projects. For larger programs, however, there will be exponentially increasing complexity that carries risk. Programs also tend to focus heavily on the successful delivery of benefits and financial goals, which may require risk trade-offs among the constituent projects. Because programs are composed of related projects, risks identified at the project level tend to be highly correlated, so overall program risk can be significantly higher than what might be expected based on individual project risk assessments.

The Focus of Portfolio Risk Management

When projects are aggregated into portfolios, the overall focus shifts even further from the results of a particular project or program. Portfolios, whether made up of stocks, bonds, subprime mortgages, or projects, focus mostly on money—delivering an expected financial return and maximizing overall value.

For portfolios of projects and programs, risk in the aggregate depends more on the average project performance than on the success or failure of any single undertaking. As discussed in chapter 1, risk for a group of investments or ventures depends on the aggregated overall collection. If the population of items making up the portfolio is independent, overall risk is moderated. Portfolios can achieve expected returns if some items can be expected to do well to compensate for those that perform poorly. Project portfolios, however, like programs, may often contain related projects that are highly correlated and result in *increased* risk.

The Focus of Enterprise Risk Management

In the abstract, an enterprise can be thought of as a bundle of projects and other activities that strives to increase in value over time through successful execution of those undertakings. Ideally the appreciation in value will be more attractive to investors and owners than alternatives such as stuffing money into mattresses. From this perspective, enterprise risk management is little different from portfolio risk management, and again the major objectives tend to be financial. At the enterprise level, though, there are other risks to manage. Some relate to the survival and ongoing health of the organization. Laws and regulations must be obeyed, and practices must be established and followed to ensure the trust of owners, customers, employees, and others in the future. Where the focus of project risk management is short-term, enterprise risk management must also consider the big picture and much longer timeframes. At the overall organization level, some of these considerations include alignment with enterprise core values, goals, and strategic plans. Effective management of future risk will require investment in long-term stability and investment in anticipated capacities and capabilities.

In addition, corporate officers of public corporations in the United States and elsewhere are now subject to significant personal penalties and potential legal prosecution if the enterprise misbehaves. The relationship between enterprise risk management and project risk management is bidirectional. The financial success and overall well-being of an enterprise depends on effective project risk management, especially for large and high-visibility projects and programs. And enterprise risk management, particularly in the recent past, has been a fertile source of projects.

PROGRAM RISK MANAGEMENT

The line between project and program management is not precise. An endeavor with ten people that delivers a result in six months is a project, and an undertaking with hundreds of people working globally in a dozen independently managed teams to deliver periodic deployments over the course of five years is a program. Between these extremes, you will find both very large projects and modest programs, and the difference between the two can be fuzzy. From the perspective of risk, though, program risk management depends heavily on the project risk management principles outlined earlier in this book, along with a number of added considerations.

The main focus of program management is dealing effectively with complexity and overwhelming detail; work that entails thousands of activities and large numbers of contributors is unwieldy to plan, and it's impossible to monitor as a single effort. Program managers have daunting responsibilities. They are accountable for the overall program objective and managing the efforts of the individual project leaders, as well as usually leading a dedicated program staff or a program office. Breaking large undertakings into chunks of work that can be effectively delegated and managed as (mostly) autonomous projects serves the same purpose as developing work breakdown structures for a project—it reduces the complexity by converting the large and complicated into a collection of smaller components that are easier to deal with. Managing risks at the program level begins with ensuring adequate planning and risk management at the individual project level. Although doing this is an effective start on program risk management, it is insufficient by itself.

It is never possible to break up a large piece of work into a set of totally disconnected pieces; interrelationships and connections remain that represent program-level risks. At a minimum, program scope links the included projects to the overall business justification for the total endeavor. From a scheduling perspective, there are always cross-dependencies connecting the projects within a program. None of these predecessor-successor linkages is entirely contained within any of the component projects, so they need to be tracked and managed at the program level. These program interconnections showed up in the PERIL database both as scope defect risks due to integration issues and as schedule dependency risks arising from project timing delays. Also, because programs are generally bigger and often longer than projects, they represent larger risk because of their scale.

For all these reasons, programs usually have a risk profile that exceeds the sum of their parts. A collection of modest-risk component projects may well aggregate into a high-risk program because of positive probability correlations for project risks within the interconnected projects. There are also cascade effects. When a risk occurs in one project, it can trigger additional problems in several other projects—quickly spinning things out of control. Managing project risks is necessary, but program risk management extends well beyond this.

Planning Program Risk Management

Chapter 2 discussed planning for project risk management, observing that for small undertakings informal risk planning is generally sufficient. Programs always need more than informal planning. They are generally large, and their risks arise from many sources. Some program risks originate from above the program. They arise from questionable benefits or ROI expectations, organizational dependencies, speculative or unrealistic assumptions, or other factors that affect the overall program. Other risks arise within the projects that make up the program, and still others are intrinsic to the program itself.

Formal program risk planning is a part of program initiation. To get started, map out how much effort this will require and verify funding support with your program sponsor (and with your other stakeholders, as appropriate). The overall process for program risk management mirrors the process for project risk management: Plan, Identify, Assess, Respond, and Monitor. The effort for managing risk for a program is often integrated with other ongoing responsibilities of the program staff (or program management office), but if you plan to use a separate staff with its own budget, secure needed approvals and funding. For the program, document:

- The risk tolerance of your sponsor and key stakeholders
- The owner for program risk management (if not the program leader) and other program staff who will participate, with their roles
- The process you will use for program risk management, including the format for the program risk register
- The planned frequency for program risk reviews
- The location where program risk information will be stored and how you will track and communicate program risks
- Any metrics to be used in monitoring program risks

As an example, for several years I was responsible for planning and risk management for a large program at Hewlett-Packard. This program was responsible for consolidating global oversight for all current fee-for-service projects under a single, consistent set of business processes and information technology applications. The program had direct responsibility for a budget of several million dollars per year and had a shifting roster of about 200 contributors working on more than a dozen project teams that were either responsible for delivery of key functions or geographically based in the regions targeted for upcoming releases. The program implemented roughly four countries in each release, and after several years of quarterly deployments the system was in operation in more than fifty countries worldwide.

Risk management was an important success factor for the program. The processes we used for this were well defined and documented. Throughout the program I led monthly program risk reviews with the rest of the program staff. In our meetings, we reviewed the risks already listed in the program risk register, retired any that were no longer of concern, and added new risks based on evolving program plans and external changes. During each meeting we reprioritized the significant risks and then reviewed or established risk responses and contingency plans associated with them. Following each monthly meeting, I distributed the updated risk register to the project leaders, and I made the current version available to everyone working on the program via the program's web-based knowledge management system. By periodically considering the risks and keeping them visible, we avoided most problems and kept the program on track.

Identifying Project-Related Program Risks and Interfaces

Program risk identification generally begins with a review of risk from below, based on the planning for each component project and identification of each project's risks. Across the entire program there may be hundreds or perhaps thousands of identified project-level risks. Nonetheless, the program risk manager should review all of them and provide feedback and assistance if any assessments appear inconsistent or flawed.

Generally, project-level risks are best managed at the project level. However, some significant project risks will also need to be "promoted" to the program risk register. Some examples are:

- Project risks that are significant enough to be program "showstoppers"
- Interproject interfaces and cross-dependencies
- Novelty or substantial technical complexity (architecture, systems engineering, and the like) that could result in integration problems or program deliverable defects

- Potential queuing conflicts involving individuals or other scarce resources needed by two or more of the projects
- Significant work done by outsourced or distributed project teams
- Similar project risks identified in several projects that in aggregate represent large overall impact
- Projects that are inherently risky overall
- Any risks that could persist as possible problems past the duration of the project where they are identified

Cross-project dependencies, or interfaces, are a substantial source of program-level risk. An effective process for documenting and managing these connections is central to managing these interconnections. It is likely that most project interdependencies will be identified during basic project planning, but the ultimate responsibility (and risk) for managing these relationships is at the program level.

Initial planning for all inter-project predecessor/successor relationships begins at the project level. However, managing these dependencies may require trade-offs or decisions that cannot be made by individual project leaders. Even when interfaces appear to be under control at the project level, each still represents potentially significant program risk.

Managing interface risks involves reliable, well-documented interproject commitments. The relationship depicted in figure 13-1 shows a typical interface. Each interface is partly within a project contained in the program, but it is also partly in "no man's land" where neither of the involved projects has full control.

The terminology of suppliers and customers is useful in analyzing program interconnections. The interface linkages initiate in the supplier project, and they terminate in the customer project.

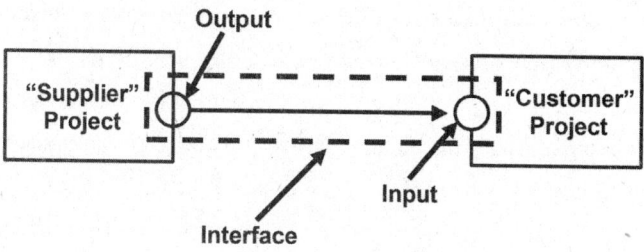

Figure 13-1: Program Interface Connecting Two Related Projects

Within any given project, at least some external predecessor dependencies are inevitable. These will surface as part of project schedule development, as discussed in chapter 4. Identification of program interfaces begins in planning for the "customer" project, the project within the program that requires an input. Every such external input for a "customer" project is a risk both for that project and for the program. Within programs, project planning processes will also uncover external successor dependencies, where projects expect to supply deliverables as outputs to be supplied to other projects within the program.

At the program level all the inputs and outputs identified by the interrelated projects must be identified and formally documented in a written description. Each input needs to be matched with an appropriate output. Program interface management strives to resolve all these connections so they can be incorporated into the overall program plan. (Any interfaces that are missed during planning are sure to be identified later—most likely as disruptive surprises for the program.)

To begin the process, the project leader of the customer project documents all inputs required, listing specifications and requested timing. Ideally, each documented input will be promptly associated with an output planned by a supplier project, and there will be quick and easy agreement by the corresponding project leader to supply it. When there are no issues with requirements or timing associated with the handoff, the two project leaders formally agree on the terms of the interface, treating it as a binding contractual commitment.

Many situations, however, are not this simple. There may be required inputs for which there are no currently planned outputs. For some of these, additional planning by a plausible supplier project may be necessary, or perhaps an outside supplier identified, to ensure that the need is met. For others, a change of scope may be necessary, or the customer project may need to plan to meet their needs internally. Even when the inputs and outputs appear to align, there may be issues. When there are differences between the input specifications needed and the output specifications planned, the program manager may need to participate in negotiations between the project leaders and guide the process to a resolution that serves the program.

Interface timing issues also are common, where inputs are needed earlier than the corresponding outputs are planned. This situation resulted in an average of nearly eight weeks of slip in the PERIL database, one of the largest averages for schedule-driven risks. Such project-level schedule delay can result in significant program-level timing exposure. The small program in figure 13-2 may look like an eight-month undertaking based on review of plans for the component projects.

After adjusting to account for interface timing, however, the ten-month schedule in figure 13-3 emerges. The program manager must coordinate reconciliation and work to resolve these conflicts.

If there are any unclaimed project-level outputs, it may reveal planning gaps in one or more other projects. For outputs that are

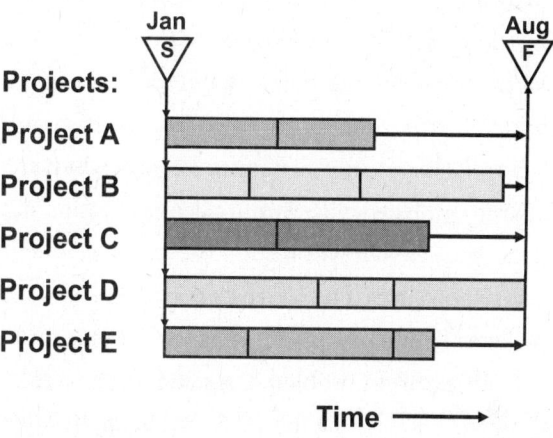

Figure 13-2: Initial Project Plans

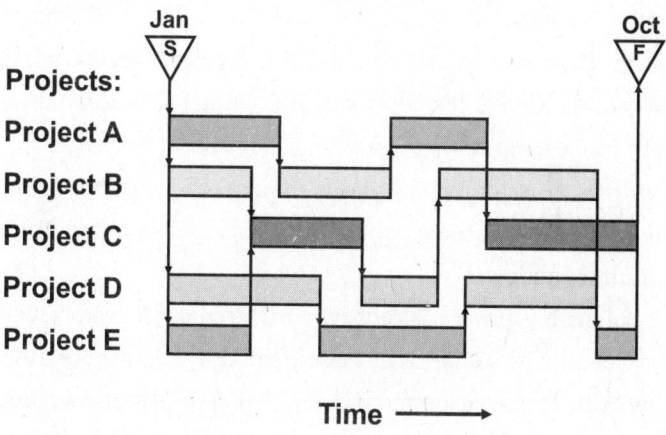

Figure 13-3: Interface Timing Connections within a Program

truly needed, the program manager will need to locate all corresponding missing inputs and work with appropriate project leaders
to integrate them into the plans. Some planned project outputs
may even prove to be unnecessary, in which case the program

manager will work with the leader of the supplier project to eliminate them, along with their related activities.

The process for identifying and documenting program interfaces also helps with another common source of program risk.
Programs regularly get into difficulty because they are quickly
chopped up into projects, with minimal consideration of the project cross-connections that will result. The more independent each
project is, the easier it will be for the project leader to manage. It
also means fewer "no man's land" issues for the program manager
to deal with. Integration problems, a substantial source of scope
defect risk in the PERIL database, are often the result of excessive organizational complexity for the program. If there are 10
projects in a program and 150 interfaces, there is almost certainly
a less complicated decomposition for the program into projects
where more dependency links lie wholly within the component
projects. Excessive interfaces connecting project teams, particularly geographically distributed teams, represent more program
failure modes and higher risk. As project plans evolve and integrated program plans take shape, monitor the number of interfaces and keep your eyes open for a logically less complicated
program breakdown.

As planning proceeds, ensure that at the program level all
interfaces are visible, formally documented, and agreed to in writing by each of the customer and supplier project leaders who are
involved. Even when interfaces are thoroughly planned and managed, they remain program risks and belong on the program risk
register.

Identifying Other Program Risks
It is rare that all program risks can be identified in project-level
planning. You will need to do additional analysis and planning at

the program level to pick up any missing program risks related to external dependencies, technical complexity, resource capacity, and other exposures.

Some program risks are a consequence of decisions and objectives above the program. Strategic risks arise from organizational decisions and objectives associated with new programs. Some assumptions made during program initiation may be realistic and credible, and others may be guesses and wishful thinking. Programs are large and complicated, so before much (or any) analysis is completed there are often significant gaps between what is expected and what is possible. Program planning provides a useful tool for identifying unrealistic assumptions and data needed for setting credible expectations and objectives. As you review overall program objectives, add any potentially problematic program constraints or assumptions that you cannot control to your program risk register.

Some program-level exposures are intrinsic to the program itself. Size and scale are significant sources of risk, even when they are only slightly larger than successful past programs. Document program risk arising from unprecedented staffing levels, budgets, duration, or other scale factors. Funding continuity is another significant exposure for lengthy programs (and projects). Programs are generally initiated and scoped in their entirety, but their budgets are approved year by year. There is always staffing and funding risk for programs when their planned duration extends beyond a fiscal boundary (and even more when they cross more than one).

Programs generally require at least some innovation and novelty, so identify sources of risk arising from "bleeding-edge" program deliverables, new development methods or equipment, and changing processes. Identify risks associated with any contributors who are geographically distributed, reporting to management elsewhere in the organization, working on a contract basis, or otherwise tenuously connected to the program. Program work can include contributions from other parts of the organization not associated with projects, so consider potential risk sources related to required support, administration, infrastructure, and other "white space" dependencies. Also consider risks related to potential program-level staff issues, such as commitment conflicts, loss of key individuals, queuing for program resources, effective program communications, and ongoing motivation (particularly for long duration programs).

Build a program risk register similar to that used at the project level, adding program-level risks to major risks "promoted" from the program's projects. Augment the list through brainstorming with the program staff, with input from key stakeholders and other organizational experts such as from a PMO. Review lessons learned from earlier similar programs, and develop relevant execution scenarios to support your analysis. The program risk register for the effort at Hewlett-Packard discussed earlier in this section started with about twenty-five items and averaged roughly thirty throughout the program. (Risks that were managed at the project level at any given time were typically about an order of magnitude more numerous.)

Assessing Program Risks

Program risk assessment does not really depart much from the principles of project risk assessment described in chapter 7. Use qualitative assessment methods based on categories to prioritize program risks. For significant risks, use quantitative analysis to refine your understanding and drive response strategies. Because some of the information for risks may come from remote or secondhand sources, be especially wary of data-quality issues and skeptical about impact and probability estimates that seem excessively optimistic. If risk consequences can be expected to vary over a wide range, be conservative and use the worst-case data for your assessments. For probability, probe for connections and similarities among risks, and increase probability and/or impact assessments for related risks. Program risks are often highly correlated, so carefully review risks having root causes in common or with comparable descriptions from project to project. Risks that might seem of modest priority for the projects within the program may actually be significant when aggregated at the program level. Some project risks may trigger a catastrophic cascade of connected problems that could derail the program.

Sort the risk list and select the most significant ones, focusing on:

- Interdependencies and interfaces between projects
- Scoping complexity and potential deliverable issues
- Staffing problems, motivation issues, and funding commitments
- All high-impact program-level risks

Responses for Program Risks

As with assessment, program risk responses primarily depend on tactics similar to those that are effective for project risks, as explored in chapter 8. For each high-priority program risk, consider options for avoidance, mitigation, escalation, or transfer. If you can find no appropriate response for a specific significant risk, or one that is only partially effective, develop contingency plans for recovery. Ensure that the individual project plans include the specifics necessary for managing the important program-level risks and determine how you plan to monitor for key risk triggers at the program level.

As with project risks, visibility is a powerful program risk mitigation strategy. When the consequences of program risks are apparent, people work to avoid them. Even if they occur, recovery from risks that people are aware of can be faster, minimizing the impact.

One final differentiator for risk response planning at the program level is the need to have an effective and well-established process for rapid escalation whenever a significant risk occurs. Quick response also depends on a pre-established program-level budget reserve for use in dealing with contingencies. Where possible, also set up adequate program-level schedule reserve to protect key program deliverable deadlines.

Monitoring and Controlling Program Risks

Disciplined monitoring is essential for program risks because they are larger, may be difficult to anticipate, and tend to quickly become major disasters. Frequent effective communication is central to avoiding this, and it's one of the main responsibilities of the program manager and staff.

For the Hewlett-Packard IT program mentioned earlier, our monthly risk management review meetings were crucial to our communication and risk monitoring. We also discussed major risks regularly at our weekly program staff meetings, and scheduled time during our semiannual face-to-face program review meetings to plan for risks associated with the upcoming releases. In addition, we discussed important upcoming risks as part of our monthly "all hands" conference calls. These "virtual" program team meetings were where the program leadership team presented current program status. We distributed all of the presentation materials for these calls in advance to the roughly 200 program contributors, and archived all the information on the program website for review by those who missed the calls.

The size of the program risk register changed over time. Although it did not drop significantly, the list of program risks we were managing also did not expand, as seen in figure 13-4. The overall severity profile of our managed risks also remained stable over time.

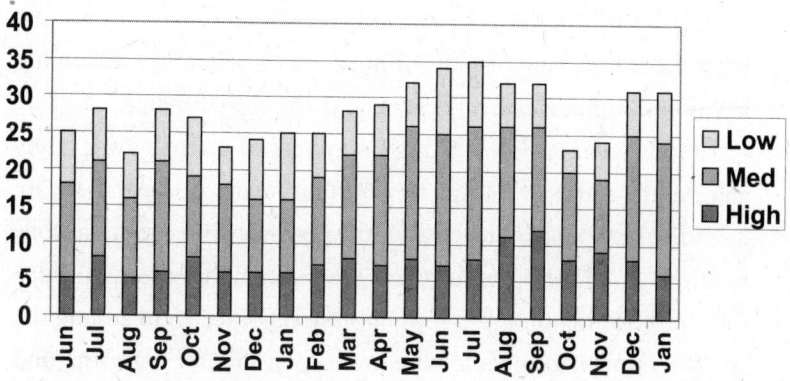

■ **Figure 13-4:** Program Risks over Time, Categorized by Severity

Effective program risk management also depends on strict control of changes. For large, complex programs, any change, regardless of how innocent it appears, can result in major unintended consequences. Program complexity also requires a hard limit on how late changes can be made; when changes are attempted too close to a release date, they often fail in test and need to be backed out at the last minute. This creates unnecessary work both to attempt the change and then to remove it, effort that could have been applied productively elsewhere in the program, such as in mitigating serious risks.

Another control strategy for programs is ongoing commitment to process review and improvement. Doing a "lessons learned" session after a project is complete is useful, but for lengthy programs there are frequent opportunities to find and deal with recurring program inefficiencies and problems.

Particularly for lengthy programs, decreasing interest and motivation can be a big risk. Work to keep people engaged by periodic program reviews, frequent implementations and delivery of incremental value, training, opportunities for advancement (or at least movement into new responsibilities), and celebrations following key program milestones, releases, and accomplishments.

Finally, programs with large numbers of contributors rarely achieve the status of a "high-performing" team, because there are just too many people involved for the necessary interpersonal connections to develop. Large programs can, however, build a high-performing program staff or program office team among the smaller number of people who are responsible for planning and managing the work over the long haul.

When I look back on the HP IT program discussed here, our biggest success factor was the investment we made, early and often, in building strong relationships and trust among the program-level staff. As a group, we all placed the needs of the program well above the specific details of our individual roles. There were never issues of coverage when people were absent from the program. Each individual had broad knowledge of the overall effort and could fill in during times of stress (which were frequent). It mattered little what our formal roles were; we all pitched in and got things done. The atmosphere of "one for all and all for one" was our most effective tactic for managing risk and ensuring a successful program.

PORTFOLIO RISK MANAGEMENT

As you move up the food chain in an organization, risk management moves from the "micro" to the "macro," as discussed in chapter 1. Where project and program risk management focus on the specific, portfolio risk management focuses more on the aggregate. Managing portfolios begins with establishing strategic objectives that serve the current goals of the organization and can be used to set criteria for evaluating potential projects and programs. Specific details do continue to matter, however, because portfolio risk management also requires the selection of projects and programs where most risks are independent. When the risks in population of items offset, the overall risk—the expected variability of the aggregate outcome—falls. Portfolio risk management tends to focus primarily on financial returns, and selecting the right mix of projects will substantially lower the variability.

Portfolio Risks: Specific and Overall

Portfolio risk management does not exclusively focus on the aggregate; obtaining the best overall return also requires working to achieve desired results for each of the projects and programs that make up the portfolio. Managing projects well depends on the techniques outlined throughout this book. People responsible for managing portfolio risk tend to delegate the risk management for a particular project (or program—for the purposes of this section, the term "project" will include programs) along with all the other management responsibilities.

Managing overall portfolio risk starts with the understanding that there is safety in numbers. Ideally, if enough projects are in plan and the organization is reasonably competent at managing the work, the few projects that fail will be more than offset by ones that surpass their objectives. If the "average project" does well, the details become less important. The performance of such a portfolio depends on large numbers and generally satisfactory performance.

A few projects in the project portfolio will be exceptions to the idea that only averages matter, though. Portfolio risk management also attempts to exclude projects having very large potential for loss, or at least minimizing their potential to do financial or other harm. Some strategic projects may carry priority based on factors beyond short-term monetary returns. As with project and program risk management, you must consider worst-case scenarios for the portfolio. Determine how much risk, overall, the organization can tolerate, in terms of financial exposure and other significant consequences. Extreme portfolio exposure—for example, one very large project that could threaten the organization as a whole—is not just portfolio risk management. It is part of enterprise risk management, which is covered in the final section of this chapter.

VUCA is another portfolio consideration. Organizational factors that contribute to volatility and ambiguity can increase overall portfolio risk substantially, and portfolio decisions should carefully consider all four factors when evaluating and selecting projects to fund and execute.

Planning Portfolio Risk Management

Project portfolio management is primarily concerned with categorizing, prioritizing, and selecting projects. Best-in-class organizations have a well-documented plan for portfolio management, including a strategy for reviewing and improving the overall portfolio management process. Some organizations make portfolio decisions annually and some do it more frequently, but the process is generally periodic, not continuous. During the times when decisions are being made, managing portfolio risk requires a good deal of interaction with project management processes.

Planning for portfolio management begins with a number of project management factors, including overall goals and the target mix of projects by type for the organization. An effective portfolio management process relies heavily on project risk management and planning data as selection and decision criteria for assessing and prioritizing project opportunities. The overall relationship between an effective portfolio management process and project management is depicted in figure 13-5.

■ **Figure 13-5:** Portfolio and Project Management Linkages

The project portfolio management process relies on feedback from projects at several stages. The list of projects to be considered for the portfolio feeds into project initiation activities, and it depends on realistic project information. A successful portfolio selection process benefits from credible project data developed in planning, especially estimates for cost, duration, and risk. As projects execute, their status provides feedback for midcourse portfolio corrections, and project metrics also feed into subsequent portfolio decision cycles.

At each stage, project risk analysis is central to a robust portfolio management process. Deciding which projects to initiate (or to continue) relies on project risk assessments to ensure that exposures remain within the organization's risk tolerances. For a startup company there will be a high tolerance for risky projects, so the portfolio process will initiate projects with considerable uncertainty. In contrast, organizations that provide custom solutions for fixed fees will tend to exclude risky projects, to protect their reputation and to avoid significant financial losses. Risk information is essential to avoiding inappropriate projects.

For all these reasons, project risk data should always be a key input for portfolio selection decisions. Because these decisions are often made well in advance of any detailed planning, it is a good idea to revisit the portfolio decisions as projects plans evolve and can provide better data.

Planning for portfolio management also requires setting decision criteria. Because the primary performance measurement for most portfolios is financial return, some version of ROI estimate is inevitably at or near the top of the list of criteria. Because all types of ROI assessment depend on two estimates—the cost of a project and the worth of a project—accurate data for both is desirable. As discussed in chapter 9, the accuracy of ROI forecasts is often poor; premature estimates of cost are generally unrealistically low and initial estimates of value are often ridiculously optimistic. Using unreliable ROI estimates increases portfolio risk.

Other criteria derived from project management include overall effort, the project risk profile (often based on a survey, such as a shortened version of the example in chapter 9), information based

PROGRAM, PORTFOLIO, AND ENTERPRISE RISK . . . | **507**

on planning, and other input supplied by project teams. It is also prudent to consider the VUCA factors for projects under consideration, examining the definition for each proposal for a clear purpose and a durable vision to minimize volatility. Explore the basis for estimates and forecasts to determine that they are based on realistic analysis (not guesses, hopes, and prayers) to decrease uncertainty. Consider the duration, effort, and overall scale of each project to recognize the complexity involved. Also examine the stated requirements and objectives for ambiguity. Include assessment of VUCA factors in your overall risk appraisals.

Portfolio decision criteria also include data unrelated to project management, such as alignment with stated business goals and strategies, assessment of markets and potential competition, and availability of needed expertise. Selecting appropriate criteria and clearly defining how each is to be used helps to minimize portfolio risk.

Once listed, each criteria needs a weight. How the criteria are weighted also affects portfolio risk, so ensure that sufficient importance is given to risk assessment and credible project information.

Not all decision criteria are created equal. Some project selection criteria tend to bypass the portfolio process altogether. One example is a project's ability to keep people out of jail. Projects undertaken to meet industry standards or regulatory, environmental, or legal requirements will also generally bypass portfolio analysis; such projects are selected and funded without much debate. In your process planning, though, work to limit the projects that can be automatically fast-tracked into plan to those that are legitimately mandatory. Bypassing the process to accept the "pet projects" of executive decision-makers without adequate analysis entails a lot of risk. Although saying "no" to such project proposals can be also risky, if you can turn them down based on objective analysis it's better for the organization, the project team, and, ultimately, even the sponsor.

Another key consideration for portfolio planning is the mix of projects. In any organization, options vary from mundane, incremental projects to high-risk efforts that may well be impossible. Typical project category types include:

- New basic research and development
- Revolutionary products, processes, or new markets
- Next generation/new platform to replace an old offering
- Evolutionary improvements to an existing product or service
- Maintenance, support, or infrastructure

Viewed from the perspective of financial return, the highest-potential projects are usually found on the bleeding-edge end of the spectrum at the top of this list. If you seek to minimize risk, however, the most desirable projects are found farther down the list with the more routine projects. For a given set of decision criteria, projects in a rank-ordered list will tend to cluster based on their category. This may result in a portfolio that is skewed, composed mostly of only one type of project. Because the balance of projects also matters, it is useful to define a target mix of project types that best aligns with the organizational strategy and risk tolerance, with percentages for each project category.

These relative proportions will vary over time and from organization to organization, but the target mix should consistently reflect current tactical and strategic objectives. The mix should also reflect a balance between projects that achieve results in the short term and longer-range projects that will best serve the organization's future needs. Managing this requires ongoing discipline. It is all too easy for a portfolio to become overloaded with projects of a given type—for example, too many "urgent" maintenance projects or an unhealthy number of projects dependent on speculative technology. When the project load deviates from the overall business objectives, it increases business risk for the organization as a whole. Define a portfolio process that strives for a focused portfolio of good projects with risk and benefit profiles consistent with business objectives.

Identifying Portfolio Risks

Project portfolio risk identification relies heavily on the project risk identification processes described in the first half of this book.

For projects that are still embryonic, detailed analysis may not be available. In these cases, at least develop a sense of potential risks by reviewing problems encountered during earlier, similar work. Brainstorming and scenario analysis done with subject matter experts can also be useful and provide a starting point for later more detailed planning and risk management.

Assessing Portfolio Risks and Overall Risk

Although the focus of project risk management is on "loss times likelihood" for an individual project, assessment of a portfolio considers risk in aggregate. Portfolio risk assessment involves both decisions about which projects to include and exclude and an understanding of how the individual projects relate to each other.

Because organizations always have many more promising project concepts than can be staffed and successfully executed, project portfolio management is a winnowing process. Determining how far down you can go in a sorted list of project opportunities begins with a realistic appraisal of capacity. Determining how much project work may be possible can be surprisingly difficult;

most organizations have an exaggerated notion of how much they can accomplish. They also make matters worse by failing to account for commitments that must be staffed for support, maintenance, operations, production, and other ongoing required work. It's not uncommon in high-tech organizations to initiate double or even triple the number of projects that can realistically be staffed. Skepticism is warranted when reviewing available capacity; the "too many projects" problem is a common and systemic portfolio risk.

The next step in the assessment process involves collecting and evaluating information on the predefined decision criteria applied to each project. As discussed earlier, relying too heavily on just estimates of ROI is problematic. Sorting a list of projects based primarily on ROI is not necessarily much better than arranging it randomly. In fact, it might even be worse, because portfolio analysis contrasts existing, ongoing projects with new project proposals. Both the cost and the value data for current projects are likely to be at least somewhat realistic, putting them at a decided disadvantage against the speculative estimates for potential new undertakings with data based on optimistic guesswork. Similar standards need to apply to all projects, with clear-eyed examination of potential return. New projects often appear to be straightforward, low risk, and high return prior to any detailed planning. Failure to account for this bias can lead to portfolio thrash, in which projects are regularly replaced in the portfolio by "better" opportunities, resulting in substantial wasted effort on projects that never complete.

Effective ROI assessment for projects also must consider uncertainty. For each project, estimate the upside potential for gain (often this is equivalent to the overall ROI assessment for new projects, since it's not likely anyone has considered much of anything that might go wrong). Also probe to realistically understand the downside potential for loss for each opportunity. Be skeptical of sales, value, profit, or other benefit estimates, especially project data described using suspiciously round numbers. Ask about the assumptions used to assess value, and find out how they were calculated. Inquire about threats, competition, or other factors that could invalidate the estimates. If there is a wide potential range, make it visible.

One additional technique for assessing financial uncertainty is "Value at Risk" (VaR). VaR is a technique for estimating the maximum amount of loss that can be expected from a financial investment. It came into widespread use in the 1990s and built on the work in portfolio theory done by Harry Markowitz. It incorporates risk analysis into ROI calculations, and attempts to show the level of risk being assumed so it can be better managed. VaR is based on some reasonable, but not completely bulletproof, assumptions. When financial markets are well behaved, VaR analysis allows financial firms to eke out a slightly larger return while remaining at the level of risk they believe appropriate. When the markets are volatile, though, as they were in the global 2007–2008 financial meltdown, VaR fails. VaR in those conditions misrepresented the risk being assumed, and it contributed substantially to the worldwide economic collapse.

The foundation of VaR is defining probability distributions for various investments in specific time frames. Using the distributions and computer simulations, potential returns (or losses) can be estimated. VaR is stated in terms such as "$100 million for one week at a 95 percent confidence interval." This means that there is no more than a 5 percent expected chance of losing more than

$100 million in the next week. An excellent description of the history and mechanics of VaR can be found in the book *Strategic Risk Taking* by Aswan Damodarian.

Using VaR requires selecting and applying an appropriate probability distribution for potential returns. Determining the distribution is done using some combination of the same three techniques used to estimate probabilities: mathematical modeling, empirical analysis of historical data, or guessing. As in most complex situations, historical analysis and guessing tend to dominate, but even plugging in a simple model such as the Gaussian distribution can provide useful insight when time frames are very short and the rising and falling variations are small and for the most part in balance.

VaR can fail, though, for a number of reasons:

- A selected probability distribution is a forecast, not a guarantee. Actual results may (and often will) vary.
- Even if the probability distribution has generally correct parameters, the "shape" may be inappropriate.
- Data used to define the distribution may be incomplete or otherwise inaccurate.
- Conditions assumed to be stable may prove to be drifting or more volatile than expected (as they have been during the recent COVID-19 disruptions).
- Other assumptions may be unwarranted due to defective analysis or dishonesty

Applying VaR to a project requires examining a longer time horizon than for many other types of investments. The time scale will need to extend out to the break-even point for the project, which can be months or even years, so "project VaR" involves investments that move in slow motion compared with the usual applications for VaR. The VaR objective, however, is the same—assessing how much money is at risk with our project investments. The analysis for a given project begins with a basic ROI analysis. Because the time horizon for a project is long, using a typical assumed distribution and a high confidence interval, VaR would be quite large compared to the project budget (unless risks are few and there is close to zero probability of cancellation).

One project under consideration for inclusion in a portfolio might be a project with expected financial benefits of $1,000,000, and a cost of $750,000. A crude ROI based on these assumptions would be $250,000, or a roughly 33 percent return. However, this is probably not a sufficiently complete story. There will doubtless be both execution risks and some uncertainty around the benefits, so a more realistic view might look like the data in this table:

	ASSUMED VALUES	ASSUMED PROBABILITIES	EXPECTED VALUES
Project Cost	$750,000	100%	$750,000
Project Benefits	$1,000,000	100%	$1,000,000
Risk 1	–$500,000	10%	–$50,000
Risk 2	–$200,000	15%	–$30,000
Risk 3	–$250,000	10%	–$25,000
Opportunity 1	$50,000	5%	$2,500
Opportunity 2	$125,000	25%	$31,250
Total Expected Value			$178,750

Assuming these probabilities to be realistic, the expected return drops somewhat, but it remains at about 24 percent—which still looks pretty good. Neither risks nor opportunities ever "partially" occur, however. Risks either happen or they don't. Given this view, the range of possible outcomes for this project will be:

Minimum value: –$700,000

Expected value (risks included): $178,750

Nominal value (certainties only): $250,000

Maximum value: $425,000

The maximum looks like very good news; if all the good stuff happens and none of the bad, the return is excellent. If the reverse happens, though—we see all of the risks with none of the upside—the result is a deep financial hole. The expenses more than wipe out the return and the project would show a significant loss.

Neither of these extremes is very likely, however. For a more nuanced view of this, computer simulation can help. Using the project data above and doing 1,000 simulation runs, the average return is about $170,400, only slightly less than the "expected" return calculated using the figures for risks and opportunities weighted using their estimated probabilities. The values can be plotted in a cumulative graph as in figure 13-6. For this project, assuming that the information is realistic, there appears a 95 percent chance of losing no more than about $250,000.

Based on the simulation, this project will either return nothing or lose money almost 20 percent of the time. About 30 percent of the time, its return will not exceed the calculated expected value. However, nearly half the time (49.3 percent), the project will return $250,000, and there is about one chance in six it will do much better than that. Of course, even this view, eye-opening as it is, is not entirely complete. The possibility that the project will fail or be canceled is not included (there could be a probability

■ **Figure 13-6:** Potential Financial Returns (Based on Simulation)

listed with an estimated cost for this), we have assumed no correlation among the uncertainties, and this excludes any discounting effect from the time value of money.

In any event, VaR analysis provides an additional tool for assessing and contrasting financial exposure across project investments.

Whatever other decision criteria may be used for portfolio analysis and item ranking, ensure that factors estimating risk (such as
ROI with range estimates or project VaR) are part of the mix.
Also strive to include input from the project team, or at least from
qualified subject matter experts, in cost estimates and other project plan-related parameters. Always provide for explicit analysis of
worst-case scenarios for any project risks that may be particularly
severe and include an assessment of risk related to the expected
scale of each project.

In determining the evaluations for all of the criteria, confront any
known organizational biases (such as a tendency to underestimate
the effort and overestimate the value for enticing novel projects

compared with boring, routine ones). Work to achieve consistent, comparable results for all the projects under consideration.

After collecting and validating the project evaluation information, use it to rank-order the list of opportunities. The first few items listed will be easy to decide on: good opportunities that can be staffed are selected and put into plan. However, the deeper in the list you go, the more complex selection becomes.

One selection strategy creates a provisional list by determining the cumulative cost of projects listed starting from the top of the sorted list and drawing a cut line below the last project that can be staffed and funded using about 90 percent of available capacity. Portfolio risk management requires that some capacity be left uncommitted, primarily to deal with project risk but also to manage organizational emergencies and to provide capacity to exploit unforeseen opportunities. The list resulting from this process is provisional because it is unlikely to conform to the target mix of project types, and it may also represent inappropriate portfolio risk.

Adjusting the relative overall investment levels dedicated to projects in different categories is straightforward. You exclude the lowest items on the list that lie above the cut line in categories that are oversubscribed, dropping projects until the aggregate investment is in line with your target. Similarly, you pull projects that are below the line into your provisional portfolio to raise the cumulative budget for categories that are too small. Further adjustments may be warranted to deal with limitations on expertise, facilities, or other organizational constraints. Additional changes may be required to ensure that related projects are either all in plan or all out of plan; if projects that are cross-dependent are not executed in sync, the value they deliver can be diminished or even evaporate.

One additional factor to consider is size. The relative scale of projects also makes portfolio management challenging. To illustrate, consider this exchange:

A university professor asked her students how many of her collected rocks she could fit into a big jar she had sitting on the desk during her lecture. Examining the pile of rocks, the class reached a consensus of perhaps six or seven. Sure enough, when she started placing the rocks into the jar, she reached the top with rock number seven. No amount of jiggling or pressing would permit her to cram rock number eight into the jar. She then asked the class if they thought the jar was full. The students looked at the jar, looked back at the rocks, and decided that the jar looked full.

At that point the professor reached underneath the desk and pulled out a bowl filled with gravel. Since these stones were smaller than the original rocks, she was easily able to pour most of the gravel into the jar. The students watched them tumble down, filling in the open spaces between the larger rocks. She asked the class again, "Now is the jar full?"

By this time the students were starting to catch on, so most answered, "Probably not."

The professor again reached under her desk, and this time pulled out a bag of sand. She was able to dump about half of it in before reaching the top of the jar. She asked again, "Now is the jar full?"

Most students thought it was, but suspiciously they replied, "Not yet."

She reached down again, lifting a bucket of water. She proceeded to pour a good portion of it into the jar. After a moment the professor looked at the jar filled with soaking wet sand, gravel, and rocks. She looked back at the class, and asked, "What's the lesson here?"

One student bravely suggested, "A vessel is not necessarily full, even when it looks like it is?"

The professor admitted that that was not a bad lesson, but not what she had in mind. From her desk, she picked up one of the remaining larger rocks that she had initially used to fill the jar. She held it over the jar and said, "If you don't put these big ones in first, you'll never get them in at all."

In a project portfolio, there will always be some way to accommodate an additional small project. Failing to consider the large, often strategic, projects at the outset of the portfolio process, however, can result in a portfolio filled to capacity with mostly smaller projects. This may leave insufficient resources to properly support the major project opportunities, so consider putting "large rocks" in first.

It may be tempting to allocate 100 percent of your available capacity when accepting projects into the portfolio. This is risky, because retaining zero slack will likely result in problems leading to adverse impact on all projects.

The final step necessary for managing portfolio risk is to assess overall risk for the proposed portfolio as a whole. This involves estimating risk correlations for the selected projects. One of the main objectives for portfolio management is exploiting negative correlations and using them to lower the overall risk. This is the reason that many people invest in mutual funds instead of individual stocks. Although the possible gains for a mutual fund are always lower than those for a single stock, so are the potential losses. The aggregate return for the "basket of stocks" in a mutual fund is more predictable and has lower risk. Even here, though, correlation matters. If all the stocks in a fund are in a single industry and subject to similar exposures and threats, they will rise and fall together. When one stock drops there is a good chance that most will follow. The fund losses will reflect the losses of the individual stocks. When project risks correlate, the same will happen in a portfolio of projects.

One tactic already discussed helps in managing this—enforcing the proportions of the portfolio that will be devoted to projects in different categories. In addition to this, the portfolio manager needs to consider the projects in the provisional portfolio, examining them for, among other factors:

- Reliance on similar new technologies or applications
- Dependence on the same resources, especially outsourced or specialized staffing
- Significant project risks listed in common by several projects
- Potential failure modes shared by the projects
- Excessive VUCA exposure

The portfolio management process seeks to select an optimal, or at least acceptable, mix of projects to undertake. Although risk is only one of the criteria applied to the decision process, it is a central one because the portfolio process is an important tactic for minimizing risks for the organization.

For each newly proposed or continuing project in a proposed portfolio, there are three possible outcomes.

1. The project is accepted into the portfolio, becoming or remaining an active project.

2. The project is accepted, but only after making changes (to scope, schedule, or resources). Some projects may be lowered to an acceptable level of risk through "transfer," by purchasing insurance to deal with excessive financial exposure, by converting the project to a joint venture and sharing the risks (and rewards) with a partner organization, or through other adjustments.

3. The project is rejected. Some (perhaps most) project ideas should be turned down or postponed for reconsideration at a later time.

Before finalizing a list of projects as the "in plan" portfolio, ensure that both the individual project risks and the overall cumulative risks have been thoroughly evaluated and the candidate list is consistent with the organization's risk tolerance. Identify any particularly risky projects that are accepted into the portfolio, and ensure that the organizational decision-makers responsible for the portfolio will have adequate visibility of project progress and will monitor it at least monthly.

Portfolio decisions are never permanent; successful portfolio management must periodically revisit the selection process, including risk assessment. Portfolio reviews are typically conducted about once per quarter, and may also be needed following the completion of major projects. Portfolio reviews revisit the portfolio assumptions and criteria and manage portfolio risk by considering project status information, especially data on troubled projects.

The portfolio review process is essentially the selection process described earlier, but one of the key risk objectives in a review is detecting and weeding out inappropriate projects early. This ensures that the mix of ongoing projects will continue to encompass the best available project opportunities. Best-in-class high-tech companies find and cancel questionable projects early, before much investment is made.

Other goals for the portfolio review are maintaining a balance of projects and keeping the project portfolio requirements within the capacity limits of the organization. Immediately after a portfolio is determined, additional good project ideas will surface. One reason for maintaining some unused capacity is to permit the organization to exploit new, unexpected opportunities, so adding some of these ideas to the portfolio is not necessarily a problem. However, there is frequently little discipline used in selecting and starting new projects, and the standards used for putting them in plan are not always as rigorous as those used for the initial portfolio decisions. This can quickly lead to a list of in-plan projects that have inadequate resources; progress will falter and stall for many of them. The "if some is good, more must be better" philosophy creates both excessive project and portfolio risk. It is not uncommon for the projects undertaken by high-tech organizations to require resources that are double, or even triple, what is actually available. Resource underestimation is a common project problem, as demonstrated by the data in the PERIL database. Making matters worse, the extra projects crammed into the plan are often "urgent," which tends to shift the mix toward short-term projects. This zero-sum game will result in inadequate resources being devoted to strategic projects that are more important overall to the organization, increasing future risk. Portfolio reviews manage risk by adjusting imbalances and trimming the project list back to what can be adequately staffed and managed.

Monitoring and Controlling Portfolio Risks

The portfolio management process is not usually something that requires a lot of day-to-day attention. Portfolio risk is mostly managed as part of the periodic selection and review processes. There are several matters, however, that do need ongoing attention.

Monitor high-level status for all the projects in your portfolio at least monthly. The portfolio monitoring process operates in parallel and depends upon the project execution and control processes, as illustrated in figure 13-4. For each project, define and track a few diagnostic project metrics such as those described in chapter 9. There are a number of software tools available for monitoring a collection of projects that can be used to implement a "project dashboard" for the portfolio. Dashboards can be quite useful, and for larger project portfolios may be necessary. For modest project portfolios, though, ongoing oversight using a handful of key measures does not usually need to be quite so complicated—a spreadsheet or a deck of presentation slides for tracking and reporting will likely suffice.

Most project portfolios have a small number of high-risk projects, and these need particular attention. At least monthly, conduct an in-depth review of progress. Work to detect issues early that might develop into major problems. For all projects in the portfolio that are currently in trouble, focus on what is necessary to bring them back under control. Allocate additional resources, revise expectations, or make other changes. Use any available resource reserves to resolve the issues, and deal promptly with any problems that are escalated by projects requiring management attention.

Managing bad news at the portfolio level, as at the project level, requires a single-minded focus on problem-solving and resolution. Responding to unfavorable status information with criticism, punishment, or even disapproval can take a situation from bad to worse. Motivation on risky projects is often tenuous, and you need a motivated, enthusiastic project team to solve tough problems. A troubled project staffed by disillusioned, depressed contributors will likely never recover.

If, after a sincere effort, there appears to be no plausible recovery scenario for a project, cancel it and get it out of the portfolio. A key job of the portfolio manager is to limit the losses when a project is headed irretrievably toward failure.

It is also necessary to monitor overall resource use, and to detect when projects are competing for the same resources. When there are resource contention issues, adjust the portfolio to deal with them, shutting projects down temporarily (or even permanently) when necessary. When key projects are delayed due to queuing for scarce resources, consider acquiring more capacity, or at least ensure that the queuing is based on project priority, not just "first come, first served."

One additional wrinkle at the portfolio level comes from the essentially financial basis used to measure success or failure. Assumptions made for projects are often overtaken by events, especially for long-duration projects. Also, as projects progress, the estimates for cost and value are likely to change. Changes inside your organization or even outside can significantly alter the overall evaluation for any given project, and some of these changes may substantially diminish a project's expected value. As new information becomes available, reevaluate the affected projects to determine whether they still deserve to be in the portfolio.

Overall, managing risk in a project portfolio involves ongoing dedication to ensuring that needed resources are available, risks are anticipated and managed, decisions and other required management actions are timely, barriers to progress are removed, and problems are solved. A portfolio filled with understaffed, poorly funded, trouble-ridden projects represents unacceptable risk for any organization.

ENTERPRISE RISK MANAGEMENT

The final section of this chapter climbs one level higher in the organization. Enterprise risk management encompasses all the project, program, and portfolio risk management concepts, and more. One type of enterprise risk management takes a traditional view of risk, "harmful uncertainty," in this case to the organization as a whole. There's also a more narrowly defined concept for enterprise risk management that has emerged recently, with government regulation and industry standards as its foundation. Both types of enterprise risk management place greater emphasis on the long term than the types of risk management discussed previously. We explore the relationship between project risk management and both of these types of enterprise risk in the remainder of this chapter, beginning with the more conventional perspective.

Organizational Threats in General

Enterprise risk relates to project risk management because projects both contribute to enterprise risk and are employed to manage it. Projects create organizational risk for all the reasons discussed throughout this book. Managing enterprise risk that arises from individual projects is generally delegated to lower levels of the organization. Risk management of this type relies on the techniques for project risk management outlined in chapters 8 and 10 for projects, and the ideas for managing program and portfolio risks explored earlier in this chapter. With the exception of extreme project risks that could materially damage the entire organization, few risks associated with projects will be actively managed at the enterprise level.

Although project risk is not generally a big concern to the enterprise risk manager, the converse is not true. The impact of enterprise risk management on projects is quite substantial. The purpose of enterprise risk management is to ensure the ongoing viability of an organization, so there are many enterprise-level concerns that affect projects, including:

- Safety and security
- Fraud and financial liability
- Casualty loss and disaster preparedness
- Organizational reputation and brand protection
- Intellectual property management

This is only a partial list, of course. There may be many other specific concerns representing potential for loss or damage to a given enterprise. One line of defense used to manage enterprise risk is defining and enforcing processes for the organization that are designed to minimize exposure. For example, legal contract templates and review processes limit financial risks. They also include mandatory provisions intended to limit other types of risk to the organization, such as nondisclosure terms protecting intellectual property. Mandatory training for well-defined, documented standards for business ethics, enterprise controls, and other business processes are essential to managing enterprise risk. Worker safety is also important to the enterprise. Reflecting the origins of the company manufacturing gunpowder two centuries ago, DuPont still requires stringent processes for safety in all locations and mandates periodic safety meetings for all employees, including people who are based in offices at headquarters where the safety risks tend toward paper cuts.

These and other actions at the enterprise level aimed at managing risk relate to project risk management because they influence the risks faced by each individual project. Conformance with risk-related policies set by the organization is intended to reduce project risk, and organization-wide standards and rules for risk management work ensure a focus on managing risks that some project stakeholders might resist. In addition to the policies and procedures for project work, other organizational mandates establish procedures for protecting confidential information, managing quality, ensuring security, and following other guidelines. Staying within the bounds of accepted organizational expectations is good risk management.

For some projects, the link to enterprise risk management is even more fundamental. In any given year, some fraction of the projects funded by an organization will address enterprise risks. Some of these projects will implement new safety procedures or replace faulty equipment. Others will develop techniques or algorithms that limit threats to security, eliminate fraud, or deal with other sources of potential loss. Enterprise risk management is a fertile source for projects, including some very large, expensive ones.

Historically, there have been many examples of this, from the thousands and thousands of projects undertaken worldwide dealing with the "Y2K" bug in the late 1990s (where the universal computer shortcut of using two digits for data relating to the year would suddenly start causing potentially catastrophic arithmetic errors dealing with time on January 1, "00") to the recent massive efforts undertaken to deal with the sudden effects of the

COVID-19 global pandemic. In early 2020, organizations everywhere suddenly found themselves with urgent projects to support
network services and other changes needed by workers, students,
customers, and others requiring safer ways to interact. (And these
projects were not only unanticipated, they faced staffing and interaction challenges as a result of the problems the projects were
attempting to address.)

In the wake of such heroic amounts of work, especially in
cases where the worst of the possible fears have been avoided,
there is an inevitable debate over how much, if any, of the work
was truly necessary. It is ironic, to say the least, that when risk
management efforts are most successful, the likelihood of later
criticism increases.

This was particularly acute in the early 2000s, when many
noted that although there were many problems (mostly small and
quickly fixed), there were few "Millennium Bug" disasters. The
absence of massive fallout from Y2K is correctly seen as a satisfactory result made possible by skillful application of risk management, not as evidence that all the project effort and investment
was much ado about nothing. There seems little doubt that the
risks to computer systems everywhere were real, and that doing
nothing would have been ugly.

Similar "Monday morning quarterback" criticisms are now
common when reflecting on all the actions mounted in response
to the disruptions caused by the global pandemic in the early
2020s. The very existence of these debates raises a fundamental
issue about risk management in general, and not just at the enterprise level. Managing risks is never free, and for these two examples the costs were enormous. For any risk we choose to manage,
we must invest real time and money. These are easily measured,
immediately. Our choice to act must be based on a belief that the

credible potential costs and consequences of inaction are much higher, as John F. Kennedy stated in the quote that starts this chapter.

A choice to manage a risk, however, changes everything. A response that removes or mitigates a risk makes it impossible to know what would have happened without that action. We cannot get in a time machine for a "do-over," where no actions are taken and we can determine with certainty the cost of inaction. It's rarely possible to "prove" conclusively that actions taken against a risk have been worthwhile. Estimates of an impact that did not occur will forever remain an uncertain forecast, open to conjecture. Particularly in retrospect, there will be people who criticize the expense of managing risk, either because they do not understand (or don't care about) the potential consequences or because they never accepted the impact or probability for the risk. Especially in the current climate of short-term organizational thinking, making investments right now to manage risks that may or may not occur in the future can sometimes be quite hard to sell.

Enterprise Risk Management Based on Standards

Over the past few decades enterprise risk management has also come to mean something much more specific, especially in the United States. There are a number of organizations that have codified practices for managing enterprise risk using this label. One of them is the Committee of Sponsoring Organizations of the Treadway Commission, or COSO, a US government–initiated organization. COSO and other groups have defined frameworks and standards for managing enterprise risk that have had substantial influence on organization-wide risk management.

Still active and quite influential, COSO is the current incarnation of a commission initiated by the US Congress in the 1980s that was formed to address issues concerning inaccurate financial reporting, particularly by companies on the brink of failure that nevertheless managed to publish healthy-looking financials. It was initially led by James Treadway, a former head of the US Securities and Exchange Commission, and comprised five US-based financial standards organizations, each involved with some aspect of financial accounting or auditing. In 1992, COSO published the *COSO Internal Control—Internal Framework*, which defined tightened standards for financial reporting. The framework addressed enterprise risk assessment, but not in much detail. It called for determining risk significance (impact) and likelihood or frequency, but it did not specify how this was to be carried out. It also outlined the need to determine how to manage the risks and what actions to take, but it left the details on this to the management of each enterprise. In the wake of additional reporting irregularities, including the now well-documented shenanigans of Enron, WorldCom, Tyco, and others, COSO expanded the control framework to include enterprise risk management. COSO initiated this project in 2001, engaging PricewaterhouseCoopers. The project culminated in 2004 with the publication of the *COSO Enterprise Risk Management—Integrated Framework*.

One of the main reasons that this framework has had such wide-ranging influence is its relationship in the United States with the Sarbanes-Oxley Act of 2002 (SOX), and increasingly with ongoing regulatory legislation around the world similar to SOX. To meet the requirements set out by SOX and equivalent laws in other countries, companies must establish and follow well-defined and controlled processes for their public reporting, and risk management has become a central aspect of this.

This book is not primarily about enterprise risk management in general or COSO in particular, but the practice and discipline of project risk management has been influenced extensively by COSO and similar standards organizations. It is useful to understand the broad outlines of the COSO enterprise risk management framework to ensure that your projects are aligned and conducted consistently with enterprise requirements.

The most recent COSO enterprise risk management framework includes five interrelated principles that are to be defined consistently at all levels of the organization, from the board of directors all the way down to the trenches where projects are managed:

- **Governance and culture:** This focuses on overall guidance and standards for managing enterprise risk, addressing ethics, behaviors, and much of what was discussed in chapter 2 on planning for risk management.
- **Strategy and objective-setting:** At the enterprise level, this starts with establishing a strategy and includes tactics, goals, and current projects. It is the foundation for identifying, assessing, and responding to risk, and includes material covered here in chapters 3–6, as well as the portfolio processes explored earlier in this chapter. Risk tolerance in COSO is referred to as "risk appetite."
- **Performance:** The focus here is on prioritizing enterprise risks and developing appropriate responses, and then communicating the results to key stakeholders. COSO processes for qualitative and quantitative assessment and developing preventative and recovery strategies mirror the content of chapters 7–10.
- **Review and revision:** This and the final item in the COSO enterprise risk management framework align with the practices outlined in chapter 11 on risk monitoring and control. The emphasis here is on

ownership and adjustment of the risk responses and on the use of retrospective analysis for feedback (as described in chapter 12).

- **Information, communication, and reporting:** Effective communications that flow up, down, and across the organization are always fundamental to good management. The emphasis for COSO is on credible, frequent reporting and retention of risk information, with a particular focus on metrics.

Overall, the roadmap outlined by COSO enterprise risk management is highly compatible with what is found in this book concerning projects, and in most other useful guidance on managing business risk in general. In early 2022, COSO developed and published guidance on "Enabling Organizational Agility in an Age of Speed and Disruption," which addresses enterprise risk management for organizations employing agile, iterative approaches for their project work.

COSO is not alone in the field of enterprise risk management standards. The Risk and Insurance Management Society is aligned with the global insurance industry and has a similar defined set of guidelines. The International Organization for Standardization (ISO) has adopted an international risk management standard, ISO 31000. The ISO standard lists seven "risk treatment options" for responding to risks, equivalent to "Avoid, Mitigate, Transfer/ Share, and Accept."

There are other standards and frameworks, and the future will doubtless bring still more standards for managing risk. That said, the basic underlying message is not likely to change materially— the fundamental ideas for understanding and managing risk that have worked in the past are quite durable. And, the future will also bring many new projects created as a direct consequence of enterprise risk management. The program that I was responsible for planning at Hewlett-Packard described earlier in this chapter was largely a consequence of the regulatory changes in the United States and elsewhere. In particular, the requirements of SOX necessitated top-down risk assessment and imposed stringent standards for reporting. This led to a tightening of processes for companies throughout the United States. At HP it also involved replacing disparate tracking and management methods in the fee-for-service project businesses worldwide to ensure consistency. The trend toward better internal controls, more audits, and improved process testing appears here to stay.

Key Ideas for Program, Portfolio, and Enterprise Risk Management

- Managing higher-level risk starts with good project risk management.
- For programs, focus on complexity-related risks, particularly those that involve cross-project dependencies, resource contention, and program "showstoppers."
- Minimize portfolio risk through use of appropriate criteria, including risk assessments and unbiased appraisals of project opportunities.
- Determine relative risks for projects and programs, and use risk correlation analysis to lower project portfolio risk.
- Manage enterprise risk through dogmatic monitoring and periodic maintenance of project portfolios.
- Understand and comply with your organization's policies and standards for enterprise risk management.

PANAMA CANAL: OVER THE YEARS

When the project finishes, the project team moves on. The deliverable remains, however, and things are rarely static. The success of the Panama Canal was as predicted, which was both good and bad. The growing traffic through the canal in its first years of operation required increasingly frequent filling and draining of the locks. The locks were filled from above using water from Gatun Lake that drained out to the sea, so the water required depended on traffic volume. The more ships that passed through the locks, the more water had to be drained from the lake. There are dry seasons even in a tropical rainforest, so it was not uncommon for the water level periodically to fall significantly. When the water was too shallow in the roughly thirteen-kilometer Gaillard Cut that sliced through the continental divide in central Panama, the canal shut down.

This enterprise risk was increasingly troublesome as the years passed. It interfered with interocean operation of the US Navy, which had been one of the main reasons for the US canal project in the first place. After several decades of periodic difficulty keeping the canal operational year-round, a sizable follow-on project was initiated to ensure a more reliable supply of water. This project constructed yet another dam, this one farther up the Chagres River above Gatun Lake. In 1935, the Madden Dam was completed, creating Alajuela Lake and the supply of additional water that the canal depends upon to this day.

CHAPTER 14

CONCLUSION

"Whether you think you can do a thing, or not, you are probably right."

—HENRY FORD

R isk management processes provide useful information about whether a project is feasible, and help you determine if you should believe it is possible. As Henry Ford said, confidence is a powerful determinant of success, especially if it is based on credible data. Project risk information can provide that data. And, when the verdict of a risk assessment looks problematic, risk information shows the way to better alternatives.

This book contains a wide range of ideas and techniques for project risk management. It is fair to ask if all of these are always necessary, and the answer is simple: No. Each is essential to some projects at some times, but it is hard to imagine any project that would benefit sufficiently from everything covered here to justify doing all of it. Besides, some of the concepts included represent alternative approaches to similar ends, and would be redundant.

So, how much is appropriate? The answer to this, like the answer to every other good question relating to project management, is: "It depends." Projects vary so widely that there can be no "one size fits all" answer. The trade-off between the value of risk information developed and the effort and cost associated with obtaining it always makes the overall investment for managing project risk a judgment call.

That said, there is at least one useful guideline. Always do at least enough planning and risk management to convince yourself that the project is, in fact, possible. The quote from Henry Ford is applicable to projects of all kinds. When people believe that they can deliver, they successfully achieve ridiculously difficult objectives with amazing regularity. Confident people persist until they find a way to get things done. Conversely, even the most trivial projects fail when the people working on them have doubts. Their expectations of failure become self-fulfilling; no one puts in much effort—why bother?

Demonstrating to all concerned that your project is at least plausible defines the minimum investment in project planning and risk assessment that is prudent. If you can do this with informal discussions and capture the necessary information on index cards or yellow sticky notes, do it that way and get to work. If your project warrants more formality, and most complex projects do, determine how to provide confidence to the project team and establish a realistic baseline for status tracking and change management. But remain practical. Investing more than necessary in computer tools and complex analysis techniques is just as inappropriate to project and risk management as doing too little.

The most successful strategy for making permanent improvements in your risk management is to define your overall objective clearly, in measurable terms, and then start to make small process additions and adjustments over time. As you proceed, assess whether your efforts are effective and helpful. Continuing this strategy over a sequence of projects will result in substantially better risk control at a modest cost in time and effort. Adding a lot of new overhead to any project environment all at once is not only expensive but also distracts at least the project leader from other project issues, and can create more problems than it solves.

Think about all the ideas and techniques in this book in the same way that a craftsperson views his or her tools. In the tool set there are tools that are used every day, tools that are used only once in a while, and a few tools that may have never been used at all. The entire set of tools is important because even the unused tools have applications, and the craftsperson knows that when the need arises, the right tool will be available.

CHOOSING TO ACT

Charles Bosler, a noted authority on project risk management, says, "Risk is simple. It is anything that requires you to make choices about the future." If you are currently doing little to manage risk, consider some of the following suggestions for your future. If your project success rate improves, this may be enough. If problems persist, add a few more ideas, and keep trying. Although risk can never be eliminated from projects completely, it can always be reduced, often with relatively minor incremental effort. Here are suggestions for getting started managing project risk.

Scope Risks

Minimize risk by a thorough definition of project scope. Every aspect of the project deliverable that remains fuzzy, ill-defined, or "flexible" represents a real failure mode. If you do not know enough to define everything, consider using agile methods to convert the project into a sequence of smaller efforts that you can define, one after the next, and perform reviews and testing as the interim subprojects complete. As you proceed, refine the scope definition and the next steps. If actually breaking the project into incremental pieces is not possible, use a "straw-man" specification to document as much specific detail as you can, and then invite feedback and criticism. Always validate the scope definition with project sponsors, customers, and key stakeholders, and set an expectation that as the work proceeds, any scope changes will require substantial and credible justification.

Schedule Risks

Project planning is the foundation for managing schedule risk, and planning for the immediate short-term activities (at minimum) is never optional. Based on the profile for the work, identify all the project activities that are similar to past work that has caused trouble. For every project estimate, set a range based on your confidence, or better yet, probe for the worst cases and document their consequences. For projects that carry significant risk, negotiate some schedule reserve, but in any case establish a believable plan that could complete at a date prior to the committed deadline.

Resource Risks

Most resource risks relate to bottlenecks, unreliable commitments, and constraints. Past project resource problems are likely to recur unless you develop plans to avoid similar situations. Perform sufficient resource analysis to reconcile your requirements and skill needs with the project budget and available staff. For particularly risky projects, negotiate a budget reserve.

General Risks

Examine your plan and brainstorm probable risks with the project team. List known risks and determine probability and impact for each risk using at least qualitative "high/moderate/low" assessments. Prioritize and distribute a risk register containing significant risks. At a minimum, use the risk register to make the project exposures visible. Develop prevention or recovery strategies for the most substantial risks. Whether you choose (or are even able) to respond to risks you have identified, awareness of them makes a difference. Risk visibility can be the factor that separates success from failure.

Overall Project Risks and VUCA

It is also essential to keep a focus on the environment surrounding a project. There may or may not be much that you can do about external forces and challenges, but awareness of them will increase their visibility and help you to minimize potential harm. Much of what you can do about two of the VUCA factors, uncertainty and complexity, falls within the project and can be minimized using many of the ideas mentioned previously, including healthy skepticism about forecasts (including those about risks), and attention to worst cases and realistic ranges for estimates. Scale is a major source of complexity, so consider options for your work that break lengthy efforts into sequences of shorter, simpler projects.

Ambiguity can be reduced through clear, thorough project documentation and early, effective stakeholder engagement to secure agreement on project specifics. Managing volatility also relies on good documentation and detailed specifications, as well as an effective process for managing changes as a project proceeds. And effective overall project risk management depends on strong, durable support from sponsors, key stakeholders, and other managers.

MANAGING YOUR RISKS

The remaining minimum requirements for risk management relate to tracking and change control. Dwight Eisenhower said, "In preparing for battle I have always found that plans are useless, but planning is indispensable." Eisenhower recognized the fact that few things ever go exactly as planned, which is especially true for projects. The exercise of planning never predicts the future precisely, but it does provide a framework for measuring progress and quickly detecting problems. For risk management, tracking progress at least once a week for all current project activities is prudent. Failure to do this periodic monitoring allows project slippage and other problems to increase quickly and cascade, and they can soon become insurmountable. Dogmatic, frequent tracking of project work is crucial to ongoing risk management. You can use thorough, disciplined tracking to detect many risk situations before they occur or at least while they are small. Small problems can be resolved quickly, preserving the project plans and objectives; large problems that go undetected can easily take a project down.

Project control is also central to risk management. During a running project there are many things going on that a project leader cannot control, so use the controls you do have to your best advantage. One of the most important controls available to project leaders is a disciplined process for managing project changes. Projects with no ability to control specification changes can collapse under scope creep or, if using agile methods, go on indefinitely. Project leaders also control the flow of information. Use project reports, meetings, and discussions to communicate risks and to keep project issues and progress visible.

Long-term improvement of project risk management relies on postproject analysis. Through this, you can assess project results and make recommendations for more (or different) processes for effective risk management and project planning, execution, and control.

Succeeding with challenging projects requires three things. The first, thorough understanding of the work based on unambiguous objectives, is the primary subject of this book. The second is diligent tracking and control of changes, covered in chapter 11. The third requirement, which is project-specific and beyond the scope of this (or any single) book, is relevant expertise.

Risk management (like life itself) is much easier when you are lucky, and this third element of success, expertise, represents the most obvious way to boost your luck. To the best of your ability, staff the project with a range of skills, including specialists in each field that the project requires. Projects with experienced practitioners are much better equipped to deal with the twists and turns in a typical project trajectory. Recovery from risks is quick and effective when there are a few battle-scarred veterans who know what needs to be done and what has worked in the past. It never hurts to recruit at least a few people for the project who have reputations as generalists known for their problem-solving talents. Once your team is together, you can boost your luck further by rehearsing contingency plans for significant potential problems. Whenever you do need to recover from a problem, you want to know what you are doing.

Through all of this, never lose sight of the main objective: to manage your project to successful completion. The project management ideas presented here provide components of the means to this end. Treat the techniques and concepts of this book as your risk management toolbox. When it makes sense, use the processes just as they are described. Or tailor some ideas to make them work in your environment. If a risk management idea promises you little current value, hold it in reserve. Above all, persevere. Inside every challenging project lies a perfectly credible one, waiting for you to break it free. Also remember that a little risk is not a bad thing; as Ferengi Rule of Acquisition 62 points out, "The riskier the road, the greater the profit."

PANAMA CANAL: THE TWENTY-FIRST CENTURY

Projects have a beginning and an end, but there is nearly always a next project. At Panama there have been many over the years, such as widening of the Gaillard Cut, and the new dam built upstream in the 1930s to ensure continuous operation through the drier seasons described at the end of chapter 13. As the twentieth century came to a close, the largest operational challenge for the canal was the limit on ship size imposed by the lock dimensions that George Goethals chose.

To accommodate larger ships, excavation began in the late 1930s for a set of larger locks for both sides of the canal. This work was interrupted by World War II and remained uncompleted until recently. Over the past century various alternatives for permitting transit by larger ships have been investigated. One proposal given serious consideration in the 1950s imagined using thermonuclear bombs to create Ferdinand de Lesseps's sea-level canal. This project was estimated to require about 300 detonations. Enterprise risk management might have been a good reason to pass up this particular project, but the main reason it was rejected appears to have been cost.

As the twenty-first century began, so did a new era for the canal. Following the 1999 turnover by the United States, the canal is currently operated by Panama. It remains a vital link in world shipping, and to ensure this into the future, planning started on the first major operational change in a century of canal operations. After a seventy-year interruption, work resumed on a new set of locks that would add a third transit across the isthmus. These new locks are now operating parallel to the older locks. They are nearly twice as wide, 40 percent longer, and 25 percent deeper. This new route supports transit of larger ships in addition to quicker transit for the PANAMAX freighters currently using the canal. As with the other transits, primary traffic flows inbound in the mornings and outbound in the evenings. The new locks require nearly four times the volume of water to operate than the original locks, and to minimize drainage losses to the sea they employ elaborate and clever plumbing to reuse much of the water. This system allows the existing lakes and reservoirs to provide an adequate supply year-round.

In 2007 the expansion project started well. Its initial budget was about 3.1 billion Panamanian balboas (or US dollars; the balboa has been pegged to the dollar since 1903) and included a contingency of about 20 percent. The target for completion at that time was in 2014, to coincide with the hundred-year anniversary of the first ship to transit Panama through the canal.

This massive project faced many of the same risks and challenges of the early twentieth-century project, including unstable soils, earthquakes, and soggy weather. As the original completion date approached in 2014, the project was $1.6 billion over budget and running about a year late. (Part of this delay was due to a lengthy work shutdown over who would bear the cost overruns.) The new transit was ultimately opened in 2016, a couple years late and over budget with a final estimated cost of about $5.25 billion. Overall, current operations are said to be profitable, with payback of the investment predicted to be about ten years.

The canal story continues to evolve. Discussions of a fourth transit in Panama continue. Climate-change-driven drought conditions challenge operations during drier seasons, spurring investigation of new reservoir capacity farther from the canal that would entail substantial pumping and additional expense. There is also growing competition. A canal through Nicaragua is (yet again) in the planning stages. The Suez Canal is widening, providing an alternate connection for shipping from Asia bound for the eastern coast of the Americas.

The future will no doubt hold many similar projects, and with plenty of risk to manage with all of them.

ACKNOWLEDGMENTS

The fourth edition of this book rests on many decades of project work, as well as many hours of discussion about project management and project risk (including more than a little good-humored disagreement). It is also the consequence of many presentations, workshops, and university classes on project risk management. Project work described in this book includes projects I have led at Hewlett-Packard, DuPont, and elsewhere, in addition to other projects done by colleagues, friends, and project leaders from an enormous diversity of project environments. The spectrum of project situations that serve as the foundation of this book ensures that it reflects the real world and that it contains ideas that are practical and effective—not just based on interesting theories.

This book would not exist without the many people I have worked with professionally over the years, especially colleagues from the Hewlett-Packard Project Management Initiative team where I spent more than a decade. Those folks served as a boundless source of wisdom and good examples, and they were always quick to point out anything that I said that was nonsense. I also must thank my many colleagues who worked as instructors at UC Berkeley and elsewhere, or as volunteers in various roles with the Project Management Institute for their support, guidance, and constructive criticism in helping to "advance the state of the art" of project risk management.

I am also grateful to the many teachers of project risk management worldwide who have adopted the earlier editions of this book as a course text and provided a wealth of helpful comments and feedback.

Finally, my largest debt of gratitude in this endeavor goes to my wife, Barbara, who encouraged this project, supported it, warned me that a new edition would be at least as much work as the first, and repeatedly reviewed the various versions of the manuscript (including the boring parts).

While many others have contributed significantly to the content of this book, any errors, omissions, or other problems are strictly my own. Should you run into any, let me know.

I also appreciate all the feedback and support from project risk management facilitators and practitioners, which has been enormously helpful in creating this fourth edition of *Identifying and Managing Project Risk*. If you are using this book to conduct training or university classes and are interested in supplemental materials, please feel free to contact me.

TOM KENDRICK
Santa Rosa, California
tkendrick@FailureProofProjects.com

SELECTED DETAIL FROM THE PERIL DATABASE

The following information is excerpted from the Project Experience Risk Information Library (PERIL) database. (These risks are an illustrative subset selected from the database, including examples representing the most significant overall impact.)

SCOPE RISKS

- Team failed to engage the critical "power-users" early enough.
- Project manager thought the solution was only one task, but there were four.
- Incomplete design was a result of not considering the particular country needs.
- Lack of consensus on the specifications resulted in later modifications.
- Survey tasks were assigned to several people in different countries, and each assumed others would complete the work.
- Development plans failed to include all of the twenty-three required applications.

- 75 percent of the requirements were unknown initially to the project staff.
- Scope for the project was never signed off by the upper management.
- A mid-project review turned up numerous regulations that were not implemented.
- The contract specified "state of the art" retrofit materials, and interpretation of this changed several times over two years.
- New technology was introduced late, and with insufficient analysis.
- The project team agreed to new requirements mid-project, some which were not even possible.
- Volume requirements were increased late in the project, requiring extensive rework.
- Engineering never stopped adding "bells and whistles" to the graphical user interface.
- Extension of scope to include Japanese users was poorly managed and controlled.
- System was expanded to include two more cities for political reasons.
- Application was changed for a prospective Chinese customer (who in the end did not buy).
- Printer project failed to meet print quality goals, requiring redesign.
- Hardware failed near the end of a three-month final test, resulting in refabrication and retest.
- Defect was discovered only after delivery to the customer.
- The software had twenty major defects and eighty other problems that prevented timely closure.

- Tests revealed a significant flaw, deferring release to next quarterly update.
- New product features were added at every weekly meeting and stage review.
- Project was based on standards still in draft form. Several options are possible, but project is staffed to pursue only one.
- Conversion from legacy system caused unanticipated problems leading to delays of three to ten days per module to fix.
- Data conversion problems made the implementation of a new system dependent on manual data reentry.
- Functionality for email was added late to a document retrieval project.
- Processes were changed and made more complex late in the project.
- A solution project was priced to win with few details on the work.
- The sponsor demanded specification changes late in the project.
- User interface requirements for a new database system were not specific enough.
- A key telecommunications requirement was detected late.
- Component failure required finding a replacement and redoing all tests.
- A 1,000-hour test was required at project end. Failure halfway required repairs and a complete test rerun.
- A critical component broke because the packaging for it was too flimsy to withstand the stress of standard shipping.

- Test hardware did not work, so all tests had to be conducted manually.
- A complex system was designed in pieces. When integration failed, redesign was required.
- Two related projects failed to synchronize, missing their release.
- A poorly implemented web tool caused ongoing support issues.
- A problem solution was developed based on assumed root cause. The cause was actually something else and resulted in a major slip.
- A purchased electronic component failed. It was necessary to design a new one late in the project.
- The delivery of the content started before the requirements were finalized.
- An application was found to need its own server, causing delay for installation.
- In a large system conversion, new applications were not able to work with existing data as expected.
- Midproject, scope was expanded to include the accounts receivable process.
- The database designed into the system was changed, requiring more resources and causing delay.
- An expected operating system release was canceled; the project was forced to use a prior version.
- A new CPU chip to be used in the product was assumed the same as the old version, but required an additional heat sink and mechanical design work.
- Original scope missed supply chain issues and could not be used without changes.

- Scoping was documented and estimated based on data from only one customer.
- The product was developed for multiple platforms but worked on only two. The project was delayed to fix some, but others were dropped.
- Market research and competitive analysis information was faulty but not discovered until late in the project.
- New technology was used, hoping for faster performance. It did not work well and resulted in redesign and rework.
- An instrument system built for a customer had been designed using the current model of PC. A new version was released that was incompatible, and project completion required finding and using an older salvaged PC.
- A system using new components failed in final tests. Obtaining replacement older components proved to be difficult.
- All the individual components passed their tests, but the assembled system failed.
- A problem with transaction volumes that was not detected in testing showed up in production.
- Purchased software was limited and inflexible, which necessitated work-arounds and additional software.
- Late design changes required manufacturing retooling at the last minute.
- "Minor" changes were added and accepted late in the project. This doubled the work in the final phase and delayed the project.

- A database set up for the client did not have sufficient free space for all the growing accounts.
- The development team misinterpreted a number of requirements.
- Documentation was provided in only one of the two required languages, causing a delay for translation.
- Network configuration sometimes caused backups to fail but only intermittently; troubleshooting was hard.
- PC board failure required redesign and fabrication.
- An upgrade to software was required. The planning and training for this caused delays.
- New software was installed by IT. It didn't work, and fixing it caused a delay.
- Metrics from many sites were required. When collected, the data was inconsistent, causing unanticipated additional work.
- The online badge printing requirement was completely missing from the scope definition.
- Proprietary data was needed, which the owners were unwilling to provide. After some delay, they finally shared partial information.
- Expected release of a new operating system expected slipped. This forced the project team to use the prior version, which was missing needed functionality.
- Although the system functioned well in Germany, it had no German documentation. Translation resulted in delay.
- A solution project elected to integrate a new, untried technology.
- Software modules in the system did not work together as planned.

- A major bug could be fixed only by moving to a later software version.
- The system move was delayed by last-minute system changes that made backups take too long.
- Scope was changed after the writers had completed their initial draft.
- A large print run of materials was scrapped and redone because of late changes required by legal.
- After the project was "complete," significant rework was required before customer approval.
- The design team failed to collect the details on what was to be displayed to users.
- The project deliverable eventually collapsed because of vibration in transit that caused nuts and bolts to work loose.
- Bugs were reported in user testing that should have been caught earlier by QA.

SCHEDULE RISKS

- Supply chain delays caused project slippage.
- The team in Germany lacked expertise needed for testing in a key intermediate step.
- New development team members were hired regardless of their lack of business knowledge.
- Ramp-up required forty new test engineers.
- Neophyte project staff lacked system expertise.
- A component ordered was too long for international shipment, so it was cut and shipped in pieces. What arrived was useful only as raw material and replacing it was expensive.

- Insufficient amount of test material was sent to the contract lab.
- Merging of multiple standards was needed to support reorganization. Lack of a consistent definition delayed project data conversion.
- Old application that had to be updated lacked documentation, and finding original code took weeks.
- The manager of a related project allowed stakeholders to make frequent scope changes, causing ripple effects and delay.
- Interdependencies in complex programs were detected late.
- Firmware needed for a key project component was dropped by another project.
- The quantity of CPU processor chips needed was not available.
- There were too few disc drives and insufficient physical space for the needed number.
- Conversion normally requires six months from the date a contract is signed, but project goal was four months.
- Software development was underestimated by a factor of three.
- None of the project staff knew the technology.
- Training for a new tool took more time than planned.
- Because the water supply available to complete the project was inadequate, water had to be trucked in.
- Expert opinion estimated two weeks, but the work took eight.
- Needed components were delayed because of an internal supplier problem.

- Work estimated displayed chronic optimism on completion dates.
- Multiple-phase rollout was delayed near the end because the systems needed were temporarily out of stock.
- Decisions were delayed without apparent reason.
- International leased line order was delayed while awaiting management approval.
- The systems required were on back order for six months, so the project was forced to use a competitor's system.
- The business counterparts were not in agreement on which option to choose.
- A special peripheral needed for the project deliverable was discontinued.
- Compilers and open source libraries needed were not available.
- Partner organizations were late with promised work, and even then their deliverables did not work as expected.
- Field engineers experienced long learning curves.
- The customer insisted on a deadline shorter than the plan.
- Development scheduled in parallel led to frequent rework.
- Needed skilled resources were unavailable.
- A three-week test took seven because of learning curves and ramping time.
- New hires were used for critical work, which required time for training.
- Senior management approval for software licenses was delayed.

- The system needed was delivered to the wrong building and was lost for weeks.
- The shipping requirements changed. Some shipments bounced, others got stuck in customs.
- Metrics required by a process improvement project were collected and delivered late.
- With a twelve-hour time difference and heavy dependence on email, even simple questions took two to four days to resolve.
- International shipment of parts was estimated to take six weeks, but it actually averages nine.
- Some parts were damaged in shipping and had to be reordered.
- Space was unavailable, so the project was forced to implement in the old space.
- Infrastructure changes caused last-minute problems.
- A sole-source chip supplier was reliable for low volume, but at high volume (and lower cost) it had quality problems that created delays.
- Components that could have been purchased were developed by the team, which took longer than expected.
- The system integration task was not broken down to small, manageable pieces in the project plan.
- There were chronic problems getting timely management decisions.
- Disaster recovery tests were delayed at project end because the hardware required was tied up solving another customer's problem.
- Some critical equipment needed for the project came from a pool of hardware in another country, which was delayed in customs.

- Parts of the development team had a twelve-hour time difference.
- Bugs took an average of two to three days longer to fix than anticipated.
- Defective parts were received, and reordering doubled the time required.
- There were frequent delivery problems on international shipments with customs and paperwork.
- Firewall changes typically had taken twenty-five days, but the estimates were capped at fifteen.
- Estimates for cabling were too optimistic.
- The deliverable expected from a related project arrived on time, but the project could not use it.
- A flood shut down the data center, resulting in delay to restore power and clean up.
- Customer supplied hardware did not work, and replacements were needed.
- A system was taken down for scheduled maintenance when needed by the project.
- There was no coordinated shipment of system components, so the last part to arrive delayed installation.
- A dependency on another project was not discovered until project end.

RESOURCE RISKS

- Multiple project contributors unavailable due to viral infections.
- Subject matter experts were let go to save money.

- Due to a layoff no writer was immediately available, so approval was delayed.
- Project was cut back. Delayed fixes cost a lot of money, and needed resources were assigned to other work.
- Project Budget was restricted to the bare minimum estimated.
- There were large funding cutbacks (66 percent of project team).
- A key supplier was purchased by another company and reorganized. Project was forced to find a new supplier.
- Research and development were outsourced, but the relationship was not managed well, and all work ultimately had to be redone.
- Contract manufacturer failed to deliver on time.
- Changes were agreed to, but the supplier shipped late and deliverables do not work.
- Components delayed, and contractors were committed to other work and were only able to work part-time.
- Expert medical specialist was no longer available.
- Product owner having unique knowledge left the company.
- Manager quit his job because of his mother's illness.
- Management mandated the project but never got team buy-in.
- Programmers were volunteers, and ultimately all of them quit.
- Staff got along poorly and frequently quarreled.
- The product manager disliked the project manager.
- Key decisions were stalled when no system architect was available.

- Several projects shared only one subject matter expert.
- Project needed $150,000 per month in supplies but had a limit of $100,000.
- The senior system analyst, who was fully trained on the application, resigned.
- The travel budget for the project was cut, which led to inefficient long-distance collaborations.
- A key subcontractor went out of business, and it took two months to find a replacement.
- Midway in the design stage, an important engineer had a family emergency and had to leave the country for a month.
- Two technicians were reassigned to a more business critical project midway through system development.
- The government contract required that the staff have only US-born nationals, but there were too few.
- The only experienced programmer gave notice and left the company.
- Halfway through the project, three of the engineers had to return to China because of visa issues.
- A key engineer was pulled off the team to work on another project.
- The project manager was unavailable because of jury duty.
- Money for needed software was not in the current budget, so the project was delayed to push the expense into the next quarter.
- Contract negotiations delayed the start of work.
- The project leader resigned and was not promptly replaced.

- Outsourcing the order entry process delayed all US-based customers.
- Legacy systems were not retired as planned, and the project team got tied up with unplanned support work.
- Critical skills unique in the head of a programmer were lost when he had a heart attack.
- Critical training had to be postponed because of last-minute emergency leave by the lead designer.
- For cost reasons, an Asian supplier was chosen, but qualification and paperwork caused delays.
- Initial stages of the project were outsourced to a professor who started late and lacked needed information.
- Last project tied up and exhausted the staff, so the following project started late and slowly.
- A key contributor was lost while solving problems related to a previous project.
- An engineer critical to the project left the company.
- Team members were reassigned to other, higher-priority projects.
- Only one employee had both the COBOL and relational database data conversion experience needed, and she had other conflicting commitments.
- A valuable resource was pulled off the project to work on a higher profile project.
- Team members were lost to a customer hot site.
- A consultant broke both arms three weeks before project end.
- Two projects depended on one resource for completion, and the other project had higher priority.

- The system architect who knew how to integrate all the components fell sick and was hospitalized.
- An earthquake in Taiwan made part of the project team unavailable.
- There was a lack of money for needed equipment.
- Pricing negotiations stalled project work until they could be resolved.
- Slow renewal of the contract for a consultant caused a work interruption.
- The contract had no penalties for missing deadlines, and a one-week task took three weeks.
- Outsourced tasks were slipping, but this was not known until too late.
- At a critical stage of the project, the medical director left the company.
- Late in the project, the budget and staff were cut. This resulted in delays, forced overtime, and team demotivation.
- Key people resigned, leaving too few to complete the project on time.
- On a very long project, enthusiasm and motivation fell, and task execution stretched out.
- Key work in flu season was delayed when most of the staff was out ill.
- The team was frequently diverted from the project to perform support work.
- A key resource was pulled off the project twice to fix bugs in a previous product.
- The lead engineer was stuck in Japan for two weeks longer than expected because of a visa problem.

- A packaging engineer was working on another high-priority project when needed.
- Key welding staff members were out with the flu.
- Manufacturing volumes spiked, which diverted several project contributors.
- An unannounced audit midproject caused a delay to participate and respond.
- An important team member was grounded in the Middle East during a regional war.

INDEX

ABOUT THE AUTHOR

TOM KENDRICK, MSEE, MBA is a consultant, educator, and author. He spent twenty years with Hewlett-Packard in its Project Management Initiative and a variety of other project, program, and management responsibilities. Tom has more than forty years of worldwide project management experience, including work for Visa, DuPont, and General Electric, and as an independent consultant. He lives in the San Francisco Bay Area.

Tom retired in 2017 as program director for the UC Berkeley Extension Project Management Curriculum. He is the author of *How to Manage Complex Programs* (AMACOM, 2016), *Identifying and Managing Project Risk*, Third Edition (AMACOM, 2015), and three other popular books on project management. Tom regularly conducts classes and presentations on program, project, and risk management.

Tom completed his BSEE at Princeton University and has an MBA from the Wharton School and an MSEE from the University of Pennsylvania. He is a certified Project Management Professional (PMP) with the Project Management Institute (PMI). Tom is a past president of the Silicon Valley PMI Chapter and frequent volunteer for many local and global PMI activities.